KV-638-501

Spenser's *Faerie Queene* and the Reading of Women

Accession no.
01090842

WITHDRAWN

Spenser's
Faerie Queene
and the Reading
of Women

Caroline McManus

1463329

CHESTER COLLEGE

ACC No.
01090842

DEPT

CLASS No.
821·3 SPE M11

LIBRARY

DELAWARE

Newark: University of Delaware Press
London: Associated University Presses

© 2002 by Rosemont Publishing & Printing Corp.

All rights reserved. Authorization to photocopy items for internal or personal use, or the internal or personal use of specific clients, is granted by the copyright owner, provided that a base fee of $10.00, plus eight cents per page, per copy is paid directly to the Copyright Clearance Center, 222 Rosewood Drive, Danvers, Massachusetts 01923. [0-87413-768-3/02 $10.00 + 8¢ pp, pc.]

Other than as indicated in the foregoing, this book may not be reproduced, in whole or in part, in any form (except as permitted by Sections 107 and 108 of the U.S. Copyright Law, and except for brief quotes appearing in reviews in the public press).

Associated University Presses
440 Forsgate Drive
Cranbury, NJ 08512

Associated University Presses
16 Barter Street
London WC1A 2AH, England

Associated University Presses
P.O. Box 338, Port Credit
Mississauga, Ontario
Canada L5G 4L8

The paper used in this publication meets the requirements of the American National Standard for Permanence of Paper for Printed Library Materials Z39.48-1984.

Library of Congress Cataloging-in-Publication Data

McManus, Caroline, 1960–
    Spenser's Faerie Queene and the reading of women / Caroline McManus.
        p.   cm.
    Includes bibliographical references and index.
    ISBN 0-87413-768-3 (alk. paper)
    1. Spenser, Edmund, 1552?–1599. Faerie queene.   2. Women—Books and reading—England—History—16th century.   3. Women and literature—England—History—16th century.   4. Authors and readers—England—History—16th century.   5. Books and reading—England—History—16th century.   6. Epic poetry, English—History and criticism.   7. Knights and knighthood in literature.   I. Title.

PR2358 .M38   2002
821'.3—dc21   2001054040

PRINTED IN THE UNITED STATES OF AMERICA

For my mother and father,
who shared with me their love of books and reading

Contents

7

Acknowledgments

An earlier version of chapter 6 appeared as " 'The carefull Nourse': Female Piety in Spenser's Legend of Holiness," *Huntington Library Quarterly* 60.4 (1997): 381–406. Parts of chapter 5 first appeared in "Reading the Margins: Female Courtiers in the Portraits of Elizabeth I," *Ben Jonson Journal* 2 (1995): 31–58; the babies and bears material in chapter 5 was first developed for a Shakespeare Association of America seminar on Spenser and Shakespeare, organized by Katherine Eggert. I would like to thank Michael J. B. Allen for his generous and wise guidance, given while the book was in its early stages and throughout the writing process. Miranda Johnson-Haddad kindly read and commented on my discussion of Ariosto in the third chapter; her shrewd professional advice and understanding friendship have helped me to persevere with this extended project while also devoting myself to motherhood and teaching. Thanks are due to the external readers, Thomas P. Roche, Jr., and Lauren Silberman, for their very helpful suggestions, and to several people associated with the University of Delaware Press, especially Jay L. Halio, Lois Potter, and Karen G. Druliner, for their interest in my project. Thanks are also due to Christine A. Retz and Julien Yoseloff at Associated University Presses and to the unfailingly patient staff of the Huntington Library. My daughter, Lora Mei, has fortunately been fascinated with the book-writing process, which helped alleviate her impatience with my time at the computer. My deepest debt of gratitude is to my husband, Jim McManus, who now knows more than he ever wanted to know about *The Faerie Queene*, but who has nevertheless given me constant, sustaining encouragement.

Abbreviations

OF   Ludovico Ariosto, *Orlando Furioso*, trans. Sir John Harington

EG   Richard Brathwait, *The English Gentlewoman*

C   Baldassare Castiglione, *The Courtyer*, trans. Sir Thomas Hoby

CW   Jacques Du Bosc, *The Compleat Woman*, trans. N. N.

DD   William Gouge, *Of Domesticall Duties*

CC   Stefano Guazzo, *The civile Conversation of M. Stephen Guazzo*, trans. George Pettie and Bartholomew Young

MM   Thomas Salter, *A Mirrhor mete for all Mothers, Matrones, and Maidens, intituled the Mirrhor of Modestie*

ICW Juan Luis Vives, *The Instruction of a christen woman*, trans. Richard Hyrde

ODH Juan Luis Vives, *The office and duetie of an husband*, trans. Thomas Paynell

Spenser's *Faerie Queene* and the Reading of Women

Introduction

... for to honour ladies this he penned ...
—Henry Stanford, 1610

When Sir John Harington, Queen Elizabeth's godson, took up residence at court, he is said to have "gained the esteem of all ranks, and both sexes." Part of his popularity with the female sex may have derived from his translation of the scandalous twenty-eighth canto of Ariosto's *Orlando Furioso*. As the story goes, the queen, pretending to be offended, banished Harington from court, but only until he had rendered the remainder of the Italian work into English. His translation, "which was highly pleasing to the Ladies," was also enjoyed by women in Ireland. As he himself relates, albeit with self-deprecating mockery, "My Ariosto has been entertained into Galloway before I came; when I got thither, a great Lady, a young Lady, and a fair Lady read herself asleep, nay dead with a tale of it." Modesty topos notwithstanding, Harington goes on to suggest that this lady would find the text compelling as he links her to an Ariostan counterpart: "The verse, I think so lively figured her fortune; for, as Olympia was forsaken by the ungrateful Byreno, so had this Lady been left by her unkind Sir Calisthenes, whose hard dealing with her cannot be excused, no not by Demosthenes."[1] Harington, and possibly the lady reader, saw in the text a mirror of her own condition.

Like Harington, many sixteenth-century authors clearly recognized and courted a female readership. Sir Thomas Elyot, George Pettie, John Lyly, Barnabe Rich, and especially Robert Greene (whom Thomas Nashe seems to refer to scathingly as the "*Homer* of Women") all sought women readers.[2] So, too, did Edmund Spenser, who in *The Faerie Queene* explicitly acknowledges the presence of women, royal and nonroyal, within the literary and political culture the poem reflects and sought to transform. In fact, electing to write his national epic in the mode of chivalric romance may have been an intentional strategy on Spenser's part to invite a female readership. Linda Woodbridge

15

notes that during the sixteenth century, epic was associated with masculinity whereas romance was "primarily a feminine genre," and she tentatively speculates, "It is not impossible that the poem's whole Arthurian framework may have been chosen with an eye to women readers."[3] Also applicable to *The Faerie Queene* are the criteria articulated by Suzanne Hull in her study of books intended for early modern Englishwomen: dedicatory sonnets to more than one woman, direct address to women within the text, discussion of women's duties and roles, and histories of famous women. Tellingly, *The Faerie Queene* incorporates practically all of the literary elements that Hull has documented as types of recreational literature read by Englishwomen in the late sixteenth century, including "the romances, the poetry, the jingles, the lusty jests, allegories, epigrams, novelle, the female biographies, and the occasional classics retold or retranslated for a female audience." Although Hull judges Spenser's poem to be "not as clearly a women's book" as *Euphues* or *The Countess of Pembroke's Arcadia*, she does allow that "The queen and her ladies were influential in popularizing the book, and it could be argued that [Spenser] wrote with their interests, tastes, and patronage in mind, as well as to glorify and advise the queen herself."[4] Spenser's text does indeed address the interests and concerns not only of his queen but also of the women who attended her at court, as the pages that follow will demonstrate.

Several of Spenser's contemporaries linked him to women readers, implying that these women were familiar with and appreciative of Spenser's poem. For example, Francis Beaumont, writing to Lady Anne Newdigate in 1612, copies an extract from *The Faerie Queene* (4.9.2) in his letter, because, he says, "I know how much you delight in all good learning, and in such honest verses." Hadrian Dorrell, in an epistle directed to "all the constant Ladies and Gentlewomen of England that feare God," praises Henry Willoby's *Willobie His Avisa, or The true Picture of a modest Maide, and of a chast and constant wife* (1594, 1609) by indirectly connecting it to the work of Sidney and Spenser: "For the composition and order of the verse, although he flie not aloft with the winge of *Astrophel*, nor dare to compare with the Arcadian sheepheard, or any way matche with the dainty Faiery Queene, yet shall you find his words and phrases neither triviall, nor absurd." As indicated by my epigraph (taken from verses accompanying a copy of *The Faerie Queene* given to Elizabeth Spencer, Lady Carey, in 1610), Henry Stanford contends that *The*

Faerie Queene was written "to honour ladies."[5] Stanford may genuinely have believed this to be one of Spenser's primary motives or he may simply have intended to compliment Lady Carey. Either way, his comment is significant evidence that at least some of Spenser's contemporaries read the poem in light of women's concerns and that Spenser's female audience was not limited to Queen Elizabeth, the poem's official dedicatee, but included nonroyal women as well.

Spenser, along with Samuel Daniel, is explicitly associated with the praise of courtly women in the concluding couplet of a dedicatory sonnet to Margaret Ratcliffe prefacing Anthony Gibson's *A Womans Woorth, Defended against all the men in the world. Prooving them to be more perfect, excellent and absolute in all vertuous actions, then any man of what qualitie soever* (1599): "Had I a *Spencers* spirit, a *Daniels* powers: / Th'extracted quintessence were only yours."[6] Gibson's strategy in his pursuit of female patronage closely resembles that of Spenser in the 1590 *Faerie Queene*. Gibson begins with an epistle and dedicatory sonnet to the "Right Honorable Lady, Elizabeth, Countesse of South-hampton," which is followed by a dedicatory epistle addressed to "the worthy Ladyes, and vertuous Maydes of Honor, to her royal Majesty: Mistresse *Anne Russell*, Mistresse *Margaret Ratcliffe*, Mistresse *Mary Fitten* and the rest, &c." Gibson endeavors, as I will argue Spenser does, to praise the mistress and the maids simultaneously, asserting to the "Vertuous Ladies, and Right Honorable Maides, attending on the only vertuous Ladye and Maide in the world" that "on you (rather then any other) the same [his book] should be bestowed, as only true Ideas of vertue, and glories of your sexe." This tribute is followed by individual dedicatory sonnets to Russell, Ratcliffe, and Fitton, the latter ironically praised as "Faire, and (for euer honord) vertuous maide" (Mary was dismissed from court in 1601 for bearing a stillborn son, the result of her affair with William Herbert). These individual sonnets are followed by a dedicatory epistle addressed collectively to "all the Honorable Ladies, and Gentlewomen of England," which extends Spenser's more narrowly defined audience of "all the gratious and beautifull Ladies in the Court."[7] Sandwiched between his long list of prominent women and a brief epistle to the (non-gendered) "Reader," Gibson's stated goal—"that by the histories of many women, every man whatsoever may perfectly perceyve, that the gifts and graces of women are infinite, and where they can alleadge any doubt in the religion of your desertes: being heerein resolved, you may re-

maine so much the more admired"—suggests more the witty hyperbole intended to amuse courtly women than a sincere
attempt to persuade a male readership.

I have been arguing that Spenser's contemporaries clearly acknowledged his awareness of a female audience and that *The Faerie Queene*'s allegory refers not only to the experiences of male
courtiers but also to those of female courtiers.[8] It behooves us,
therefore, to broaden the scope of Spenserian scholarship by
positing, in addition to the "Irish" Spenser, the "Protestant"
Spenser, the "laureate" Spenser, and the "poets'" Spenser
(among others), a "ladies'" Spenser, taking seriously the inter-
play between *The Faerie Queene* and this early female community of readers. Despite the textual and historical evidence that
women constituted part of Spenser's intended and actual readership, few critical studies have considered the relationship between the female characters Spenser constructs in his poem and
those he sought to fashion as readers. Those critics who have attempted to explore this dynamic have primarily focused on
Queen Elizabeth. The poem's major female figures, including
Una, Belphoebe, Amoret, Florimell, and Britomart, have received much critical attention as "shadows" of various aspects of
the virgin queen's nature: her Protestantism, her power and sexual inviolability, her beauty, and her embodiment of national ideals.[9] Several more recent studies, particularly those with new
historicist and feminist orientations, have usefully examined the
poem in light of the eroticized political dynamic operative at the
Elizabethan court. Yet even those books that specifically ask
questions about gender and readership focus almost exclusively
on the depiction and imagined response of the queen, who is
clearly unique as a female reader.[10] Such readings are certainly
valuable in that they acknowledge the impact of gender on literary production and, to some extent, reception, but they pay little
to no attention to female readers other than Elizabeth, Spenser's
primary and most illustrious, but by no means sole or even representative, female reader.[11]

Spenser marks his awareness of an aristocratic female readership in a variety of ways, one being the deliberate inclusion of
courtly women in his poem, both within the narrative and in the
dedicatory and explanatory apparatus that accompanies it. Although most critics are willing to acknowledge that Spenser does
not limit his "shadows" of the queen to Gloriana and Belphoebe
but hints at her presence in other powerful or iconic female figures such as Diana, Mercilla, Pastorella, and Radigund, the at-

tendant women who serve as markers of that royalty have often
been overlooked. The "beuie of faire Virgins clad in white"
(5.9.31) that attends Mercilla is the most explicit mirror image of
Elizabeth's maids of honor, customarily dressed in white to underscore the cult of the virgin queen, but the ladies' courtly roles
could also be suggested by the nymphs who jealously guard
Diana, the shepherdesses who encircle Pastorella, and perhaps
even the female warriors who accompany a less flattering royal
analogue, Radigund.[12] Following Ariosto's example, Spenser addresses his female readership directly in several narrational
asides, as in 3.1.49, 3.5.53–54, 3.6.1, 3.9.1–2, and 6.8.1–2.

Although many of these references are tongue in cheek, and
are required by the Ariostan formula, Spenser expressly courts
an aristocratic female audience in his 1590 dedicatory sonnets to
the "*right honourable and most vertuous Lady, the Countesse
of Penbroke,*" the "most vertuous, and beautifull Lady, *the Lady
Carew,*" and "all the gratious and beautifull Ladies in the Court."
David Miller claims that the flirtatious tone Spenser adopts in
the dedicatory sonnets reveals how little is really at stake in his
seeking their patronage; he is essentially "patronizing" them. Yet
Carol Stillman has argued that the second issue of the 1590 edition reflects Spenser's conscious revisions, including the addition of the Countess of Pembroke sonnet prior to the Lady Carey
sonnet. This reordering of the sonnets addressed to women follows the social protocol laid out in Sir William Segar's *Honor,
Military and Civil* (1602), whereby a countess outranks a viscountess.[13] This attention to the women's social rank (even
though it is derived from that of their husbands and fathers)
would imply that Spenser might have taken their influence more
seriously than Miller suggests. All of the dedicatory sonnets,
whether addressed to men or to women, were omitted from the
1596 edition; the 1611 edition retains the Countess of Pembroke
sonnet (on the overleaf of the sonnet to Raleigh, with ornamental
borders above and below) but not those to Lady Carey and the
ladies of Elizabeth's court, perhaps because the single leaf on
which they were printed was inadvertently omitted. Spenser,
having died in 1599, was obviously not overseeing the publication
of this edition as he did the first two. Even the dedicatory sonnets
addressed to men might pertain to "invisible" female readers. As
Susanne Woods points out, Aemilia Lanyer was the mistress of
Henry, Lord Hunsdon, in the late 1580s and early 1590s; Woods
claims, "there is every reason to believe that Lanyer was familiar
with *The Faerie Queene.*"[14] Given our increasing awareness of

women's participation in Elizabethan literary culture, we should attend to the dedications to female courtiers as carefully as we do those addressed to male courtiers. What do we know, for example, of Spenser's relationships with Mary Sidney, the Countess of Pembroke, and Elizabeth Spenser, Lady Carey? Moreover, how might his designation of an aristocratic female readership ("all the gratious and beautifull Ladies in the Court") affect our understanding of the poem?

Although the extent of the contact between Spenser and the Countess of Pembroke, one of the most eminent female literary patrons of the period, is unclear, Spenser does allude to her "manie singular favours and great graces" in the dedication of *The Ruines of Time* (1590), and in *Colin Clouts Come Home Againe* (1595), he praises her as "Urania," claiming that she "graced" him "goodly well."[15] The evidence linking Spenser to Lady Carey is more substantial. Nashe's dedication to *Christes Teares Over Jerusalem* (1593) addresses her as that "Excellent accomplisht Court-glorifying Lady" and observes, "Divers wel-deserving Poets, have consecrated their endevors to your praise. Fames eldest favorite, Maister *Spencer*, in all his writings hie prizeth you." He certainly seems to do so in his *Faerie Queene* dedicatory sonnet, confessing that he would need a "golden quill" and "siluer leaues" to accurately portray her virtues. Instead, he will simply "make humble present of good will: / Which whenas timely meanes it purchase may, / In ampler wise it selfe will forth display." Spenser seems to promise additional work in praise of Carey, although it may be contingent on her provision of the "timely meanes." Carey is punningly reminded in Stanford's presentation verses of Spenser's attention to her as well as of their family relationship: "the autour when he liv'd did beare your name."

The second daughter of Sir John Spenser of Althorpe, Elizabeth married Sir George Carey in 1574. Her husband, who in 1596 became the second Lord Hunsdon, was the queen's cousin (Anne Boleyn was his grandmother's sister); he served as a member of the privy council and as Lord Chamberlain, Lady Carey as a lady of Elizabeth's privy chamber. Lady Carey was thus closely linked to the court's inner circle. After her first husband's death in 1603, she married Ralph, third Baron Eure; she died in 1618.[16] Several writers in addition to Spenser and Nashe addressed sonnets and epistles to Lady Carey or dedicated works to her, among them "A Tragical Discourse of the Haplesse mans life" in Thomas Churchyard's *Churchyards Challenge* (1593), Thomas Playfere's

The Meane in Mourning (1595, 1616), and Henry Lok's *Ecclesiastes, Otherwise Called the Preacher* (1597), bespeaking her interest, or perceived interest, in devotional literature as well as Spenserian epic romance (and the multiple genres it comprises).[17] This generic range and Carey's worldly experience suggest a sophisticated female reader, one who belies the stereotyped images of completely passive or uncontrollably lascivious female readers conveyed by the diatribes of Tudor moralists (to be discussed in subsequent chapters).

Spenser's dedication of *Muiopotmos* (1590) to "the right worthy and vertuous" Lady Carey reinforces her image as a witty, adept reader, given the complaint poem's complexity, tonal range, and thematic concerns (the nature of art and, probably, contemporary politics).[18] We may never know why Spenser dedicated this particular poem to this particular lady,[19] but we can look to the dedication's language for clues about the way Lady Carey was invited to interpret the poem. In addition to Spenser's conventional (and not necessarily insincere) desire to advance the lady's "excellent partes and noble vertues" and the more personally charged desires to express gratitude for her "great bounty" and to affirm his familial connection to her (the "name or kindreds sake by [her] vouchsafed"), he credits her with a degree of moral autonomy in praising, above all, the honorable name she has "by [her] brave deserts purchast to [her]self, and spred in the mouths of al men." She has, in other words, caused men to speak of her, but virtue, not loose living, makes her a byword.

Spenser beseeches her to value his poem and asks her "of all things therein according to your wonted graciousnes to make a milde construction." He thus links her temperament and past practice—her "wonted graciousnes"—to a precisely nuanced, "milde" reading of the poem, clearly acknowledging that it could very well be read otherwise, whether by her or by other readers. "Milde construction" paradoxically reinforces gender stereotypes of women as gentle rather than harsh while also acknowledging her independence of those stereotypes—she now will exercise power over the text in an individual act of interpretation. This implication is taken for granted in the Yale edition footnote: "Sometimes held to be Sp[enser]'s way of discouraging allegorical interpretations and sometimes his way of encouraging them, the phrase ["milde construction"] in all likelihood simply asks Lady Carey to indulge the work with her 'wonted graciousnes.'" Yet it is precisely the question that the footnote raises only to dismiss that seems crucial—is Spenser inviting her to read allegorically or to dissuade her from reading allegorically? To what degree is such a request individuated or comprehensive (reflective of Lady Carey's personality or a general hermeneutic philosophy), and to what degree is it gendered? In other words, would Spenser have defined the task of reading in similar terms had he been addressing a non-gendered reader or a male patron? Moreover, what kind of "construction" might she and other female contemporaries have given *The Faerie Queene*?[20]

The complexities and ironies of Spenser's poem would not, I suggest, have been lost on Lady Carey and the female reading community she formed with her sisters Anne (d. 1618) and Alice (d. 1637), the Phyllis, Charillis, and Amaryllis of *Colin Clouts Come Home Againe*, a community representative of the female readers who constitute the focus of my study. Alice, having married Ferdinando Stanley, Lord Strange, in 1579, became the Countess of Derby in 1593 when Ferdinando succeeded his father as the fifth Earl of Derby. Alice entertained Queen Elizabeth several times during the 1590s, and she participated in many of Queen Anne's masques. With her second husband, Thomas Egerton, Baron Ellesmere, whom she married in 1600, Alice worked to establish the notable Bridgewater Library. Alice was the dedicatee of John Davies' *The Holy Roode, Or Christs Crosse* (1609) and Thomas Gainsford's *The Historie of Trebiszond* (1616), and she received dedications from Sir John Harington, John Marston, Samuel Daniel, John Donne, Ben Jonson, and John Milton as well as from Spenser. Still buying arrows and thread to equip her crossbow for hunting at age seventy-five and endowing an almshouse in 1636 for six poor widows of the parish,[21] Alice reminds us that behind Spenser's distant and iconic images of feminine virtue (Belphoebe and Dame Caelia, for example) were women who actually embodied some of the tastes, dynamism, and piety to which those textual figures allude.

Spenser's entire oeuvre, in fact, reflects his attentiveness to a female readership. Many of his works include flattering attendant roles for female courtiers. The woodcut accompanying the April eclogue in *The Shepheardes Calender* (1579), for example, depicts Elizabeth with her ladies, some of them singing and playing musical instruments, and in *Colin Clouts Come Home Againe*, the shepherdess Lucida desires news of Cynthia's retinue of nymphs, providing Colin with the opportunity to describe several ladies of the court in rarefied terms as patterns of true womanhood and flowers of chastity, virtue, grace, and learning. *Astrophel* (1595) is dedicated to Frances Walsingham, the Countess of Essex, and the *Fowre Hymnes* (1596) to Margaret Russell Clifford, the Countess of Cumberland, and Anne Russell Dudley, the Countess of Warwick.[22] In addition to his dedication of *Muiopotmos* to Elizabeth, Lady Carey, *The Teares of the Muses* (1590) to Alice, Lady Strange, and *Mother Hubberds Tale* (1590) to Anne, Lady Compton and Mounteagle, the three Spencer sisters, Spenser singled out the Marquess of Northampton as the dedicatee of *Daphnaida* (1591). In fact, the number of aristocratic women designated as Spenserian dedicatees is cited by William Ponsonby as a rationale for gathering together the poems that constitute the 1591 *Complaints*. In "The Printer to the *Gentle Reader*," he explains that he has included these particular poems, "To which effect I understand that he besides wrote sundrie others, namelie Ecclesiastes, and Canticum canticorum translated, A senights slumber, The hell of lovers, his Purgatorie, being all dedicated to Ladies; so as it may seeme he ment them all to one volume."[23] Whatever the amount of actual patronage Spenser received from these women, he seems to have consciously and repeatedly chosen to link his work to them. Tellingly, the first to erect a burial monument to Spenser in Westminster Abbey was a female reader, Lady Anne Clifford.

This study, therefore, asks new questions of Spenser's text, questions having to do with the nonroyal women featured in the poem and those who formed a significant portion of *The Faerie Queene*'s early readership. Research on early modern women writers suggests that many contested or at least freely adapted the male-dominated literary tradition they inherited. Unfortunately, seeking similar responses from Spenser's female readers is more difficult, given the paucity of extant reading journals, the generic conventions governing the content of those journals that do survive, and the lack of substantive marginal annotations in copies of the poem owned by women. One can, however, ask how *The Faerie Queene* participates in its culture's construction of women as readers. Drawing on feminist, cultural materialist, and reader-response theories, I argue that Spenser's text in many ways resembles popular didactic literature in its advocacy of modesty, chastity, and piety, but that the rhetoric of feminine virtue he presents is rendered ambiguous by his conflation of courtesy literature with the genre of romance, which effectually undermines any reading that is narrowly prescriptive in nature and provides a broader spectrum of female exemplars for women

readers to appropriate. This conflation of often contradictory generic discourses serves to destabilize critical assessments of
Una, Britomart, Amoret, Florimell, and Serena, all of whom wander the world in search of their lovers. Judged by the conventions
of courtesy literature, such wandering can be read as sexual errancy, but within the romance paradigm, wandering can signify
chaste, even heroic constancy. This combination of disparate discourses calls attention (perhaps unintentionally) to the different
ways in which female behavior could be scripted and thus broad-
ens interpretive options for women readers, many of whom enacted a variety of (often contradictory) cultural roles: daughter,
lover, wife, mother, patron, courtier, friend, Christian, Englishwoman, writer, along with reader.

In fact, the polyvalence of Spenser's women and the freedom
with which they move among different genres can be related to
sixteenth- and seventeenth-century debates about female literacy. Literacy enabled women to read not only those texts that
might inculcate in them socially desirable qualities but also more
dangerous, proscribed literary material. Above all, literacy enabled women to adapt at will certain fictional roles to their own
methods of self-presentation. Spenser's poem registers a remarkable awareness of women's encounters with texts and the
interpretive autonomy women were capable of exercising. My
study (as the intentional ambiguity of its title suggests) explores
the ways in which Spenser's text attempts to "read" women at
the same time that it anticipates the ways women may have read
it, the tension between the text's designs on women and women's
designs on the text.[24]

In keeping with recent studies of Tudor and Stuart interpretive
practices, which generally suggest that reading in Spenser's day
was a highly contingent and intertextual activity,[25] I will examine
The Faerie Queene in conjunction with other early modern
works written for or about women, particularly other romances,
didactic works of courtesy literature, and devotional material.
The questions Robert Hume lists as he outlines his proposed
methodology are essentially the same questions that I have been
asking of Spenser's text: "Why did the author write what he or
she wrote? What reactions did the work generate around the
time of its original publication or performance? What audi-
ence(s) did the author address? How would various members of
the postulated original audience have understood or reacted to
the work? What do we learn from parallels to and differences
from related works at about the same time?"[26] Interpreting *The*

Faerie Queene's depiction of the "priuate morall vertues" of Aristotle, as Spenser, in the letter to Raleigh, claims the poem does, becomes a more complex process when taking into account the gendering of virtue that strikes modern readers as reprehensibly sexist but that may have been taken for granted (and manipulated) by sixteenth- and seventeenth-century readers. The notion of virtue seems to have been gendered (at least in theory) during Spenser's day; Antonio Montecatini's *In politica progymnasmata* (Ferrara, 1587) argues, as Ian Maclean summarizes, "Woman possesses the virtues of temperance, liberality, justice and all others but of a different class (*species*) and in a different way (*modus*) from man. Her role in life causes them to be expressed differently."[27] Sidney's well-known remark in his *Defence of Poesy* (1595), "Truly, I have known men that even with reading *Amadis de Gaule* (which God knoweth wanteth much of a perfect poesy) have found their hearts moved to the exercise of courtesy, liberality, and especially courage,"[28] raises questions about the ways in which women readers might have been moved by Spenser's (more poetically perfect) romance to exercise their own gendered versions of "courtesy, liberality, and especially courage." Would Sidney have singled out modesty, chastity, and piety had he made an analogous statement about the benefits of romance to women readers? Much less sanguine than Sidney's description of the *Amadis*'s effect on male readers, Jacques Du Bosc's assessment of its effect on female readers is couched in gendered terms: "They *read* more willingly the bookes, which corrupt manners, then such as order them, and there are more Ladyes who learne by heart, the tales of the *Amadis*, then the histories of the holy writ."[29]

How, then, might *The Faerie Queene*, given its ostensible intent to instruct readers both morally and socially by fashioning "a gentleman or noble person in vertuous and gentle discipline," speak to the experience of Spenser's female readers? My first two chapters—" 'Some comfortable and wise discourses': The Reading of Early Modern Englishwomen" and " 'How doubtfully all Allegories may be construed': Women's Interpretive Strategies"—provide an overview of the reading practices of late sixteenth- and early seventeenth-century Englishwomen and place them within a context of contemporary assumptions about female interpretive activity. I incorporate within the second chapter reflections on how Spenser's poem reinscribes early modern anxieties about women's literacy and reading practices. Many of the women in Book 3, primarily Britomart but also Malecasta and Hellenore, exercise a surprising degree of interpretive agency as they selectively appropriate established literary roles to serve their own erotic interests. Chapter 3, " 'Don Quixote's Sisters': Lady Knights and Reading Women," provides a comparative analysis of scenes of female reading in *The Faerie Queene, Orlando Furioso* (in Harington's 1591 translation), and *The Mirrour of Princely Deedes and Knighthood* (1578–1601). Spenser's employment of common romance motifs constitutes an essentially conservative courtship script for women (represented by Merlin's mirror and oral prophecy), yet Britomart's decision to become a lady knight in response to Glauce's revisionist version of Merlin's history lesson serves as an uneasy reminder of the contestable nature of the reading act—women's potentially subversive appropriation of male-authored texts might transform them into metaphorical, if not literal, female warriors.

The second part of the book focuses on the "vertuous and gentle discipline" of modesty, chastity, and piety, the feminine virtues one would expect to find promulgated in a work of courtesy literature. In chapter 4, " 'Put on your vailes': Reading Modesty," I focus on Books 2 and 4 and their depiction of female courtiers who faced the double bind of remaining above sexual reproach while negotiating the transition from chaste maid to chaste wife. The female modesty advocated by Spenser's poem, and by Juan Luis Vives's *The Instruction of a christen woman* (1523), Baldassare Castiglione's *The Courtyer* (1528), and Stefano Guazzo's *The civile Conversation* (1574),[30] is ultimately destabilized by the fact that all women, modest and immodest alike, adopt various guises or "veils" of modesty (blushes, hair, etc.), in order to deflect or to invite the male gaze. My fifth chapter, "Courtship and the Female Courtier: The Problem of Chastity," explores a similar double bind, that experienced by Amoret, Priscilla, and Serena, who must simultaneously exhibit the sexual desire and restraint demanded by the genres in which they are situated. As romance, *The Faerie Queene* valorizes their devoted quests for their loves; as courtesy literature, the poem condemns their wayward errancy and questions their chastity. Elizabeth's maids of honor, especially during the 1590s, may have found themselves in a similar dilemma at court, expected by their queen "Diana" to perform as devoted virginal nymphs while simultaneously expected by their families and culture at large to form advantageous marriage alliances.[31] The struggle of Spenser's ladies illuminates the paradoxes inherent in courtesy literature itself, which draws attention to the practice of modesty and chastity

(virtues highly dependent on interpretation) as cultural performance. The final chapter, "Chaste but Not Silent: Reading and Female Piety," examines aristocratic women's roles as devout
wives and mothers in light of religious discourse. I suggest that
the care for the Redcrosse knight demonstrated by Una and the
female inhabitants of the House of Holiness effectually literalizes
the allegory of the Mother Church, in that they serve as exemplars of the good mother, who was to nurture her children physically, by breast-feeding, and metaphorically, by catechising and
teaching. The latter responsibility, however, elicited concern
among Spenser's contemporaries about the potential abuses of
female literacy and the extent to which women should be allowed
to use their voices in God's service. Not surprisingly, Spenser's
text simultaneously praises and limits the authority of the holy
women in Book 1. Una achieves a precarious balance of wifely
submission and strong leadership, but not without drawing attention to the autonomy and power exercised by women who
read and taught God's word. Throughout the poem, Spenser's female characters exemplify not only standards of conduct, but
also the various modes of reading available to his female audience.

Theorizing an aristocratic female reader as both the subject
and the object of Spenser's poem will, I hope, provide a new way
of looking at *The Faerie Queene* and speak to Spenser's engagement in the ongoing *querelle des femmes*. Additionally, and perhaps more importantly, I hope my study will illustrate the
necessity of constructing a history of early modern women readers to complement the recent progress made in constructing a
history of early modern women writers. Underlying my analysis
of Spenser's text are questions about the ways readers and authors negotiate social scripts and the opportunities for readers,
especially female readers, to find in literature alternatives to paradigms imposed by a dominant culture. Carol Neely has suggested that a feminist critique of Renaissance literature must of
necessity "over-read, . . . read to excess, the possibility of human
(especially female) gendered subjectivity, identity, and agency,
the possibility of women's resistance or even subversion."[32] As I
attempt to do exactly that in speculating about *The Faerie
Queene*'s original female readers, I am reminded of Spenser's
defense of his own project in the proem to Book 2: like him, I
"vouch antiquities, which no body can know." I am, however, encouraged by his reminder that "of the world least part to vs is
red" and his protestation that "later times things more vn-

knowne shall show. / Why then should witlesse man so much misweene / That nothing is, but that which he hath seene?" The reading protocol Spenser describes in the proem to Book 3—"In mirrours more then one her selfe to see, / But either *Gloriana* let her chuse, / Or in *Belphoebe* fashioned to bee" (my emphasis)—is explicitly linked to the queen, yet Spenser's poem as a whole suggests the implicit applicability of this interpretive freedom to all female readers, royal and nonroyal alike.

1
"Some comfortable and wise discourses": The Reading of Early Modern Englishwomen

Rivers used to read to me in Montaigne's Plays [Essays] and *Moll Neville* in the Fairy Queen.

—Anne Clifford, 1617

There is, as Robert Darnton reminds us, "a history as well as a theory of reader response," and a feminist reader-response criticism, according to Elizabeth Flynn, "would look at the responses of real readers in real contexts in an attempt to link those responses to the social and political matrices which constitute them."[1] The difficulty of trying to historicize sixteenth- and seventeenth-century Englishwomen's readings of Spenser's *Faerie Queene* lies in defining accurately the experience of "real readers." An obvious starting point is to examine the relationship of women to books during Spenser's day and the ways their reading experience may have been gendered. We must also attempt to ascertain the reading preferences, motivations, and interpretive strategies associated with and practiced by Elizabethan and Jacobean Englishwomen. In this chapter, I will briefly describe the rationales used for teaching women to read and look to journals and biographical writings for evidence of the books that gentlewomen of the period owned or to which they had access. What emerges from such a survey is the range of women's reading—in addition to the romances and devotional literature with which they are so frequently linked, secular histories (charged with contemporary political implications) also engaged the interest of female readers. Having briefly summarized what women seem to have read (and what they were admonished to read) in chapter 1, I will consider in my second chapter how women read, or at least how they were assumed to read, docu-

menting the often-conflicting assumptions about sixteenth- and
seventeenth-century women's hermeneutic practices dissemin-
ated by authors of didactic literature. Read together, the two
chapters serve as an introduction to the literary and educational
context in which female readers first encountered Spenser's
poem.[2]

Despite the difficulties of reconstructing the reading experience of a group of women living 400 years ago, we do at least have
evidence that some women *were* readers. Two examples are emblematic of both the desire of women to read and also the antipathy that that act could engender: one night in 1607, Elizabeth
Baker, the wife of an Otham yeoman, was "at her book reading
as she uses many times to do before she goes to bed," a habit
that evokes no surprise in the reporter; however, when a Faver-
sham woman "had been reading and leaving her book in some
place," her husband, Bartholomew Dann, "would catch the book
out of her hands and tear it in pieces or otherwise fling it away."[3]
Reception studies are needed at all levels of the social hierarchy,
but, given the courtly female readership Spenser identifies in his
final dedicatory sonnet, the readers most germane to my examination of *The Faerie Queene* are women of the gentry, aristocracy, and nobility, the literate class that David Cressy numbers
at less than 5% of the population. Cressy's literacy figures, derived from the number of men and women able to sign their
name on a legal document, have, however, been challenged by
Keith Thomas as being far too conservative. Thomas argues that
women would have been more likely to read than to write, given
that reading was taught before writing and that girls received
less formal education than did boys. Additionally, women were
considered in need of moral instruction (available to them by
means of reading) and were expected to teach their children to
read but certainly were not encouraged to express their own
ideas in writing.[4]

Thomas's more generous assessment of women's literacy
rates is supported by Elizabethan educator Richard Mulcaster,
Spenser's headmaster at the Merchant Taylors' School, who indicates that women were more frequently taught to read than to
write. In his 1581 treatise *Positions wherin those primitive circumstances be examined, which are necessarie for the training
up of children, either for skill in their booke, or health in their
bodie,* Mulcaster observes in regard to girls' studies:

> To learne to read is very common, where convenientnes doth
> serve, & *writing* is not refused, where oportunitie will yeild it.

> *Reading* if for nothing else it were, as for many thinges else it is, is verie needefull for religion, to read that which they must know, and ought to performe, if they have not whom to heare, in that matter which they read: or if their memorie be not stedfast, by reading to revive it. If they heare first and after read of the selfe same argument, reading confirmes their memorie.[5]

The preeminent place given religion in Mulcaster's statement suggests that encouraging personal and familial devotion was the most obvious and palatable rationale for female literacy during the period. Erasmus had urged earlier in the century that vernacular translations of the Bible be provided so that "even the lowliest women" could read the gospels and the Pauline epistles for themselves.[6]

In addition to the devotional rationale (particularly the Protestant imperative that all believers be able to read the word of God) that was adduced to support female literacy, social pressures dictated that aristocratic women attain a certain level of education in order to be eligible for positions at court and to marry educated (and preferably wealthy and prominent) men. Lady Lisle, for example, when trying to obtain places for her daughters Anne and Catherine in the households of Anne Boleyn and Jane Seymour, had the girls taught "to read and to write French and English, to play the lute and the virginals, to choose and to wear stylish clothes properly, and to sew."[7] Stefano Guazzo's 1574 conduct manual, translated into English by George Pettie and Bartholomew Young as *The civile Conversation of M. Stephen Guazzo*, advocates a similar program: "it is needefull to instruct [daughters] in things meete to get the favour of their Mistresse, if the father meane to set them to the court to [the] service of some Princesse, so that it behoveth the[m] to learne to reade, to write, to discourse, to singe, to plaie on instruments, to daunce, and to be able to perfourme all that which belongeth to a Courtier to doe" (*CC*, 158r). Fathers are advised in *The Court of good Counsell* (1607) "to consider of what calling his Sonne in law is like to bee, and so to frame his Daughter accordingly: as, if he purpose to marry her into the Countrey, to bring her up in Countrey huswiferie. If the Father meane to marry his Daughter to a Courtier, he must set her to the Court to the service of some great Lady, and must be learned to read, to write, to discourse, to sing, to play on Instruments, to daunce, and to be able to performe all that, which belongeth to a Courtier to do: by this meanes many are marryed to great Gentlemen, without one

penny dowrie given by their Father."[8] Although the assumption
that a good education obviates the need for a dowry seems overly
optimistic, this advice suggests that, to some extent, class and
profession took precedence over gender in dictating the nature
of early modern education. However, gender did obviously influence the duties assigned male and female courtiers; noblewomen were not expected to advise their prince as their male
counterparts were and hence, if they did receive humanist training, did so for reasons consistent with gender ideology.

Most aristocratic families seem to have provided their daughters with the rudimentary training deemed necessary by Mulcaster and Guazzo, namely that gentlewomen be taught to
"reade plainly and distinctly, write faire and swiftly, sing cleare &
sweetely, play wel & finely, understand & speake the learned lan-
guages, and those tounges also which the time most embraseth
[usually French or Italian], with some *Logicall* helpe to chop, and
some *Rhetoricke* to brave."[9] Young gentlewomen received this
instruction either at home or in the home of another family of
equal or higher status. Grace Sharington Mildmay (1552–1620),
the daughter-in-law of Walter Mildmay, Queen Elizabeth's chan-
cellor, was taught by a governess and recollects learning to ci-
pher, writing imaginary letters, reading Scripture, herbals, and
books of physic, practicing the lute and singing, and executing
her own designs in needlework.[10] Sir Robert Sidney's London
agent describes a similar regimen when reporting on the progress of the young Mary Sidney, who "is very forward in her learning, writing and other exercises she is put to, dancing and the
virginals."[11] Retha Warnicke contends that only sixty or so
women received the more extensive humanist training in sixteenth-century England and that they did so not because of any
egalitarian belief in women's intellectual ability or protofeminist
agenda but in order that they might be extraordinarily accomplished. Even more specifically, she attributes the humanist
training given to certain daughters of the dukes of Somerset and
Suffolk and the earls of Surrey and Arundel (all conveniently
named Jane) to a hope that the girls might be considered as potential brides for Edward VI.[12] Rather than use their learning to
assist their sovereign as "governors," as male courtiers were to
do, these women were expected to use their learning as a means
of first attracting and then serving their prince in the role of con-
sort. As Mulcaster notes, only "such personages as be borne to
be princes, or matches to great peeres, or to furnish out such

traines, for some peculiar ornamentes to their place and calling, are to receive this kinde of education in the highest degree."[13]

Other rationales provided for the education of women rein-scribe their established gender roles in relation to others, as a social duty rather than a realization of their intellectual potential. Sir Thomas More, for example, believed that women would be more entertaining companions for their husbands and wiser mothers for their children when educated in the classics.[14] Mul-caster reiterates More's point that education in a wife is advanta-geous, since it also produces physical benefits; the education of girls serves to strengthen their bodies as well as their minds so they will be improved as "the seminary of our succession." Mul-caster later waxes lyrical over the advantages reading provides women: "Or is there any better meane to strengthen their minde, then that knowledge of God, of religion, of civil, of domesticall dueties, which we have by our traine, and ought not to denie them, being comprised in bookes, and is to be compassed in youth?" However, Mulcaster is careful to qualify some of his more expansive claims by invoking a woman's primarily domes-tic responsibilities: "Here I may not omit many and great content-mentes, many and sound comfortes, many and manifoulde delites, which those wymen that have skill and time to reade, *without hindering their houswifery*, do continually receive by reading of some comfortable and wise discourses, penned either in forme of historie, or for direction to live by" (my emphasis).[15] Occasionally the advocates of female literacy present reasons that grate harshly on modern ears, being based on assumptions that women, if allowed to remain idle, will indulge their "innate" propensity for wrongdoing. Richard Hyrde argues that "Redyng and stydyeing of bokes so occupieth the mynde that it can have no leyser to muse or delyte in other fantasies[,] whan in all handy werkes that men saye be more mete for a woman the body may be busy in one place and the mynde walkyng in another while they syt sowing and spinnyng with their fyngers may caste and compasse many pevysshe fantasyes in theyr myndes."[16]

Hyrde may have had reservations, however, about some of the books owned and read by women later in the century. Although book ownership is no guarantee that the works were read (merely possessing books, expensive material objects, bespoke gentility), the fact that many gentlewomen did own copies of *The Faerie Queene* and a variety of other poetic, historical, and devo-tional texts suggests that women constituted a more significant readership than has hitherto been assumed. What were some of

the specific titles owned by Englishwomen during the period?
Lady Mary Grey at her death bequeathed three editions of the
Bible, the *Book of Common Prayer*, a French dictionary and an
Italian commentary, several published sermons, Foxe's *Actes
and Monuments*, and other religious works, whereas Bess of
Hardwick named only three books in her will, all of which were
in English: the Proverbs of Solomon, Calvin's discussion of Job,
and a book of meditations.[17] Such selections might at first seem
rather tame for the redoubtable Bess of Hardwick. Carol Meale
argues that testaments function as rhetorical documents, attesting to the dying person's spirituality and relinquishment of
earthly goods, so they often emphasize devotional rather than
secular works.[18] Conversely, the books recorded in Bess's will
may have been all she owned and simply constitute part of her
net worth. The pragmatism of Solomon's proverbs would not
have been inconsistent with Bess's hardheaded approach to life,
and perhaps Calvin's disquisition on Job was a gift—a rather obvious hint that patience and submission were virtues she might
well afford to develop.

One of the more extensive sixteenth-century women's collections belonged to Jane, the daughter of the Earl of Arundel; her
husband, John, Lord Lumley, continued to add to the library
after her death in 1577. Jane had been given a humanist education, as is apparent from the books belonging specifically to her.
These included two theological and three historical works in
Latin, some genealogical lists relating to her family, works by
Cicero, Greek and Latin exercises she completed when young,
and her translations of Isocrates and Euripides from Greek into
Latin. However, the Lumley collection also contains such "diver-
sionary" works as Elyot's *The Defence of Good Women*, an En-
glish translation of Petrarch's *Trionfi*, and Castiglione's
Courtyer in the Hoby translation of 1561, all of which share with
The Faerie Queene a concern with fashioning women.[19]

The Countess of Pembroke is said to have formed an extensive
collection of books, including "a great many Italian bookes; all
their poets; and bookes of politie and historie"; her library was
unfortunately destroyed by fire in 1647.[20] We have more specific
information about the library of Lady Anne Clifford (1590–1676),
Countess of Dorset, Pembroke, and Montgomery. A portrait of
her at fifteen features as a background numerous books, presumably read under the guidance of her tutor Samuel Daniel and her
governess Mrs. Anne Taylour. The authors include Epictetus,
Boethius, St. Augustine, Eusebius, Ovid, and Agrippa; more re-

cent works (*Don Quixote*, Sidney's *Arcadia*, the works of Spenser and Chaucer, Montaigne's *Essays*, Daniel's verse and his *Chronicles of England*) are also identifiable.[21] Perhaps even more indicative of personal ownership and frequent use of books is Clifford's diary entry for May 1617: "The 24th we set up a great many of the books that came out of the North in my closet, this being a sad day with me thinking of the troubles I have passed" (her mother had recently died and she was involved in continuous disputes about land ownership with her husband and relatives). Clifford's will (made in 1676) bequeaths "books" from various castles she owned, but without naming them by title.[22]

A catalogue of books owned by Lady Frances Stanley Egerton, Countess of Bridgewater, is equally informative, especially since the catalogue excludes works in the general family collection. (Frances was Alice Spencer's daughter by her first husband, the Earl of Derby; she married John Egerton, who was the son of Alice's second husband Thomas Egerton, and she seems to have shared her mother's literary interests.) As might be expected, many of the 241 books were of a devotional nature or dealt with ecclesiastical and religious matters, including works by Launcelot Andrewes, John Donne, Joseph Hall, and Richard Hooker. She owned works in French as well as English and, in translation from the Latin, such authors as Tacitus, Petrarch, and Boethius. She seems to have shared the predilection of many of her female contemporaries for history, indicated by her possession of a Turkish history and Thomas Heywood's *The History of Women* (1624).[23] The library of Lady Anne Southwell (1573–1636) included the Bible, editions of Calvin and Hooker, and other devotional works (such as Michael Sparke's *Crumms of comfort*), an English dictionary, Daniel's history of England, Philippus Camerarius's *Historicall Meditations* (listed in the *STC* as *The walking librarie, or, meditations and observations historical, natural, moral, political, and poetical*, 1621), as well as Gerard's herbal, Montaigne's essays, Ariosto's *Orlando Furioso*, and "Spensers ffayrie Queene in ffolio."[24] The Duchess of Suffolk owned a "chestful of books," and Anne, Viscountess of Dorchester possessed seventy-seven pounds worth of books (probably equivalent to at least 100 volumes). Heidi Brayman notes that "Printed book labels survive for another 18 women between the 1590s and 1670. For these women to have had book labels formally printed suggests that they had sizeable collections to monitor."[25]

Although a member of the gentry rather than the courtly aristocracy, Frances Wolfreston (1607–77) also possessed a sizeable library. Her collection—English literature (48%), theology (24%), history (10%), current affairs (7%), medicine (3%), works in Latin (3%), miscellaneous, including French (5%)—indicates that women's reading interests ranged far beyond the domestic and devotional spheres to which they are assumed to have been consigned. Although brief, her annotation of *The Good Womans Champion, or A Defence for the Weaker vessell* (1650?), "in prais of women, a good one" (written after the identification "frances wolfreston hor bouk"), hints at her appreciation of female causes, if one construes the "goodness" of the book as being a consequence of its subject matter ("in prais of women"). Her interest in history is represented by such works as William Camden's *Britannia* and various civil war tracts, and the presence of *The Queene's Majestie's Entertainment at Woodstocke* (1585) suggests a fascination with Elizabeth or at least the idylls of the rich and famous. Wolfreston owned numerous dramatic texts, including plays by Chapman, Dekker, Heywood, Marlowe, Massinger, Shirley, and Shakespeare (ten quartos of the latter, in fact). She also read poetry, possessing works by Donne, Drayton, Wither, Gascoigne, and Shakespeare (notably *Venus and Adonis*, 1593, and *The Rape of Lucrece*, 1594). Representative prose titles include Greene's *Mamillia: The second part of the triumph of Pallas* (1593) and Pettie's *A Petite Pallace of Pettie his pleasure.* Miscellaneous titles (Puttenham's *The arte of English poesie* [1589], Dorothy Leigh's *The mothers blessing* [1616], and collections of conceits and riddles) attest, respectively, to her awareness of language, concern for her children, and sense of humor.[26]

Knowledge derived from these libraries about women's reading tastes can be supplemented by evidence of women's actual reading practices. Such evidence is necessarily anecdotal and incomplete, given the different generic conventions and rhetorical strategies dictating what material was considered appropriate for inclusion in journals and biographies, but these sources provide crucial information about the extent to which the books owned and read by English gentlewomen correspond (or fail to correspond) to moralists' prescribed lists of salutary reading material for young women. Authors of educational and conduct literature for women did not hesitate to enumerate particular works for women that would presumably lead them in the paths of moral virtue. Juan Luis Vives recommends "the gospelles, the actes, the epistoles of the apostels, and the olde Testament, sainct Hieronyme, sainct Ciprian, Augustyne, Ambrose, Hillary,

Gregorye, Plato, Cicero, Senec, and suche other" (sig. D4r–v), but he cannot resist cautioning elsewhere, "lette her have no bookes of Poetrye."[27] He relents eventually by allowing her to read Christian poets, but he still carefully admonishes that the wife should read only such books as will "inflame her to live vertuouslye" (*ODH*, sig. P8v). He persists in his view of reading as a corrective for woman's putatively "natural" moral infirmities: "Let her read many thinges to subdue & bring under the affections & to appeace and pacifie the te[m]pestes & unquietnesses of the minde " (*ODH*, sig. Q1r).

In *A Mirrhor mete for all Mothers, Matrones, and Maidens, intituled the Mirrhor of Modestie* (1579), which was dedicated by printer Edward White to Lady Anne Lodge (mother of author Thomas Lodge), Protestant divine Thomas Salter generally agrees with Vives as to what women should read. Salter does allow the addition of some contemporary works, provided that they contain adequate role models: the maiden is "to reade (if she delight to bee a reader) the holie Scripture, or other good bookes, as the bookes of *Plutarche*, made of such renowmed and vertuous women as lived in tyme paste, and those of *Boccas* [Boccaccio] tendyng to the same sence, or some other nerer to our tyme."[28] Elsewhere he explains exactly the means by which the texts are to inspire imitation and morally transform their readers:

> But in steede of suche [unsuitable] bookes and lacivious ballades, our wise matrone shall reade, or cause her maidens to reade, the examples and lives of godly and vertuous ladies, whose worthy fame and bright renowne yet liveth, and still will live for ever, whiche shee shall make choice of, out of the holy Scripture, and other histories, both auncient and of late dayes; whiche bookes will not onely delight them, but as a spurre it will pricke and incite their hartes to follow vertue, and have vice in horror and disdaine. . . . for you shall never repeate the vertuous lives of any suche ladies as *Claudia, Portia, Lucretia*, and such like were, but you shall kindle a desire in them to treade their steppes, and become in tyme like unto them. (*MM*, sig. C2r)

Salter's metaphor for the reading process—a "spurre" that will "pricke" hearts—equates women's hearts to horses that must be controlled and dominated by their masters, in this case the books' content. Salter occludes the possibility that women might instead "master" the content.

Richard Brathwait's *The English Gentlewoman* (1631) repeats and elaborates on Vives's list of books prescribed for young women, praising Plato for his philosophy, Cicero for his rhetoric, and Seneca for his morality. He continues:

> But for as much as it is not given to most of you to be Linguists, albeit many of their workes be translated in your mother-tongue, you may converse with sundry English Authors, whose excellent instructions will sufficiently store you in all points; and if usefully applied, conferre no small benefit to your understanding. I shall not need particularly to name them to you, because I doubt not, but you have made choyce of such faithfull Retainers and vertuous Bosome-friends, constantly to accompany you.[29]

Brathwait's metaphor for books ("faithfull Retainers and vertuous Bosome-friends") grants women a greater degree of power in the reading process than does Salter, the women being either the employers or the intimate equals of the books they read, but Brathwait also seeks to limit the scope of women's reading ("*sundry English* Authors . . . will *sufficiently* store you in all points," my emphasis). Here the woman is depicted as a mere repository, a storehouse for the authors' meanings, but Brathwait's conditional phrasing ("*if usefully* applied," my emphasis) acknowledges, as Salter does not, that the outcome of the reading process cannot be predicted or controlled with any certainty. The best Brathwait can do in this regard is to socialize the young woman into making the "right" interpretive choices consistent with the religious and domestic agenda he advocates: "Some Bookes shee reads, and those powerfull to stirre up devotion and fervour to prayer; others she reads, and those usefull for direction of her houshold affaires. Herbals she peruseth, which she seconds with conference: and by degrees so improves her knowledge, as her cautelous care perfits many a dangerous cure" (sig. Gg1r).

Devotional and domestic reading indeed figure prominently in the extant reading journals of English gentlewomen. Born in 1571, Margaret Dakins Hoby served her youthful education in the Puritan household of Catherine, Countess of Huntingdon. Margaret was married three times, first in 1589 to Walter Devereux, a brother of the second Earl of Essex, then to Thomas Sidney (one of Sir Philip's brothers), and then in 1596, when she was twenty-five, to Sir Thomas Posthumous Hoby (a son of Lady Elizabeth Russell). She notes reading or being read to almost daily, and seems, either out of enjoyment or a strict sense of duty, to have missed no opportunity to do so. When staying for a period in London, she writes: "I went to a standinge to se the quene Come to London, were I Reed a serome [sermon]" (13 November 1600). Depicting herself as genuinely reluctant to put down her book, she records, "I . . . gott Mr Hoby to Read some of perkines to me, and, after dinner, I red as Longe as I Could my selfe" (9 March 1599), but she is careful to defend herself against charges of frivolity or laziness by claiming (especially on Sundays) to be reading of a "good" book.[30]

Hoby does occasionally record variations from the theological in her reading regimen. She notes that on 11 June 1600, she "reed a litle of humanitie," and the matter mentioned in her entry for 14 May 1601, bespeaks an interest in the use of language: "after diner I went about the house, and kept with my Maides tell all most night: then I went in to my Chamber and did some busenis: and, this after none, tooke a Lecture of Rhetorike." (Dorothy Meads speculates that this was a reading from Sir Thomas Wilson's *The Arte of Rhetorique*, first printed in 1552, but with many editions throughout the century; it was dedicated to John Dudley, brother of Catherine, Countess of Huntingdon, in whose house Margaret was brought up.) Other entries recording secular literature are domestic in nature, dealing with medicine or the garden. On 12 October 1599, Hoby "reed of Bright of Mallincocolie," probably Timothy Bright's *A treatise of melancholie* (1586), which combined medical with metaphysical information, and on separate occasions in 1599 she "read of the arball" (probably Turner's or Gerard's).[31] Regrettably, Hoby's diary does not mention the copy of *The Faerie Queene* (the 1590 edition) which her husband owned and annotated. Either Hoby never read the poem or heard it read, or, which is perhaps more likely, she may have felt the poem was not in keeping with the more serious works she records reading in her daily account.

Numerous critics have noted the degree to which women were admonished to confine their interests to the domestic and the devotional, yet what is less frequently discussed is the degree to which history was also considered a morally edifying genre for women readers. Knowledge of civic duty is included in Mulcaster's list of the advantages reading provides women, and Salter also urges women to use their literacy to heighten their devotion to their country: "Lette her reade, I saie, and with the same print in her minde, the lives of suche noble ladies as lived in *Troie*, *Sabina*, *Phocia*, *Argiva*, and *Rome*; for no doubte she shall learne greate example of pitie to her countrie by *Megestona*, *Aretaphila*, *Policreta*, and by *Judith* and *Hester*" (*MM*, sig. D3v).

Samuel Daniel's *The Civile Wares* (1609), dedicated to the
Countess of Pembroke, assumes a female readership, to which
he alludes explicitly in his prefatory apology: "And if I have erred
somewhat in the draught of the young Q. Isabel (wife to Ric. 2) in
not suting her passions to her yeares: I must crave favour of my
credulous Readers; and hope, the young Ladies of England (who
peradventure will thinke themselves of age sufficient, at 14
yeares, to have a feeling of their owne estates) will excuse me in
that point."[32] Jacques Du Bosc, in a section of *The Compleat
Woman* (1639) entitled "Of Courage," advocates history as suitable reading matter for women; histories "are full of their [wom-
en's] generous actions for the conservation of their Country, for
the love of their Husbands, and for the religion of their Ances-
tors" (sig. Aa1r). Superior to the "poyson" of romances, histories
combine "recreation with instruction" (sig. H3v).

    One of the most significant sources of evidence that early mod-
ern women were, or were at least encouraged to be, readers of
history is Thomas Danett's dedicatory epistle in *The Historie of
France: The Foure First Bookes* (1595), addressed to Anne,
Countess of Warwick, Katherine, Baroness Howard of Effing-
ham, and "to the rest of the illustrious Ladies of her sacred Majesties most Honourable privie Chamber." Danett praises the
reading practices of these ladies, recalling of Lady Katherine,
"you are accustomed to retire your selfe to your Bookes and
Muses. Verified is that in you, that never, Les alone; then when
most alone, for the more part spending your vacation of time, either in Meditation of holie letter, or conference and reading of
some notable and famous Historie." He then provides a veritable
pantheon of English women readers, including Margaret, Countess of Lennox, Anne, Countess of Oxford, Frances, Countess of
Sussex, Elizabeth, Countess of Lincoln, Mary Sidney, Countess
of Pembroke, Frances, Baroness Cobham, and Mildred, Baroness Burleigh, "manie high and loftie Ladies, who often times to
be meete with wearisomnes, exercised themselves in studie, &
reading of worthie writers . . . . to the end to incite you to treade
in their steps, and imitate their examples."[33] By valorizing these
women as readers, Danett is, in effect, creating contemporary
exemplars of avid reading as well as of virtuous living.

    Danett's catalogue of illustrious readers is significant for at
least two reasons. He implicitly suggests that a woman's life experience informs her understanding of the works she reads, and
he also comments on the individual tastes of the women he
praises.[34] For example, he remarks that "That grave Matron,

harmelesse Courtier, and faithfull servant *Francis Barones* of *Cobham*, (late wife to the noble L. and trustie Councellor yet living) to whome I was so much bound (in many duties being likewise to the whole house) as that both in her health and languishing Maladie, she sundrie times admitted me, to conferre or reade with her, finding in the Ecclesiasticall Historie her most delight," perhaps inferring that her sickness rendered her even more receptive to contemplating the history of the church than she had been formerly. Lady Katherine Howard's experience as a seasoned courtier and as the wife of a soldier-statesman is invoked in the description of her "reading of some notable and famous Historie, which whether it treate of peace, pollicie, war, or martiall exploits, can hardly discover ought, new or strange unto your wisedome, the one by your high place, long services, and Courtelie conversation, made familiar unto you, the other by nothing more, then the signall acts, and heroicall prowes of Magnanimious [*sic*] and victorious *Charles*, your Lo. and husband." The climax of Danett's epistle is his praise of Lady Burleigh's "knowledge in the Latine letters, (wherein of a subject she excelled) such were her studies, exercises, and continuall Meditation in the Greeke Doctors of the Church, (especially *Basil, Ciril, Chrisostome* and *Nazianzene*,) as a chiefe reader in that tonge (*Laurence* by name) hath ere now confessed unto me, that in his judgme[n]t she Egalled if not overmatched any, in whose profession (as expected so) most was to be required."[35]

Danett is, however, careful to subordinate Lady Burleigh's admirable scholarship to her exemplarity as a pious and domestic woman, introducing her as "that famous Religious and learned Ladie (flower of her familie,) provident mother, blessed in her posteritie." Underlying Danett's praise of Lady Burleigh's charitable acts is the assumption that a woman's reading should not be pursued as an end in itself but serve as the inspiration to perform good works, indicated by his shift of emphasis away from her reading, conducted in isolation, to her bountiful deeds, performed in the social community:

Neither were these excellent parts of hers, onely Theoricall, but still put in practise like an other *Dorcas*, full of piety and good works, as without any ostentation . . . besides her readines in solliciting for poore and distressed sutors unto her deare Lo. (the auncients Councellor of *Europe, Pater Patriae*, piller of the state, thorough whose prudent pollicie, and carefull watchings justly may be applied, *Neque periculum in R. P. suit gravius unquam, nec maius otium*) in her life time setting on her owne charge so many poore aworke, her exhitition [*sic*] to Schollers, liberallitie to Universities, bountie to exiled strangers, and her most abounding charitie everie quarter to all the prisons about London hath manifestly declared.[36]

Danett's peroration combines elements of the humanist ideal of public service with the standard move of subordinating the importance of women's reading to their imitation of the busy matron idealized in Proverbs 31. Danett's construction of the reading woman, then, both acknowledges women's intellectual acumen and interest in the political world they were (almost) as fully invested in as their husbands, while gently constraining them to limit the scope and nature of their historical inquiries. Caught in something of a double bind, Danett attempts to praise the intellectual talents of his dedicatees and their delight in reading history, thus hopefully generating additional female readers of his own volume of history (who will, presumably, be eager to imitate the exemplary women he addresses) and simultaneously to accommodate and reinscribe gender roles that shape women as pious caregivers rather than scholarly readers.

Elizabethan and Jacobean women readers seem to have shared their male counterparts' antiquarian and political interests. William Harrison's description of the intellectual accomplishments of Elizabeth's ladies, despite its hyperbolic nature, attests to the diversity of their tastes in reading, including history:

And to say how many gentlewomen and ladies there are that, beside sound knowledge of the Greek and Latin tongues, are thereto no less skillful in the Spanish, Italian, and French, or in some one of them, it resteth not in me, sith I am persuaded that, as the noblemen and gentlemen do surmount in this behalf, so these [the ladies] come very little or nothing at all behind them for their parts; which industry God continue and accomplish that which otherwise is wanting! Beside these things I could in like sort set down the ways and means whereby our ancient ladies of the court do shun and avoid idleness ... some in continual reading either of the Holy Scriptures or histories of our own or foreign nations about us, and divers in writing volumes of their own or translating of other men's into our English and Latin tongue.[37]

Harrison is careful to point out that female courtiers conform to the moral standards promulgated by conduct literature (they read merely to avoid idleness), but their attention to history and public affairs suggests that the intellectual horizons of these women may have been wider than is sometimes assumed. Grace Mildmay, after advocating knowledge of the Bible and religious doctrine, extends the range of women's necessary interests to the political:

> Also to make ourselves expert in the understanding and knowledge of the chronicles of the land, what matters of moment have passed from the beginning under the government of our royal and annointed Princes. Whereby we may be instructed to imitate and to follow the good examples of true and faithful subjects and to have their worthy acts and exploits in memory . . . whereby we may avoid and shun all treasons and treacherous attempts and all unfaithful combinations with plotters and devisers of evil.[38]

Mildmay's fervor suggests that despite women's exclusion from overt participation in affairs of state, they were nevertheless keenly aware of political events. Lady Katherine Manners (1603–49), the daughter of Francis Manners, sixth Earl of Rutland, kept a manuscript notebook before she was married in 1620; it contains three excerpts describing the French religious wars in 1562 and discussing the actions of the Dukes of Guise and Montpensier.[39] The author of *The French Historie* (1589), Anne Dowriche, writes in her dedicatory epistle: "This hath beene my ordinarie exercise for recreation at times of leasure for a long space togeather: If I were sure that you would but take halfe so much pleasure in reading it, as I have in collecting and disposing it: I shoulde not neede anie farther to commend it."[40] Such information has important implications for any reconstruction of an early modern Englishwoman's response to *The Faerie Queene* in that Spenser's female contemporaries may have enjoyed the history chronicles in Books 2 and 3 much more than the modern reader is likely to and may have found particularly resonant Britomart's pride and sorrow as she responds in Book 3 to accounts of her national history.

The diaries of Hoby and Clifford affirm the political awareness characteristic of Spenser's female readership. Two of Hoby's entries deal with the Essex uprising. On 16 July 1600, she writes: "I spent the after none in my Chamber and hard Mr Rhodes [the chaplain] read a book that was mad, as it was saied, by my lord of Esex in defence of his owne Causes." Although Hoby is not given to much personal commentary on the recorded events of her life, her coolness and lack of personal reaction to this event is particularly striking, given that the Earl of Essex was her brother-in-law by her first marriage. She refers to the Essex tragedy again, on 12 May 1601, in terms no less calm: "I hard this day, after I had praied, Mr Rhodes read the booke of my lord of Esixe treason, and I wrought."[41] Such detachment, while it is typical of Hoby's restrained style, would also have been circumspect in such a case, when other women closely related to Essex and much less discreet than Hoby were implicated in his crime.[42]

Lady Anne Clifford read about continental as well as English history, recalling of September, 1616, "This month I spent in working and reading. Mr *Dumbell* read a great part of the History of the Netherlands." Numerous entries mention her reading or being read to without citing specific titles, but in January, 1617, she heard "Mr *Sandy's* book . . . about the Government of the Turks," and sometime around April, 1617, she recalls sitting in her husband's closet where she "read much in the Turkish History [presumably the same text] and Chaucer." Wat Conniston (probably a young man in service in the Clifford household) seems to have read exclusively historical or theological works, leaving the essays and romances to the women. He is linked with "the book of *Josephus*" and "a book called *Leicester's* Common Wealth, in which there's many things concerning the reignment and death of the Queen of *Scots,* which was all read to me."[43]

Not surprisingly, records of women's reading and the books they owned did not always align neatly with those works they were admonished to read for their own spiritual, domestic, or political good. Revealing the discrepancy between what the moralists advocated and what women may have spent a good part of their time reading are the numerous secular, diversionary works enjoyed by some of these female readers, such as Sir Thomas Overbury's *Characters* (1614) and *A quip for an upstart courtier* (1620), the works of Michael Drayton and Ben Jonson, Fulke Greville's *The tragedy of Mustapha* (1609), Lady Mary Wroth's *The Countess of Montgomery's Urania* (1621), and of course *The Faerie Queene,* all part of the Countess of Bridgewater's collection. Lady Mary Wroth (1587–1653?), another exceptionally well-read woman of the period, drew heavily on the third and fourth books of *The Faerie Queene* in writing her prose romance *Urania.*[44] Anne Clifford, suffering from an unhappy and often-tempestuous marriage, notes that in her country retirement she made "good books and virtuous thoughts [her] Companions." Some of those "companions," however, would cause Vives to shudder; they include romances and poetry, particularly Spenser's, mentioned in a 1617 diary entry describing an attendant named Moll Neville reading *The Faerie Queene* aloud to her mistress. Neville seems to have preferred, or been asked to read romances, for she also read Sidney's *Arcadia* during August of 1617.[45] Clifford also read Montaigne, which is not surprising, given that John Florio had dedicated his 1603 translation of the *The essayes or morall, politike and millitarie discourses of Lo: Michaell de Montaigne* (as well as his dictionary *A worlde of wordes*, 1598) to another lady of the court, Lucy, Countess of Bedford.[46] In addition to romances and essays, Clifford relished Ovid ("All this week I spent at my work and sometimes riding abroad. My Coz. *Maria* read *Ovid's* Metamorphoses to me").[47] Clifford displayed a natural interest in her father's maritime adventures; in November of 1619, Sir Francis Slingsby "came hither to me and read to me in the sea papers about my Father's voyages." The scope of her knowledge earned for her the following encomium from John Donne: "she knew well how to Discourse of all things, from Predestination to Slea Silk."[48]

Yet another avid and eclectic (and independently minded) female reader was Elizabeth Tanfield Cary (1585–1639), Lady Falkland, who, according to her daughter's *The Lady Falkland: Her Life*, "learnt to read very soon and loved it much." Cary's daughter attributes her mother's scholarly nature to the fate of being much alone as a child: "She having neither brother nor sister, nor other companion of her age, spent her whole time in reading; to which she gave herself so much that she frequently read all night; so as her mother was fain to forbid her servants to let her have candles, which command they turned to their own profit, and let themselves be hired by her to let her have them, selling them to her at half a crown apiece, so was she bent to reading."[49] Whether Cary's daughter is trying to downplay the origins of her mother's writing career or rhetorically shaping her account of her mother's life to conform to culturally acceptable standards of femininity, she often explains her mother's literary interests as a matter of merely adapting to social circumstances rather than crediting her mother with unusual ambition. When living with her formidable mother-in-law soon after marriage, Cary was confined to her chamber, "which seeing she little cared for, but entertained herself with reading, the mother-in-law took away all her books, with command to have no more brought her; then she set herself to make verses."[50]

Cary's fondness for reading is illustrated in her daughter's amusing recollection of her mother's elevating books above such

CHESTER COLLEGE LIBRARY

practical matters as dressing: "her women were fain to walk around the room after her (which was her custom) while she was seriously thinking on some other business, and pin on her things and braid her hair; and while she writ or read, curl her hair and dress her head." After her husband's death, she lived very frugally and "spent her own time almost wholly in reading." Again, the range of these reading interests is remarkably extensive:

> She had read very exceeding much: poetry of all kinds, ancient and modern, in several languages, all that ever she could meet; history very universally, especially ancient Greek and Roman historians, and chroniclers whatsoever of her own country; and the French histories very thoroughly, of most other countries something, though not so universally; of the ecclesiastical history very much, most especially concerning its chief pastors. Of books treating of moral virtue or wisdom (and natural knowledge as Pliny . . . Seneca, Plutarch's *Morals*, . . . and of late ones, such as French Mountaine [Montaigne], and English Bacon) she had read very many when she was young, not without making her profit of them.[51]

This comprehensive statement occurs near the end of the *Life*, and it clearly emphasizes Cary's "serious" reading, that which reflected her earnestness in seeking moral and religious truth, as would befit a daughter's hagiography. It therefore does not include details about the poetry she must have read early in life, or other fictional literature she may have read following her conversion.

Books, according to this account of Cary's life, had a powerful impact on her. This emphasis on Cary's reading may serve her daughter's Roman Catholic, polemical purposes[52] in constructing an image of her mother that is saint-like in its devotion to the life of the mind and spirit, piously disregarding the life of the flesh and its material comforts. In describing her mother's conversion experience, she may even be drawing a parallel to St. Augustine's conversion by singling out a particular text. The author's Catholicism, though never shrill, may inform her citing, and subtly criticizing, the Anglican apologist Hooker, which, counter to his text's intent, caused Cary to question her faith: "She continued to read much, and when she was about twenty year old, through reading, she grew into much doubt of her religion. The first occasion of it was reading a Protestant book much esteemed, called Hooker's *Ecclesiastical Polity*." In the same paragraph, she mentions that Cary's doubt was unintentionally furthered by her brother-in-law, who "was a great reader of the

Fathers, especially St. Augustine, whom he affirmed to be of the religion of the Church of Rome. He persuaded her to read the Fathers also (what she had read till then having been for the most part poetry and history, except Seneca, and some other such, whose Epistles it is probable she translated afore she left her father's house."[53] Cary indeed read Hooker, Calvin, and the church fathers recommended to her (as prescriptive moralists had recommended these texts to a general female readership), but the use to which she put them, the way she "translated" them experientially—using them to confirm her own conversion to Catholicism and thus reinforce her independence of and resistance to her husband, eldest son, and the English church—was clearly not part of the anticipated result.

What, then, can we conclude about late sixteenth- and early seventeenth-century Englishwomen's attitudes toward reading and the ways various authors tried to shape those attitudes? Although the intellectual curiosity demonstrated by Cary and Clifford may have been exceptional, the scope of their interests may have been relatively representative of many of their female contemporaries, who, based on the limited evidence we have, evinced similarly varied tastes in books. Clearly, many women did indeed align their reading interests with those religious and domestic subjects prescribed for them, and it would be grossly inaccurate to suggest that women universally contested these prescriptions as radically "resistant" readers. Yet we need to recall that women were not mindless automatons, completely programmed by oppressive patriarchal discourses to read only works that promoted the health of their souls, the chastity of their bodies, and the successful functioning of their homes. Far from being prohibited intellectual engagement with political issues and the way those issues shaped national histories, women readers were taken seriously as interested, if not publicly active, members of the commonwealth. That women's reading interests extended beyond the genres and authors prescribed for them also indicates the autonomy women exercised as readers and reminds us that overtly didactic strictures about social behavior, whether in educational treatises or fictionalized courtesy literature such as *The Faerie Queene*, might, or might not, have been carried out. As suggested by the histories of Anne Clifford, who may have been more interested in books and property than husbands, and Elizabeth Cary, who read the "right" texts but then defiantly refused to be dissuaded by them from becoming a Catholic, women could be wayward in their use of literacy. My next chapter will focus in more detail on the anxiety this potential waywardness generated, particularly in connection with women reading romance literature, and the ways Spenser's *Faerie Queene* comments on this anxiety in its depiction of autonomous female readers.

2

"How doubtfully all Allegories may be construed": Women's Interpretive Strategies

> . . . seldome is the tale carried cleane from an others mouth.
> —Margaret Tyler, *The Mirrour of Princely Deedes and Knighthood* (1578)

Isabella Whitney, in "The Auctor to the Reader" preceding *A Sweet Nosgay* (1573), observes that the ability or willingness to appropriate texts for one's own edification varies dramatically from reader to reader:

> But as we are not all a lyke,
> nor of complexion one:
> So that which helpeth some we see,
> to others good doth none.

Spenser's contemporaries were constantly reminded (most often in prefatory material, as in Whitney's case) of the multiple interpretations a given text might generate and of the variety of readerships it might be addressing. Gender was one, but by no means the only, marker of distinct readerships signaled in dedicatory sonnets and epistles. For example, George Gascoigne's *The posies* (1575) contains addresses to young gentlemen, divines, and readers in general (the latter group is further categorized by their degree of curiosity, ignorance, etc.). In his discussion of this "reader diversity," John Kerrigan cites Thomas Dekker's analogy likening authors to cooks who must please "A thousand palats. . . . A hard taske: one sayes, it is too harsh[:] another, too supple: another too triviall: another too serious."[1]

Motivations for reading, being influenced by gender, class, occupation, religious beliefs, and even pragmatic agendas that changed from day to day, differed tremendously from reader to reader during the sixteenth and seventeenth centuries, as they do today. Although reader-response theorists have only relatively recently popularized this notion, it was an early modern commonplace. Philemon Holland's 1603 translation of Plutarch's "How a yoong man ought to heare poets, and how he may take profit by reading poemes" is a case in point:

> Moreover, like as in pasturage and feeding, the Bee setleth upon flowres: the goate searcheth after greene leaves and brouseth yoong buds: the Swine searcheth for roots, and other beasts for the seed & fruit; Even so in reading Poems, one gathereth the flowre of the History: another cleaveth to the elegancie of phrase and furniture of words, . . . Others there be who affect morall sentences aptly fitted to the reformation of maners.[2]

Lisa Jardine and Anthony Grafton have documented the ways Gabriel Harvey employed a variety of reading strategies and goals, reading a poem politically one day and morally the next.[3] Meaning appears to have been highly contingent, dependent in large part on the locale and company in which one read, in addition to the purposes for which one read. These were often frivolous, according to Susan Du Verger, who laments in the dedicatory epistle to her translation of John Peter Camus's *Admirable Events* that "many reade books for curiosity, others for variety, or to passe time, and for want of other imployment, another with envy, few with sincerity, few with a desire to profit, and to put in practise the good instructions they finde therein."[4] Such an assessment suggests that Spenser's female readers might, or might not, have taken to heart the explicit morals addressed to them throughout *The Faerie Queene*, or might have freely appropriated aspects of the text for their own ends. John M. Wallace's examination of early modern commentaries on the classics, mythological literature, and Renaissance epic suggests that a "wide latitude of response [was] permitted within the pale of unstrained interpretation."[5]

Given the wealth of readership studies produced in the 1980s and 1990s, postulating a generic, monolithic "reader" of English Renaissance poetry is even less acceptable today than when Paul Alpers denounced this practice in 1967: "Modern scholars often refer to 'the Elizabethan reader' or 'sixteenth-century readers' as if all Spenser's contemporaries had the same attitudes and responses to his poem, or indeed any poem."[6] I confess to using the similarly generic term "female reader" in this study of *The Faerie Queene*'s engagement with Elizabethan and Jacobean female courtiers, but I have done so of necessity, given the paucity of detailed reading records, and in full awareness that it glosses over important differences among these women. Although lack of detailed historical evidence makes such a semi-generic term unavoidable, we can at least inquire as to how these women may have read, or were taught or expected to read, and, in particular, how they might have interpreted and perhaps even appropriated significant aspects of *The Faerie Queene*. Kerrigan has argued that Gabriel Harvey, as he read Gascoigne, looked "for strategies which would advance his own career in the courtly world inhabited by 'F. I.' "[7] Why could not the women closely linked with the court and contending for privileges dispensed by the queen have similarly interrogated fictional texts for clues about maintaining and advancing their own "careers" or social positions?

Another challenge to reconstructing early modern women's readings of the Spenserian text lies in the particular openness of allegorical epic romance to multiple interpretations, as Harington acknowledges repeatedly throughout his annotations of *Orlando Furioso*. Demonstrating readers' tendencies to construct meanings that go beyond an author's intention, Harington disarmingly observes of the allegory in the initial book, "I find not much to be said, except one should be so curious to search for an allegorie where none is intended by the Author him selfe," but then goes on to expound not one but four possible meanings.[8] Later he confirms, even invites individual interpretations: "For the Allegorie of this booke [Book 4] much might be said of *Atlant*, of his horse, and his shield, but I will only touch what I thinke will be thought most worth the noting, and let passe the rest for each mans private conceipt" (30).

Extant annotated copies of *The Faerie Queene* confirm that multiple perspectives and goals resulted in highly individual interpretations of the poem. The annotations in William Drummond of Hawthornden's 1609 edition of *The Faerie Queene* reflect, not surprisingly, his literary interests. Drummond marks primarily the sources of Spenser's allusions, annotates characters and places, and signals passages of "special effectiveness or beauty," such as the *blason* of the captive Serena (perhaps with an eye to imitation in his own work).[9] The notes of John Dixon, penned in 1597 in the copy of the poem belonging to the Earl of Bessborough (the 1590 edition of Books 1–3), are less concerned with aesthetics than with politics and theology. Given Dixon's ardently Protestant and nationalistic focus, the notes are most numerous for Book 1, which Dixon reads as an allegory of the English Reformation, explicitly identifying Redcrosse with Leicester, Duessa with Mary Queen of Scots, and Una with the true church and Elizabeth. He thus equates the six-year delay in the marriage of Una and Redcrosse with the six years of Mary I's reign, and equates Una's betrothal with the day of Elizabeth's coronation, the marriage of the true English church to Christ. The marginalia include references to relevant scripture texts and glosses on the chronicle histories in 2.10 and 3.3. According to Graham Hough, Dixon was "indifferent to the courtly and romantic aspects of *The Faerie Queene*; it is the Protestant divinity, the ascetic morality, and the national history that concern him." Dixon glosses the reconciliation between Britomart and Guyon, "Unitie between Temperance and Chastitie," and elevates allegorical meaning over comprehension of the literal plot. In Book 3, for example, Dixon "gets hopelessly mixed up in the complicated narrative and makes mistaken identification of the new characters with others whom he has already met." Dixon's gender may only be registered in his (comparatively heavy) annotations of Book 2, cantos 10 through 12. Dixon comments, for example, on the wiles of sirens in 2.12.32–33: "womanish alluringe baites, and perswasions, wherby fonde intemperat men, are ofte over-come, to the hurte both of soull and bodye."[10]

As an alternative to Dixon's allegorically oriented notes, other early readers might have simply tried to keep the story line straight. Paul Alpers cites the annotations of Sir Thomas Posthumous Hoby (Margaret's husband), which trace literal plot developments.[11] A much more sophisticated reader of the poem, Ben Jonson, seems to have read at least one intriguing episode in a highly intertextual manner. Jonson's annotation of 3.2.1 reads, "<W>omen in former / <a>ges have excelld in / <b>old deeds of armes. / <S>ee. Sands Ovid." James Riddell and Stanley Stewart infer that Jonson is referring to George Sandys's 1632 Folio commentary on *Metamorphoses* Book 8, in which he links the story of Atalanta to Plato's endorsement of women being trained in arms. "For Jonson, Spenser's text—like Sandys's commentary on the passage from Ovid—is seen to indict men for weakening the state by refusing to recognize the martial power of women."[12] Although Riddell and Stewart do not analyze Jonson's (surprisingly) neutral observation in light of the attitudes toward women he expresses in his own poetry or of the contra-

2: "HOW DOUBTFULLY ALL ALLEGORIES MAY BE CONSTRUED" 53

dictory attitudes toward women's rule in Spenser's text, it stands to reason that if Jonson made this connection, a female reader such as Anne Clifford (who also owned and read a copy of Sandys's Ovid) might have done so as well.

Commonplace books provide another way of ascertaining how poems in general and *The Faerie Queene* in particular were read. Excerpts from *The Faerie Queene* figured in personal commonplace books and published anthologies of the period, including those authored by women. Daniel Tuvil's *Asylum Veneris, or a sanctuary for ladies* (1616) quotes *The Faerie Queene* 5.8.1 on women's beauty and 3.5.52 on their chastity, as does the 1600 work *England's Parnassus*, a dictionary of quotations on such topics as "Beauty," "War," and "Life."[13] Elizabeth Grymeston (ca. 1563–1603) also borrows from Spenser's poem in her *Miscelanea, Meditations, Memoratives* (1604). Elaine Beilin notes that by appropriating such quotations Grymeston is taking possession of "jealously guarded masculine knowledge and language by making it a quintessentially feminine gift, a mother's advice to her son."[14] The same could perhaps be said of M. R., the author of *The mothers counsell* (1630), who also borrowed from *The Faerie Queene* (notably quotations from Books 2 and 5) to suit her purpose.[15]

The only extant annotations of *The Faerie Queene* by a woman seem to be the minimal ones of Lady Raleigh in the edition given to her son, Carew Raleigh. Walter Oakeshott hypothesizes that Sir Walter Raleigh had begun annotating the work in his later years and that following his execution the text passed into Lady Raleigh's hands, who was eager for her son to have some of his father's books. Approximately 3,394 lines have been marked, presumably by Raleigh, and more than 2,000 of them comprise passages that could be read as allusions to Raleigh: Belphoebe's first appearance, the Belphoebe/Timias passages, the Marinell passages, and those relating to Sir Calidore (Raleigh, like Sir Philip Sidney and other courtiers out of favor with the queen, had been forced to withdraw into the pastoral realm). Lady Raleigh annotated Raleigh's two commendatory verses as "bothe thes of your fathar's making" and connected the Fox in *Mother Hubberd's Tale* with "Burly." Oakeshott suggests that Lady Raleigh valued the book as a relic of her husband and hence did not add any of her own annotations, which is understandable but disappointing to those who wonder what she might have made of Amoret, Florimell, and especially Serena.[16] Although the material conditions of this particular reading—a wife and mother preparing the text for her son in an attempt to vindicate her dead husband—may have necessitated a particularly passive interpretive stance, her response to Spenser's text may have differed considerably when read from the perspective of an exiled maid of honor and Raleigh's lover.

The presentation verses penned in 1610 by Henry Stanford to Elizabeth Carey, Lady Hunsdon, are suggestive of how Stanford wished or expected her to read Spenser's poem:

> h. st. to yᵉ lady Hunsdon 1610. faery quene
> Having no other gift right noble dame
> to testifie my mynde this booke I send
> the autour when he liv'd did beare your name
> & for to honour ladies this he penned
> here may you reade in sugred verse set out
> the praises of *Belphebe* worthie Quene
> & faery landes adventures all about
> wᵗʰ other exploites worthie to be seene
> here Georges holines may us direct
> to conquer all the monstrous shapes of sin
> & Guions temperance make us suspect
> the sugred baites of pleasures wanton ginnes
> > Deign it to reade & reape such fruites it beares
> > I still will wishe you long & happie yeares.[17]

Stanford quickly moves from Spenser's (and his own) complimentary purpose ("to honour ladies") into the political ("the praises of *Belphebe* worthie Quene") and especially the moral ("Georges holines" and "Guions temperance"). The slippage from the initially open-ended "here may *you* reade" (my emphasis) to the didactic collective pronoun of "may us direct" may indicate Stanford's conscious or unconscious instinct to hold up the Redcrosse knight and Guyon as moral exemplars rather than the more inflammatory, ambiguous Britomart, the knight of chastity, who might well have been singled out (as Spenser's text in fact does) as particularly germane to a female recipient of the poem. Stanford's verses may ultimately tell us more about how he read the poem or *wanted* Elizabeth Carey to read it than about how she actually read it.[18]

Stanford's references to the knights of holiness and temperance underscore one of the primary tenets of Renaissance reading theory: although the texts are remarkably open to diverse interpretations, the end or goal of reading is moral application. John Wallace argues that an important source text for this combination of openness tempered with morality is Philemon Holland's translation of Plutarch. Holland states that the text "pertaineth unto those onely who read ancient Poets, as well Greeke as Latin, to take heede and beware how they take an impression of dangerous opinions, in regard either of religion or manners: yet a man may comprehend likewise under it all other profane authors, out of which a minde that is not corrupt may gather profit, so they be handled wisely and used with discretion." With certain qualifications ("a minde that is *not corrupt may* gather profit, *so* they be handled *wisely* and used with *discretion*," my emphasis), Holland grants the male reader access to profane authors, trusting him to exercise discrimination and moral rectitude. "And for that there be some hard and difficult places, which like unto forked waies, may leave the mindes of the Readers doubtfull and in suspense: he sheweth that it is an easie matter to apply the same well, and that withall, a man may reforme those sentences ill placed, and accommodate them to many things."[19] In other words, the reader is to "re-form," "reverse" the author's words in accordance with the culture's prevailing moral code. Content becomes less important than employing the proper reading protocol: "children and yoong men if they be well nourtured and orderly inured in the reading of Poemes, will learne after a sort to draw alwaies some holesome and profitable doctrine or other, even out of those places which move suspition of lewd and absurd sense."[20] What constitutes a "holesome and profitable" reading is one, presumably, that reinforces the dominant social order and the gender roles it inscribes.

Yet situating the responsibility for extracting and applying morals within the mind of the reader, the hallmark of Renaissance reading theory, becomes extremely problematic when the reader is a woman. "N. N.'"s English translation of Jacques Du Bosc's *The Compleat Woman* includes a sixteen-page section entitled "Of Reading" that, as Plutarch's *Philosophie* does with young men, defends women's right to read secular material as long as the reader's goal is the achievement of virtue: "The helps of learning fortifies the best inclinations, and they who are perswaded that reading of Books is a Schoole to learn to do ill with the more dexterity, might do better to beleeve that women finde therein more meanes to correct then corrupt themselves" (sig. Dd1r). Du Bosc seems relatively enlightened and moderate, seeming to refute assumptions about women's excessively wayward inclinations as he maintains "that a woman should be intelligent to appeare in conversations, it may be this opinion at first would offend the ignorant and simple, who imagining all like themselves, think a woman cannot study or reade without proving vitious, or at least without being suspected" (sig. Dd1r). (His willingness to indict members of his own sex resembles that of Mulcaster, who admits honestly that men as well as women have abused their learning: "Some wymen abuse writing to that end, some reading to this, some all that they learne any waye, to some other ill some waye. And I praie you what do we?")[21] Both Du Bosc and Mulcaster before him may be responding to such carpers as Edward Hake: after grumbling that few women of his time are eager to pursue either virtue or learning, Hake claims that "that same small number which have anye knowledge at all, doe so greatlye abuse it, that much better were it they shoulde unlearne that againe which they have alreadie learned, then miserably to abuse it as they doe, or at the least wise (as we see them) to make equalle Pampheticall trifles with wholesome Doctrine and tryall of lyfe."[22] Du Bosc argues:

> what can be desired for ornament of the minde, which is not in bookes? where they [women] finde instructions of all sorts, where they see Vertue under all kinds of visages; where they discover Truth in what maner soever they desire it, they behold it with all its force in Philosophers, with all its purity in Historians, with all its beauty, dresses, and artificiousnesse in Oratours, and Poets. (sig. G3r-v)

Acknowledging that women are not all the same and that their reading tastes will be affected by their social position and temperament, Du Bosc continues, "It is in this pleasing variety, that all sorts of humours and conditions finde wherewith to content themselves, and wherewith to be instructed" (sig. G3v).

However, Du Bosc is of his age in prohibiting the reading of prose romances as "poysonus" and highly unsuitable for women. Rather unusually, and at great length, he gives voice to the women's anticipated objections to this prohibition:

> Why shall they forbid, say they the, [*sic*] *reading* of these Pamphlets, while they permit those of Poets; and what likelyhood is it to thinke that fictions are more dangerous in prose, then in Poesie? What need is there, for so light considerations, to deprive ones self of the sweet pleasure of life? and what greater contentment can be imagined, then to *read* in those quaint Pamphlets, so many different successes, where we feel our passions moved according to the adventures treated of. And likwise though we know well, how the objects that

touch us, have never been, or are no more, yet have we sometimes, a true compassion for fained miseries, and we shed tears for imaginary Shepheards. (sig. H2r)

This objection emphasizes the passions, perhaps to be expected in a male author's ventriloquized account of a woman's reading affect, but his feigned female response then articulates a version of the Plutarchan (and Sidneyan)[23] defense:

Wee should not, say they, renounce bookes, because we may meet therein with some thing evill, as if indeed wee should never take the Sea, for feare of the rocks; or that the art of navigation were not most certaine and profitable, because now and then, there are some who suffer shipwrack through disastre, or ignorance. There is no reason, to leave the good, because often mixed with evill. Prudence teacheth to sever vice from vertue, and not to fly them both at once; otherwise we should pluck out our eyes, for feare of abusing them with our lookes, we should stand stock still for feare of falling. (sig. H2r–v)

Du Bosc repeats this defense, however, only to refute it, citing the "lewdnes, wherewith many of these Pamphlets, are fraught" and advocating instead the reading of histories: "And truly to examine this well, what contentment can there bee in these Pamphlets, which is not found in History? See we not successes, adventures, and events, faire and Tragick enough as well in love, as in fortune, to move, to teach, and to recreate with?" (sig. H2v–H3r).[24]

Despite his ultimately conservative stance, Du Bosc's reservations about the potentially deleterious effects of reading on women's morals are phrased much more pacifically than the concerns of most sixteenth- and seventeenth-century moralists. Much of the didactic literature of the period voices deep anxiety about female interpretive autonomy, and it sexualizes the experience of women's reading to a far greater extent than it does men's when expressing concern about the moral impact of reading. The potential advantages of women's reading were, to some minds, outweighed by the concomitant dangers, notably that women might feel empowered to form their own interpretations of the book's subject matter, as Juan Luis Vives fears: "But as touchyng some [works], wyse and sad [serious, learned] men must be asked counsayle of, in them. Nor the woman oughte not to folowe hir owne judgemente, lest whan she hath but a lyght entring in learning, she shoulde take false for true: hurtfull in stede of of [sic] holsome folyshe and pevysshe for sad and wyse. . . . Therfore on holy daies continnally, and sometyme on workynge dayes, let hir reade or here such as shall lifte up the mynd to god, and set it in a Christen quietnes, and make the living better" (*ICW*, sig. D4v). With a tongue-in-cheek humor evocative of Christine de Pizan, Isabella Whitney playfully assumes the stance of Vives's ideal, ever-so-humble female reader: because she is sick and is out of service, she

> Had leasure good, (though learning lackt)
>   some study to apply:
> To reade such Bookes, wherby I thought
>   my selfe to edyfye.
> Sometime the Scriptures I perusd,
>   but wantyng a Devine:
> For to resolve mee in such doubts,
>   as past this head of mine
> To understand: I layd them by,
>   and histories gan read. . . .[25]

Whitney's seeming humility serves her own rhetorical purpose, however; by reading and then rejecting men's books (because they depress her and fail to satisfy her current interest), she prepares a space for her own work, a free adaptation of Hugh Platt's *The Floures of Philosophie* (1572).

Even worse than practicing her own judgment and thus risking "misinterpretation," a woman might rebel against a strict diet of morally edifying works, as Puritan Thomas Salter fears:

> Some perhaps will alledge that a maiden beyng well learned, and able to searche and reade sonderie authors, maie become chaste and godlie by readyng the godlie and chaste lives of diverse: but I answere, who can deny, that, seynge of her selfe, she is able to reade and understande the Christian poets, too wete, *Prudentio, Prospero, Juvenco, Pawlino, Nazianzeno,* and suche like, that she will not also reade Lascivious bookes of *Ovide, Catullus, Propercius, Tibullus.* . . . (*MM*, sig. C4v–D1r)

Salter's grim judgment is that "the evell use of learnyng hath more often tymes beene cause of discommodytie and domage, then the right and laudable use of it hath beene of profitte and benyfite" (sig. C4r). As Elaine Beilin remarks on the uneasiness present even in the work of the fairly tolerant Mulcaster, "Tudor educational theorists were at best ambivalent and at worst prohibitive when considering how women might use their education."[26] Even Anniball Magnocavalli, the moral spokesman of Guazzo's *The civile Conversation*, who must respond to William Guazzo's concern that "in teaching our women to write and reade, we doe but give them occasio[n] to turne over the hundred Novelles of *Boccace*, and to write amorous & lascivious letters," sounds unconvincing and overly optimistic as he contends, somewhat feebly, that literacy also enables women to "reade the lives of Saints, to keepe the accounts of the house, and to write their mindes to their absent husbands" (*CC*, 158v). Clearly, female literacy was considered by many male educationalists to be a double-edged sword.[27]

Educational rhetoric is thus characterized by a tremendous uneasiness about the volatile interaction of women with texts and the operation of female interpretive agency. Fears about how women *might* read constantly undercut pronouncements about how they *ought* to read, and injunctions about how women are to read are often fraught with contradictions. Women are enjoined to invent "better" (i.e., acceptable in light of gender norms) meanings to impose on secular material, drawing on the Plutarchan paradigm that implies women possess a degree of intellectual sophistication and moral responsibility. Yet the same author might then argue against women being allowed to read at all, suggesting that women are so passive and malleable, so vulnerable to textual designs upon their virtue, that their behavior will inevitably be dictated by whatever they read. Conversely, authors occasionally express concern that women will read extremely actively, even subversively, by intentionally elevating the literal over the allegorical meaning.[28] Such fears reveal discrepancies in the moralists' assumptions about female interpretive agency; sometimes they radically underestimate women's intellectual and discriminatory capabilities while grossly overestimating the power of texts, and then, conversely, assign wayward interpretive tendencies to the powerful female readers of the passive texts.

Women's reading, whether constructed as stupidly gullible or willfully rebellious, is almost always sexualized. As Mary Ellen Lamb comments, "when men were represented as reading Sidney's *Arcadia*, it was usually described as a work replete with political or moral precepts; when read by women, however, it was represented as dangerously or titillatingly sexual."[29] This obsessive sexualization constitutes the main difference between prohibitions on men's and women's reading material. Fearing that women would be incited by reading to commit adultery (shades—

pun intended—of Paolo and Francesca), Heinrich Bullinger recommends stringent restrictions on the reading of daughters: "let
them avoyd ydlenes, be occupied ether doing some profitable
thyng for your family, or elles readynge some godly boke, lette
them not reade bokes of fables, of fond and lyght love, but call
upon God to have pure hartes and chaste, that they might cleve
only to theyr spouse."[30] Edward Hake views the negative sexual
effects of female literacy to be inevitable: "Eyther shee is alto-
gither kept from exercises of good learning, and knowledge of
good letters, or else she is so nouseled in amorous bookes, vaine
stories and fonde trifeling fancies, that shee smelleth of naughtinesse even all hir lyfe after, as a vessel which being once seasoned, doth never forgo the sent of the first licour."[31] Not even
Lucrece, the oft-cited exemplar of absolute chastity, is free from
suspicion when depicted as a reader: "*Erubuit posuitque meum
Lucrecia librum; / Sed coram Bruto. Brute recede, leget. Lucrecia* (by which he [Martial, whom Harington is quoting] signifies
any chast matron) will blush and be ashamed to read a lascivious
booke, but how? not except *Brutus* be by, that is if any grave man
should see her read it, but if *Brutus* turne his backe, she will to
it agayne and read it all."[32]

Richard Brathwait reminds his female readers that "*Books*
treating of light subjects, are Nurseries of wantonnesse: they instruct the loose Reader to become naught, whereas before,
touching naughtinesse he knew naught" (*EG*, 139). Brathwait
here seems to be articulating a generality, as his use of the masculine pronoun suggests, but after listing such examples of "light
subjects" as accounts of Ganymede's rape, lais in Euripides, and
the poetry of Anacreon, he focuses his argument more specifically on female readers: "*Venus* and *Adonis* are unfitting Con-
sorts for a Ladies bosome. Remove them timely from you, if they
ever had entertainment by you lest, like the *Snake* in the fable,
they annoy you" (*EG*, 139). Situated in a section entitled "Fancy,"
Brathwait's admonition indicates the troublesome relationship
between text and reader and the general inability to determine
which takes precedence in the hermeneutic process.

Brathwait expresses similar concern over women's prurient
reading tastes in *The English Gentleman* (1630). At first, he
chastises the youthful male appetite and urges studious exercise
("conversing with the *Muses*"), because it "draweth the mind
from effeminacie, as remisnesse feeds the desire, and addes fuell
to unlawfull heat. And no lesse occasion gives wanton discourse,
or Lascivious Bookes to the enraged affections of distempered

Youth." Citing the poetry of Anacreon and even the philosophical writings of Plato as being morally tainted, he recommends,

> Such Discourses should be throwne to the darkest corner of our studies, as that of *Ovids* was by *Augustus*, which tend to corrupt *Youth*, and divert his minde from the exercise of vertue. But alas; to what height of licentious libertie are these corrupter times growne? When that *Sex*, where Modesty should claime a native prerogative, gives way to foments to exposed loosenesse; by not only attending to the wanton discourse of immodest Lovers, but carrying about them (even in their naked Bosomes, where chastest desires should only lodge) the amorous toyes of *Venus* and *Adonis*: which Poem, with others of like nature, they heare with such attention, peruse with such devotion, and retaine with such delectation, as no Subject can equally relish their unseasoned palate, like those lighter discourses.[33]

Tellingly, Brathwait begins by chastising the amorous tendencies of young men, but when the issue of reading erotic literature comes up, he focuses on *women's* susceptibility. Brathwait continues his vilification of lascivious women readers, distinguishing them from their more virtuous counterparts: "I will not insist upon them, but leave them, to have their names registred amongst those infamous Ladies; *Semphronia, Scribonia, Clitemnestra, Cleopatra, Faustina, Messalina*, whose memories purchased by odious *Lust*, shall survive the course of time; as the memory of those famous Matrons, *Octavia, Porcia, Caecilia, Cornelia*, shall transcend the period of time." He finally returns to his focus on young men, noting male exemplars of sexual continence (Alexander the Great, Scipio, Marius), but his ultimate exhortation to redirect youthful energies away from sexual pursuits—"amongst employments, ever mix such *Readings* as may minister matter, either *Divine*, or *Morall*, to allay the heat of this distempered *passion*"—is still marked by a gendered double standard: "for *Idlenesse* maketh of *men, women*, of *women, beasts*, of *beasts, monsters*."[34] Succumbing to the seductions of the text render men effeminate, women subhuman.

John Davies implies that women intentionally read erotic poetry to excite their lust:

> Another [poet] (ah Lord helpe) mee vilifies
> With Art of Love, and how to subtilize,
> Making lewd *Venus*, with eternall Lines,
> To tye *Adonis* to her loves designes:
> Fine wit is shew'n therein: but finer were

If not attired in such bawdy Geare.
But be it as it will: the coyest Dames,
In private read it for their Closet-games:
For, sooth to say, the Lines so draw them on,
To the venerian speculation,
That will they, nill they (if of flesh they bee)
They will thinke of it, sith *loose* Thought is free.[35]

"Coyest Dames" assume the guise of shyness, retiring quietly to the seclusion of their chambers, but they are also "coy" in that they are "lascivious" readers (listed in the *Oxford English Dictionary* as a possible synonym).

Whores especially are depicted as reading such material, which seemingly confirms the concern expressed by Vives that romances were "bokes of baudes craftes." Harebrain, a citizen in Thomas Middleton's *A Mad World, My Masters* (1608) is obsessively focused on maintaining the virtue of his wife. When the courtesan Frank Gullman visits Mistress Harebrain, Harebrain (unaware of Gullman's profession) encourages her to instruct his wife, whom he has left inside at her lute. "I have convey'd away all her wanton pamphlets, as *Hero and Leander, Venus and Adonis*; oh, two luscious mary-bone pies for a young married wife. Here, prithee, take the *Resolution*, and read to her a little."[36] Harebrain urges Gullman to read the chapter on hell to his wife: "Terrify her, terrify her; go, read to her the horrible punishments for itching wantonness, the pains allotted for adultery; tell her her thoughts, her very dreams are answerable." Gullman happily instructs Mistress Harebrain, but rather than advising her to replace her "naughty" books with morally edifying tomes, she imparts female stratagems for preserving their autonomy as readers:

If he chance steal upon you, let him find
Some book lie open 'gainst an unchaste mind,
And coted [quoted] scriptures, though for your own pleasure
You read some stirring pamphlet, and convey it
Under your skirt, the fittest place to lay it.

These deceitful measures prove effective. Harebrain muses in 3.1,

Come I at unawares by stealth upon her,
I find her circled in with divine write
Of heavenly meditations; here and there

> Chapters with leaves tuck'd up, which when I see,
> They either tax pride or adultery.[37]

Harebrain's removal of his young wife's books fails to contain either her sexual activity or her determination to read what she wills. Although the hoodwinking of possessive husbands is a standard motif in city comedy, the form this example takes attests to the ability of early modern women to resist restrictions on their autonomy as readers, a resistance Spenser also addresses in *The Faerie Queene*.

What other strategies, more subtle than Harebrain's, were employed to control women's interpretation of texts and limit the meanings they might construct? One, used by John Lyly in his *Euphues and his England* epistle "To the Ladies and Gentlewomen of England," was to depict women's reading as a thoroughly frivolous activity and thereby render it less threatening:

> It resteth Ladies, that you take the paines to reade it, but at such times as you spend in plaieng with your little Dogges . . . that when you shall be wearie in reading of the one, you may bee readie to sport with the other: or handle him as you doe your Junkets, that when you can eate no more, you tye some in your napkin for children, for if you bee filled with the first part, put the second in your pocket for your wayting maides: *Euphues* had rather lye shut in a Ladies casket, then open in a Schollers studie.
>   Yet after dinner, you maye overlooke him to keepe you from sleepe, or if you be heavie to bring you a sleepe. . . . I woulde you woulde reade bookes that have more shewe of pleasure then ground of profit, then should *Euphues* be . . . often in your hands. . . . If a Tailour make your gowne too little, you cover his fault with a broade stomacher, if too greate, with a number of plightes . . . my trust is you will deale in the like manner with *Euphues*, that if hee have not fead your humour, yet you will excuse him more then the Taylour: for could *Euphues* take the measure of a womans minde, as the Taylour doth of her bodie, hee would go as neere to fit them for a fancie, as the other doth for a fashion.[38]

Lyly tries to have it both ways: he first dismisses the importance of women's mental activity by equating reading with eating candy and playing with lapdogs, but then appeals to women's imaginative capabilities, asking them to piece out the imperfections of his own work. The impossibility of ever taking "the measure of a womans minde" and his fashion metaphor speak to the volatility of women's interpretations—ever-changing and superficial, they can therefore be easily dismissed.

Another means of limiting the autonomy of female readers was to allow women only positive exemplars by prescribing selected books (as discussed in chapter 1) and emphasizing the imitation of ideal types such as Penelope and Lucrece. Book dedications indicate that one of the key interpretive strategies prescribed for (and quite possibly practiced by) women was that of imitation. Sir Thomas Elyot's *The Defence of Good Women* (an account of Zenobia as ideal queen, wife, and mother) had been intended to teach "good wives to know well their duties," as Elyot claims in the preface to *The image of governance* (1540).[39] Prefacing *Willobie his Avisa*, an epistle by Hadrian Dorrell addresses "all the constant Ladies and Gentlewomen of England that feare God," encouraging them to emulate textual models and thereby perhaps earn an exemplary place in another author's book: "If mine Author have found a Britaine Lucretia or an English Susanna, envie not at her life (good Ladies) but rather endevor to deserve the like."[40]

Yet texts also register awareness that such a strategy was not foolproof, as suggested by Ariosto's tale of the cuckolded Mantuan knight, whose wife has been brought up in isolation, surrounded by images of only the most chaste women. Employing the strictness called for by Vives, Salter, and others, the young woman's father "caused chast old women, her to nourish" and decorates her domestic interior with figures to emulate:

> In this same house, in which she grew most faire,
> And in those years when youth doth chiefly florish,
> He let not any thither to repaire
> That were in looks, or speech, or manners whorish
> But contrarie, he causd in marble faire
> Or else on tables to be drawne and carved,
> All such whose chastities had praise desarved.
>
> Nor onely such as have in auncient times,
> Bene patterns true of manners chast and pure,
> And have opposd against all fleshly crimes,
> Most chast and vertuous thoughts (a buckler sure)
> By which their name to such hye honour climes,
> As their great praise shall evermore indure:
> But such as shall excell in times to come,
> Of which those eight, that erst you saw be some.
>
> (*OF*, 43.15–16)

Ariosto's literary depiction reconfigures the painted and carved images of exemplary ladies, the eight referred to in the final line of stanza 16 being the "chast and sober dames / That now do live, but were unborne as then" (42.74) whose forms are carved (appropriately) in white marble and decorate the fountain described in 42.72 ff. (They are positioned above two male figures, the poets who praise the ladies' virtues, in a metafictional invitation to Ariosto's female readers to become the ladies rendered famous in his text.) Despite this careful upbringing, however, the young wife succumbs to the lure of wealth promised by her seducer, suggesting that fictional constructs of chaste exemplars may ultimately prove ineffectual—control of a woman's reading material cannot ensure control of her sexual behavior, which is shaped by a multitude of social and cultural pressures that moralists choose to ignore in their fixation on women's imitation of either chaste or wicked textual exemplars.

An alternative to providing positive exemplars was, of course, to limit women's access to dangerous texts, hence the numerous proscriptions for women's reading in Renaissance educational treatises. One of the genres most frequently denounced was the chivalric romance.[41] Nevertheless, many sixteenth- and seventeenth-century women, whether in a spirit of defiance or indifference to the admonitions of moralists, did read the oft-condemned romances. Professional writers who sensed profit from an expanding new market ignored humanist and Puritan concerns regarding the inflammatory nature of romances and frankly catered to women's tastes. Suzanne Hull argues persuasively that the female readership of romances expanded considerably in the latter part of the sixteenth century. She notes an increase from 1573 to 1582 in the number of books addressed to women; at the same time fiction and recreational literature became a greater part of the book market. She concludes that "a mini-explosion of female literature took place in the last quarter of the sixteenth century beginning with a new emphasis on fiction for women in the 1570s."[42] Romance-reading continued to be popular in the seventeenth century as well, as attested by the proclivities of Susan Herbert, the Countess of Montgomery. In addition to being the dedicatee of Lady Mary Wroth's *Urania*, she is said to have encouraged Anthony Munday in his translation of *Amadis de Gaule* (1618–19) with "urgent importunitie."[43]

Chivalric romances had been reviled in the writings of early humanists, notably Vives, Erasmus, and More, who were concerned that such works made light of adultery and glorified war. Vives, in a chapter entitled "What bokes be to be redde, and what not," laments, "There is an use nowe a daies worse than amonge the pagans, that bokes written in our mothers tonges, that be made but for idel men and women to reade, have none other matter but of war and love" (*ICW*, sig. D1v). Vives's concerns were evidently ignored by many readers, who continued to consume Elizabethan prose romances avidly—A. C. Hamilton acknowledges the strong market for literary sex and violence by citing the increase from ninety-eight prose romances published between 1580 and 1589 to the 165 between 1590 and 1599.[44] Claiming that he has "never founde in them [romances] one stepe either of goodnes or witte" (sig. D3r), Vives derides the silliness of their plots. But even more repugnant to Vives are the violence and illicit sex characteristic of many romances. In *The office and duetie of an husband,* Vives rails against inflammatory popular reading material such as "the workes of Poetes . . . and manye other whiche are written in the vulgar tonge, as of Trystram, Launcelote, Ogier, Amasus [Amadis] and of Artur the whiche were written and made by suche as were ydle & knew nothinge. These bokes do hurt both man & woman, for they make them wylye & craftye, they kyndle and styr up covetousnes, inflame angre, & all beastly and filthy desyre" (*ODH*, sig. O7r-v). The humanist condemnation of romances later took on more strident political and religious overtones, reflected in Roger Ascham's scathing denunciation:

> . . . whan Papistrie, as a standyng poole, covered and overflowed all England, fewe bookes were read in our tong, savyng certaine bookes of Chevalrie . . . for pastime and pleasure, which, as some say, were made in Monasteries, by idle Monkes, or wanton Chanons: as one for example, *Morte Arthure*: the whole pleasure of which booke standeth in two speciall poyntes, in open mans slaughter, and bold bawdrye: In which booke those be counted the noblest Knightes, that do kill most men without any quarell, and commit fowlest aduoulteries by sutlest shiftes . . . . What toyes, the dayly readyng of such a booke, may worke in the will of a yong gentleman, or a yong mayde, that liveth welthelie and idlelie, wise men can judge, and honest me[n] do pitie. And yet ten *Morte Arthures* do not the tenth part so much harme, as one of these bookes, made in *Italie*, and translated in England.[45]

These condemnations, despite their ostensible applicability to both sexes, must be weighed against the common assumption that women were more passionate and less capable of exercising moral restraint than were men. As Vives notes, a woman's mind "is unstable, and abideth not longe in one place, it falleth from the good unto the bad without any labour"; he has argued earlier that men are "more stedefast and constant" (*ICW*, sig. G1r). Vives's pronouncement is (predictably) severe: "For many, in whome ther is no good mynd al ready, reden those bokes, to kepe the[m]selfe in the thoughtes of love. It were better for them not only to have no learning at all, but also to lese theyr eies, that thei shuld not reade. . . . I mervaile, that wyse fathers will suffre their doughters, or that husbandes will suffre their wyves, or that the maners and customes of people wyll dissemble and over loke, that women shall use to reade wantonnes" (*ICW*, sig. D2r–v). Thomas Salter recommends that maidens be forbidden "to reade anye suche bookes or ballades as maie make her mynde (beeying of it self verie delicate) more feeble and effemynate, but also from all those thynges that any waie maie make her unworthie of a laudable reputation" (*MM*, sig. C2r). Given the double standard that prevailed throughout the period, the humanists' objections to romances on the basis that they idealized and encouraged adultery (sentiments not limited to humanists alone) would have been more readily applied to women, whose sexual sins were judged, on the whole, much more severely than men's. A young man's indulgence in a sexual affair, inspired by the "bold baw-drye" of a romance, would in general have fewer social repercus-sions than would a woman's, whose physical purity was closely linked to the purity of the family's blood line and hence the integ-rity of inheritance. Extramarital affairs among women at court may have been less severely punished when the offender was of a high-ranking family, but the effects of sexual indiscretion were, in general, more severe for women than for men.[46] Consequently, Tudor and Stuart educational literature contains countless dia-tribes about the dangers of women reading contaminating light works and therefore becoming "light" women.

Since it is ultimately impossible to control a woman's interpre-tation of romantic texts, Vives resorts to a forceful if unrealistic solution: if a woman persists in reading books on love, he sug-gests that "she shulde not onely be kepte from theim, but also if she reade good bokes with an yll wyll and lothe therto, hir father and frendes shulde provide that she maie be kept from all readyng, And so by disuse, forget learnyng, if it can be done" (*ICW*, sig. D4r). Vives certainly never threatens such extreme measures if a boy is caught reading romances. Not all fathers were this strict, however, suggesting the inevitable gap between theory and practice, moralists and fathers, and publicly and pri-vately expressed views on women's reading. One Englishman,

Sir Ralph Verney, flies in the face of Vives's dire warnings by holding out romance-reading as a lure to get his goddaughter to practice her French. Subordinating the potential immoral influence of romances to his desire that the young woman might gain suitably "feminine" accomplishments, Verney here vilifies not romances but the learned woman who might herself scorn romances and the domestic realm: "In French you can not be too cunning for that language affords many admirable books fit for you as Romances, Plays, Poetry, Stories of illustrious (not learned) Woemen, receipts for preserving, makinge creames and all sorts of cookeryes, ordering your gardens and in Breif, all manner of good housewifery."[47] Mary Boyle Rich (b. 1624), Countess of Warwick, enjoyed romances and plays, and the copy of Sidney's *Arcadia* presented to her at the age of twelve by her father, the Earl of Cork, must have fed her interest.[48] (The equanimity with which these fathers encourage their daughters to read romances may reflect the social utility of courtship narratives, a topic I will address in chapter 3.)

The Faerie Queene, like the didactic literature of its time, links promiscuous women with morally questionable genres. It is no accident that the narrative of Venus and Adonis (frequently cited as emblematic of women's wanton taste in reading) figures preeminently in the apartments of Malecasta's Castle Joyeous, a setting evocative of the vilified medieval romance. (As Brathwait complains, "I have heard of some, who for want of more amorous or attractive Objects abroad, have furnished their private Chambers with wanton pictures, *Aretine* tables, *Sibariticke* stories. These were no objects for Christian eyes: they convay too inordinate an heat from the eye to the heart," *EG*, 49.) Spenser constructs Malecasta as an unchaste reader in direct contrast to Britomart, whose heroic resistance to the texts Malecasta proffers refutes assumptions that female readers are inevitably susceptible to the seductiveness of chivalric romance. A woman disguised as a male knight, Britomart is aptly suited to correct even those male misreadings that concerned Vives and Ascham. Britomart enters the Castle Joyeous only as a result of assisting Redcrosse, who is notoriously prone to reading his martial encounters as tests of his knightly valor rather than the spiritual trials of an embattled Christian soul.[49] Redcrosse and Una's story (known both as "the Legende of the Knight of the Red Crosse, or of Holinesse" and "Th'aduenture of the *Errant damozell*," 2.1.19) operates as the locus for Spenser's refutation of humanist critiques of romance, which may be one reason Red-

crosse appears, albeit briefly, at the beginning of the romance-
driven Book 3.[50] Redcrosse's inability to withstand the wiles of
the false Una and Duessa suggests that he will prove no match
for Malecasta unless he is rescued by Britomart, a reader more
chaste than he. The false Una has addressed Redcrosse as her
"liege Lord and my loue," subtly reducing the true Una's politically and spiritually charged apostrophe "my Lyon, and my noble
Lord" to an erotic appellation. In asserting "Your owne deare
sake forst me at first to leaue / My Fathers kingdome," the false
Una posits a univocally romantic motive for Una's quest. (This
explanation is more suited to Britomart than to Una; Britomart's
quest for Artegall is a political reprise of Una's spiritual quest for
Redcrosse, and in both cases Spenser is redeeming his romance
genre.) His sexual fantasy stimulated by the false Una's fiction,
Redcrosse consequently dreams of romance topoi: "bowres, and
beds, and Ladies deare delight," an image that looks forward to
the dallying that takes place at the Castle Joyeous. Duessa also
anticipates Malecasta's stratagems as she sets Redcrosse, Sans-
foy, and later Sansjoy against one another, eagerly embracing
her chivalric role as the meed of any knight who wins her in battle. Malecasta picks up where the false Una and Duessa left off,
urging the knight to indulge the lust and senseless violence that
characterized the romances excoriated by Vives and Ascham.
Despite his heroic resistance when attacked by Malecasta's six
knights, Redcrosse is not unscathed. He "breathlesse grew" and
"lost much bloud through many a wound" (3.1.21) before Britomart comes to his rescue.

Once inside the castle's inner room, Britomart and Redcrosse
wonder at its decor, the "image of superfluous riotize," and "each
gan diuersely deuize" "whence so sumptuous guize / Might be
mayntaynd," suggesting that each is beginning to develop distinct interpretations of the castle's owner. The erotic text provided them is the Venus and Adonis tapestry. Despite Britomart's
resemblance to Venus (each one experiences "the bitter balefull
stowre, / Which her assayd with many a feruent fit, / When first
her tender hart was with his beautie smit," 3.1.34; Britomart is
seeking Artegall to woo him "her Paramoure to be," although by
more heroic means than those employed by Venus; and both are
destined to lose their loves to a violent, untimely death), she refuses to use literature to incite unchaste desire. She and Redcrosse (now accompanied by chastity) condemn the tapestry and
the behavior it prompts: "with scornefull eye, / They sdeigned
such lasciuious disport, / And loath'd the loose demeanure of that

wanton sort" (3.1.40; note the typically Spenserian pun on "demean-ure").

In contrast, Malecasta indulges herself by entertaining romantic fantasies inspired by her sight of Britomart's face. Ignorant of Britomart's sex, Malecasta

> greatly gan enamoured to wex,
> And with vaine thoughts her falsed fancy vex:
> Her fickle hart conceiued hasty fire,
> Like sparkes of fire, which fall in sclender flex,
> That shortly brent into extreme desire,
> And ransackt all her veines with passion entire.
>
> (3.1.47)

Malecasta's thoughts are "vaine" and her fancy "falsed" not only because Britomart is not what she appears to be but also because Malecasta's intentions are lascivious. Spenser thus credits women with a degree of will and autonomy as they project their own desires onto the texts they read. Throughout the banquet, Malecasta continues to "feed" her "flit fancy" (3.1.56). Malecasta's epithets, "the Lady of delight" and "this Lady free" (3.1.31, 44), underscore her generic and sexual status; closely allied with the romances decried by Vives and Ascham, she reads for (guilty) pleasure.

Of central importance in the Castle Joyeous are women's interpretive skills. As the ambiguity of being "brought to that great Ladies vew" suggests, Malecasta not only eyes the newcomers, assessing their potential as sexual partners, but she also invites them to view her beauty and engage in courtly dalliance with her. Hence Spenser's emphasis on her "wanton eyes, ill signes of womanhed," which "Did roll too lightly, and too often glaunce, / Without regard of grace, or comely amenaunce" (3.1.41). Such wanton eyes suggest wanton reading habits, the reading of texts and bodies for purposes of sexual titillation. In 3.1.49, Spenser expounds an explicit moral for his female readers:

> Faire Ladies, that to loue captiued arre,
> And chaste desires do nourish in your mind,
> Let not her fault your sweet affections marre . . .

Such an admonition, while employing the rhetoric of love taking women "captive," acknowledges that they are not without agency in that they are held responsible for selectively "nourishing" only their "chaste" desires and regulating their affections.

Britomart tactfully tries to avoid reading the text Malecasta proffers (Malecasta "told her meaning in her countenaunce; / But *Britomart* dissembled it with ignoraunce," 3.1.50), judging such behavior as too light. (Unlike the bold Malecasta, Britomart will later feign with "womanish art" to *hide* her love from Artegall as he woos her.) Just as Britomart intentionally resists interpreting Malecasta's textual and sexual designs on her, Malecasta willfully chooses to misinterpret Britomart's courtesy, reading it as evidence of mutual sexual attraction. Once Malecasta invades her bed, however, Britomart must of necessity put an end to all interpretive ambiguity. In unsheathing her "weapon" (sometimes a sword is just a sword), Britomart ironically literalizes the sexual double entendre of 3.1.60 ("She softly felt, if any member mooued"). After Gardante wounds Britomart (she, like Malecasta, has fallen in love with the face of a knight whose visor is uplifted), she rapidly and indignantly rearms herself, echoing (or foreshadowing, depending on whether one is tracking the teleological progression of the story or Spenser's structural logic) her heroic response to Merlin's prophecy in the upcoming cantos. Escaping from Malecasta's promiscuous chivalric romance text, Britomart reenters Spenserian epic romance in pursuit of a more worthy literary paradigm of love.

In Hellenore, Britomart encounters an even more overtly libidinous and wayward female reader who, in Spenserian terms, abuses her imagination, willfully misreads texts in playing her love games, and shapes her destiny according to skewed literary topoi. Hellenore seems to have inflamed her erotic imagination with a variety of literary paradigms drawn from such genres as medieval fabliau and the Petrarchan lyric (in contrast to Amoret's resistance to or enforced participation in Busirane's Petrarchan discourse, Hellenore willingly embraces her Petrarchan role as a "castle to be breached").[51] She also situates herself happily within Ovidian literature, both the *Ars amatoria*, suggested by her knowing responsiveness to Paridell's love games played with wine, and the *Metamorphoses*, suggested by her complacently hedonistic life with the satyrs.[52] The foremost literary model to which she adheres in her elopement with Paridell is, of course, the Homeric story of Helen of Troy. The ignoble couple appropriates the narrative irresponsibly, selectively identifying with the nonheroic elements of the saga, in contrast to Britomart's more reverential reading. Hellenore's creative intertextuality bears out Thomas Salter's concern that women, once taught to read the Bible and Christian poets, might "also reade Lascivious bookes of *Ovide*, . . . and in Virgill of *Eneas*, and *Dido*; and amonge the Greeke poettes of the filthie love (if I maie terme it love) of the Goddes themselves, and of their wicked adulteries and abhominable fornications, as in Homer and suche like" (*MM*, sig. D1r).

Britomart's admission to castles throughout the poem usually entails combat, because her readings are disruptive; they threaten the inhabitants' interpretive practices and the literary genres associated with those literal structures (castles, houses) that contain female inhabitants. Although Britomart does come out slightly ahead of Paridell in their initial hostile encounter, it is a somewhat hollow victory, in that Hellenore will prefer his self-indulgent reading of the Troy story to Britomart's more heroic version, which she feels compelled to render as a supplement to his misreading. In addition, Britomart's bruising blow to Paridell ironically affords him the occasion to remain in the castle and thus seduce Hellenore. The knight of chastity has inadvertently enabled Paridell to literalize the Petrarchan metaphor, to gain access both to the fortified castle and the female body it represents. Unwittingly, Britomart assists in Hellenore's downfall when the knights agree to set fire to the gates; Malbecco does let them in, but the burning gates serve as a sexual double entendre for Paridell's and Hellenore's desire. Britomart's lament for the destruction of Troy (she "was empassiond at that piteous act") certainly underscores her feeling for her native country, but it is also consistent with her identity as the knight of chastity. Her mournful statement "In one sad night consumd, and throwen downe" prophesies, as does her elegiac description of the once fresh but soon faded flower, Hellenore's fiery destruction of Malbecco's home as well as her refusal to defend her bodily "castle" adequately. Britomart cannot remain in the castle because Hellenore is allegorically as inhospitable to marital chastity as Malbecco is to "knightly" competition.

Tellingly, Britomart's connection with Hellenore is not nearly as sustained and affectionate as her relationship with Amoret, for the simple reason that Hellenore does not wish to be rescued by Britomart. Hellenore prefers the less noble constructs of her own imagination to Britomart's heroic glory. Critics have focused on the male knights' reaction to Britomart's spectacular revelation of herself as a woman warrior, but few have speculated about Hellenore's response to such a visitor. She has been presented with a heroic female archetype in Britomart, a martial maid who nevertheless loves, in contrast to the roles of the vir-

ginal Penthesilea or the seductive Helen. Yet Hellenore is conspicuously silent, seemingly unaffected by the alternative ways a
woman can figure textually in an epic. Hellenore rejects Britomart as a model, repudiating her heroic quest for a husband and
substituting her own less noble wandering, which takes her away
from Malbecco and toward a succession of lovers.

Paridell reads the Troy story self-servingly, casting himself
(and the irresponsibly reckless lover Paris) as the hero and using
it as an instrument of seduction.[53] He also adopts the personas of
epic heroes such as Aeneas and Odysseus who relate their adventures to the admiring, receptive (textually and sexually) female auditors Dido and Nausicaa (a situation anticipating
Desdemona's fascination with Othello and his stories). Paridell,
a truly corrupt Aeneas, delays his quest in order to dally with a
debased version of Dido. In his free reworking of the Homeric
and Virgilian materials, Paridell thus usurps the roles of poet and
central character in an abuse both of words and female audience.
Hamilton's gloss notes that Paridell depicts Aeneas first resisting and then regretting his marriage to Lavinia, which should
alert Hellenore to the limits of Paridell's sexual commitment. Yet
Hellenore eagerly drinks in his words and meets Paridell's advances with her own suggestive behavior. Words are Paridell's
most efficacious weapon as he assaults Hellenore, and she participates willingly in the deception, using his words to inspire her
own fictions:

> But all the while, that he these speaches spent,
> Vpon his lips hong faire Dame *Hellenore*,
> With vigilant regard, and dew attent,
> Fashioning worlds of fancies euermore
> In her fraile wit, that now her quite forlore:
> The while vnwares away her wondring eye,
> And greedy eares her weake hart from her bore:
> Which he perceiuing, euer priuily
> In speaking, many false belgardes at her let fly.
>
> (3.9.52)

Paridell continues to "fe[e]d her fancie" through his manipulation of words, literary snares reminiscent of the "ditties of dali-
ance" mentioned by Salter:

> Now singing sweetly, to surprise her sprights,
> Now making layes of loue and louers paine,
> Bransles, Ballads, virelayes, and verses vaine;

Oft purposes, oft riddles he deuysd,
And thousands like, which flowed in his braine,
With which he fed her fancie, and entysd
To take to his new loue, and leaue her old despysd.

(3.10.8)

Hellenore embraces the cynically Ovidian *Ars amatoria* role, indicated by her adeptness at playing love games with wine. (As Edward Hake would argue, Hellenore should never have been taught to read; he laments that those parents who "doe bring up their daughters in learning, do it to none other ende, but to make them companions of carpet knightes, & giglots, for amorous lovers," an apt description of the pair.)[54] Much as Dante's Francesca does with her misreading of the story of Lancelot and Guenevere, Hellenore romanticizes adulterous literary amours and allows herself to be carried away (literally) by identifying herself with Helen, who is described by Paridell as the "flowre of beautie excellent, / And girlond of the mighty Conquerours" (3.9.35). Using Paridell's prompts, Hellenore easily envisions herself in the epic role of the well-traveled Helen rather than the long-suffering, domestic Penelope or the doomed, noble Dido. The link with Helen is made explicit in 3.10.12. Having set fire to Malbecco's wealth, Hellenore rejoices "As *Hellene*, when she saw aloft appeare / The *Troiane* flames, and reach to heauens hight / Did clap her hands, and ioyed at that dolefull sight."[55]

Part of Hellenore's spite in setting fire to Malbecco's treasure store as she runs off with Paridell could stem from resentment of her husband's tendency to read her as a fabliau wife to be possessed but not "used," as her frequent equation with his goods suggests. She seeks to rewrite her own narrative, to interpret her behavior in more grandiose epic terms, but without the nobility and integrity demonstrated by Britomart. However, the fabliau genre's insistence on humor and her natural, almost innocent animal sexuality undercuts Hellenore's aspirations to enact the tragic and epic. Spenser's description of Hellenore, while not especially laudatory, is not unsympathetic: she is "a louely lasse, / Whose beauty doth her bounty far surpasse," and she "does ioy to play emongst her peares, / And to be free from hard restraint and gealous feares." Malbecco, in contrast, "is old, and withered like hay, / Vnfit faire Ladies seruice to supply"; he "in close bowre her mewes from all mens sight, / Depriu'd of kindly ioy and naturall delight" (3.9.4–5). Admittedly, the Squire of Dames is our source for this information and may take pleasure in exaggerating Malbecco's impotence, but Satyrane's response suggests that Hellenore is not completely to blame for her misbehavior:

> It is not yron bandes, nor hundred eyes,
> Nor brasen walls, nor many wakefull spyes,
> That can withhold her wilfull wandring feet;
> But fast good will with gentle curtesyes,
> And timely seruice to her pleasures meet
> May her perhaps containe, that else would algates fleet.
>
> (3.9.7)

Her final pastoral setting and the culpability and ridiculousness of her fabliau husband moderate the narrator's condemnation of Hellenore, who seems simply a young, vulnerable, and highly sexed reader, rather than a hardened, sophisticated manipulator of texts like Malecasta. Once living among the satyrs, she evinces neither guilt for deserting Malbecco nor pain at Paridell's desertion but instead a high degree of sexual satisfaction, which is more than many of the nobler wandering women in the poem achieve.

Spenser rings changes on yet another genre when Malbecco dresses as a pilgrim to seek his wife, reversing the romance topos of the faithful wife dressing as a page to seek her unfaithful or jealous husband. Parodying the other more noble love quests in the poem, Malbecco seeks Hellenore "endlong, both by sea and lond. / Long he her sought, he sought her farre and nere" (3.10.19), but she is "farre wandered," morally as well as geographically. When at last the cuckolded Malbecco locates Hellenore, he magnanimously invites her to return home, "where all should be renewd/ With perfect peace, and bandes of fresh accord, / And she receiu'd againe to bed and bord, / As if no trespasse euer had bene donne" (3.10.51). This is a less glamorous role to play, that of the penitent wife of domestic tragedy (Malbecco here anticipates the role of John Frankford in Thomas Heywood's *A woman kilde with kindnesse*, 1607), and she refuses, thoroughly satisfied with the Ovidian role that has succeeded her Homeric epic persona. In contrast to Britomart's chastely heroic quest for a husband, Hellenore uses literary models to pursue her own "errant" course, deserting her husband for a succession of increasingly base lovers. Spenser concludes this story of female agency in reading with an acknowledgment of the interpretive choices exercised by his own female readers, urging them to adopt Britomart as a literary model:

> And ye faire Ladies, that your kingdomes make
> In th'harts of men, them gouerne wisely well,
> And of faire *Britomart* ensample take,
> That was as trew in loue, as Turtle to her make.

(3.11.2)

Although Spenser may hold up Britomart's constancy as exemplary, the context of the passage indicates that "faire Ladies" can, and frequently do, use their erotic and imaginative power in much less restrained ways.

Spenser employs here one of the conventional strategies designed to guide or limit women's interpretation: articulating explicit, gendered morals for female readers. Salter carefully designates certain female worthies as exemplars of particular virtues: women will learn "pitie to her countrie" from Judith and Hester, "true love and loialtie to their husbandes" from Lucrece, Portia, and Camma, and "vertue, religion, and holinesse" from virgin saints (Cecilia, Agatha, Barbara, etc.) (*MM*, sig. D3v). Harington also moralizes sporadically throughout the *Orlando*, observing at the conclusion of Book 13 that from Isabella's tragedy "young Ladies may take this good lesson, that though they make choise of most worthie men (as *Isabella* did) yet if it be without their parents good will, it seldome prospers, but is full of diverse misadventures and hazards, that many times be the cause of their utter ruine" (101). Later he apostrophizes Isabella (perhaps with ironic exaggeration) as an ideal exemplar: "Oh worthy *Isabella*, that deservest to be painted in Tables, and set foorth in clothes of Arres, for an example to all young Ladyes of constant chastitie" (412). Yet Harington also dryly acknowledges that the efficaciousness of such literary exemplars cannot be taken for granted, given women's "willful" autonomy as readers: "In *Olympia* we may see a rare mirror of constancie, which I doubt too few of her sex will imitate" (the moral to Book 9, 71). Glossing exemplary warrior women proves even more problematic. Harington's final (and clearly reductive) assessment of Bradamante is that she is "a patterne of honest and commendable love before marriage" (411). Reading Bradamante's violence as acceptable service to the state and to God, and thus minimizing its radical implications, Harington resorts to biblical terms in his commentary on Book 35: "*Bradamant* a woman, overcomming *Rodo-*

mount, a most terrible Turke, alludes to the notable History of *Judith,* that cut of [*sic*] *Holofernes* head" (296).

The deferment to which Harington resorts (rather than encouraging his female readers to imitate Bradamante's actions, he directs them to reading another, "safer" text—the Bible) draws attention to the dilemma confronting those authors who use heroic exemplars to teach feminine virtue: how could female readers be prevented from interpreting the lives of the female worthies literally and instead be taught to allegorize, to draw appropriately gendered morals that would reinforce their own culture's sex/gender system? A "subtle way of discrediting the Worthies," according to Celeste Wright, "is to deny their authenticity—to say that Penthesilea, Camilla, and Judith were invented as examples.... The religious writers ... [could] proclaim that the Jewish Worthies should not be copied today." The story of Judith was particularly troublesome. Its account of a woman righteously exercising violence on a man demanded further refinement into a tropological interpretation. Women could be reminded, for example, that Judith, "until strengthened, was an ordinary weak woman," or the allegorical significance of the story—"a widow cutting off the Devil's head through continence and virtue"—could be emphasized to the exclusion of any literalizing interpretation.[56] Guazzo does exactly that in his discussion of Judith. Having stated that because women ought not to be "*Amazones,*" they should be trained in modesty. He then adduces as an exemplar the "renowned widow *Judith,* whome though her great riches, her young yeeres, and her singuler beautie, perswaded to marrie againe: yet she was content to preferre her wydowhood before wedlocke, her wollen garments, before gorgeous apparell, abstinencie before gluttonie, watching before sleeping, praying before loytering, and armed with these weapons, she cut of [*sic*] the head of *Holofernes,* that is, the divel" (*CC,* 160v).

The challenge of interpreting violent women warriors correctly confronts Spenser's Cymoent. Proteus has bidden her to keep her son Marinell "from womankind . . . / For of a woman he should haue much ill, / A virgin strange and stout him should dismay, or kill" (3.4.25). Cymoent misinterprets Marinell's prophesied fate in metaphorical, Petrarchan terms, assuming that he is to be kept from amorous rather than literal warfare. Cymoent's overreading points to the highly subjective nature of interpretation, which is inevitably influenced by the reader's fears and desires (in this case, maternal protectiveness or perhaps even

desire for her son). Ironically, Cymoent is reading as a good
woman probably should have, translating unconventional female
activity directly into the private sphere of erotic relationships,
rather than crediting women with literal martial roles. In doing
so, however, Cymoent underestimates the heroic potential of
women in Spenserian epic, being too gender-specific in her assignment of physical force to men. The prophesied hurt she
"vainely did expound, / To be hart-wounding loue," and she continues to deny the intensity and power of a woman's love when
diagnosing Marinell's literal wound: "Not this the worke of womans hand ywis, / That so deepe wound through these deare members driue" (3.4.37). She mistakenly refuses to acknowledge
women's capacity for intense erotic and political devotion.

She thus practices a very narrow understanding of women's
participation in the sexual arena, limiting them to enactment of
(and inadvertently causing Marinell to assume) the Petrarchan
archetype of the cold, indifferent lady. This is clearly an inappro-
priate literary paradigm, not only for Britomart but also for Marinell's future mate, the passionate and loving Florimell, who
courageously seeks out her reluctant male beloved. Not all
women disdain their lovers, as Britomart tries to indicate by forcibly literalizing and thereby correcting Cymoent's flawed interpretation. Cymoent operates as a negative analogue to Merlin,
Glauce, and the poet in her attempts to influence the romantic
destiny of her youthful charge. She warns Marinell daily

> The loue of women not to entertaine;
> A lesson too too hard for liuing clay,
> From loue in course of nature to refraine:
> Yet he his mothers lore did well retaine.
>
> (3.4.26)

Her "lore" replaces his rightful "love"; Marinell unquestioningly
obeys his mother in matters of love, whereas Britomart defies
her father. Hamilton glosses Cymoent as "wave-tamer," but Britomart doesn't want the tempestuous surging of her passion
quieted, preferring instead to have it requited. Her assault on
Marinell occurs immediately after Glauce has redirected Britomart's passion away from self-pitying Petrarchan reflection
toward active pursuit of Artegall, and Glauce's forceful recollection of Merlin's positive prophecy (the children Britomart is destined to bear) counters Cymoent's less daring interpretation of
Proteus's negative prophecy. Britomart fights not only for her

right to pursue her destined course toward Artegall across Marinell's land but also to defend her unorthodox role as a heroic female lover. Britomart's action justifies Florimell's quest and prepares Marinell and Cymoent to accept her gentler version of the lady knight's sexual aggression.

Warrior women were not the only literary figures who were "translated" into contemporary, sanitized moral terms. The practice of adducing contemporary social and domestic morals from ancient literature was endemic. Some of the lessons strike modern readers as so forced that they seem almost unrelated to the narrative. For example, the narrator of George Pettie's *A Petite Pallace of Pettie his pleasure* follows the tale of Alcestis's sacrifice of her life to revive Admetus with this *sententia*:

> This seemeth strange unto you (Gentlewomen) that a woman should die, & live againe: but the meaning of it is this, that you should die to your selves, and lyve to your husbandes, that you shoulde count theyr life your lyfe, their death your destruction ... that you should in al thinges frame your selves to theyr fancies, that if you see the[m] disposed to mirth, you should indevour to be pleasaunt ... if they delight in haukes, that you should love Spaniels: if they hunting, you houndes.[57]

Some women may readily have drawn these morals themselves, but the degree to which others would construct or even accept such overt moralizing could not be guaranteed. John Ferne expresses some doubts on this head in *The Blazon of Gentrie* (1586), in which Collumell responds anxiously to Berosus's digressive account of the nine female worthies (Minerva, Semiramis, Tomyris, Jael, Deborah, Judith, Maud, Elizabeth, queen of Aragon, and Joanna, queen of Naples):

> Byr Lady maist story man, I am well apaid thou hast doone with that talke: I rather woulde have hard, some thing sayd, of gentle and meeke women: for it is evill examples, to let them understande, of such sturdye and manlye women, as those have beene, which erewhile thou hast tolde of. They are quicke inough (I warraunt you, now adayes) to take hart a grace, and dare make warre, with their husbandes: I woulde not vor the price of my coate, that *Jone* my wyfe, had hard this geare: she would have carried it zoner away, then our ministers tale, of his *Sara* and *Rebecca*.[58]

Given Collumell's lowly status in the social hierarchy (he is a plowman), his fear is treated merely as an amusing interlude in

Ferne's analysis of knights, their arms, and heraldic devices, and
the antiquarian and scholar Berosus quickly dismisses the belli-
cose Joan as a typical shrew to be tamed ("If thou hast a shrewd
wyfe, give her as shrewde a wintring, and turne her off, to hard
meat"). Physical subjugation, however, fails to address Collumell's more astute observation—that he cannot control his wife's
interpretive activities and that her status as a reader or aural recipient of dangerously ambiguous texts could render her a figurative amazon, ready to contest her husband's authority. Joan's
minister has tried to inculcate wifely obedience and female godliness with his stories of Sarah and Rebecca, but Collumell suspects that his wife will find martial, combative women more to
her taste.

This taste was not limited to women of the lower classes but
was evident among the gentry and aristocracy as well. Aemilia
Lanyer appropriates such biblically militant women as Deborah,
Jael, Hester, and Judith in her prefatory epistle "To the Vertuous Reader" of *Salve Deus Rex Judaeorum* (1611). The poem
was designed to win patronage from politically powerful and
prominent literary women, such as Anne of Denmark, Mary Sidney, the Countess of Pembroke, Lucy, Countess of Bedford, Margaret, Countess of Cumberland, and Anne, Countess of Dorset.
Lanyer's tone is decidedly contumacious as she argues that
women

> are not to regard any imputations, that they ["evill disposed men"]
> undeservedly lay upon us. . . . Especially considering that they have
> tempted even the patience of God himselfe, who gave power to wise
> and virtuous women, to bring downe their pride and arrogancie. As
> was cruell *Cesarus* by the discreet counsell of noble *Deborah*, Judge
> and Prophetesse of Israel: and resolution of *Jael* wife of *Heber* the
> Kenite . . . blasphemous *Holofernes*, by the invincible courage, rare
> wisdome, and confident carriage of *Judeth* . . . with infinite others.[59]

Lady Anne Southwell also appropriated powerful female exemplars. In the midst of her poem retelling the creation story, she
breaks off to threaten would-be critics:

> & now mee thinkes I heare some wizzard <gazeling> <gallant>
>   say
> how dares this foolish woman bee soe bold.
> ask Jahells nayle y^t Siseraes head did stay
> & Judiths sword that <soone> made her <a> hott love cold
>   Hee that enabled them, enables mee.[60]

It would be anachronistic to credit these early modern women with a political agenda of conscious, consistent resistance. Many female readers probably did recast the heroic deeds of historical female figures into the "appropriate" (i.e., private, domestic) social contexts. Sara Mendelson's study of three Stuart women argues that although they "sometimes expressed resentment at the limited role assigned to them . . . . they did not challenge . . . the whole complex of cultural axioms about gender, with its implicit assumption that the two sexes were polar opposites with two sets of mutually contradictory traits . . . . Most women did not venture beyond the traditional virtues assigned to their sex."[61] Such gendered interpretations may have been commonly practiced, given contemporary assumptions that women were considered to have different moral virtues than did men or were to express the same virtues as men but do so according to their gendered role in society. Maclean discusses commentaries that "first argue the equality of male and female virtue by citing the examples of women who, for their acts, have achieved public fame and honour; but then translate these examples into domestic terms, use them to encourage women to be chaste, obedient, thrifty, silent and so on."[62] However, the frequency of strident strictures urging women to perform such translations suggests that some women evinced a tendency to forge their own, less passive interpretations of the literature they read. As Sara Jayne Steen observes, "if women always had fulfilled the ideal or even attempted to, there would have been little need for conduct books or cautionary negative stereotypes."[63]

To what extent did sixteenth- and seventeenth-century Englishwomen consciously or unconsciously participate in the practice of a "textual feminism" (defined by Nelly Furman as "a recognition of the fact that we speak, read, and write from a gender-marked place within our social and cultural context")?[64] Did these women in fact perceive themselves to be speaking and reading from such a "gender-marked place" or even constitute themselves as speaking subjects? Catherine Belsey thinks not:

Permitted to break their silence in order to aquiesce in the utterances of others, women were denied any single place from which to speak for themselves. A discursive instability in the texts about women has the effect of withholding from women readers any single position which they can identify as theirs. . . . Legally the position of women was inherently discontinuous, their rights fluctuating with their marital status. From the discourses defining power relations in

the state women were simply absent; in the definitions of power relations within the family their position was inconsistent and to some
degree contradictory. While the autonomous subject of liberalism
was in the making, women had no single or stable place from which
to define themselves as independent beings. In this sense they both
were and were not subjects.[65]

Yet Belsey's premise, that early modern women had no fixed
place in society from which to position themselves as subjects,
could also be read, conversely, as enabling them to embrace a
greater variety of subject positions, at least in terms of their interpretation of literature. Female readers may have been more
able than male readers to identify with fictional exemplars of
both sexes. Fulke Greville certainly sees nothing incongruous in
advising the recipient of his "Letter to an Honorable Lady" to imitate the stoicism of Ulysses as well as the virtue of the arche-
typal wronged wife Octavia, but rarely are male readers urged to
imitate the prowess of Penthesilea.[66] We might therefore fruit-
fully investigate the ways in which women, as readers and as fictional characters, seem to have negotiated or occupied the space
between two different senses of subjectivity, "the construction of
the gendered subject and the ideology of women's submission or
subjection to men."[67]

In theorizing a female subject, we must be cautious not to replace one totalizing image ("the" sixteenth-century reader) with
another one, that of "the" female reader as a helpless victim of
oppressively patriarchal texts. Roberta Krueger's point that the
female reader of Arthurian romance "hears a discourse that
casts her not as subject but as object" presents a necessary revisionist perspective, as does Sheila Cavanagh's similar point
about *The Faerie Queene*'s objectification of female characters,
yet we should also take into account the numerous examples of
early modern women who did not dutifully conform to their culture's gender codes and might very well have been capable of
reading against the grain.[68] Certainly by 1640, some women were
becoming very outspoken about gender-based discrimination:

> when a Father hath a numerous issue of Sonnes and Daughters, the
> sonnes forsooth they must bee first put to the Grammar schoole, and
> after perchance sent to the University. . . . When we, whom they stile
> by the name of weaker Vessells, though of a more delicate, fine, soft,
> and more plyant flesh, and therefore of a temper most capable of the
> best Impression, have not that generous and liberall Educations
> [*sic*], lest we should bee made able to vindicate our owne injuries, we

are set onely to the Needle . . . or else to the Wheele. . . . : If wee be
taught to read, they then confine us within the compasse of our Mothers Tongue, and that limit wee are not suffered to passe; . . . and thus
if we be weake by Nature, they strive to makes [sic] us more weake
by our Nurture.[69]

Although aristocratic women may have been less likely to articu-
late such grievances openly, their class status providing them
material benefits of wealth and privilege that to some extent
counterbalanced their inferior gender status, other women (such
as Lanyer) did voice resentment on their behalf. Steen's analysis
of Arabella Stuart (1575–1615) points to the middle ground that I
am proposing many women readers may have occupied; Steen
concludes that Stuart was "aware of the social and literary conventions as conventions and saw that they could be manipulated
to her advantage."[70]
    Studying the reading strategies of women throughout history
is a project that stems naturally from the recent trend in feminist
criticism to recover a female literary tradition. Analyses considering how female-authored texts "revise, appropriate, and subvert the established male literary tradition"[71] can be extended to
include female readers as well as writers, if our definition of
"texts" encompasses the potential "texts" or mental scripts produced by women reading within their own historical contexts.
Christine de Pizan's *The boke of the cyte of ladyes* (translated
into English by Brian Ansley and published in 1521) provides one
example of a woman reading herself as both subject and object
within a single text. She acknowledges that male authorities
have frequently "subjected" women in their texts, but she simultaneously practices an empowering strategy of rereading those
women as acting subjects in their own right, thus producing
some startlingly positive depictions of such women as Medea,
Circe, and Dido. Susan Schibanoff has explored the ways in
which Christine's persona and Alison, Chaucer's Wife of Bath,
"reread and thus reclaim their own history from antifeminist
texts."[72] Jocelyn Wogan-Browne makes a similar point in relation
to medieval texts and readers: "there is often, even in stereotypi-
cal representation of women, the potential of slippage between
particular hagiographic texts and their readers' responses to
them . . . . meaning is in any case complex and to a significant
extent negotiable between reader and text, rather than automatically fixed by the text. Though a clerical and aristocratic culture

allowing access to privileged women may remain 'overwhelm-
ingly male,' this does not mean that the saints' lives have nothing
to say to women or that women can say nothing in, through, or in
response to them."[73]

We will probably never know to what extent sixteenth- and
seventeenth-century women, especially those reading Spenserian texts, were passive "consumer[s] of male-produced literature" socialized to accept their reflection in literary mirrors, and
to what extent they were "resisting" readers,[74] reconstructing female images in a text to validate their experience or desires, but
the ways early modern women "reread" their source texts in the
translations and original literature they produced suggest that
many were engaged in the task of reforming the image of women
by their choice of subjects and presentation of character. Jane
Lumley, the first known English translator of a Greek dramatist,
selected Euripides' *Iphigenia at Aulis* (in which Clytemnestra,
as well as Iphigenia, figures as strong and sympathetic); the
translation "emphasizes female heroism and self-sacrifice."
Lumley's choice of subject matter, "a situation of familial conflict
that bore striking resemblances to dilemmas in her own aristocratic patriarchal family" (her father supported Mary Queen of
Scots' claim to the throne and helped hasten the execution of his
wife's niece, Lady Jane Grey),[75] suggests that the personal and
political were clearly interrelated for this female reader. The
Countess of Pembroke elected to translate works featuring Cleopatra and Laura, women traditionally defined only by their sexuality, in order to render them more complex figures. Elizabeth
Cary's closet drama, *The tragedie of Mariam, the faire queene
of Jewry* (1613), explores the sexual and political conflicts plagu-
ing a tragic heroine, and Mary Wroth revises the conventional
portrayal of the romance lady and sonnet mistress in her *Countess of Montgomery's Urania* and *Pamphilia to Amphilanthus*.[76]
Karen Newman concludes from this evidence that these women
were clearly not prevented from writing by social expectations of
female submission and silence. It cannot be denied, however,
that the voices of women writers could be muted, if perhaps not
silenced altogether—consider Wroth's being abjured, when her
Urania provoked an angry reception, to follow her aunt's pious
example and limit herself to devotional subjects. Women writers
were inevitably influenced, if not completely defeated, by contemporary constructions of gender, which, as Mary Ellen Lamb
remarks, exerted "formative pressure upon what [women]

wrote, how they wrote, and the ways their writings were received,"[77] and, I would add, how they read.

Female readers of this period (or any other) obviously cannot be neatly categorized into a homogeneous group. Intellectual tastes, religious beliefs, and changing material and political considerations affected women's as well as men's choices of reading material and modes of interpretation. Some women authors refer to erotic or romance motifs only to criticize them. For example, a letter written by Lady Anne Southwell in 1627 to her friend Lady Ridgway[78] (both of whom had served as maids of honor to Elizabeth I) presents the former's defense of poetry against the latter's preference for prose. Southwell's own poetry was mostly devotional, and in marshaling arguments to defend her choice of genre, she blames inferior works for prejudicing her friend's taste. Southwell praises the divine poetry of the Davidic psalms (much as Sidney had done in his *Defence*) but criticizes immoral poems, admitting that "To heare a Hero & Leander or some such other busye nothing, might bee a meanes to skandalize this art. But can a cloud disgrace the sunne[?]" Stating that "It is the subject, that comends or condemmes the art," she suspects that "some wanton venus or Adonis hath bene cast before your chast eares, whose evill attyre, disgracing this beautifull nimph, hath unworthyed her in your opinion."[79] Despite the moralists' anxieties, women could, it seems, withstand the seductiveness of texts such as *Venus and Adonis* and *Hero and Leander*. Yet Southwell was no dull religious prude; her commonplace book contains a spirited defense of women's abilities as she refutes men's "wilfull herresye" of "thinkinge ffemales have so little witt / as but to serve men they are only fitt."[80] Later in the century, perhaps indicative of her desire to be taken seriously as the intellectual equal of men, Margaret Cavendish, the Duchess of Newcastle, dismisses the work (and by implication the reading tastes) of her female counterparts with derision: "when any of our Sex doth Write, they Write some Devotions, or Romances, or Receits of Medicines."[81]

The vast majority of women, however, from the sixteenth to the twentieth century, have been characterized as avid consumers of literary romances. Suzanne Hull's attitude—"Probably then, as now, more women than men were attracted to romantic fiction"[82]—has become something of an unexamined truism among critics, most of whom assume that women of the period simply wished or needed to escape into fictional worlds. Gamaliel Bradford, for example, asserts that the Elizabethan woman's chief reading "was very much the same as that of most women for a great many years after her: the Bible with other religious literature, and romances. Indeed, the Elizabethan romance is in most cases manifestly intended for women and has often the advantage of combining the edification of a moral tract with the less legitimate attractions of fiction."[83] Bradford, however, overlooks the problematic nature of this combination of discourses—moral tract overlaid with enticing fiction. How could authors be sure that the moral would automatically take precedence over a potentially subversive literal interpretation of the independent and sexually assertive women depicted in many sixteenth-century romances?

Whatever their individual tastes and to whatever degree they internalized and reproduced their culture's distrust of romance literature, women readers nevertheless functioned as figurative women warriors, engaging the texts they read in battles for contested meaning, the outcomes of which were never certain. The interpretive independence exercised by early modern women readers can be illustrated by Margaret Tyler's and Susan Du Verger's adaptations of the martial motif for very different rhetorical purposes. Tyler, writing in 1578, defends romances and, indeed, helps to initiate their popularity in the later sixteenth century. Du Verger, writing in 1639, ridicules the overworked cliches of the romance genre. However, both women use their pens as the weapons with which they take captive or appropriate the scripts of others.

Du Verger targets romances in the authorial epistle to the reader prefacing her translation of John Peter Camus' *Admirable Events*. Using a romance motif against itself by adopting the role of the only hero able to defeat a monstrous foe, she announces:

> The enterprise which I have taken in hand, is to wrastle, or rather to encounter with those frivolous books, which may all be comprized under the name of Romants, which would require the hands which fables attribute unto *Briarius*, or the strength which Poets give unto *Hercules*: the hands of that Gyant to handle so many pens, and the vigour of that *Heros* to undergoe so painefull a labour: but what cannot a courage do, animated by a zeale of pleasuring his neighbour, and provoked by desire to advance the light of vertue, and to lessen vice. O why hath not my pen the vertue to cure the wounds that these wicked books [later referred to as "Romants, Adventures, Chivalries, and other such trash"] cause in this world! or at least, why cannot it devoure those monsters, which the writers of those aforesaid workes,

meere inchanters of mindes cause to appeare in the formes of bookes?[84]

Du Verger rejects the Sidneyan-Plutarchan defense, arguing that "although fables, parables, and poeticall fictions, do sometimes hide in them good precepts, and many serious examples, yet the instructions loose [sic] much of their credit when they are mixed amongst vaine inventions."[85] Yet she employs romance metaphors to express her own power; the use of the pen to cure wounds connotes the magical healing properties possessed by certain romance heroines, and if used to "devoure" monstrous books or make them disappear, the pen becomes a type of magic wand. Du Verger's use of her pen renders her a literary warrior, as her initial combative metaphor of wrestling implies; she fashions herself as a reluctant fighter forced to engage in a battle of books.

Du Verger's appropriation of the armchair amazon stance was anticipated by Margaret Tyler, who translated Diego Ortuñez de Calahorra's *The Mirrour of Princely Deedes and Knighthood* (1578), which proved to be one of the most popular sixteenth-century chivalric romances and a source of plot material for Spenser, Shakespeare, and Bunyan.[86] Tyler's prefatory epistle to the reader registers consciousness of the early modern anxiety about female literacy by alternately teasing and appeasing her readers, defusing suspicions about her project only to raise them again.

Tyler attempts to disarm the inevitable objections to a female writer departing from the usual devotional mode in choosing to translate such unsuitable matter (which she openly acknowledges, hoping her work will be accepted "the rather for that it is a womans work, though in a story prophane, and a matter more manlike then becometh my sexe. But as for the manlinesse of the matter, thou knowest that it is not necessary for every trumpettour or drumstare in the warre to be a good fighter," sig. A3r). Here she disclaims the role of warrior, describing herself merely as the one whose music calls others to action or proclaims the outcome of battle. As might be expected, she attests to the profit and delight the work offers, but employs a double diversionary tactic by deflecting attention away from her own role as translator as she emphasizes Ortuñez de Calahorra's role as author. She also ignores altogether the touchy subject of possible deleterious effects on female readers as she focuses on the advantages to male readers: "The authors purpose appeareth to be this, to animate thereby, and to set on fire the lustie courages of you[n]g gentlemen, to the advauncement of their line, by ensuing such like steps" (sig. A3r).

Although she claims to desire only the freedom to write of battles, not the right to fight in them, Tyler's allusions indirectly link her to other female figures who have challenged gender distinctions, notably the martial maids of epic literature: "it is no sinne to talke of Robinhood though you never shot in his bow: Or be it that the attempt were bolde to intermeddle in armes, so as the auncient Amazons did, and in this story *Claridiana* doth, & in other stories not a fewe, yet to report of armes is not so odious but that it may be borne withal, not onely in you men which your selves are fighters, but in us women, to whom the benefit in equal part apperteineth of your victories" (sig. A3v). Her acknowledgment of women's potential for exhibiting martial skill and political power (the amazonian allusion might even constitute a veiled threat) is supplemented by an inverse tactic of protesting her own powerlessness. Disarmingly assuming the virtues of obedience, diligence, and responsiveness to the desires of others, she claims she did not willingly choose her subversive subject matter: "the first motion to this kinde of labour came not fro[m] my selfe, so was this peece of worke put upon me by others, & they which first counsailed me to fall to worke, tooke upon them also to bee my taskemasters and overseers least I should be idle." She admits that she will still probably be held responsible for complicity and her "easie yelding" (sig. A3v), indicating some awareness of a double standard that first teaches women to be submissive and then blames them for it.[87]

Tyler's ultimate salvo (her claim that men have dedicated books on war, medicine, law, government, and theology to women) disingenuously takes the dedications of male authors at face value while disregarding the possibility of men dedicating works to women in attempts to gain the favor of their more powerful husbands or to win financial remuneration: "And if men may & do bestow such of their travailes upon gentlewomen, then may we wome[n] read such of their works as they dedicate unto us, and if we may read them, why not farther wade in the[m] to the serch of a truth. . . . it is all one for a woman to pen a story, as for a man to addresse his story to a woman" (sig. A4r–v). Her ease in moving from an implicit reassurance that women will not seek to emulate in literal fashion the amazons of romance to an extremely literal interpretation of dedications confirms the dominant fear of the moralists: that women's interpretations of a given text could not ultimately be controlled and might readily challenge the literary and social status quo. Translation serves as a useful metaphor for the process of appropriating, and adapting, texts; the practice of reading is always inevitably an exercise in translation.[88] As Tyler notes, "seldome is the tale carried cleane from an others mouth" (sig. A3r). Women writers and women readers, by virtue of their power to "rewrite" or interpret texts for themselves, can, like Tyler, envision themselves as literary, if not literal, amazons.

A more socially conservative use of the amazon motif occurs in the preface by "O. F." to Du Bosc's *The Compleat Woman*, which suggests that female readers are indeed to become warriors, but only in a moral sense: "Women are to learne in bookes the rule of their duties, that evill examples may never corrupt them, that they may discern falshood from truth, and may have Arms to defend themselves against those, who study but to abuse and seduce them, and who make it a trophy to illude them, and to leade them into a fooles Paradise" (sig. B4v–C1r). O. F. concedes that women can and must contest the meanings of the texts they read. In inciting women to arm themselves, O. F. may be drawing on the gender-neutral image of the Christian soul as warrior, fighting sin in a psychomachia, but the possibility of slippage from this type of "armed" woman to a more ideologically threatening one is ever-present if one chooses to read the figure of the woman warrior literally rather than metaphorically; in contrast, the notion of a man as warrior is consistent with, not antithetical to, cultural norms. In my next chapter, I will examine this type of interpretive slippage in *The Faerie Queene*'s third book, Ariosto's *Orlando Furioso*, and *The Mirrour of Princely Deedes*, which all depict lady knights as readers, but I wish to conclude the present chapter by examining one of *The Faerie Queene*'s most notoriously cryptic episodes, Britomart's rescue of Amoret from the House of Busirane, which can be read as a commentary on the experience of the poem's female readers.

A repository of erotic fantasies and romantic paradigms, the House of Busirane is markedly metapoetic. Thomas Roche's reading of Busirane's masque hints that gender might influence one's interpretation of literary depictions of love affairs; he suggests that from the figure of Daunger on, the masque figures constitute "both sonnet conventions and visions of the horrors of love, depending on whether we read them from the man's or woman's point of view."[89] The narrator seems to imply that the horrifying fantasies derive from Amoret's vulnerable imagination, but at the same time, Busirane is identified explicitly as the author of the masque that objectifies, tortures, and misrepresents Amoret's love. Whose imagination is actually in control in this contest of fantasies, the male poet's or the female reader's? This apparent contradiction is precisely the point—literary paradigms inevitably shape female readers' constructions of their love affairs, but female readers exercise a degree of choice about which models they will employ. Adding to the impenetrability of the episode is Britomart's experience. She is depicted as "reading" Busirane's masque and tapestries assiduously and yet seems unable to comprehend or evaluate their meanings until she at last witnesses Busirane writing with Amoret's blood. What exactly are Britomart and Amoret, and especially Spenser's female audience, to read in the House of Busirane?[90]

One way of coming to terms with this ambiguous episode is to read the House of Busirane intertextually with the cave of Artidon, described in *The Mirrour of Princely Deedes and Knighthood*. It is not inconceivable that Spenser's female readers may also have done so, given that the English translations of the first five parts of *The Mirrour* had been published between 1578 and 1586 (the Artidon episodes occur in chapters 4–5 of the second part, 1585, and chapter 27 of the third part, 1586). Indeed, Dorothy Atkinson has argued that Spenser, who was working on Book 3 during the 1580s, used *The Mirrour* as a source, pointing to obvious parallels between the texts (fire blocks the entrance to each dwelling, both Rosicleer and Scudamour are identified as knights of Cupid, and the sight of a lover's open breast and bleeding heart is the central spectacle in each).[91] *The Mirrour* has otherwise received little attention in relation to Spenser's text, perhaps because, as a popular romance, it has been dismissed as lowbrow "women's" fare, unlike the more respectable genres of classical epic and Italian dynastic romance, which are more obviously linked to public affairs and the consolidation of the state's hegemonic power. Although in both *The Faerie Queene* and *The Mirrour* a lady is released from a magician's power, Britomart's engagement with Busirane is depicted as being much more oppositional than either Rosicleer's or Claridiana's with Artidon. Aware of the woman reader's latent power, *The Faerie Queene* comments metafictionally on its own reception, as women readers watch a remarkably resistant reader, Britomart, reject the literary paradigms utilized by the poet-mage and insist on a more congenial romance model.

One striking distinction between the two texts is the representation of the poet-mage. Both Busirane and Artidon are cruel and vengeful toward women they ostensibly love—Busirane torments Amoret in an attempt to gain her favor and Artidon seeks revenge on Artidea, the princess who has refused to requite his love. Yet Artidon is praised as being "a knight of great courage and high linage" as well as "the wisest in the magicall art" in many countries (Bk. 1, pt. 2, ch. 4, 16v). He, like Busirane, works his charm at night, an appropriate time for the manifestation of erotic fantasies: "So on a night by his great learning, he toke the Queene out of hir bed and brought hir unto his cave" (17r). As readers enter and view Artidon's cave through Rosicleer's eyes, the scene is devoid of dramatic tension, partly because Artidon is, in a sense, dead and has foregone all attempts to woo Artidea; his intent now is to force her to witness his own suffering and to rue the death she has caused. Artidon dismembers himself, not the lady. Rosicleer sees a stage upon which is a

> chaire verie richlie wrought, the Queene *Artidea* who was verie faire & royallie apparailed, who leaned her head upon her arme, and there was beholding a knight of a verie good countenance and disposition, who was all armed with guilt armour, and brodered with precious stones, kneeling upon his knees before her, having his breast open, shewing unto the Queene his bloudie heart, and although his countenaunce did shew him to be dead, yet the wound and the bloud was so fresh, as though at the same instant it had bene done. This knight was the wise *Artidon,* who willingly and with his owne hands did wound and open his breast, after that he hadde brought the Queene thether. (ch. 5, 23r–v)

Onlookers are less horrified at Artidon's project than filled with pity for his plight. When Prince Luziro (who has been ruling Artidea's kingdom as governor during her imprisonment) enters the cave with various shepherds and attendants after Rosicleer has broken the enchantment, they interpret the violent sight from their own perspective as lovers: "they were moved and had great compassion on him, & did verie much extoll and praise his wisedome and bountie, in that he wold rather die then profite himselfe of the Queene against her will" (26v). Rosicleer, like Artidon, suffers from unrequited love, as does the female knight Claridiana, who later seeks out the magician desiring to know whether her steadfast love for the vacillating Knight of the Sun is or is not returned. All are aligned with Artidon in their empathy for him rather than expressing antipathy, as Britomart does for Busirane.

Artidea's punishment takes the form of having to constantly read the pitiful sight, an enforced rereading of the lover she had earlier refused to look upon. She thanks Rosicleer for releasing her from "this heavie and sorrowfull prison, in the which I have ben so many yeeres, doing no other thing but live in continuall sorrow and lamentation for the death of this knight" (23v). This marks her as a compliant reader who has extracted precisely the meaning Artidon intended: she reads herself as he has read her—a cruel mistress who needs to be taught repentance and sympathy. *The Mirrour* does not consistently invite allegorical readings, but "Art-idea" suggests poetic inspiration, just as "Art-a-done" suggests the completed fictional construct itself: the image of the suffering male lover. Artidea has served as Artidon's mouthpiece during her captivity, compelled to tell the "truth" about love to visitors, and her truth has been brought into complete conformity with his.

Conversely, Amoret resists Busirane's inscription. She is the object of the onlooker's gaze in Spenser's text, and her suffering is much more severe than that of Artidea. A plaintive Scudamour describes Amoret's plight in 3.11.10: "Why then is *Busirane* with wicked hand / Suffred, these seuen monethes day in secret den / My lady and my loue so cruelly to pen?" Amoret could function here as a single referent, Scudamour's ladylove, or the lines could indicate two referents as Busirane attempts to constrain both Scudamour's lady and his love affair, rewriting them according to a courtly standard of love involving pain, separation, and betrayal. Busirane takes feminine love (represented by Amoret) captive in order to reinscribe the limiting roles and emotions enacted in his masque of Cupid.[92] To counteract the literary paradigms guiding Amoret's sexual, philosophical, and social instruction in the Garden of Adonis and the Temple of Venus, Busirane must use force. But Amoret incurs Busirane's anger by unequivocally rejecting his advances. When Scudamour claims Busirane "by torture . . . would her constraine / Loue to conceiue in her disdainfull brest," her disdain is not that of the unresponsive Petrarchan sonnet mistress but moral indignation directed at Busirane's concept of love and the role she is expected to play in it. Busirane is like Lechery, who "ioyd weake wemens hearts to tempt and proue / If from their loyall loues he might then moue" (1.4.26), but Amoret staunchly resists his attempts to woo her heart away from Scudamour. (The steadfast loyalty of Amoret can be contrasted with the more malleable affections of Artidea, who, within a few pages of text, is depicted as refusing

Artidon, desiring to wed Rosicleer, and then, upon discovering that he loves another lady, pledging herself to Prince Luziro.) The constancy Amoret displays looks forward to Richard Brathwait's idealized depiction of female fancy, in which a lady utilizes the motifs of portraits, wounded hearts, and burning fire to express constancy rather than the desire to seduce and dominate:

> FANCY is featured with a lovely and lively presence; fixing her eye intentively on a *Tablet*, presenting the portrature of her *Lover*: Drawing aside a Curtaine, she discovers an *amorous Picture*, and compares it with her *Tablet*, which enshrines her *best feature*. In the middle of the *Picture* is engraven a *wounded heart*, implying loves intimacy; above it, a *burning Lampe*, importing loves purity; below it, a paire of *Turtles* mating, inferring loves constancy. All which expressive Emblemes of her minde, she seconds with this Mot. *My Choyce admits no Change*. (*EG*, "The meaning of the Frontispice")

Amoret remains within the discourse of courtesy literature, stubbornly rereading Busirane's torturous afflictions as "expressive Emblemes of her minde," which "*admits no Change*."

Busirane seems to assume that women readers will passively allow themselves to be "charmed" into love affairs and texts, that the site/sight of the female body is to be inscribed with meaning by the male poet alone. He exhibits no compunction about violating Amoret's body in order to draw forth the means and matter for his sadistic poetry. Although Busirane's "thousand charmes could not her stedfast heart remoue" on the metaphorical level— having first been moved to love Scudamour, her heart refuses to be re-moved to alter her love—he attempts to cause her physical pain. In his analysis of Greek amatory magic John Winkler describes a related erotic phenomenon involving transference, whereby the male mage projects his suffering onto the woman who has remained impervious to his "charms":

> The erotic spells, found in great numbers in the Greek magical papyri, are full of violent imagery in which the lover performs a ceremony aimed at making the woman he desires burn and suffer until she gives herself to him. Yet the underlying scenario of these performances suggests that it is the lover himself, alone at night and feeling victimized by a helpless passion, who is symbolically projecting his own distress onto his putative victim.[93]

Winkler's theory could be expanded to include the male poet, who depicts himself as (almost) all powerful in the Spenserian text, yet who is ultimately frustrated by the superior power of the resistant reader.

Despite her suffering, Amoret stands firm. Although Artidon is actually dead (his body somehow retains sufficient animation to engage in conversation and act as soothsayer to his visitants), Amoret is still alive, albeit with "deathes owne image figurd in her face." However, her torture is rendered in much more graphic terms and is much more aestheticized. Artidon is presented as simply "having his breast open, shewing unto the Queene his bloudie heart," while Amoret's heart is actually being removed from her breast (see 3.12.20–21).[94] The epithet "that Lady trew," assigned to her as Busirane launches his final attack, emphasizes the heroics of her constancy and renders her more than a mere victim. She is a remarkably resistant female reader, preferring the faithful lover/wife archetype to that of the haughty sonnet mistress or the slyly adulterous courtly lady, and her defiance suggests that women exercise significant choice in reading themselves into particular texts. Indeed, we have some evidence that Spenser's female contemporaries may have been attuned to such an emphasis. Lady Mary Wroth provides a re-reading (or re-versing) of this episode in her prose romance *The Countess of Montgomery's Urania* (1621), in which Pamphilia's inconstant but beloved Amphilanthus is tortured by vengeful women. As Maureen Quilligan remarks,

> What is most striking about Wroth's revision of Spenser's scene is that the moral values are completely reversed. Pamphilia tries vainly to come to Amphilanthus's rescue but she is unable to, not because she may, like Scudamour, be implicated in some way in the torture or because she has no powers of aggression (like Britomart's magic—and some have thought phallic—lance), but because only *false* lovers are able to enter such an arena. She is *too* true and constant (read "chaste") to have an impact. . . . The entire pressure of the narrative of the *Urania* insists upon the moral virtue of constancy (the titular virtue for the incomplete seventh book of Spenser's epic). Pamphilia is heroine because she is the truest, most constant lover, the most all-loving, that is, "Pam-philia." In Wroth's text women are, for the most part, better lovers than men.[95]

Amoret's determination to act as a chaste, unyielding heroine effectively counters Busirane's determination to act as omnipotent magician-author, but only a third reader, Britomart, will be able to resolve the interpretive stalemate. Amoret needs the alternative literary paradigm of love represented by Britomart, who will

release Amoret into either the rapturous Ovidian hermaphroditic embrace of the 1590 ending or the epic quest narrative of
the 1596 conclusion.

Artidon's cave is constantly referred to as a source of enlight-
enment, an oracle to which lovers may repair to learn the fate of
their love (Claridiana, for example, seeks to "know the trueth of
that which had brought her into so great care and heavinesse,"
Bk. 1, pt. 3, ch. 27, 121v); read in this light, Britomart's visit to the
House of Busirane seems a reprisal of her earlier visit to Merlin's
cave. As the Spenserian analogue of Artidon's cave, the House of
Busirane provides a false truth that is resisted rather than dutifully accepted by Britomart and Amoret. (The knights in both
texts have different agendas when reading in the magicians'
abodes, agendas distinguished by varying degrees of purposive-
ness and assertiveness—Rosicleer loves Princess Olivia but
does not choose to consult Artidon regarding the fate of his own
love; Claridiana seeks confirmation of her hopes; and Britomart
contests the mage's proffered meaning.) Both sites are highly
metafictional, literally marked with language. Writing at Artidon's cave recounts the narrative even as it is being scripted and
rescripted. When Rosicleer first visits, he encounters a legend
engraved in rock:

> This is the cave of the wise *Artidon*, who died for the love of *Artidea*,
> daughter unto king *Liberio*, the onely heire of this kingdome, who in
> recompence of her crueltie doeth and shall remaine heere, giving
> true aunsweres unto all that shall be demaunded of her, till such
> tyme as a knight shall come, who with his great bountie and force
> can overcome the terrible keepers of the entrie heereof, and let her
> at libertie, and then shall this entrie be free unto all those that will
> know anie thing of the wise man. (Bk. 1, pt. 2, ch. 4, 15v)

Rosicleer, in typical romance-hero fashion, reads this as an invitation to prove his mettle and enters to free the lady. After he
does so, the inscription is magically revised to read: "This adventure was finished by the knight of *Cupid*, who did set at libertie
the Queene *Artidea*, and in remembraunce thereof there doth re-
maine within the wise *Artidon*, of whom all those that are
touched with amorous passions, may passe the flames of fire
without anie impediment, and knowe of him all that ever they will
aske" (ch. 5, 25v). Artidon's straightforward account makes no
demands on the reader, in contrast with the subtler riddles of
Busirane, whose enigmatic phrases "Be bold," "Be bold," "Be

not too bold" demand greater hermeneutic skills and invite allegorical rather than literal interpretation (the "ridling skill, or
commune wit" Britomart utilizes in 3.11.54).

Busirane's text resists penetration in other ways, one being
the fire that burns in the castle porch. In *The Mirrour*, "amorous
passions" provide visitants with magical power to pass unscathed through the flames at the entrance to Artidon's cave.
Claridiana and her companions Elizea and Elizea's knight find
the fire more a nuisance than a threat: "when they came unto
the entrie thereof, they were greatly amazed to see the wonder-
full fire that came foorth thereat, which seemed to be some infernall thing. But when they had read those letters and understoode
the propertie of the fire, they straight waies entred in thereat"
(Bk. 1, pt. 3, ch. 27, 121v). The Spenserian flames, in contrast, are
indeed "some infernall thing," almost animate in their vicious-
ness and designed to obscure interpretation and prevent entry
into the house-as-text—the fire is "ymixt with smouldry smoke, /
And stinking Sulphure, that with griesly hate / And dreadfull hor-
rour did all entraunce choke" (3.11.21). Denied the gloss that re-
assures Claridiana, Britomart reads, and rereads, the flames'
significance, assuming initially that she and Scudamour are
transgressing against gods, but, when Scudamour despairs, re-
fining her interpretation to postulate that the fire may represent
only "*shew* of perill" (my emphasis) (3.11.24). Unlike the flames
marking Artidon's cave, Busirane's fire will ultimately be extin-
guished, indicating that, as a product of the poet-mage's imagination, it cannot endure unless readers are willing to sustain the
image's effect with their own imaginative belief.

As Susanne Wofford has pointed out, Britomart's exploration
of her strange surroundings "is glossed by Spenser as an activity
like reading, and like other inner worlds, the House of Busyrane
is treated as textual space, furnished with a multiplicity of intertextual references."[96] Britomart's lengthy progress from the
porch to the room where Busirane holds Amoret captive is
marked by a gradual increase in textuality, as she must first determine the meaning of the glossless fire, then numerous visual
images (the tapestries depicting Cupid's wars, the altar to Cupid
inscribed with "*Vnto the Victor of the Gods this bee*," the golden
bas-relief of the second chamber, which she spends an entire day
perusing, the allegorical figures performing in the masque of
Cupid), and finally Busirane's language in the inscriptions over
the three doors ("Be bold," "Be bold, be bold," "Be not too bold")
and the "bloudy lines" he pens in 3.12.36. Britomart's martial

might is utilized only after a prolonged series of interpretive trials, and only three stanzas are devoted to it; her heroic reading is emphasized instead.

James Broaddus contends that Britomart exhibits only "wonderment," "naïveté," and a virtuous determination to be constant and courageous rather than any extensive perspicacity in the House of Busirane.[97] John Watkins also notes Britomart's lack of ability or desire to interpret Busirane's tapestries; Spenser "attributes both her triumph over Busirane and her subsequent rescue of Amoret to her powers not as a reader but as an agent of heavenly chastity."[98] Designating Britomart a mere "agent," however, denies her the autonomy suggested by the text's emphasis on her "busie" eye, which is described as active in the liminal moment between the received sense impression of the artistic construct and the final imposition of meaning on it. Later her eyes become "greedy" (3.11.53) and then "heauy" (3.11.55), but once in Busirane's chamber the first thing she does is cast her eyes about, and her eye remains "stedfast" while Busirane reverses his enchantment (3.12.37). She is neither an illiterate fool nor indifferent to the tapestries and bas-relief—Britomart's response to what she reads is, significantly, much more intense than the responses depicted in *The Mirrour*. Rosicleer's admiration or wonder (the conventional romance response) is described only briefly, whereas Spenser recounts in detail the effect of Cupid's altar on Britomart: "That wondrous sight faire *Britomart* amazed, / Ne seeing could her wonder satisfie, / But euermore and more vpon it gazed, / The whiles the passing brightnes her fraile sences dazed" (3.11.49). The Cupid image serves as both an intimidating warning about love's power and as a decoy meant to absorb completely the onlooker's attention so that she will not further venture to read Busirane's "bloudy lines" but instead remain mesmerized by the artistic image that feeds the viewer's insatiable desire for wonder. She would thereby be absorbed into, rather than resist, the artist's designs. The failure of this diversionary attempt is implied by the word "Tho," which marks the transition from stanza 49 to stanza 50:

> Tho as she backward cast her busie eye,
> To search each secret of that goodly sted,
> Ouer the dore thus written she did spye
> *Be bold*: she oft and oft it ouer-red,
> Yet could not find what sence it figured:

> But what so were therein or writ or ment,
> She was no whit thereby discouraged
> From prosecuting of her first intent,
> But forward with bold steps into the next roome went.
>
> (3.11.50)

Not content with mere wonder and amazement, Britomart looks beyond or behind the dazzling statue in her persistent effort to understand Busirane's house and thereby rescue Amoret. She is determined to "search each secret."

Critics who are themselves uncertain of the exact meaning of "Be bold" (myself included) should perhaps hesitate to assume Britomart lacks perspicacity. Often characterized as a noncomprehending reader, Britomart *does* make a crucial critical judgement—when she enters Busirane's chamber, she is described as being "Neither of *idle* shewes, nor of *false* charmes aghast" (3.12.29, my emphasis). Having repeated the reading protocol she practiced at the entrance, a hermeneutics of suspicion, Britomart tests the truth of the images she sees against her experience. She is a discriminating reader: the images are not intended for her in the same way that the vision in Merlin's mirror was, but instead pertain to Amoret—as Busirane's fantastic house dematerializes, the distressed magician is said to have created "all that fraud ... To haue efforst the loue of that faire lasse" (3.12.43). Britomart is initially startled by the Masque of Cupid, but she does not find it at all threatening and in fact dismisses it as irrelevant to her life and purpose. Just as Shakespeare's Lucrece reads the Troy painting in order "To find a face where all distress is stell'd"[99]—in other words, to view her own image—so Britomart seeks but does not find her own image, an image of heroic, mutual love, in Busirane's gallery. When Britomart looks at Busirane's texts, nothing "to the looker appertaynd" (3.2.19). Britomart's stoic (some might say stolid) response to Busirane's depictions of what Salter terms "the filthie love (if I maie terme it love) of the Goddes themselves, and of their wicked adulteries and abhominable fornications" (*MM*, sig. D1r), admiring the style but not the content, reveals that a heroic woman reader can reject what a wanton woman reader such as Hellenore might affirm. (As Nicholas Breton notes, "as all Women are not of one nature, so neither are all Natures of one disposition: as one loves to be flattered, so other love to be flatlie dealt withall.")[100] Spenser thus acknowledges contemporary anxiety about women's potential responses to erotic literature but defuses it to some extent by asserting that female desire can be appropriately sublimated and channeled into epic rather than Petrarchan or Ovidian discourse.

That Britomart is depicted as a spirited and contestable reader becomes clearer when her experience is contrasted with that of Rosicleer, who acts more than he reads, and of Claridiana, who is vulnerable and acquiescent in Artidon's presence. Neither Rosicleer nor Claridiana is depicted as reading as much or as thoughtfully as Britomart, and the type of reading they exercise (rendered metaphorically in the opening of literal doors) differs qualitatively. Rosicleer, too, reads an inscription over a closed door ("When this doore shall bee open, then shall the Queene *Artidea* be at libertie, and the entrie heerein shall bee free unto all people," ch. 5, 22v), but the nature of the inscription is descriptive and prophetic rather than paradoxically cryptic—nowhere must he practice the subtlety of interpretation that Britomart must. For example, when entering the magician's chamber, Rosicleer's force, not his circumspectness, is emphasized. The Knight of Cupid wrests the mace away from the giant who guards the door and the giant thereupon vanishes. Rosicleer says as he takes the mace, "It dooth come all to one purpose to breake thee by force, as to open thee by policie or art," and then breaks open the door (23r).

For Claridiana, doors open magically. Having once entered Artidon's cave, Claridiana "never rested till she came unto the dores of shining steele that were shutte, which was the entrie into the inchaunted hall, but so soone as she had layd hand on them for to open them, they straight waies opened of themselves with so great a noyse, that [the] all mightie woorke seemed as though it woulde have sonke" (ch. 27, 122r). Unlike Britomart, who must wrest meaning from the cryptic codes of Busirane's house and ingeniously devise a way to enter the inner room, Claridiana does not have to strategize a way into Artidon's presence because she approaches the mage reverently and respects his "authority"—a much more passive reader, she has already resigned herself to believing whatever he will tell her. More vulnerable than the armed and watchful Britomart, Claridiana mounts the stairs "shaking with all parts of her bodie, for the sorowfull or heavie newes which shee looked to receive" and addresses Artidon only after "humbling her selfe unto him" (122v). The "sweet and peaceable Musicke" (122v) that sounds when Claridiana enters Artidon's enchanted hall she happily interprets as a sign that Artidon's pronouncement will support her own desire to be married to the Knight of the Sun. Britomart, however, must resist Busirane's music and fight against the seductiveness of the "lay of loues delight" composed and performed by the "wanton Bardes, and Rymers impudent" (3.12.5) prior to the masque's performance.

As Claridiana approaches Artidon, she is shown "the whole historie of the mightie and perillous battailes there, done by Rosicleer, and of all that had happened unto him in that Cave," and she reads this narrative in light of her own desires. Because Rosicleer is the Knight of the Sun's brother, his deeds remind her of the nobility of her own lover, and this explains her passionate response: "the which being well understoode by the roiall Princes, [she] greatly wondered at those worthie actes, not without shedding of a few teares which trickled downe her rubicall cheekes" (122r). Claridiana is moved to apostrophize Trebatio (the father of Rosicleer and the Knight of the Sun), praising him and hoping that her destiny will link her to his noble family. Claridiana makes no distinction between the manner in which she and Artidon love and even likens herself to him ("The great care which hath ben the occasion of my comming hether, (although I doe beleeve that thou doest know it) yet will I declare it unto thee, for that he that loved so faithfully and firmely in his time, will not mervaile at any force whatsoeuer it be that love doth upon humaine hearts," 123r), whereas Britomart sets herself in opposition to Busirane and his definition of love. Claridiana relinquishes her own power as a reader to Artidon, expressing her willingness to be guided by his response to her question about the Knight of the Sun's reported love for the lady Lindabrides: "I doe desire thee for to tell mee if it be true, and put me out of all doubt, for whatsoever that thou shalt tell mee, I shall beleeve it to be true, and conformable thereunto I wil take order with my selfe what is best to be done" (123r). Both Claridiana and Elizea[101] are reassured that their knights are true and faithful, and Claridiana is urged by Artidon to seek the Knight of the Sun and save him from despair (which she consequently does). In contrast, Britomart and Amoret are confronted with a hostile poet-mage whose message that love is essentially predatory and mutable engenders resistance in his two female readers.

In contrast to the interpretive nature of Britomart's and Claridiana's encounters with Busirane and Artidon, Rosicleer's trials are generically conventional acts of martial might. After Rosicleer passes through the fiery entrance and kills a large bull and a dragon, his prowess is validated by its immediate transformation into lifelike art:

> and as hee looked about him, hee sawe upon a wal that was right before him under one of the galleries in that court, a thing which put him in great admiration, which was, that he saw there portraied his owne figure and likenesse, with the device of his armour, and the entering into the cave, and all that happened in the contencion hee had with the Bull and the Dragon, till such time as they were consumed into the earth, everie thing perticularlie as it was, that hee himselfe could not declare it so perfectlie as it did appeare there upon the wall, and the Bull and the Dragon appeared there so fierce and furious, as though they had bene a live. (21v–22r)

He acts, and art then mirrors his actions; he is not expected to refashion himself according to the images he sees. Additionally, Rosicleer battles literal monsters; Britomart encounters artistic depictions of the "thousand monstrous formes" of false love, which she must distinguish from the image of true love she has chosen to embrace. Rosicleer sees his own heroic deeds, but Britomart is shown not her own power but Cupid's. With such a buildup, one expects Rosicleer's final showdown with Artidon to be action-packed, but it is strangely anticlimactic: "at the houre that the knight of *Cupid* entered into that Quadran and sawe all this, the same houre was the inchauntment undone, and the Queene was at libertie" (23v). Politely, Artidea stands up and thanks Rosicleer for releasing her. Rosicleer simply has to perceive Artidon's tableau (mere perception being one of the most elemental components of the interpretive process) to effect Artidea's release, whereas Britomart must force Busirane to "reverse" his image of love altogether. The contrast further underscores the contumacious nature of Britomart's face-to-face encounter with the magician-poet.

When Rosicleer speaks to Artidon, he does not chastise him for imprisoning Artidea; rather, he wishes he too could open his breast and show his heart to his own cruel lady, Olivia. When Britomart encounters Busirane in the act of composition, drawing on Amoret's bleeding heart for the source of his poetry, however, she registers extreme horror.[102] After Busirane sees Britomart, "His wicked bookes in hast he ouerthrew," and she "His cursed hand withheld, and maistered his might." In the ensuing struggle, Busirane wounds Britomart's breast; Hamilton notes that the wound, though "nothing deepe imprest," suggests imprinting. Yet Britomart's heart is less susceptible to being "written"

or "scripted" than Amoret's. At this point, however, Britomart
has succeeded only in halting Busirane's scripted words, his
"hand"; Amoret's reminder that "none but hee, / Which wrought
it [her pain; note the pun on "wrote"], could the same recure
againe" (3.12.34) initiates Britomart's forceful attempt to make
Busirane rewrite the conclusion to Amoret's love story. Busirane
must

> ouerlooke
> Those cursed leaues, his charmes backe to reuerse;
> Full dreadfull things out of that balefull booke
> He red, and measur'd many a sad verse,
> That horror gan the virgins hart to perse,
> And her faire locks vp stared stiffe on end,
> Hearing him those same bloudy lines reherse;
> And all the while he red, she did extend
> Her sword high ouer him, if ought he did offend.
>
> (3.12.36)

In mastering Busirane, elevating her sword (a metaphorical
pen) over him, Britomart finally claims for women the power that
much male-authored love literature has pretended to ascribe to
them. In binding the enchanter, Britomart attests to the triumph
of the female imagination, which can "re-verse" texts that either
dictate or falsify women's experience. Moreover, her action may
even speak to the (possibly resented) power exercised by Spenser's female patronesses, who, as his revision of *Fowre Hymnes*
(1596) to accommodate the wishes of Margaret Russell Clifford
and her sister Anne Dudley suggests, may not have refrained
from voicing their criticism of his work.[103] Britomart then binds
Busirane with the same "great chaine" (3.12.41) with which he
had bound Amoret—perhaps the revised lines of poetry. Susan
Frye has expressed dissatisfaction with the lack of ultimate punishment for Busirane,[104] but then Acrasia also escapes punishment; this seems a characteristically Spenserian way of
reminding readers that the dangers represented by these figures
are ever-present. Spenser's female readers are, like Britomart,
to be bold but not too bold, resisting Busirane's construction of
love but acquiescing to that of Merlin. Behind both mages lurks
the Spenserian author, whose poetic charms will prove fully efficacious only when fully affirmed by women readers. In this
sense, Britomart's encounter with Busirane represents the
Spenserian female reader's story of her own (potentially resistant) reading of *The Faerie Queene*. The remarkable range of

Britomart's responses (indifference, aesthetic pleasure, horror) to the texts she reads in the House of Busirane resists codification (and hence containment). Critics' failure to pin down the exact meaning of Britomart's reading experience may be precisely the point—that female reading will not ultimately be consistent or controlled.

3

"Don Quixote's Sisters": Lady Knights and Reading Women

> Shee reads *Greenes* workes over and over, but is so carried
> away with the *Myrrour of Knighthood*, she is many times re-
> solv'd to run out of her selfe, and become a Ladie Errant.
> —Sir Thomas Overbury, *Characters* (1614)

> She reades now loves histories as *Amadis de Gaule* and the
> *Arcadia*, & in them courts the shaddow of love till she know
> the substance.
> —Wye Saltonstall, "A Maide," *Picturae Loquentes* (1635)

In a diatribe against the masculine fashions being adopted by
seventeenth-century Englishwomen, the anonymous author of
Hic Mulier (1620) admonishes his female readers:

> doe not become the idle Sisters of foolish *Don Quixote*, to beleeve
> every vaine Fable which you reade, or to think you may bee attired
> like *Bradamant*, who was often taken for *Ricardetto* her brother;
> that you may fight like *Marfiza*, and winne husbands with conquest,
> or ride astryde like *Claridiana*, and make Gyants fall at your stir-
> rops, (the Morals will give you better meanings) which if you shunne,
> and take the grosse imitations, the first will deprive you of all good
> societie; the second, of noble affections; and the third, of all beloved
> modestie: you shall lose all the charmes of womens naturall perfec-
> tions, have no presence to winne respect, no beauty to inchaunt mens
> hearts, nor no bashfulnesse to excuse the vildest imputations.[1]

Although encompassing a range of subversive female behaviors,
the author's critique focuses on the potentially transgressive
ways women can read, and the texts to which he alludes (Diego
Ortuñez de la Calahorra's *The Mirrour of Princely Deedes and
Knighthood* and Ludovico Ariosto's *Orlando Furioso*) were indeed read by women. The first part of *The Mirrour* was trans-

lated by a woman, Margaret Tyler, in 1578, and the translator of
a subsequent portion declares that he has "in many places . . .
directed the Historie as it were particulerly to one or to more Ladies or Gentlewomen."[2] Sir John Harington's 1591 translation of
the *Orlando* purportedly originated in his providing an English
version of the provocative Book 28 for Elizabeth's gentlewomen
and then of the work as a whole for the queen. Female readers,
the *Hic Mulier* author proclaims, should seek allegorical meanings for the heroines' martial virtues, meanings consistent with
what the dominant culture identified as a woman's "naturall"
perfections rather than constructing aggressively literal meanings (those "grosse imitations") that would threaten established
gender paradigms. He prescribes a protocol of reading that radically limits the meaning of fictional lady knights, yet the very fact
that he needs to scold women readers does not bespeak confidence that his instructions will be carried out.

What is perhaps most intriguing about the *Hic Mulier* passage
is its omission of Spenser's lady knight Britomart.[3] That the author of *Hic Mulier* was aware of Spenser's *Faerie Queene* is indicated by his quotation of 5.5.25 ("Such is the cruelty of women-
kinde, / When they have shaken off the shamefac't band . . .") several pages after the Don Quixote's sisters passage. The author
thus appropriates the text of "the Poet" (glossed in the margin
as "E. S.") for his own polemical purpose: to chastise women who
have turned "Maskers, Mummers, nay Monsters in their disguises."[4] The quotation could have been culled from an anthol-
ogy, but the author, given his own argument that women should
submit themselves to male rule, would more likely have been
keenly aware of Britomart's suppression of Radigund and the
overthrow of the amazonian state only two cantos later in 5.7.
Was the *Hic Mulier* author simply vilifying "foreign" Italian and
Spanish romances and complacently overlooking the presence of
a woman warrior in Spenser's native English romance? Was he
undisturbed by Britomart, convinced that her actions as the
knight of chastity constituted no potentially incendiary exemplar
for "errant" female readers? Or, conversely, was he so concerned about the British martial maid's impact on Englishwomen that he purposely omitted her, as being too dangerous a
model of female reading to evoke in his diatribe against women's
interpretive agency?

This chapter will examine the contexts in which Britomart and
her fellow lady knights read texts, noting ways *The Faerie
Queene*, *Orlando Furioso*, and *The Mirrour* metafictionally rep-

resent the dynamic engagement between literary romance and the erotic imagination of female readers.[5] In the pages that follow, I discuss the scenes of reading that precipitate Bradamante's, Claridiana's, and especially Britomart's falling in love, readings that are all mediated by poet-mages. I include in my definition of "reading" the interpretation of visual images and the auditory reception of texts. That "Poesie is a speaking picture, and picture a dumbe Poesie"[6] was a commonplace of the time. For example, Britomart thinks of Artegall's "faire visage, *written in her hart*" (3.2.29, my emphasis), and the proem to Book 3 refers to the poem as both a painting and a mirror. Early modern women of the middle and upper classes would have been expected to read images of famous biblical and mythological women depicted in civic pageantry or in material household objects such as embroidered bed hangings; they also would have been read to or preached to much more often than are their modern counterparts. I will pay particular attention to the reception of these texts or images, analyzing the lady knights' uses of literary paradigms and female exemplars to structure both their erotic experiences and their martial identities.

The epigraphs to this chapter mock certain responses of women romance-readers (deemed "errant" either for their sexual desires or for their desire for power and autonomy or both).[7] Spenser's Britomart narrative, of course, links the two, in that the heroine adopts a knightly role in order to find her destined husband. In so doing, *The Faerie Queene* attempts to refute the concern common in sixteenth-century didactic literature that reading might teach women to be "subtile and shamelesse lovers" (*MM*, sig. D2r),[8] suggesting instead that reading functions in these texts to socialize women into culturally acceptable paradigms of romance, teaching them to be "good" (i.e., obedient and constant) lovers by scripting marriage as the necessary and ultimate goal of literary heroines. As a character within Spenser's fiction, Britomart dutifully acquiesces to Merlin's patriotic and patriarchal agenda. However, the *manner* in which she does so (appropriating literary images of women, particularly women warriors) provides early modern women with a potentially radical exemplar of a female reader, a more subtle but ultimately more threatening role (and certainly one more easily practiced) than that of lady knight.

The predominant focus of this chapter, then, is the texts' staging of the dynamic of literary influence, as the lady knights selectively appropriate literary discourses and imitate female exemplars in their originary moments as women warriors. These investitures, as enacted in the text, symbolize the transformation of women readers into metaphorical knights who can exploit either or both of the primary narrative trajectories: martial quest and courtship. Spenser's text is particularly vulnerable to female "misreading" and appropriation, in that it simultaneously addresses Queen Elizabeth and nonroyal female readers. Although it would be impossible to prevent nonroyal female readers from appropriating the models of martial women included as complimentary to the queen, the text at least tries to counterbalance this possibility by also demonstrating how books socialize women into certain courtship scripts that, if adopted, promote dutiful obedience to the state and its extension of power into patriarchal households. Spenser's inclusion of predatory poetic analogues and of a variety of competing literary images of passionate women necessarily emphasizes the choice women readers exercise in accepting or resisting particular literary conventions and in allowing their romantic fantasy to be abused, either by irresponsible poets or their own desires. He is far from assuming that women are unconscious consumers of literary fictions; if anything, he seems slightly uneasy about the ramifications of their imaginative autonomy.

* * *

Spenser's linkage of Britomart's sexual and imaginative maturation is consistent with sixteenth-century assumptions about the interconnectedness of female physiology and psychology.[9] The uterus was thought to cause many ailments, hysterical illnesses that provoke lovesickness, melancholy, listlessness, and general irrational behavior. Renaissance physiologists also believed that a woman's cranial structure provided insufficient means for allowing humors to escape, and they concluded that women were therefore more subject to perturbations or passions than men. These physiological singularities had moral implications: the imagination (thought to be very active in women because cold, moist objects are subject to metamorphosis and mental changeability) could easily lead to deceit, inconstancy, and infidelity. The overall effect of the uterus on a woman's mind, then, was a presumed weakening of rational powers and strengthening of all passions, both positive and negative.[10] The homily on matrimony read in churches throughout England helped to institutionalize such beliefs. The wife was clearly considered less stable than her husband: "For the woman is a weake creature, not indued with like strength and constancie of minde, therefore they be the sooner disquieted, and they be the more prone to all weake affections & dispositions of mind, more then men bee, & lighter they bee, and more vaine in their fantasies & opinions."[11]

The power of the female imagination was taken extremely seriously, considering that Renaissance embryologists blamed monstrous births on the mother's fantasies when the child was conceived or in the early weeks of fetal development.[12] In warning against women's reading loose "pamphlets" in contrast to truly good books, Du Bosc argues, "for since Mothers cannot eye certaine pictures, without leaving the markes in their Infants; why should wee not beleeve, but that the lascivious stories of these loose pamphlets may have the same effect on our imagination, and alwayes leave behinde some touches in our soule" (*CW*, sig. H3v–H4r). Decorating Phantastes' chamber in the House of Alma are shapes "Such as in idle fantasies doe flit," and the conclusion of the list with "fooles, louers, children, Dames" (2.9.50) implies that women as a sex are particularly susceptible to these perturbations. (Britomart, who as a "fantastical" female reader is read or lectured to and who views images more often than she reads written words, is thus distinguished from Arthur and Guyon, who read their histories in Eumnestes' library and are associated with the more positive aspects of the intellectual faculties.) Spenser acknowledges the more disturbing ramifications of a misdirected female imagination by concluding his lurid description of Busirane's masque with an inexpressibility topos couched in precisely these psychological terms:

> There were full many moe like maladies,
> Whose names and natures I note readen well;
> So many moe, as there be phantasies
> In wauering wemens wit, that none can tell,
> Or paines in loue, or punishments in hell.
>
> (3.12.26)

In using his magical powers to attempt a seduction of Amoret, Busirane recalls the figure of the magician used by Vives to warn women, whom he believes to be particularly susceptible to the enchantments of love, against would-be seducers: "This affection of love taketh wonders sore the myndes of all folkes, and specially of women. Wherfore they had nede to take the more heede, least it steale in upon theim. . . . Gyve none eare unto the lover, no more than thou woldeste dooe unto an inchauntoure or a sorcerer" (*ICW*, sig. O1v–O2r). Likewise, Busirane's "penning" of Amoret, his attempts to script her erotic experience, speaks to the parallel Thomas Nashe draws between mage and poet in *The Anatomie of Absurditie*. Nashe very explicitly links romance-writers with magicians and romance-reading with falling in love:

> Are they not ashamed in their preffred posies, to adorne a pretence of profit mixt with pleasure, when as in their bookes there is scarce to be found one precept pertaining to vertue, but whole quires fraught with amorous discourses, kindling *Venus* flame in *Vulcans* forge, carrying *Cupid* in tryumph, alluring even vowed *Vestals* to treade awry, inchaunting chaste mindes, and corrupting the continenst.[13]

Authors, like lovers and magicians, can use words as erotic charms. Nashe's mockingly self-righteous castigation of romance-writers expresses in exaggerated terms women's vulnerability to textual designs upon their virtue and clearly assigns too much agency to male authors and not enough to their female readers. Spenser's description of Lechery explicitly connects the sin with men's use of romantic literature to ensnare women, as Nashe does, but Spenser also acknowledges women's complicity in the process, as they are capable of inexplicable waywardness in interpretation. Lechery is an

> Vnseemely man to please faire Ladies eye;
> Yet he of Ladies oft was loued deare,
> When fairer faces were bid standen by:
> O who does know the bent of womens fantasy?
>
> (1.4.24)

Lechery's technique, which involves consultation of erotic texts, is amplified in stanza 25:

> And in his hand a burning hart he bare,
> Full of vaine follies, and new fanglenesse:
> For he was false, and fraught with ficklenesse,
> And learned had to loue with secret lookes,
> And well could daunce, and sing with ruefulnesse,
> And fortunes tell, and read in louing bookes,
> And thousand other wayes, to bait his fleshly hookes.

Yet women often exercise their own will in choosing whether or not to take the literary bait.

Spenser appropriately uses his legend of chastity to explore the dynamics of female interaction with seductive texts, the diversity of women's ways of reading, and the extent to which they imaginatively project sexual desires and moral values onto the texts they read. In Book 3, Paridell, Proteus, and especially Busirane, motivated either by lust or simply a wicked determination to disrupt the course of heroic love, act as usurpers of Spenser's persona as *praeceptor amoris*, challenging his (and his surrogate Merlin's) efforts to script female roles in the poem.[14] By manipulating established poetic constructions of the woman in love, they strive to lure Hellenore, Florimell, and Amoret into inconstant erotic roles. Yet all these characters, whether they resist or succumb, exercise autonomy in selecting, rejecting, or modifying the roles available for them to play, an autonomy epitomized by Florimell's staunch resistance to the enamored Proteus's designs to engage her in fictional role-playing (3.8.40).

Merlin and Britomart constitute Spenser's ideal model of the relation of male poet to female reading subject. The heroic Britomart, having been inspired by Merlin's prophecy of her political and sexual destiny, remains chaste and true to the literary paradigm of her dynastic epic vision, despite the alternatives she encounters during the course of her quest, and thus disproves Nashe's cynical assertion that romances corrupt even "the continenst." Her adventures may teach her not so much how to be chaste as how to read texts chastely. Her course is ultimately, as Susanne Wofford observes, "an amorous *dis*course."[15] She seems to falter only when she relinquishes her ability to transform the genres in which she finds herself being scripted, as, for example, when she lapses into the role of the passive victim of Petrarchan paradigms.[16] However, even Britomart cannot be contained completely within the dynastic script Merlin provides for her, as suggested by her responsiveness to Glauce's revisionist history of Britain's women and by her yearning to hear the love story of Scudamour and Amoret.

Nashe's equation of romance-writers and enchanters points to a motif common to all three of the romances under discussion here: Claridiana and Britomart fall in love, not with actual knights, but with images of those knights in scenes of reading mediated by mage figures, and Bradamante's love for Rogero is fomented through similar mediation.[17] Bradamante's initial encounter with Rogero at the end of Boiardo's *Orlando Innamorato* leads her to admire his valor but her erotic feelings, unlike his, go unrecorded. In *Orlando Furioso*, she "Disdained not"

Rogero's love "Although he had but seeld bene in her sight" (2.32); Book 4 reiterates the minimal contact between Bradamante and Rogero: "But till this present time they had no meeting, / Nor given by word nor writing any greeting" (4.31). It is the prophecy of Merlin and Melissa in Book 3, given in Rogero's absence, that significantly strengthens Bradamante's love. The effect is that of having fallen in love with the *story* of Rogero, with a fictional ideal. Ariosto's Melissa, Ortuñez de Calahorra's Oligas, and especially Spenser's Merlin act as author-substitutes in providing the prophetic scripts that channel the lady knights' erotic energy into a (heterosexual and monogamous) love quest for the man of "their" (culture's) dreams. These scenes of reading dramatize the role books play in establishing sexual paradigms by enlisting women's fantasy to shape their expectations of romance.

Illustrating Bradamante's receptivity as a reader is the engraving that prefaces Book 3 of Harington's edition of the *Orlando*.[18] Melissa holds open her magic book, turning her head toward Bradamante, whose eyes are fixed on the text before her. Bradamante's physical stance reflects the efficacy of the prophetic words: her left arm rests on her sword hilt (affirming her initial commitment to serving Charlemagne, her king, and her subsequent task of rescuing her lover Rogero), and her right hand gestures toward her breast as if applying the book's words to herself. Indeed, Bradamante later describes the confirmation of her love as a textual encounter. Despairing of a happy resolution to her love affair, Bradamante curses not Rogero, but Merlin and Melissa, whose words seduced her into increased desire. For example, in Book 32, Bradamante rails at herself for her susceptibility to Merlin's and Melissa's narrative:

> Beside my destinie which drew me on,
> By others sugred speach I was entrained,
> As though I should by this great match anon,
> Another Paradice on earth have gained:
> But now their words into the wind be gon,
> I in a Purgatorie am restrained:
> Well may I curse *Marlin* the false deceaver,
> Yet my *Rogero* I shall love for ever.

> (32.24)

Her word choice ("entrained," "restrained") suggests her perceived powerlessness to resist the enchanters' "sugred speach."

She continues in this vein, still blaming both the mages but now also her own acquiescent fantasy:

> I hop't of *Merlins* and *Melissas* promises,
> Who did such stories of our race foretell.
> This is the profit of beleeving prophesies,
> And giving credit to the sprites of hell;
> Alas, they might have found them better offices,
> Then to flout me, that trusted them so well:
> But all for envie have they wrought me this,
> For to bereave me of my former blis.
>
> (32.25)

The renewed power of Bradamante's love for Rogero attests to the power of the prophetic words, considering that he "had but seeld bene in her sight," and to her willingness to accept the structuring of her love as a teleologically driven dynastic romance, rather than a recursively patterned one. Bradamante's final curse of Melissa and the "Oracles perswasion blind, / That lapt her in this Laberinth of love, / Whence she her selfe knowes not how to unwind" (42.26) precedes her retelling of the story to Marfisa, which draws attention to the repeated narratives of the love affair that substitute for the affair itself. In the absence of the physical Rogero, Bradamante gains some solace in his imagined presence as she recounts repeatedly the story of their love.[19]

Merlin had foretold the coming of Bradamante to his cave and, during her night in his tomb, "with talke did her still entertaine: / Emboldning her to give her free consent, / To love where she should sure be lov'd againe" (3.52), yet Melissa serves as the active agent of magic and Bradamante's tutelary spirit. A skilled manipulator of magic texts, Melissa is specifically associated with books: "Her gowne ungyrt, her heare about her hed, / Much like a priest or prophetesse arraid, / And in her booke a little while she red, / And after thus unto the damsell said . . ." (3.10). Once Merlin's disembodied voice has urged Bradamante to persist in her pursuit of Rogero (3.20), Melissa, using a "triple clasped booke" to work her spell (3.22), stages the pageant of Bradamante's descendants. Treating Bradamante as a text to be inscribed, Melissa leads her by the hand into a circle and places characters over the woman warrior's head (3.23), a benign version of Busirane "penning" Amoret. Although Merlin's invisibility might be said to enhance his mystique, his absence from most of the text's action and his static position in captivity provide a striking contrast with the energetically shape-shifting Melissa, who assumes male as well as female disguises. Harington allegorizes Melissa as God's grace, but she could also function as Bradamante's imagination, in that Melissa accompanies Bradamante as a guide, suggests strategies for action, and even doubles for Bradamante. Melissa's remarkable activity reminds us that the seemingly invincible Merlin has been subdued by the Lady of the Lake, a woman who learned to use his own charms against him. Harington comments forebodingly on the means used by the Lady to entomb Merlin: "This I thought good to set downe for expounding the 11. staffe of this booke the plainer, not that any matter herein is worth the noting, without it be to warne men not to tell such dangerous secrets to women, except they will take occasion to imitate the wisedome of *Cato* in repenting it after" (22). Melissa and the Lady of the Lake serve as emblems of powerful female readers who appropriate for their own purposes the words or "charms" of the male writer of romance. Harington's grudging admission of this power attests to the tension between the desire to withhold literacy from women and thereby preserve masculine power and the desire to employ literacy as an instrument of socialization, a tool whereby women could be brought into conformity with idealized images of chaste, obedient femininity.

The Mirrour contains similar scenes that conflate female reading with falling in love, although the text does not link love to the fulfillment of political and religious duty as do the *Orlando* and *The Faerie Queene*, both of which combine romance with dynastic epic. Palisteo, father of the knight Flamides and the lady Lindaraza, draws in a gallery "manie histories of thinges passed in the worlde, and among other the pictures of many valiant knightes which were the[n] on live"; this gallery functions as an analogue for the romance text itself. As Flamides explains to Trebatio (the emperor of Greece), who has been held in enchanted captivity to serve Lindaraza's desire, "with the rest you were so lively drawen that it happening my sister to enter one day where the Imagery was, by the sight of your picture she was surprised with your love. Our father *Palisteo* knowing hir disease devised you should be brought by following your owne wife carried from you" (Bk. 1, pt. 1, ch. 44, 148v). *The Mirrour*'s version of this motif is striking in that it (rather radically) legitimizes female desire without containing it in a compensatory fiction of dynastic necessity, as the Ariostan and Spenserian texts do.

When Trebatio's son, the Knight of the Sun, views the gallery and the same images that Lindaraza did, he is not moved to fall in love but to perform the courageous action of rescuing his noble father, underscoring the gender-inflected nature of romance-reading. Paintings of famous knights move other knights to imitation of their glorious deeds (as in the *Amadis* when Leonides views paintings of King Arthur, Charlemagne, and their knights). (In contrast, when Pyrochles falls in love with the princess Philoclea's painted image in Sidney's *Arcadia*, the effect—his transformation into an amazon—renders him more effeminate.)[20]

The scene of reading in *The Mirrour* most analogous to those involving Bradamante and Britomart features Claridiana, a royal princess who delights in hunting and who has ventured (with her parents' permission) into the mountains to slay bears, boars, and lions. Carrying a boar spear and dressed in green velvet, her golden hair "knit up in a call of golde" and covered with a green velvet hat, she pursues "a verie great Hart, faire, & as white as snow" (a prophetic symbol for the Knight of the Sun, with whose image she is soon to fall in love; see Bk. 1, pt. 2, ch. 26, 89v). The hart leads her to a cave, at the mouth of which she kills, "with a valiant & manlike courage," a huge lion and then a mighty serpent with her "warlike and strong arme" (90r). Reminiscent of Scudamour's succession of trials-by-combat as he fights his way into the Temple of Venus to claim Amoret as his prize, Claridiana's martial prowess is rewarded with a lover, but as yet only the image of that lover. She is welcomed by Oligas, an old woman "who seemed by her personage and apparell to bee a person of authoritie" and who is famed for her "knowledge & understanding . . . in the art Magicke" (90v–91r). After awarding Claridiana Penthesilea's suit of armor and watching her charge put it on, Oligas takes Claridiana by the hand and leads her into "a fayre and great hall, wher, upon the walls was painted all the fairest damosells that were in all the world: and such as in times past had the fame to be faire and bewtiful. Amongst the which the princes did see hir owne face pictured" (91r). Prior to viewing her future husband, therefore, Claridiana's own identity (as a warrior and a beautiful woman) is firmly established; the implication is that her love quest is not the sole purpose of her being, and her identity as a warrior is not causally linked to her quest for the Knight of the Sun, as Britomart's is with her quest for Artegall.

In a second hall, Claridiana is shown painted images of "all the famous knights that hath bene and wer at that present in all the world, and all such as wer dead and past" (91v). Unlike Britomart, who is shown only one male image, Claridiana is presented with numerous images,[21] and, again unlike Britomart, *she*, not her magician guide, does the choosing, as her fancy is caught by one knight in particular:

> And as the royall Princes, did cast hir eyes upon him, and did conci-der his mightie stature and gentil disposition, and his severe coun-tenaunce, who seemed to be more a celestiall creature then any humaine knight. And joyning therunto his great and mightie wonder-full deedes and prowesse, which was portraied there before him. She straight waye found hir selfe wounded with his love, in whose hero-ical and liberal heart, dyd never enter any humaine thought before: was now all onely with that sight, taken prisoner in such sorte, that lyfe should first want, before that she should be released and at liber-tie. And bicause she would desemble that new & amourous passion, she asked of that olde Lady, who that knight should be, then the Ladie, who dyd well understand hir thought, sayde: you shall under-stand faire Princes, that this knight is called the knight of the Sunne.
> (91v)

Like Britomart, Claridiana is virginal in heart, mind, and fancy as well as body. Oligas's assurance that the knight is the most valiant in the world merely feeds Claridiana's passion. The en-couraging role played by Oligas, as by Melissa and Glauce, sug-gests that women are complicitous in employing fictional constructs to initiate younger women into the sexual cycle.

The reading-loving motif recurs with Archisilora, queen of Lyra, who "being a horseback and armed in hir armour, proved another *Claridiana*" (1583, *The Second part of the Myrrour of Knighthood* [i.e., Books 4 and 5], ch. 8, 48v). Like Claridiana, she is led toward love through the efforts of a magician, in this case Lyrgandeo, who endorses both her knightly identity (he has ear-lier provided her with armor, referred to in ch. 27, 152r) and her identity as a lover. Archisilora has secretly armed herself, plan-ning to challenge Claridiana to a fight, but Claridiana is engaged in fending off Brufaldoro, a Mauritanian pagan knight, who had attempted to carry off Briana, Claridiana's mother-in-law. Archi-silora, in her guise as the Knight of the Lilies, intervenes, and her valor and policy win the admiration of Trebatio and the Knight of the Sun. While pursuing the Mauritanian to continue the fight, Archisilora encounters a damsel (the magician Lyrgan-deo in disguise), who invites her onto a sailing vessel with this enigmatic (and not altogether cheerful) prophecy: "if thou wilt have that thou seekest, it behooveth thee to enter into this Barke

with me, that I may carrie thee whereas thou shalt loose on a
sodaine thy great mirth and gladnesse, thy heart remaining in so
great captivitie, that the best remedie that thou shalt conceive,
shall be to desire the death" (ch. 28, 159r). At sea, Lyrgandeo reveals his identity and, before vanishing, says: "Worthie Ladie,
feare you nothing in this journey, for by me thou shalt be carryed
whereas thy fame shall be exalted, till such time as the brave
Lyon doth rob thy heart, & thou remaining overcome, shalt overcome one of the best knights in all the world" (159r).

Once ashore, she comes to a palace wherein lie what seem to
be the bodies of the dead Claridiana and the Knight of the Sun,
surrounded by mourners, whom she joins (almost as if she is rereading the story of her exemplar's bravery and love and is now
poised to imitate it). Her hand is taken by a lady "of great authoritie" (163r), who proceeds to show her the palace, a sight not
granted to any other; she invites Archisilora to "rejoyce thy selfe
in the sight of that which heereafter shall come to passe, without
all doubt" (163v). The lady displays fair buildings and great
riches,

> but especiallye shee carryed her into a verie faire and foure square
> Court, which had at everie corner foure pillers, and upon the toppe
> of eyther of them an Image, mervailously wrought, and everie one of
> them had his title written what it did signifie, and shee tolde her that
> those which shee had shewed her, were kings and Princes, and fa-
> mous Lordes, that were there inchaunted. And how that all that
> should be made frustrate by one of the best knightes in all the world,
> who shall bring for his device blased on his sheelde, a braunch of
> golde. (163v)

Archisilora's curiosity is piqued, and the lady narrator postpones
telling the remainder of the story until the end of the third book
"where you shall receive more contentment in the reading: Lyrgandeo will now goe no farther heerein" (163v). Repeating the
Merlin/Melissa and Artidon/Oligas pattern, Lyrgandeo, not the
lady, seems to be scripting the palace tour, which culminates in
the sight of

> manie and fayre halls, the which were adorned with the stories of the
> notable actes of worthie knights, but in one hall, in the middest of a
> Cloth, shee sawe the Picture of a knight of a greate stature, who was
> nine foote in height, and armed with Purple armour, and his sheelde
> of the same coulour, without having anie device, and his face was
> verie fayre. The Queene coulde not by any meanes, but by sight

thereof staie a while and beholde his greate beautie, and felt within her heart a new and strange wrastling of love, which tourned afterwarde into an amorous fire. This Ladie did well perceive her newe imaginations, and with a gracious smiling shee tooke her by the hande, and carried her out of that Chamber (although shee coulde not bring her out of her newe conceit) shee went out so troubled, that all which the Ladie shewed her afterwardes, shee little respected. (163v–164r)

The impact of the knight's portrait has been so great that, once outside the palace, Archisilora behaves "even as one that had beene newe awaked out of his sleepe" and, "dissembling her newe paine" (164r), asks the lady a question she thinks unrelated to the image she has seen. The silver branch she requests is placed into her helm as though wrought by workmanship where, the lady says, it will remain "till such time as by the hands of a fierce Lyon it shall be throwen downe, leaving his heart wounded, and he remaining unto thee submitted" (164r). (In Book 7 [1598], Archisilora will recall her vision as she does battle with the knight, who, in an interesting reversal of the gendered terms of the common marriage topos, "embraced her with more strength then doth the Ivie incompasse the straight towering Elme," sig. H3v–H4r.) The textual image works as literary romance does, stirring and shaping the incipient love that has not yet come to be. Archisilora rides toward the sea "without any remembraunce of all that which shee had seene, neither did she thinke of it, till such time as she didde see the perfect figure of that knight, which she sawe in the hal, as shall be tolde you heerafter" (164v). Significantly, *The Mirrour*'s lady knights embrace their martial identity prior to becoming lovers; their roles as warriors are not contingent upon their acquiescence to the courtship script.

As with the loves of Bradamante, Claridiana, and Archisilora, Britomart's love for Artegall originates in a scene of reading. Spenser's text carefully draws attention to its romance genre and the common topos of magically falling in love at first sight, marking Britomart's vision of Artegall in the mirror as a distinctly literary experience:

> By strange occasion she did him behold,
> And much more strangely gan to loue his sight,
> As it in bookes hath written bene of old.
>
> (3.2.18)

The antecedent of "it" is ambiguous—Spenser alludes most obviously to the love-at-first-sight motif, but "it" might also refer to versions of Britomart's love story that predate his own, marking the intertextual nature of the literary enterprise. The mirror functions here as a metaphor for a love text, this one authored primarily by Merlin. *The Faerie Queene* dwells insistently on the efficacy of textually generated love; Britomart has never before seen her future lover, thus suggesting the supreme power of Spenserian romance (analogous to Merlin's mirror) over its female readers.[22] But *The Faerie Queene* also acknowledges the ways female readers can exert power over texts. Behind Merlin's mirror is the guiding power of Venus (3.1.8 refers to Britomart seeking the lover "Whose image she had seene in *Venus* looking glas"), suggesting that not only the author/Merlin but also the female erotic imagination helps to frame the mirror's revelations. What has helped to shape the imagination of the female reader is, of course, other texts or romance scripts.

Merlin's looking glass is reminiscent of the Fountain of Love featured in the *Roman de la Rose* and of other mirrors in courtly love poetry. Donald Stump reads in Britomart's story the traditional medieval romance conventions: the lover being stricken by Cupid's arrow "while gazing at an idealized image of the beloved," the knight seeking and serving the beloved through a quest that involves trials of character, and the knight's "rescue of the beloved from the dungeon of an unchivalrous tyrant," an ennobling process that ensures that the lover has become a suitable match for his lady.[23] But Britomart here assumes the subject position traditionally assigned to the male lover, anticipating her later decision to become a lady knight.[24]

Britomart's consultation of Merlin's mirror can also be linked to English folk traditions that used a mirror to ascertain the identity of one's future husband. As Burton comments in *The Anatomy of Melancholy*:

> They will in all places be doing thus, young folks especially, reading love stories, talking of this or that young man, such a fair maid, singing, telling or hearing lascivious tales, scurrile tunes; . . . hence it is, they can think, discourse willingly, or speak almost of no other subject. 'Tis their only desire, if it may be done by Art, to see their husband's picture in a glass, they'll give anything to know when they shall be married, how many husbands they shall have, by Cromnysmantia, a kind of Divination with Onions laid on the Altar on Christmas Eve, or by fasting on Saint Agnes' Eve or Night, to know who shall be their first husband.[25]

This passage illustrates the degree to which love is socially constructed, a communal activity, and Burton foregrounds the role of literature in the process (reading "love stories" precedes all other activities).

It is no coincidence that Britomart's vision of Artegall marks her transition from being "fancy-free" to actively using her erotic imagination; the vision serves to initiate her as a fully engaged reader of texts. Spenser emphasizes her essential freedom from sexual desire, even though after recalling the rules governing the mirror's function, her immediate thought of what "mote to her selfe pertaine" is her future marriage partner.[26]

> So thought this Mayd (as maydens vse to done)
> Whom fortune for her husband would allot,
> Not that she lusted after any one;
> For she was pure from blame of sinfull blot,
> Yet wist her life at last must lincke in that same knot.
>
> (3.2.23)

Sixteenth-century women were, with rare exceptions, expected to marry, and this would especially have been the case for Britomart as Ryence's sole heir.[27] Her lack of unchaste desire and indeed agency at this stage is underscored by Spenser's use of the passive voice: "Eftsoones there was presented to her eye / A comely knight, all arm'd in complete wize." Although Merlin's prophetic and scriptive powers are lurking behind that passive construction, Britomart is, unlike Bradamante and Claridiana, alone when she first sees her future husband's image, which suggests a private act of silent reading. The initial effect on Britomart is negligible; she "well did vew his personage, / And liked well, ne further fastned not, / But went her way" in her "vnguilty age." Britomart here exemplifies the dutiful but chastely nonspecific desire that Juan Luis Vives advocated: "it is not comely for a mayde to desyre mariage, and muche lesse to shewe hir selfe to longe therfore. . . . Therfore whan the father and the mother be busye about their doughters mariage, let hir helpe the matter forwarde with good praier, and desyre of Christe and his mother with pure affection, that she maie have suche an husbande, whiche shall not let nor hinder hir from vertuous livynge, but rather provoke, exhorte and helpe hir unto it" (*ICW*, sig. P2r–v). The same general desire is illustrated by Grace Sharington Mildmay, who claims to have prayed as a girl, "Oh Lord, if ever I marry, send me a man after Thine owne hearte."[28]

Soon, however, the vision triggers the onset of menarche and, along with the physical suffering of sexual desire, troubling apparitions of an overactive imagination. Britomart becomes "Sad, solemne, sowre, and full of fancies fraile" and finds her sleep destroyed by dreams and "fantasticke sight / Of dreadfull things." In other words, just as her body is undergoing a sexual transformation, so her fantasy is being transformed by desire. When she has realized that her pain derives from love of Artegall's image, she recoils from the discomfort of her sexual development, assuming that this metamorphosis of her body foreshadows her own death rather than her potential to breed new life. According to Britomart, the image of Artegall has been fixed within her

> bleeding bowels, and so sore
> Now ranckleth in this same fraile fleshly mould,
> That all mine entrailes flow with poysnous gore,
> And th'vlcer groweth daily more and more;
> Ne can my running sore find remedie,
> Other then my hard fortune to deplore,
> And languish as the leafe falne from the tree,
> Till death make one end of my dayes and miserie.
>
> (3.2.39)

Britomart's tragic plaintiveness echoes not only the exact tone of adolescent love's emotional confusion and intensity but also Petrarchan hyperbole.[29] The inception of Britomart's love has a distinctly literary quality, as if she is seeking textual paradigms that will help her define, categorize, and thus comprehend her bewildering and traumatic experience.

Britomart's engagement with the mirror's image, her love of a fictional construct of a knight prior to loving the knight's physical person, resembles the action of the maiden described by Wye Saltonstall in chapter 19 of *Picturae Loquentes* (1635), who reads "loves histories as *Amadis de Gaule* and the *Arcadia*, & in them courts the shaddow of love till she know the substance." Britomart's passionate reaction to the vision, however, indicates fear that her shadowed love may never materialize into substance, that she will be left only with the fictional image. She agonizes over her inability to distinguish fantasy from reality:

> Nor Prince, nor pere it is, whose loue hath gryde
> My feeble brest of late, and launched this wound wyde.
>
> Nor man it is, nor other liuing wight;
> For then some hope I might vnto me draw,

> But th'only shade and semblant of a knight,
> Whose shape or person yet I neuer saw,
> Hath me subiected to loues cruell law.
>
> (3.2.37–38)

She even complains of becoming a shadow in a negative identification with the beloved "shade," as her body, suffering from lack of physical fulfillment, languishes and seems on the verge of death (3.2.44).

The severity of Britomart's reaction can be measured by juxtaposing it with that of Claridiana, who, rather than bewailing her plight, responds much more actively to her own love torment. Rather than indulging in ontological debate, she simply feels a "great desire to passe into Grecia, & to see with hir eyes, that knight whose picture had robbed hir of hir libertie" (Bk. 1, pt. 2, ch. 26, 92r). Much more confident of her ultimate success in love than Britomart, Claridiana is "fully certified with in hir selfe, that if the knight of the Chariot [the Knight of the Sun in disguise] dyd once behold hir beautie & fairenesse, that he would quickly forget that Princesse, whose beautie he doth now defend [Lindabrides, with whom he is pictured in Oligas's cave]" (92r). Claridiana's delight in hunting is diminished by the new desire that has entered her heart, but she is still "verye glad & joyfull for that precious armour which shee hadde wonne" (92v). Her passion is certainly not life-threatening; she never goes into a protracted decline as Britomart does. When she does finally exchange mutual love blows in the field with her knight, Claridiana measures his physical presence by the earlier image: "But when the royal princes did see that pleasant countenaunce, whose all onely picture did wound hir unto the heart, and made hir to come into those partes, the great joy and pleasure which she received, I am not able to expresse: and hir love dyd the more increase, for that it semed unto hir, that by a great deale, that royal presence that she had before hir, might be compared unto the figure which she saw in the mountaines of *Oligas*" (ch. 31, 106v).

Predisposed to love the Knight of the Sun because of her mental image of him, Claridiana's love continues to be mediated and shaped by various texts and literary paradigms as she attempts to order her newly ignited passion. When Claridiana later discovers that the Knight of the Sun is engaged to marry Lindabrides, her first reaction is to swoon for an hour (her attendant Arcania fears that she is dead). However, upon recovering consciousness, she bursts into a love lament addressed to the sun, whereby (in a play on her lover's epithet) her "heart is fired" (Bk. 1, pt. 3, ch. 5, 12r). This lament seems initially to resemble Britomart's in its hyperbolic anguish and its literary allusiveness. Yet Claridiana cites as analogues to her grief primarily classical figures, several of whom, unlike the Petrarchan lover-victim Britomart evokes, take revenge for the hurt they have sustained:

> If that my singuler beautie & highnesse were not, I might put remedie in my great griefe, as *Ariadne* that was left of *Theseus*, and *Medea* forgotten of *Jason*. But who is there now in all the world, with whom I may make change of so faithfull love? What woman is there in all the world, that ever felt so great griefe for love? Trulie there is no comparison to be made unto mine: no not that of a *Deyamira*, whom *Hercules* changed for *Yole*, nor that of *Penelope* for *Ulysses*, nor of *Phillis* for *Demophoon*. (ch. 5, 15v)

Continuing the catalogue, she cites the experience of other women who have suffered for love (Io, Biblis, Thisbe, Dido, Hero, Gofreda, Hecuba, Sophonisbe, and Cornelia), but rather than condemning them and herself for experiencing desire, Claridiana simply identifies with their pain. Self-victimization (she envies Cleopatra for the opportunity to commit suicide [16r] and wishes "Oh that he were now in this countrie, surely I would be slaine in battaile with him") is replaced with anger at her beloved ("or else his great disloyaltie should be revenged by mee" [16v]). Matter of factly acclaiming herself as the most beautiful woman in the world and therefore deserving of the most valiant knight (12v), she feels cheated of her due. Lacking the one partner who could prove her equal in marriage,

> she desired no other thing but to die the death, for to evitate the suffering of so great evill, and from that daie forwards hir life was cleane changed over that it was before, neither did she exercise hir selfe in armour nor in hunting, as at other times, but as one that was past all hope ever to be married, and as a widowe, shee spent her time in her closet all alone, occupying her selfe alwaies in praier, leading the lyfe more of a religious woman, than of so high a Ladie as shee was. (17r)

However, her resignation and withdrawal from the world are only temporary. The passage continues, describing her as "alwaies waiting the comming of the knight of the Sun for to bee revenged on him." She is thus constructed here as an agent waiting to avenge herself rather than a passive victim.

Britomart also draws on classical literature as she reads her passion, doing so not only in hyperbolically Petrarchan terms but also in inappropriately Virgilian and Ovidian terms, assuming that her love, like Scylla's in the pseudo-Virgilian *Ciris*, will bring about the downfall of her nation. Britomart would presumably be aware of the political significance of the mirror's visions (Merlin has given "the glassie globe" to Ryence so "That neuer foes his kingdome might inuade, / But he it knew at home before he hard / Tydings thereof, and so them still debar'd," 3.2.21). She must be equally aware of her own political importance; she is quite at home in her father's closet, "For nothing he from her reseru'd apart, / Being his onely daughter and his hayre." Spenser's spelling suggests a pun on hair and may refer to Scylla's treacherously cutting her father Nisus's purple lock out of love for Minos, an allusion underscoring Britomart's self-imputed culpability. Britomart may be equating her body with Ryence's kingdom, which is being "invaded" by the foreigner Artegall. Her consternation could also result from her feeling the tug of separate loyalties to her new beloved and to her father as she considers the political ramifications of her private acts and despises herself for capitulating to the "enemy." Hence her harshness in labeling her anguish a "crime" (3.2.37), either of treason or of unseemly sexual desire or both. Britomart's self-condemnation is precisely the type of application advocated for women by George Pettie, who also reads Ovidian tales of unnatural love in terms of female conformity to sixteenth-century standards. For example, as Pettie concludes his retelling of Scylla's story, he addresses his gentlewomen readers: "But I am by this story cheefely to admonish you, that you pull not of your fathers heare, that is, that you pul not theyr hartes out of theyr bodyes, by unadvisedly castyng your selves away, in matchyng in mariage with those who are not meete for you. That is to pul of your fathers heare, when you shal cast of the bridle of obedience, rashly runne at randon, rudely neglect his preceptes, & presumptuously place your selves in mariage contrary to his pleasure." Similarly, Pettie concludes the Pasiphae story with a lengthy tirade on the importance of a woman's bridling her desire and maintaining her chastity at all costs.[30] Britomart may be reading her desire, then, as a "good" female reader of Spenser's time was enjoined to do, in line with the most severe of the moralists' strictures.

Glauce, however, refuses to accept any connection between Ovidian lust and Britomart's innocent love (demonstrating the variety of constructions female readers might place on these stories) and in fact urges her to love on. In order to convince Britomart of the normality of her emotional state, Glauce resorts to sensationalized love literature, in effect rereading Britomart's erotic dilemma within the same context of Ovidian narratives of perverted love that her charge has invoked. Launching into an admonitory lesson detailing the unchaste passions of Myrrha, Biblis, and Pasiphae, Glauce exemplifies precisely the method Salter recommends for matrons seeking to influence their charges. Perhaps it is significant that the first Ovidian figure Glauce mentions is Myrrha, who committed incest with her father—the nurse seems relieved to discover that she has not been scripted into a scandalous love story involving incest between Britomart and Ryence.[31] Glauce also counters Britomart's self-incriminating reading of herself as a female Narcissus by vowing to find Artegall, the physical object of her longing.

Glauce answers Britomart with a combination of magical, Petrarchan, and mythological discourses, urging her to acquiesce to the "tyranny of love" that the Petrarchan script demands, but also reminding Britomart that the love tradition can be read more positively, since Cupid "Another arrow hath" to wound her beloved:

> Daughter (said she) what need ye be dismayd,
> Or why make ye such Monster of your mind?
> Of much more vncouth thing I was affrayd;
> Of filthy lust, contrarie vnto kind:
> But this affection nothing straunge I find;
> For who with reason can you aye reproue,
> To loue the semblant pleasing most your mind,
> And yield your heart, whence ye cannot remoue?
> No guilt in you, but in the tyranny of loue.
>
>   (3.2.40)

After providing Britomart with these alternative readings, Glauce also resorts to incantations and other rituals of amatory magic, none of which prove effectual. Neither Glauce nor, later, Busirane, as practitioners of love magic, will be able to "reverse" or otherwise affect Britomart's constant love; the power to control her romantic destiny is located only within Britomart's imagination, and despite her pain, she does not wish to excise Artegall's image from her heart. Glauce and Britomart seek out Merlin for an alternative erotic paradigm, what will essentially be a lesson in rereading Britomart's fate. As Glauce suggests in her description of the "sore euill" tormenting Britomart,

what thing it mote bee,
Or whence it sprong, I cannot read aright:
But this I read, that but if remedee
Thou her afford, full shortly I her dead shall see.

(3.3.16)

Spenser's Merlin is invested with more authority than Ariosto's
Merlin and is revealed in the very act of authorship when Britomart and Glauce seek him out. "Deepe busied bout worke of
wondrous end," Merlin is seen "writing strange characters in the
ground" (3.3.14), which bind the spirits to his service, but the
"worke of wondrous end" may also refer to the dynastic romance
in which he will place Britomart. If, as Hamilton's gloss suggests,
Merlin's posture recalls that of Christ in John 8:6 as he traces
figures in the dust, mercifully rewriting the punitive Old Testament script for women who transgress the cultural norms for female sexual expression, female desire here is affirmed (even if
co-opted) rather than rebuked.

Merlin redirects Britomart's reading from mere romantic
wandering and self-indulgent, circular Petrarchan complaints
into a "streight course," a teleological narrative:

It was not, *Britomart*, thy wandring eye,
Glauncing vnwares in charmed looking glas,
But the streight course of heauenly destiny,
Led with eternall prouidence, that has
Guided thy glaunce, to bring his will to pas.

(3.3.24)

Lest this reduce Britomart to a passive object rather than an active subject, Spenser underscores the necessity of her cooperat-
ing with her providential destiny by making her the active
grammatical subject and Artegall the passive object in Merlin's
description of her task: "From thence, him firmely bound with
faithfull band, / To this his natiue soyle thou backe shalt bring."
Britomart will also contribute her "prow valiaunce" to Artegall's
martial efforts until her labor shifts to that of bearing Artegall's
child. Her role throughout is one of a highly active cooperation
with the text provided her. Expanding Britomart's reading of
Merlin's mirror into two episodes (in contrast to the single love-
vision/prophecy episodes in the *Orlando* and *The Mirrour*)
serves to foreground matters of reception and interpretation and
exposes the political purposes of the romance paradigms used to
structure the lady knight's erotic experience. Whereas Brada-

mante and Claridiana encounter their beloveds' images in the
course of their martial activities, without actively seeking the
services of a mage, Britomart is more purposive, first in desiring
(however casually) the vision in the mirror and then in pursuing
an interpretation of that vision from an authority figure.

Britomart may have anticipated Merlin's call to noble, active
love by projecting her own desires onto the image viewed in the
mirror. The Artegall she envisions (described as "comely" and
possessing "Heroicke grace, and honorable gest," 3.2.24) differs
strikingly from the occasionally surly character we encounter
later in the poem, particularly in his guise as the salvage knight,
whose motto is "*Saluagesse sans finesse.*"[32] The discrepancy
suggests that her fantasy is actively engaged in shaping her love
affair according to existing literary paradigms. As Wofford suggests, Britomart constructs Artegall's image from "fragments
taken from the epic and romance traditions,"[33] perhaps an indi-
cation that Britomart is predisposed to read her life in these generic terms. This imaginative activity constitutes a necessary
condition of reading the mirror's images (and literary texts as
well). Lauren Silberman notes Spenser's ambiguity in describing
the mirror's capacity "to shew in perfect sight, / What euer thing
was in the world contaynd. . . . So that it to the looker appertaynd" (3.2.19): "The double meaning keeps unclear to what extent the vision in the mirror is a subjective transformation of the
object—that whatever appears in the mirror is distorted to pertain to the looker—and to what extent the pertinence of the object to the subject is a necessary precondition for the magic
vision—that you can see anything you want, just as long as it pertains to you."[34] This allows for both agency and obedience on Britomart's part. We (and perhaps early modern female readers)
could interpret her behavior as dutiful acceptance of the patriarchal will of Merlin, her father, and her "author" Spenser in immediately acquiescing to her romantic destiny and transferring her
loyalties to her designated husband. Julia Walker argues that
"the paradigm of reflection" is used in Britomart's case "as a
strategy of containment rather than a consistent definition and
representation of female selfhood."[35] However, we can also interpret her as shaping her own destiny, taking advantage of the rel-
ative freedom and agency women have traditionally enjoyed in
the romance genre to fall in love without being constrained by
patriarchal controls. Britomart assumes the role of desiring subject, rendering Artegall the object of her own gaze and fantasies
in a reversal of the usual Petrarchan pattern.

Britomart's interpretation of the crowned ermine on Artegall's shield provides an example of her determination to read him as virtuous, the animal's ambiguous iconographic significance open to translation as either promiscuity or chastity. Alciati's Emblem 79 associates the ermine with the former because of its softness and luxuriousness (Malecasta's mantle is appropriately trimmed with ermine), whereas Elizabeth I's "Ermine Portrait" is intended to signify the queen's chastity.[36] Initially, Britomart attributes the more positive significance to Artegall, but in 5.6 she falls prey to destructive fantasizing, envisioning Artegall as unfaithful and casting aspersions on her beloved's integrity (although, one might argue, with some justification, given his susceptibility to female beauty). When Artegall hasn't returned by the promised time, Britomart "gan to cast in her misdoubtfull mynde / A thousand feares, that loue-sicke fancies faine to fynde." She acknowledges that he may have been trapped or overcome by accident,

> But most she did her troubled mynd molest,
> And secretly afflict with iealous feare,
> Least some new loue had him from her possest;
> Yet loth she was, since she no ill did heare,
> To thinke of him so ill: yet could she not forbeare.
>
> (5.6.4)

She vacillates between blaming herself and him, but is subject to "Many vaine fancies, working her vnrest," and her uncertainty in interpreting the ermine's significance as chastity or wanton luxury is apparent in her confusion when determining on a course of action:

> Now she deuiz'd amongst the warlike rout
> Of errant Knights, to seeke her errant Knight;
> And then againe resolu'd to hunt him out
> Amongst loose Ladies, lapped in delight:
> And then both Knights enuide, and Ladies eke did
>   spight.
>
> (5.6.6)

When Talus initially refuses to speak, "As if that by his silence he would make / Her rather reade his meaning," and then reveals that a female tyrant has taken Artegall captive, Britomart lapses into an even more destructive type of reading, interpreting his captivity metaphorically, as Petrarchan love, or as fulfilling the conventional epic script, which calls for the hero to be ensnared by a female temptress. She gives full rein to her negative fantasies, preferring to indulge her jealousy rather than hear Talus's words: "Cease thou bad newes-man . . . The rest my selfe too readily can spell." Just as she had earlier idealized Artegall in her imagination, here she vilifies him, creating in her mind a despicable, cad-like knight.

Britomart's habit of constructing her own version of Artegall is long-standing. She uses her early companion, the Redcrosse knight, to augment the erotic vision derived from the mirror by encouraging him to expatiate on Artegall's noble qualities. After Redcrosse has challenged her defamation of Artegall's character, Britomart continues to prevaricate, in order "To feed her humour with his pleasing stile," and she asks Redcrosse for a detailed description of the man she claims has done her wrong. Redcrosse complies, and Artegall "in euery part before her fashioned" (3.2.16). Spenser leaves Britomart suspended in eager absorption of Redcrosse's description, breaking off at this point to introduce the flashback recounting the mirror episode, the original fashioning of Artegall's image, thus enclosing the account of one reading of Artegall within another. When the narrative of her quest continues in 3.4.5, we see just how effective Redcrosse's words have been and how complicitous Britomart is in actively engaging her imagination to elaborate on Merlin's fictions: she "Grew pensive through that amorous discourse" and

> A thousand thoughts she fashioned in her mind,
> And in her feigning fancie did pourtray
> Him such, as fittest she for loue could find,
> Wise, warlike, personable, curteous, and kind.
>
> (3.4.5)

Britomart thus aggravates her love wound with "selfe-pleasing thoughts."[37] Wroth's Pamphilia also consciously utilizes her fancy to indulge her desire: "for though the sight which she desired, was hid from her, she might yet by the light of her imaginations (as in a picture) behold, and make those lights serve in his absence."[38] Pettie's Alcest similarly recreates a mental image of her beloved: "For as women be of delicate and fine mettal, and therfore sone subject to love, so *Alcest* after this first sight was so overgone in goodwil towardes *Admetus*, that she fixed her onely felicitie, in framing in her fanc[i]e the fourme of his face, & printing in her hart the perfection of his person."[39] Pettie's use of the word "printing" suggests not only the permanency of this impressed image but also the means by which erotic desire is rendered materially—through the publishing and dissemination of books.

Britomart continues to feed her fancy, perhaps in an attempt to satisfy vicariously her yearning for union with Artegall, in her encounters with Amoret and Scudamour. Set apart from the central action as she wistfully observes Scudamour and Amoret's loving embrace at the conclusion of the 1590 edition of the poem and "halfe enuying their blesse," Britomart figures Spenser's female readers, whose own desires have been fed by witnessing the happy outcome of another couple's relationship.[40] In Book 4, on another occasion that should mark Amoret's restoration to Scudamour, Britomart's romantic imagination manifests itself in her desire to hear love stories. When Sir Claribell entreats Scudamour to "recount to vs in order dew / All that aduenture, which ye did assay / For that faire Ladies loue" (4.9.40), Spenser singles out Britomart as the most avid auditor:

> So gan the rest him likewise to require,
> But *Britomart* did him importune hard,
> To take on him that paine: whose great desire
> He glad to satisfie, him selfe prepar'd
> To tell through what misfortune he had far'd.
>
> (4.9.41)

Britomart's desire for romantic stories that will feed her fantasy is never sated. As *The Faerie Queene* thus anatomizes in great detail the textuality of sexuality, the means by which romance narratives can generate and give form to erotic desire, Spenser thus inscribes within his own romance narrative a desire for just such a text as his own.

*   *   *

Spenser begins canto 4 of Book 3 with a seemingly nostalgic lament for the bygone accomplishments of martial women:

> Where is the Antique glory now become,
> That whilome wont in women to appeare?
> Where be the braue atchieuements doen by some?
> Where be the battels, where the shield and speare,
> And all the conquests, which them high did reare,
> That matter made for famous Poets verse,
> And boastfull men so oft abasht to heare?

Bene they all dead, and laid in dolefull herse?
Or doen they onely sleepe, and shall againe reuerse?

(3.4.1)

He goes on to enumerate the valorous deeds of such heroic women as Penthesilea, Deborah, and Camilla, exclaiming, "For all too long I burne with enuy sore, / To heare the[ir] warlike feates," and yet the response he records to such stories is oddly discordant: "But when I read . . . I swell with great disdaine" (3.4.2). The *Oxford English Dictionary* lists three meanings for "disdaine": "the feeling entertained towards that which one thinks unworthy of notice"; "indignation"; and "loathing, aversion, dislike." Hamilton glosses Spenser's usage as meaning "pride for women or contempt for men; or indignation that he does not have such matter for his song," yet although the context would suggest the latter as the more positive meaning, Hamilton's suggestion seems contradictory, given that the narrator shifts rapidly away from these militant characters to boast in the following stanza that the more feminine Britomart outdoes all other martial women: "Yet these, and all that else had puissance, / Cannot with noble *Britomart* compare, / Aswell for glory of great valiaunce, / As for pure chastitie and vertue rare, / That all her goodly deeds do well declare" (3.4.3). The narrator here records his own conflicted reaction, marked by admiration of valor, envy of other heroic poets' subject matter, and veiled criticism of the unladylike behavior of these powerful women, but what of the reactions of Spenser's female readers? These three stanzas point to the dangers inherent in women's reading histories of exemplary martial women and the tendency of the Spenserian text to direct female readers away from literal interpretation toward allegorical, moral application, as the *Hic Mulier* text recommended.

The discussion above focused on the sexual affect of reading, the ways texts can incite and shape personal romance. But *The Faerie Queene* foregrounds (as do the *Orlando* and *The Mirrour*) additional textual designs on women readers, including that of inculcating loyalty and service to the "motherland" through the reading of history, particularly stories of heroic foremothers. How do the texts under discussion here represent lady knights, or, more specifically, how do they depict lady knights being read? In other words, how do Bradamante, Claridiana, and Britomart respond to stories of martial women, and how might their responses serve as models for the female readers of the *Orlando*, *The Mirrour*, and *The Faerie Queene*?

As I noted in chapter 1, history was considered a highly suitable genre for women readers, yet, as postmodern historiographers might point out, "history" is notoriously unstable and can be reshaped, consciously or unconsciously, according to the values and biases of the teller. The figure of the woman warrior serves as a lightning rod for such contested readings. Examination of the originary moment of a woman's transformation into a lady knight reveals the danger implicit in women's reading history: the ability of women readers to appropriate the autonomous power and perhaps even the gender subversion enacted by many female exemplars of civic virtue.[41] How, then, do the texts confront (or expose only to deny) the opportunities for subversive interpretation afforded female readers by tales of martial women? And what is the significance of the female tutelary figures—Melissa, Oligas, and especially Glauce—who teach their charges how to read and to negotiate martial and marital imperatives?

Although Spenser's proem to canto 4 fails to include the perspectives of female readers, we do see possible responses figured in the characters Marfisa, Bradamante, Claridiana, and Britomart, who are depicted as readers not only of romances (usually their own) but also of history, even as they themselves exemplify civic virtue. For example, Marfisa is singled out as expressing curiosity about the allegorical images decorating one of Merlin's caves: "Chiefly *Marfisa* wisht to heare it told, / What men these were" and if the images were historical or prophetic (26.33). In Book 33, women again constitute the primary audience for the prophetic history of the Italian military resistance of the French drawn on the walls by Merlin: "oft they read the writings were between, / That in fayre Roman letters all of gold, / The circumstaunce of ev'rie picture told. / Now when *the Ladies fayre*, and all the rest, / Had seen and askt, as much as they desired. . . ." (st. 52–53, my emphasis). The poets thus inscribe desire for their own texts into the texts themselves, creating a fictional female audience craving to hear more histories of women. Not surprisingly, having heard Melissa tell stories about the virtuous progeny born of Bradamante's union with Rogero, Bradamante specifically asks for stories about women:

> Now when *Melyssa* sage such things did show,
> The noble Lady modestly replide,
> Sith God (quoth she) doth geve you skill to know,
> The things that shall in future times betide,

> And meanes on me (unworthy) to bestow,
> An issue such as few shall have beside,
> Tell me among so many men of name,
> Shall there no woman be of worthy fame?
>
> (13.49)

Here Ariosto, perhaps as a strategy to limit literal interpretation and offset the Marganorre episode in which Marfisa establishes amazon rule, emphasizes women's chastity, modesty, and maternal nature as Melissa explains that many will achieve fame as "Mothers to such as beare imperiall crownes, / Pillers and stayes of roiall families, / Owners of realmes, of countries and of townes" (13.50) rather than as rulers in their own right. Ariosto, through Melissa, coyly explains that if only Bradamante had asked about women at first in Book 3, she could have seen some, but that now, it is too late. Melissa continues to instruct Bradamante (as Astolfo had instructed his nephew Rogero) in the comprehension of their illustrious posterity as depicted on the walls of the wedding bower wrought by Cassandra: "Onely by good *Melyssas* wise instruction, / Dame *Bradamant* did know their whole construction" (46.82). Melissa has magically conveyed the bower to Bradamante for her wedding night, because the bride will presumably produce that which she looks on, physically conceiving heroes as she mentally "conceives" the images of the heroes she views. Sexual desire is thus co-opted by the state and transformed into the obedient performance of duty to the dynastic family.

Marfisa serves the state as Rogero's sister rather than as his wife; her amazonian origins resemble those of Camilla, Penthesilea, and Tasso's Clorinda and follow the common literary prototype. Just as Clorinda was suckled by a tigress, so Marfisa is suckled by a lioness (36.61) and fostered for seven years in the wild (38.15). The powerful but nurturing lioness doubles for Marfisa's mother Gallacell, who was also a lady knight. A king's daughter, Galacell "In feates of armes so valerous did prove, / That divers Palladines she overlayd; / And then with that, *Rogero* fell in love, / And of her fathers anger not affrayd, / Marrid in Christen state, as did behove" (36.72). Unwittingly imitating her mother's defiance, Marfisa (having been stolen as a child and sold as a slave to a Persian king for her virginity) kills the king and goes on to win eight crowns before she is twenty years old (38.16). Bradamante's martial origins are more self-consciously intertextual, as her explanation to Fiordispina indicates: "the worthy fame, / *Hippolita*, and stout *Camilla* wonne, / In deeds of armes, mov'd her her mind to frame, / To do the like, while others sowd and spunne: / And that she thought it to her sex no shame, / To do as women of such worth had done" (25.26). Neither Marfisa's nor Bradamante's transformation into woman warriors are staged in the narrative but are merely described and taken for granted by the fiction.

Like Marfisa, Claridiana is the daughter of a warrior mother, yet Claridiana has been reared by her actual rather than a surrogate mother, and Claridiana consciously expresses a desire to imitate her. As she explains to the princes Zoylo, Bargandel, and Liriamandro, "Wit you now that I am called *Claridiana* the daughter to *Theodoro* Lord of this Empyre and to the Empresse *Diana* Queene of the *Amazones*. . . . I am their onely childe which since my young yeares have bene brought up in hunting and I am promised to be made knight, for my mother being but young achieved such enterprises that in hir time there was no knight more famous, and I am desirous to be somewhat lyke unto hir especiallye in that poynte" (Bk. 1, pt. 1, ch. 45, 151r, misnumbered 142). (In contrast, Britomart's mother is never mentioned, and Britomart's surrogate mother, Glauce, is rendered as a comic rather than heroic figure when she assumes a martial role as Britomart's squire.) Claridiana's self-construction, like Bradamante's, is marked by heroic, epic allusions; when she rides ahead of her entourage during the hunt, she engages in conversation with the young men: "The Lady delighted in the good behaviour of the three knights and tickeled with the wordes of the *Tartarian* [Zoylo has compared her to Diana], in greate majestye aunswered him. Assuredly sir knight I knowe no cause you have to mervayle at me, but rather I at you. For if I seeme to you lyke to *Diana* the goddesse of the Gentiles, you lykewise seeme to me the three sonnes of *Priamus*: *Hector, Paris* and *Troylus*" (150v), thus capping their classical allusion with one of her own. When first glimpsed by the princes, she is identifiably a gentlewoman rather than a knight, and her transformation into a lady knight is progressively staged throughout the narrative. In fact, she invites the princes to witness the ceremony of her investiture. That the princes have a month earlier sailed from "the haven which was neerest to *London*" (150r) and have lighted by chance in Claridiana's country of Trabisond may imply (*pace* the author of *Hic Mulier*) that lady knights inhabit locales closer to England than one might otherwise think. When Claridiana meets Oligas, she has received the order of knighthood but has not yet been invested; the public ceremony staged by her father and graced with the presence of visiting princes is complemented by the private female investiture conducted by Oligas.

Even more so than Melissa, Oligas seems to possess her power in her own right. She mentions a "wyse man" (Artidon, the magician who will later supply the magic spears with which Claridiana and the Knight of the Sun wound each other with love) who has brought Penthesilea's sword and armor to Oligas's cave after the amazon's death on the battlefield at Troy, knowing "that it should be achived by a damosell, who in force of armes, and beautie, should farre surmount that famous queene" (Bk. 1, pt. 2, ch. 26, 91r). However, no man is present in the cave to prophesy Claridiana's future, and Oligas is the one who grants Claridiana the arms, having judged her worthy by her prowess in slaying the beasts. Only after Claridiana arms herself with Penthesilea's armor (an intertextual gesture, in that Claridiana now "tries on" epic as well as romance) does she enter the room in which she falls in love with the image of the Knight of the Sun. *The Mirrour*'s depiction of Claridiana's gradual transition from maid to knight in such detail encourages, or at least allows, female readers to assume that identity is not fixed and that a martial identity can be assumed at will.

In addition to being inspired by the deeds of her mother and Penthesilea, whose armor she has won, Claridiana inspires other women to imitate her valorous deeds by becoming lady knights themselves. Archisilora, the queen of Lira, has heard Claridiana "teil [*sic*] of some feates of knighthoode that had passed by her, the which the Queene with great contentment gave eare unto, imagining within her selde to be of as good disposition, and have as much strength as she, yea, and rather more: and knowing that her strength was much, she purposed verye secretlye to prove her selfe" (1583, *Second Part*, [Bks. 4–5], ch. 27, 152r). The Liran queen dons armor covered with golden lilies and makes her first appearance by assisting Claridiana in her battle against a Mauritanian knight. He becomes enraged when he realizes he is fighting a woman, and the Knight of the Lilies taunts him by citing the deeds of her chosen exemplar: "for heere I doo certifie thee, that the Empresse *Claridiana* hath brought into subjection many better then thou art, and made them to stoope. And for that thou shalt understand how little thou art esteemed in *Greece*, and how much more thou maist complaine thy unhappinesse, knowe that I am lykewise a woman as she is, and am called *Archisilora Queene of Lira*" (154v). Lady knights breed other lady knights, both physically and metaphorically. Rosamond, the daughter of the king of Callidonia, also models her life upon the exemplary Claridiana in defiance of patriarchal control:

being brought up together with my brothers, seeing them so greatly affected and given to hunting, I determined also to keepe them company, refusing no danger that might be offered me, untill our more yeares inabled us, to presume to mount on horses, and with Boare speares follow the cruellest beastes that we met. My brothers attaining to the age of xvi. yeares, were by my Father knighted, who denyed me that honour, supposing I would absent my selfe fro[m] him, because he heard me divers times say, how greatly I desired to passe unto *Graecia* to visite the Empresse *Claridiana*, whose fame through all the world, especially in these kingdomes, glorifies her with the name of a sole Paragon of beautie, and only Myrrour of chivalrie. I could not but grieve with my Fathers denyall (yet I dissembled it) still following the chase, untill this day two moneths, there befell me what I will now tell you.

We came, my brothers and I a hunting to this Forest, (called of the fair Fountaine,) and parting from them in pursute of that Hart, on the toppe of a mountaine, on the sudden a beauteous Lady set her selfe before me, crying, stay: for without armour, you cannot well passe forwards: and unbynding a little packet shee there had, shee gave me this armour, saying they were them wherewith *Semyramis* did winne Babylon, and that with them I should overcome one of the best knights of the world. (*The Seventh Booke of the Myrrour of Knighthood* [1598, i.e., the second book of the third part], ch. 2, sig. E1r–v)

Yet another lady knight, Floraliza, uses Camilla's sword in battle (1598, *Seventh Booke*, ch. 8, sig. O1r). Arms and weapons serve metaphorically as representations of a power passed on from woman to woman through oral history, weapons these women use both defensively and offensively.

Whereas Claridiana is initiated into knighthood prior to her vision of the Knight of the Sun (which then marks her initiation into love), Britomart's love for Artegall works her transformation from a lovesick maiden into a lady knight, thus valorizing love over martial deeds,[42] and nowhere in *The Faerie Queene* do we see other female characters consciously imitating Britomart as they do Claridiana in *The Mirrour*. It is hard to underestimate the significance of this Spenserian adaptation of the romance topos—Galacell, Claridiana, and Archisilora all devote themselves to martial pursuits prior to falling in love, at which point, having already established a militant, autonomous identity, they

can marry whom they choose. (Bradamante experiences slightly
less freedom, as she is torn between her desires to marry Rogero and to obey her parents.) Spenser seems to have very intentionally reversed the motif of the woman warrior turning
lover—Britomart is a lover emboldened by her love to become a
warrior.[43]

Britomart's transformation into a knight is also staged within
the course of the narrative, but, despite Spenser's attempt to
contain the autonomous impulse within the boundaries of marital love, Britomart's may constitute an even more radical transformation than Claridiana's, who has always possessed the
desire to emulate her martial mother. Even more consciously literary than Claridiana, Britomart's knightly origins are rooted in
a retelling of women's history, her new role a response to texts
she has read or heard, rather than observed firsthand. Britomart
functions as a seemingly exemplary reader/auditor of historical
texts, particularly as she responds with nationalistic fervor to the
accounts of British history provided by Merlin and Paridell in
3.3.43 ff. and 3.9.38 ff., becoming "full deepe empassioned" in
each case. Yet Britomart's public response to British history and
the version of that history she receives differ according to the
company and material circumstances in which she finds herself
as she reads. Both at Malbecco's castle and earlier in Merlin's
cave, Britomart hears a male-centered version of history and
acts in accord with civic virtue in the presence of the male narra-
tors and her fellow auditors, but when alone with Glauce she responds quite differently to the feminized alternative history
recounted by her nurse.

According to Merlin's history lesson, Britomart's preeminent
service to the state will not be to perform her own martial deeds
but to bring Artegall back to Britain so that *he* can fight: "From
thence, him firmely bound with faithfull band, / To this his natiue
soyle thou backe shalt bring, / Strongly to aide his countrey, to
withstand / The powre of forrein Paynims, which inuade thy
land" (3.3.27). Her martial actions are subordinated as merely
complementary or supplemental to Artegall's:

> Great aid thereto his mighty puissaunce,
> And dreaded name shall giue in that sad day:
> Where also proofe of thy prow valiaunce
> Thou then shalt make, t'increase thy louers pray.
> Long time ye both in armes shall beare great sway,
> Till thy wombes burden thee from them do call.

(3.3.28)

All of the historical figures in Merlin's lesson are male, and Britomart registers no heightened interest even in the culminating
figure of Merlin's narrative, her counterpart the "royall virgin"
Elizabeth. Britomart is moved to interrupt only once, in response
to Merlin's cue ("O who shall helpe me to lament, and mourne /
The royall seed, the antique *Troian* blood," 3.3.42), sighing and
asking when the heavens will be kind again to her fellow Britons,
a response that reveals her dutiful subordination of her own
erotic longing to her desire for her nation's good.

Yet Glauce gives Britomart another history lesson almost immediately after Merlin's, the rhetorical purpose of which is to encourage Britomart to emulate martial women in her own right.
Although Glauce's ultimate purpose may be to unite Britomart
with Artegall and therefore to inscribe her surrogate daughter
within the patriarchal order, the means by which she effects this
are potentially subversive. She reminds the lovesick Britomart
that

> it ought your courage much inflame,
> To heare so often, in that royall hous,
> From whence to none inferiour ye came,
> Bards tell of many women valorous
> Which haue full many feats aduenturous
> Performd, in paragone of proudest men:
>
> (3.3.54)

The "performance" of noble deeds suggests that female valor is
not innate but rather can be learned.

Glauce then proceeds to appropriate the bards' sanctioned authorial role by detailing the exploits of several notable women,
urging Britomart to emulate the deeds of

> The bold *Bunduca*, whose victorious
> Exploits made *Rome* to quake, stout *Guendolen*,
> Renowmed *Martia*, and redoubted *Emmilen*.
>
> (3.3.54)

Glauce seems at first simply to be following Salter's recommendation that wise matrons inspire their charges with tales of virtuous women: "But in steede of suche [unsuitable] bookes and
lacivious ballades, our wise matrone shall reade, or cause her
maidens to reade, the examples and lives of godly and vertuous
ladies, whose worthy fame and bright renowne yet liveth, and
still will live for ever, whiche shee shall make choice of, out of

the holy Scripture, and other histories, both auncient and of late dayes" (*MM*, sig. C2r). The desired effect, of course, is to "not onely delight them, but . . . [to] pricke and incite their hartes to follow vertue, and have vice in horror and disdaine. . . . for you shall never repeate the vertuous lives of any suche ladies as *Claudia, Portia, Lucretia*, and such like were, but you shall kindle a desire in them to treade their steppes, and become in tyme like unto them" (*MM*, sig. C2r). However, Glauce, unlike Ariosto's Melissa, selects for her pep talk tales not of chaste wives but rather of valorous women who assume public authority and exercise considerable political influence. Pamela Benson makes a similar point, observing that Glauce's exemplars are not the classical, lifelong amazons Camilla and Penthesilea but instead are Englishwomen who "took up arms for a particular cause. . . . These are women whose female virtues lead them to find the strength to act in the interests of family and nation."[44] Although I agree with her that the Spenserian text does attempt to contain the subversive energies associated with these figures ("their actions do not challenge the traditional order of society as those of Amazons do"), I question the ultimate effectiveness of this containment strategy. The fact that Glauce's exemplars are *not* typical literary amazons but instead "ordinary" women who can transform themselves into martial women when necessary may make them more suitable for appropriation by Spenser's female readers and thus ultimately encourage rather than contain subversion. The fact that the exemplars are British suggests that Britomart, a British rather than Greek or Roman or Italian lady knight, can, in turn, be appropriated all the more easily by her female readers.

Just as Melissa's power may have originally been derived from Merlin but is then exercised independently, so Glauce follows Merlin's example of instructing Britomart in the history of her country, but looks backward rather than prophetically forward, providing a feminized version of the *Briton moniments* featured in 2.10. Unlike Merlin, whose only female exemplar is the "royall virgin" whose reign is not yet concluded, Glauce's history consists only of women. She glosses for female readers the account they have read earlier through Arthur's eyes in Eumnestes' library; her account, delivered by a female narrator to a female auditor, emphasizes only the positive aspects of the notable women described in *Briton moniments*.[45] Glauce's partiality and selectivity as an historiographer illuminates the comparable partiality of *Briton moniments*, and this foregrounding of Spenser's manipulation of his source material allows, even invites, the reader to imitate that selectivity. Glauce's ordering principle appears to be the ways each of these historical exemplars' lives overlaps with that future prophesied for her charge Britomart. By juxtaposing *Briton moniments* and Glauce's retelling of that text, Spenser's poem acknowledges the existence of "authorized" versions of history and of subversive feminine readings of that history (and, by implication, the Elizabethan history constituted by his own poem). Glauce's technique will later be imitated by Britomart, as she does not hesitate to correct Paridell's masculinist (and egotistically biased) construction of British history. Granted, her correction conforms to official Tudor propaganda, but she nevertheless demonstrates the ease with which women can contest the seemingly "authoritative" versions they are given. If, as Mihoko Suzuki suggests, Paridell functions as an "epic poet *manqué*,"[46] Britomart functions as the alert female reader who does not hesitate to note the omissions that are relevant to her quest. She thus models how Spenser's female readers might similarly challenge his own version of history.

Anticipating Britomart's combined political and maternal concerns, Emmilen (presumably the queen of Cornwall and mother of Tristram [6.2.29] as Hamilton suggests in his annotation) takes the initiative to safeguard her son from his jealous uncle. Taking counsel of a wise man (as Britomart does of Merlin), she sends Tristram out of Cornwall into Fairyland, where he can be safely prepared for public service. Spenser's account depicts Emmilen as more heroic and politically engaged than does Malory's, in which the Emmilen counterpart, called Elizabeth, dies in childbirth.[47] "Renowmed *Martia*," or Mertia, also resembles Britomart in her role not as mother but as wife. Mertia's husband is described as just, carrying out the laws she has written (2.10.42), thus anticipating the dynamic to be enacted by the just Artegall and the equitable Britomart in Book 5. The text of *Briton moniments* is ambivalent about Mertia's power and agency: Guitheline "had to wife Dame *Mertia* the fayre,/ A woman worthy of immortall prayse, / Which for this Realme found many goodly layes, / And wholesome Statutes to her husband brought" (2.10.42). "Found" and "brought" suggest that she merely introduced the laws of others, but the final line of the stanza ("of her be *Mertian* lawes both nam'd and thought") suggests that the laws indeed originated with her.[48]

Like Britomart, Bunduca (Boadicea) becomes a warrior maid out of necessity and passion for country (although Britomart's motivation is erotic as well as heroic). Seeing that her country "did her selfe in sundry parts diuide" and the Romans were sub-duing the weak, Bunduca "vp arose, / And taking armes, the *Britons* to her drew; / With whom she marched streight against her foes, / And them vnwares besides the *Seuerne* did enclose" (2.10.54). Glauce mentions only Bunduca's victories, whereas the chronicle featured in Book 2 conspicuously downplays these. The contrast between the two versions is heightened by the struc-tural parallel—Bunduca's exploits are described in the fifty-fourth stanza of both Books 2 and 3. As Carrie Harper notes, stanzas 54 and 55 "gave no opportunity" for the triumphs praised in stanza 56, "as Bunduca is there described as fighting only twice and being defeated both times. The fifty-sixth stanza there-fore in part contradicts and in part repeats the narrative in the preceding stanzas. . . . All previous versions of the story . . . repre-sent Bunduca as victorious in her early battles."[49] Spenser adds defeats not mentioned by other chroniclers, perhaps in an effort to diminish the power of the warrior queen, whereas Glauce, tai-loring her account to her immediate audience, is unequivocal in her praise of Bunduca. Spenser's ambivalence regarding wom-en's rule may be present in the noncommittal description of Bun-duca as "Matchable either to *Semiramis*, / Whom antique history so high doth raise, / Or to *Hypsiphil*, or to *Thomiris*" (2.10.56); "antique history," not the author, raises her to these heights. She does display courage, but fortune, not her own skill, is credited with her victories ("Who whiles good fortune fauoured her might, / Triumphed oft against her enimis"). Spenser may have, consciously or unconsciously, perceived her as too danger-ous a precedent for his own female readers.

Guendolen (2.10.17–20), like Bunduca and Britomart, *becomes* a warrior woman, "gathering force, and courage valorous" in the interests of both radical marital chastity and her country's wel-fare. She has proved "alwaies faithfull" to her husband, Locrine, but when Locrine "fell to vaine voluptuous disease" and "lewdly lou'd" the lady Estrild, Guendolen "Would not endure to be so vile disdaind" and takes arms against him. He is constrained to flee after she vanquishes him, "But she so fast pursewd, that him she tooke, / And threw in bands, where he till death remaind" (2.10.18). The conclusion Spenser uses here is highly unusual in its emphasis on the wronged wife's aggression and power to ef-fect her husband's lingering death; other chronicle accounts de-scribe Locrine being killed by an arrow in battle.[50] Spenser's version also accentuates Guendolen's active engagement in battle, her direct and immediate confrontation of her husband, whereas in the *Mirror for Magistrates* account she "mou'de the Cornish men to fight."[51] Guendolen's power does not diminish once her husband has been subdued; as Britomart is destined to do, she rules as regent for her infant son, "During which time her powre she did display / Through all this realme, the glorie of her sex, / And first taught men a woman to obay" (2.10.20). Yet Spenser omits a key phrase included in the Stow account: she was "by common assent of all the Brytaines, made ruler of the whole Ile of Brytaine."[52] The effect of this omission is to emphasize her power as "displayed" (and therefore inauthentic) and as imposed on her male subjects rather than welcomed. The Stow account calls her "ruler" whereas Spenser only implies this, remarking "In her owne hand the crowne she kept in store," which diminishes her autonomous strength. However, we have evidence that at least one seventeenth-century female reader freely adapted the story of Guendolen (perhaps mediated by Milton rather than Spenser) in Margaret Cavendish's play *The Apocriphal Ladies* (1662). Cavendish's "mind was occupied with the question of Gwendolen's claim to the throne after Locrine's marriage to Estrildis; and in order to make this problem more difficult [and perhaps to vindicate Guendolen's actions and augment her political power] she supposes that Gwendolen was the rightful heir and Locrine king only by virtue of being his wife's husband."[53]

Glauce's exemplars culminate with one "which more then all the rest may sway" (perhaps because she is "Late dayes ensample" and therefore more compelling than earlier exemplars or because Glauce is an eyewitness of her glory). Glauce invokes Angela, the virginal Saxon leader: "Therefore faire Infant her ensample make / Vnto thy selfe, and equall courage to thee take" (3.3.55, 56). Angela seeks revenge on Ulfin, who, according to Hamilton's note, assisted Arthur in his seduction of Igerna and has therefore offended female chastity, a cause Britomart will also defend. Her interest especially piqued by Angela, Britomart is moved to ask the Saxon virgin's name and interrupts Glauce's account to do so: "Ah read, (quoth *Britomart*) how is she hight?" This question is much more personalized than the public lament Britomart utters in the presence of Merlin and of Paridell. Benson assumes Angela is "the kind of woman warrior Britomart pretends to be when describing herself to Red Cross, one schooled in fighting since infancy,"[54] yet the text is silent about Angela's upbringing. For all we know, Angela may have become

rather than been born a lady knight. Harper observes that the
story of Angela is less well documented than many of the others
Spenser relates and that Holinshed refuses to acknowledge the
story's authenticity.[55] Harper admits defeat in her attempts to locate Spenser's source for the story of Angela beyond mention of
her name.[56] Significantly, Angela, whose arms Britomart is to
bear, is the only female exemplar not validated by inclusion in
another of *The Faerie Queene*'s history chronicles—she is *sui
generis*. The fact that Angela serves as Glauce's most compelling, climactic example underscores the powerful effect that even
fictional exemplars can have on female readers. Britomart's primary inspiration is thus founded on the most historically dubious
example, thus establishing a precedent for female readers to be
inspired by Britomart herself, who is not a historical personage
but rather an intertextual composite of numerous literary heroines.

   Glauce feeds Britomart's fancy with positive images, offsetting
the negative images of Ovidian unnatural passion she referred to
earlier, and to good effect:

> Her harty words so deepe into the mynd
> Of the young Damzell sunke, that great desire
> Of warlike armes in her forthwith they tynd,
> And generous stout courage did inspire,
> That she resolu'd, *vnweeting to her Sire*,
> Aduent'rous knighthood on her selfe to don,
> And counseld with her Nourse, her Maides attire
> To turne into a massy habergeon.
>
> (3.3.57; my emphasis)

The phrase "Her harty words" (which punningly inspire "courage") emphasizes that Glauce is appropriating the words of male
authors for her own rhetorical purposes. Omitting the negative
details included in *Briton moniments*, Glauce heightens the
strength of these women in her narrative, with the result that
Britomart is inspired to emulate them and their defiance of male
authority.[57] Britomart's decision to become a knight implies a
measure of female autonomy, a rejection, however temporary, of
the role of dutiful daughter as she moves from the restricted domestic world of the castle to the freer landscape of the romance
world. King Ryence has had Angela's armor hung in the chapel
as a sign of his victory over the warrior maiden, but ironically
this act brings about his loss of control over another female war-

rior, his own daughter, as Britomart moves into the liminal space between submission to the desires of her father and those of her husband, an independent space that she occupies throughout most of the narrative. (Recall that Claridiana's, Bradamante's, and Marfisa's parents have no qualms about their daughters becoming lady knights; these heroines have no need to go undercover, as it were.) Glauce, reinforcing her "leading" narrative, physically leads Britomart to the church where Angela's armor has been hung and dresses her in it (3.3.59). Britomart literally puts on the image of the warrior woman as women readers imaginatively try on and thereby reanimate various literary roles in the reading process. She enacts the dire effects of women's reading romances predicted by Du Bosc: "what liklyhood is there for them, to *read* many passages of these sorts of bookes, and not put innocencie it self in danger? where they see often how this leaves her Country and her parents to run after a stranger, she is in love within a moment" (*CW*, sig. H4v). Britomart's choice of the martial role is also highly ironic in light of Vives's concern about women's reading chivalric literature: "What shoulde a maide do with armoure? Whiche ones to name were a shame for hir." Recalling that women have been known to behold "merveilous busily" the jousts of men and to judge them, he complains, "It can not lyghtly bee a chaste maide, that is occupied with thinkyng on armoure, and turney, and mans valiaunce, What places amonge these before chastite unarmed and weake?" (*ICW*, sig. D1v–D2r). Britomart reverses these terms, arming herself to exemplify chastity in her imitation of the chaste warrior Angela.

We should remember that the lady knight is not Britomart's first or only disguise and that her choice of role results from the "secret counsell close conspird" between the older and the younger woman. Before assuming this warrior role, borrowed from classical epic, Renaissance epic romance, and English chronicle history, Britomart tries out the romance convention of a princess disguising herself in "straunge / And base attyre" to visit Merlin (perhaps along the lines of Sidney's heroines in *The Countess of Pembroke's Arcadia*), a disguise that is singularly unsuccessful. Although Merlin prophesies Britomart's eventual participation in feats of arms alongside Artegall, he does not prescribe her immediate course of action, demanding that she rely primarily on her own ingenuity and courage.[58] In an odd textual disjunction, Britomart does not immediately assume the woman warrior role. Glauce and Britomart first collaborate in devising

an appropriate script ("Now this, now that twixt them they did
deuise, / And diuerse plots did frame, to maske in strange disguise"), their literary indebtedness underscored by Spenser's
pun on "diuerse plots." Demonstrating the dismissive derisive-
ness often used to describe female romance-readers, the narrator expresses little approbation for Glauce's final proposal: "At
last the Nourse in her foolhardy wit / Conceiu'd a bold deuise"
(3.3.52). Glauce promotes the knightly role for pragmatic reasons
as well as heroic ones; it will provide them protection and is ad-
mirably suited to Britomart's physique,[59] but it is also the one
Britomart becomes most eager to take on, having been inspired
with Glauce's storytelling:

> Let vs in *feigned* armes our selues disguize,
> And our *weake* hands (whom need *new* strength shall *teach*)
> The dreadfull speare and shield to exercize:
> Ne certes daughter that same warlike wize
> I weene, would you misseeme; for ye bene tall,
> And large of limbe, t'atchieue an hard emprize,
> Ne ought ye want, but skill, which *practize* small
> Will bring, and *shortly make* you a mayd Martiall.
>
> (3.3.53; my emphasis)

The text clearly insists that Britomart's role as a martial maid is
new and consciously chosen.

However, Britomart's later fiction of being trained from childhood as a warrior (derived from Virgil's, Ariosto's, and Tasso's
accounts of Camilla, Marfisa, and Clorinda; see 3.2.6–7) con-
vinces not only Redcrosse of her martial upbringing but also
some critics, who have taken her at her word. Marie Buncombe,
for example, assumes that the desire to be "a knight in arms"
has been Britomart's "ambition ever since she left the nursery,"
and Cavanagh asserts that "even though Britomart stays at
home until puberty, she was raised 'to tossen speare and
shield.' "[60] The language of 3.2.27 may contribute to the confusion: after Britomart has viewed Artegall in the mirror, "the
feather in her loftie crest, / Ruffed of loue, gan lowly to auaile, /
And her proud portance, and her princely gest, / With which she
earst tryumphed, now did quaile." "Crest" need not be limited
to the meaning of "helmet" but rather could signify any kind of
headdress, and the feather could have served to decorate a
lady's hunting ensemble.[61] Britomart is here described in regal
but not necessarily martial terms. Similarly, when first seen,

Claridiana, who was "brought up in hunting" but is not yet a knight, carries "a Boare Speare in hir right hande, hir hunters weede was all of greene velvet, hir tresses hanging downe in colour lyke the golde of *Araby*, in hir left hand a wande of golde and two rich Pearles hanging at hyr eares" (1578, Bk. 1, pt. 1, ch. 45, 150r). Britomart's fictional account of her childhood is plausible precisely because the warrior maid motif is so common in literature; life imitates art as art does life.

Glauce's fiery reminder of bold Britonesses may have affected Britomart to such an extent that her boast to Redcrosse, "All my delight on deedes of armes is set, / To hunt out perils and aduentures hard, / . . . Onely for honour and for high regard," may be taken at face value. Conversely, Britomart may be mocking even as she performs aggressive masculine virility. *Hic Mulier* denounces masculine women, who are "man-like . . . in every condition: man in body by attyre, man in behaviour by rude complement, man in nature by aptnesse to anger, man in action by pursuing revenge, man in wearing weapons, man in using weapons: And in briefe, so much man in all things, that they are neither men, nor women, but just good for nothing."[62] Yet when she hears Redcrosse's description of Artegall's honorable reputation, she seems to delight more in his fame than to thirst for her own personal glory. Her martial stance is also qualified by the maternal analogy comparing her delight to that of a woman after delivery:

> The louing mother, that nine monethes did beare,
> In the deare closet of her painefull side,
> Her tender babe, it seeing safe appeare,
> Doth not so much reioyce, as she reioyced theare.
>
> (3.2.11)

Silberman's observation that "Britomart appropriates the childhoods of the epic characters Camilla and Clorinda, just as Spenser adapts his literary predecessors Virgil and Tasso"[63] points to yet another level of adaptation or appropriation, that open to Spenser's female readers, who can imitate author and fictional character in laying claim to whatever aspect of the lady knight tradition they choose—perhaps, in Britomart's case, her "puissaunce" and "glory of great valiaunce" or, alternatively, depending on the proclivities of the reader, her "pure chastitie and vertue rare" (3.4.3).

Britomart's disdainful repudiation of ladies' skill in fingering "the fine needle and nyce thread" in favor of handling a lance can plausibly be interpreted either as part of her self-consciously assumed martial stance or as genuine disgust, which might constitute a critique of the limited ways women can manifest their virtue. Mary Ellen Lamb notes the "long tradition according to which working with cloth signified women's chastity," Penelope and Lucrece being the primary exemplars; and Rozsika Parker draws similar connections between embroidery (which is done within the home, usually for domestic purposes) and the ideal purity of the chaste, non-erring wife.[64] Britomart proposes a more militant option for women to assert their chastity, one which some early modern women may have found more appealing than that represented by Penelope. However, unlike Bradamante and Marfisa, who enact a type of feminine justice in establishing an amazonian regime in the *Orlando* (37.97) to punish Marganor, Britomart restores the amazonian inhabitants of Radegone to male subjection in 5.7.42, indicating the limits the Spenserian text imposes on "misreadings" of the woman warrior role. If Britomart's originary moment as a lady knight occurs within the context of radically open-ended literary appropriation, her final action as a lady knight is that of iconoclastically dismantling the potential misreading that could ensue—she destroys Radigund. Britomart appears no more in Spenser's text, situated in a liminal space between martial activity and the fulfillment of her destined roles of wife and mother. She is defined, ultimately, by her openness to the projections of the reader.

What, then, can be said about the *Hic Mulier* author's omission of Britomart from his diatribe against literal readings of lady knights? The narrator's assertion that Britomart will surpass the Camillas and Penthesileas of the epic tradition in "puissaunce" and "glory of great valiaunce" as well as in "pure chastitie and vertue rare" (3.4.3) exacerbates the interpretive dilemma, especially for female readers inclined to seek textual exemplars. Were they to admire Britomart's chastity but dismiss her subversive disguise as a knight as an unrealistic romance topos? Was her armor to be read as a mere symbol of chastity and thus an armor all women should possess, or as literal armor, which some Renaissance women (Caterina Sforza, for example) had been known to don? Britomart is both less and more radical than her fellow woman warriors—less because the catalyst for her transformation is civic duty couched as love, more because she reveals that one's chance of becoming a lady knight is not dependent upon having had the good fortune to be suckled by a lioness in the wilderness but more upon having read a sufficient range of books. Britomart's decision to become a martial maid could be viewed as obedience to the state and submission to Merlin's prophecy or, conversely, as a desire to emulate her powerful female forebears. Similarly, her desire for Artegall could be viewed as compliance with the patriarchal order that calls for the husband's priority over the wife or, in light of the fact that she makes her own match without her father's direct intervention, as a subversion of sociosexual conventions. Her overdetermined pairing with Artegall illustrates the Spenserian mystification of "one true love" (which is thrown into relief by the multiple marriages often made by Spenser's early readers—three for Alice Spencer, three for Anne Clifford, etc.), but it also gives her the power to rule without an attendant husband. Such openness is inevitable, given the tension in the text between competing, generically coded paradigms of courtesy literature and romance.

In acknowledging that Don Quixote might have had sisters whose femininity could affect their interpretive choices, the author of *Hic Mulier* voices concerns that had engaged Spenser thirty years earlier in *The Faerie Queene*. Indeed, the *Hic Mulier* author had good reason to be concerned about female readers' emulation of women warriors. Such female self-fashioning was not unheard of in early modern England, as Elizabeth I's donning armor to inspire her troops at Tilbury indicates. James's daughter, the Princess Elizabeth, and Arabella Stuart both adapted romance paradigms to their own political and erotic ends, as Barbara Lewalski has argued. Elizabeth seems consciously to have styled herself as a romance heroine, while Stuart, like Britomart, disguised herself as a man in a clandestine attempt to join her bridegroom.[65] In "Elegie III," French poet Louise Labé signals her own combativeness by linking herself to the warriors Bradamante and Marfisa, although acknowledging that love ultimately proves the victor.[66] *The Faerie Queene* suggests that women could exercise a remarkable degree of interpretive agency in reading the texts that sought to read them by affirming, adapting, or challenging literary roles at will. Female literacy was indeed a double-edged sword, one that could in effect arm women and transform them into literary, if not literal, woman warriors. Just as Britomart draws on a vast literary and historical tradition for suitable female models in fashioning and altering her own persona, so her readers may—indeed, must—impose their own values and desires on Spenser's text as they construct their own image of Britomart. Britomart's transformation of history into romance also opens the possibility of turning romance into history, of staging the insertion of the lady knight into the public order.

Appropriating male and female roles to suit herself, the knight of chastity provides Spenser's female readers with a potentially subversive role model, one who moves easily between epic and romance genres, between masculine and feminine modes. Not all of Spenser's ladies have the protection of Britomart's armor, however, and can pursue their love with the impunity and bravado of the lady knight. What is the fate of more conventional women who also love constantly and choose to wander in pursuit of that love? How does their negotiation of Spenser's multiple genres differ from the solution worked out by Britomart? How might their experience, even more than Britomart's, exemplify the tensions inherent in using texts to fashion the female self? In the next three chapters, I will address these concerns in light of contemporary assumptions about modesty, chastity, and piety, focusing on the extreme instability of Spenser's poem as a work of courtesy literature for women.

4

"Put on your vailes": Reading Modesty

> ... doe you discover unto men all things that are fit for them to understand from you: as bashfulnesse in your cheekes, chastitie in your eyes, wisedome in your words, sweetnesse in your conversation, pitie in your hearts, and a generall and severe modestie in the whole structure or frame of your universall composition.
>
> —*Hic Mulier* (1620)

Sir Thomas Hoby's popular 1561 translation of Baldassare Castiglione's *The Courtyer* was, according to the title page of the 1577 edition, "very necessarie and profitable for yong Gentlemen & Gentlewomen abyding in Court, Palace or Place," and the title page of the third book reads "Englisshed at the request of the Lady Marquesse of Northampton." (Helena Von Snakenborg, the third wife of William Parr, the first Marquis of Northampton, had served as one of Elizabeth's maids of honor; she was the chief mourner at the queen's funeral.) Juan Luis Vives's *The Instruction of a christen woman* was dedicated to Katherine of Aragon and written in large part as an educational program for her daughter, the Princess Mary. George Pettie's 1581 translation of a 1574 Italian courtesy book, *The civile Conversation of M. Stephen Guazzo*, was dedicated to Marjorie, Lady Norris, who served for several years as one of Queen Elizabeth's favorite ladies of the bedchamber. The dedications of all three of these texts bespeak the female courtier's desire or need for social instruction (probably projected onto her by male authors), a desire embedded in Castiglione's text in the form of Elisabetta Gonzaga's fictionalized command: "fashion us suche a Gentlewoman, that these our adversaries may be ashamed to say, that she is not equal wyth the Courtier in vertue" (*C*, sig. N4r). This request leads to Book 3's lively discussion of the attributes of the ideal courtly lady.

Spenser's poem serves a similar purpose. Without denying the allegorical import of *The Faerie Queene*'s female figures, we can also read them as exemplars in the courtesy literature tradition Spenser refers to in his letter to Raleigh ("The generall end therefore of all the booke is to fashion a gentleman or noble person in vertuous and gentle discipline"). Although Frank Whigham, in *Ambition and Privilege: The Social Tropes of Elizabethan Courtesy Theory*, links Spenser's text to the "heroically self-fashioning" Renaissance man producing himself as a commodity for courtly consumption, Whigham limits his consideration to the male sex: "my concern in this book is with courtesy for *men* at court. I have chosen to bracket for the moment issues regarding courtesy and women, whose situations were distinctly different, both in life and in the literature, owing to complex interactions of social and gender codes."[1] Therefore, in an attempt to elucidate issues Whigham acknowledges but does not discuss, in this and the following chapter I would like to read Spenser's poem in light of early modern conduct literature's pronouncements on the modesty and chastity courtly women were expected to display and the problematic nature of that display.

Significantly, most of the female characters in the poem are married or destined for marriage. Elizabeth could, of course, identify with them metaphorically, given her self-proclaimed role as England's spouse, but on a more literal level Spenser seems to have been appealing to women other than the queen, women whose vocation was clearly marriage. As Maureen Quilligan points out, "Spenser may counsel his female readers to follow Belphoebe's example of virginity, but the chastity he truly extols is Amoret's; it is the chastity not of a virgin queen, but of a wedded wife."[2] Yet the transition from the state of virginity to that of wife proved highly problematic for the Elizabethan ladies who had to negotiate the demanding civil conversation of the mixed-sex court. Spenser's poetic depiction of this dynamic is no less problematic. What seems to be *The Faerie Queene*'s most obvious textual strategy for inculcating such admirable traits as modesty and chastity in female readers (contrasting idealized characters such as Medina and Alma with disreputable ones such as Phaedria and the bathing nymphs in the Bower of Bliss) is ultimately an extremely unstable technique. Reading the female modesty advocated by Spenser's poem, and by treatises such as Castiglione's and Guazzo's, becomes much more challenging than it might initially seem, given that the virtue is notoriously contextual and demands an audience if it is to be recognized as a virtue. On the other hand, modesty must seem to be oblivious to such an audience if it is to be recognized as genuine. My discussion of the poem's dialogue with early modern courtesy literature and representation of the courtly virgin will focus primarily on Books 2 and 4, dedicated respectively to the virtues of temperance and friendship. If, as Quilligan has suggested, Spenser's text produces the reader "as social hero—someone who acts within society,"[3] how might Spenser's nonroyal female readers have been expected to interpret and emulate the poem's exemplary female figures, particularly in their attempt to temper with modesty the friendships demanded of them by virtue of their participation in courtly society?

Spenser's conflation of chivalric romance with courtesy literature would not have struck his female readers as unusual. Sidney's *Arcadia* was mined as a social handbook addressing a variety of subjects, among them political theory, conduct in love, and the use of rhetoric, and most examples of Elizabethan popular fiction, especially the works of John Lyly and George Pettie, attempt to inscribe desirable behavior patterns, usually in a much more openly didactic fashion than that practiced by Spenser. In the preface addressed to readers of *The civile Conversation*, Pettie asserts that its seriousness will compensate for his earlier *A Petite Pallace of Pettie his pleasure*, that "trifling worke of mine" (sig. A5r), yet the guidelines for female behavior in both the fictional work and the conduct manual are remarkably similar, as is his assumption of a female readership for both works.

Defining early modern woman's nature was a highly popular activity, especially during the period from 1580 to 1630, and Spenser's readers may have been conditioned to interpret the poem as a contribution to this subgenre. The common practice of extracting quotations along thematic lines from favorite poems for spiritual or rhetorical commonplace books or literary anthologies implies that Spenser's contemporaries did indeed adapt his allegory to respond to relevant social concerns and practices, including the ongoing controversy about women's nature, nurture, and social function. For example, *Hic Mulier* alludes to 5.5.25 (in which the narrator excoriates Radigund's abandonment of her lawful yoke of submissiveness) as an example of notorious and unfeminine behavior. Therefore, Venus's commissioning Psyche to be the preceptress for Amoret, in order to teach her "true feminitee" in the Garden of Adonis, may be informed not only by Neoplatonic allegories of love and generation but also by the common practice of an aristocratic young woman being sent away from the parental home to be groomed for her social role.[4]

Despite the oppressive nature of the courtesy literature discourse and the culture that shaped it, I wish to consider not only what authors prescribed but also what female readers might have preferred to extract from such texts and to what ends women may have practiced socially endorsed virtues. Some women may have looked to courtly fiction and courtesy literature for exemplars as they attempted to embody contemporary constructions of femininity and thereby achieve sociopolitical advancement through advantageous marital alliances. In other words, some women must have manipulated these prescriptions for their own ends.[5] As Ann Rosalind Jones reminds us, "The uproar over upstart women had some basis in an actual increase in women's opportunities. Like men, a few women were encountering new milieux outside the private domestic sphere—local and national courts, humanist coteries—where 'merit,' in the form of beauty, polished manners, and verbal skill, could improve the principal employment available to them: marriage into a higher rank."[6]

This is not to say that courtesy literature did not inscribe within its own genre numerous contradictions about the behavior of women, the most obvious of which Jones points out:

> These discourses [medicine, philosophy, religion, law, etc.] represented female character and status as fixed—eternal givens founded on nature, Scripture, and precedent. Conduct books appear to be based on a different assumption: men and women can be *produced*. They are malleable, capable of being trained for changing roles; proper instruction can fashion them into successful participants in new social settings and the etiquettes belonging to them. . . .
> . . . once a conduct-book writer like Castiglione or Guazzo admitted the presence of women at court and in other masculine gathering places, he faced the contradiction between longstanding discourses that condemned the public woman as a whore and the courtly code, which constructed women as decorative and inspiring adjuncts to men, necessary partners in the outward show of country house, palazzo, and literary salon.[7]

Lucy Murray, in *The Ideal of the Court Lady, 1561–1625*, identifies two distinct ideals for Renaissance women inherited from the medieval tradition, that of the good wife, deriving from the Church Fathers, and that of the court lady who served a distinct function in the chivalric system: "Good manners, correct deportment, skill in all the courtly accomplishments, as well as ease and grace of manner, were necessary for her. The pleasant conversation, the poise and charm of this lady contrasted vividly with the silence, the unassuming manner, and the sober gravity of the good wife." Murray contends that during Elizabeth's reign "the ideal of the court lady had included the ideal of the good wife, so that writers such as Sidney, Lyly, and Greene could write in praise of both ideals," but she fails to consider the resulting ambiguities this conflation of dichotomous ideals could produce in day-to-day behavioral choices or in the reading process, as women attempted to model their behavior on that of literary exemplars.[8]

Spenser's poem explores in surprising detail the range of behaviors available to courtly women and the challenge of maintaining their ever-tenuous honor within such a system. Court ladies were expected to be chaste (or else the queen's reputation would be tainted), but they were also to participate in courtly games and witty conversations with male courtiers, a practice that demanded a degree of sexual sophistication. Jones concludes that the courtly lady's task in light of such contradictions was to contrive a means of "feminine self-display" that would not violate the code of chaste conduct.[9] Spenser's text reinscribes this complex system of checks and balances, as his convoluted and constantly qualified description of Canacee demonstrates. After stressing her great learning (some, if not all, of which derives from her magic ring) in 4.2.35, Spenser hastens to emphasize her more traditionally feminine virtues—beauty and desirability, but also, in accordance with courtesy literature's relentless emphasis, her modesty and chastity: "And, that augmented all her other prayse, / She modest was in all her deedes and words, / And wondrous chast of life, yet lou'd of Knights and Lords." (Spenser deliberately adds modesty and chastity to the initial description of Canacee; Chaucer mentions only her beauty.) Stanza 36 elaborates on her sexual temperance and, more importantly, on her self-consciousness about the need to maintain her reputation for chastity:

> Full many Lords, and many Knights her loued,
> Yet she to none of them her liking lent,
> Ne euer was with fond affection moued,
> But rul'd her thoughts with goodly gouernement,
> For dread of blame and honours blemishment;
> And eke vnto her lookes a law she made,

> That none of them once out of order went,
> But like to warie Centonels well stayd,
> Still watcht on euery side, of secret foes affrayd.

(4.2.36)

Knowledgeable yet modest, attractive yet chaste, Canacee is so careful that her behavior not be misconstrued as sexually inviting that she achieves, paradoxically, precisely that effect: "So much the more as she refusd to loue, / So much the more she loued was and sought" (4.2.37).

Spenser explores this and other paradoxical dynamics of feminine behavior throughout the poem, yet critics have, for the most part, overlooked his commentary, probably because they have unwittingly accepted the male reading subject as the norm. For example, A. Bartlett Giamatti proposes a teleological progression in the poem's structure, from youth to adolescence to maturity, although he does not distinguish how one's sex would have influenced the differently gendered virtues requisite at each step in the process.[10] Benjamin Lockerd's Jungian schema comes closer to doing so by tracing "the normal maturation of the relation between the sexes" and thus associating Book 2 with an early adolescence not yet touched by love, 3 with adolescence eroticized, 4 with the maturation of love, and 5 with the celebration of marriage. The power of eros, which threatens to weaken society in Books 2 and 3, becomes in 4 and 5 "the preserver of society" through "the discipline of friendship and with the social sanction and religious sanctification of matrimony."[11] Although Spenser's poem is, I believe, too complex a structure to be reduced to a neat progression from maid to wife to widow in the typical manner of Renaissance courtesy literature, it does nevertheless provide extensive commentary on the range of social and sexual behaviors expected of women who could not be so neatly pigeonholed and who often occupied the interstices of prescribed sexual categories, especially the liminal space between complete naïveté and utter depravity.

*   *   *

Castiglione, like Spenser, addresses a dual-gendered audience, referring in his third book to "al the readers of this our travayle (if at the least wise it shal deserve so muche favour, that it may come to the sight of noble men & vertuous Ladies)" (sig. N5r). Both men and women, we assume, would have profited from descriptions of courtly behavior, gendered or not, just as all

of Spenser's readers could benefit from allegorical presentations
of virtues pertinent to the Christian soul. In fact, Dain Trafton
reads Magnifico's discussion of the attributes of the courtly lady
as "a vehicle for political ideas intended to have a general applicability to both sexes" on the grounds that the subtle manipulation
practiced by women as an oppressed (or at least subdominant)
social group resembles the indirect techniques subservient
courtiers were forced to employ in advising headstrong and
touchy rulers.[12] Yet the danger of such an interpretation is that it
diverts critical focus once again to a predominantly male readership and the public political arena. Castiglione's women seem
particularly eager to extend the evening's discussion of role
models that pertain specifically to themselves, suggesting that
the obverse of Trafton's hypothesis is not true (i.e., that standards of masculinity are not as readily applicable to dominant
constructions of femininity). For example, the indomitable Emilia Pia demands the full story of the wise Jewish queen Alexan-
dra, refusing to be satisfied by a mere allusion (sig. O6v). Later,
after Lord Julian has related a few more anecdotes, Lady Margaret Gonzaga questions the strength of his devotion as a champion
of women's cause: "Me seemeth that yee make too brief rehersall
of these vertuous actes done by women," noting that revilers of
women are reluctant to acknowledge noble women's contribu-
tions to history (sig. O7r). When Julian ceases several pages
later, with the excuse that he fears he might be boring his audience with stories of virtuous women, Emilia Pia again reminds
him that women are a significant part of his audience: "Do you
not deprive . . . women of the true praises due unto them. And
remember thoughe the L. *Gaspar* and perchaunce the L. *Octav-
ian* to, heare you wyth noysomnesse, yet doe wee, and these
other Lordes harken to you wyth pleasure. Notwythstandyng the
L. *Julian* wold there have ended, but all the Ladies began to en-
treat him to speake" (sig. Bb1r, 1588 ed.; this is an interesting
alteration of the 1561 and 1577 editions, which use "Lordes" in
the final clause).

The reaction of the female members of the court of Urbino suggests that despite any superficial inclusiveness, Castiglione does
in fact reinscribe substantial gender differences in his virtuous
models. Wayne Rebhorn suggests that Castiglione may have
worried that the courtly ideal could be attacked as too effeminate, hence his frequent emphasis on the virility of the courtier
as opposed to the emphatically chaste, traditionally feminine
lady who is strongly discouraged from impinging on masculine

territory.[13] For example, Lord Julian disagrees with Lord Gaspar's assertion that the discussion of the female courtier could be curtailed in order to spend more time fashioning the male courtier, given that "the very same rules that are given for the Courtier serve also for the woman" (Julian here paraphrases Gaspar's position, sig. N6v) and instead carefully distinguishes between qualities appropriate to the construction of masculine and feminine social identities. He admits that they will share some qualities, such as the "vertues of the minde," and certain social obligations, such as demonstrating wit, refraining from contentiousness, being able to please superiors, and so on, but he contends that beauty "is more necessarye in hyr than in the Courtier" (sig. N6v), and delimits most behaviors as unmistakably gendered:

> But principally in hir fashions, manners, wordes, gestures and conversation (me thinke) the woma[n] ought to be much unlike the man. For right as it is seemely for him to shew a certaine manlinesse ful & steady, so doth it wel in a woma[n] to have a te[n]dernes, soft and milde, with a kind of womanlye sweetnesse in everye gesture of hirs, that in going, standing, and speaking what ever she lusteth, may alwayes make hir appeare a woman w[ith]out any likenes of man. (sig. N6v)

This emphasis on maintaining distinct gender differences is common to the courtesy literature popular in sixteenth-century England. Sir Thomas Elyot's *The Boke Named the Governour* inscribes gender difference similarly: "A man in his natural perfection is fierce, hardie, strong in opinion, covetous of glory, desirous of knowledge, appetiting by generation to bring foorth his semblable. The good nature of a woman, is to bee milde, timorous, tractable, benigne, of sure remembrance, & shamefast."[14] Stefano Guazzo concurs, although his emphasis on *learning* to act modestly demystifies what Elyot terms the "good nature" of a woman:

> a Mayde ought to frame her behaviour in such sort, that above all things shee shew both inwardlie and outwardlie, that maidenlie modestie which is proper to Maydes: for it is a monstrous and naughtie thing, to see a young Gyrle use such libertie and boldnesse in her gesture, lookes, and talke, as is proper to men: and therefore let maydes learne in all their behaviour to expresse the modestie, which is so seemelie for their estate, assuring themselves, that though they be furnished with all other beauties, graces, & vertues of the world,

yet if that bright Sunne shine not in them, all the other as starres borrowing light of that, wil make no shew at all. (*CC*, 159r)

Despite the suspiciously arbitrary nature of the assignment of skills and activities to the two genders (Castiglione's Lord Cesar Gonzaga interjects that he has seen women "play at tenise, practise feates of armes, ride, hunt, and do (in a manner) all the exercises beside, that a gentleman can doe," sig. N8v), the lady is to eschew participation in such "manly" exercises. Even in her dancing and musical performance she is to demonstrate a feminine "sweet mildenesse" and should reveal reluctance when requested to perform, evincing "a certain bashfulnes, that may declare the noble shamefastnesse that is contrary to headinesse" (sig. N8v). That she will have "al those parts that belong to a good huswife" is taken for granted (sig. N7r).

In many ways, Castiglione's ideal lady of the court is the prototype for Spenser's Amoret, whose unquestionably feminine character and social training is reconstructed by Scudamour in a setting similar to that of *The Courtyer*'s Urbino, a company of male and female courtiers engaged in conversation.[15] Even Castiglione's emphasis on the women's particular investment in the story is replicated, in that Britomart has urged more strongly than the others that the love story be recounted. Hamilton notes that when Scudamour addresses the "gentle knights and Ladies free" in his audience (4.10.3), "Ladies free" indicates those of gentle birth and also those who have not been taken captive as Amoret has, i.e., those who have not yet begun to love, and who therefore have much to learn about the behavior appropriate to the negotiations of courtship (in both senses of the word).

Representing respectively Spenser's royal and nonroyal female readers, Belphoebe has been taught "perfect Maydenhed" whereas her slightly younger twin sister Amoret has been "lessoned / In all the lore of loue, and goodly womanhead." Spenser explicitly designates Amoret as an exemplar when, following the pattern of many noblewomen of the period, she is deemed ready to demonstrate her virtues at court and hopefully contract an advantageous marriage:

> In which when she to perfect ripenesse grew,
> Of grace and beautie noble Paragone,
> She brought her forth into the worldes vew,
> To be th'ensample of true loue alone,
> And Lodestarre of all chaste affectione,

To all faire Ladies, that doe liue on ground.
To Faery court she came, where many one
Admyrd her goodly haueour, and found
His feeble hart wide launched with loues cruell wound.

(3.6.52)

Despite her popularity, however, Amoret chastely loves only one knight, Scudamour, "To whom her louing hart she linked fast / In faithfull loue, t'abide for euermore." In the narrative sequence, then, her love for Scudamour is made known to readers prior to the description of his conquest of her in the Temple of Venus, which suggests that her reluctance when he attempts to claim her as his prize constitutes a conscious and socially requisite display of maidenly modesty, rather than a lack of love or sexual desire.

Amoret enters the Garden as a baby and resides in the Temple as an adult, suggesting two separate phases in a woman's education, although C. S. Lewis argues that Amoret's sojourns in the Garden and the Temple are co-temporal rather than "successive stages in a biography."[16] Inherent in both the developmental and the allegorical readings, however, is a disturbing potential contradiction for Amoret and female readers alike as they attempt to fulfill the social mandate of living modestly and loving chastely. Amoret's upbringing in the Garden of Adonis, where she is reared as Pleasure's half sister and is presumably made aware of the physical cycle of sex, reproduction, and death, seems somehow incongruous in light of her education in the Temple, where she is surrounded, even constrained, by a very different vision of female sexuality, one that is almost at odds with her service to the fertile *Venus genetrix*.

In both locales female sexuality is figured by the landscape, yet the fertile, inviting Mount of Venus at the center of the Garden contrasts sharply with the image of the island, heavily guarded against any who would invade the innermost sanctum of the Temple. Here Womanhood resists Scudamour's determination to undo the tight knot formed by Amoret and her companions. In the Garden, Venus "enjoys," "possesses," and "reaps" pleasure of Adonis, whereas in the Temple, the social code demands that Scudamour aggressively claim a much more passive Amoret. Love in the mythological Garden of Adonis is explicitly sexual yet resists any moral judgment based on the complexities and interpretive pitfalls of social intercourse:

For here all plentie, and all pleasure flowes,
And sweet loue gentle fits emongst them throwes,

Without fell rancor, or fond gealosie;
Franckly each paramour his leman knowes,
Each bird his mate, ne any does enuie
Their goodly meriment, and gay felicitie.

(3.6.41)

In contrast to the frankness of the lovers in the Garden as they engage in "goodly meriment," those in the Temple gardens act out "spotlesse" pleasures, indicating an awareness of a prevailing sexual code that distinguishes between pure and impure love and defines goodness in negative terms. Whereas the Garden is characterized by sexual fulfillment and an absence of jealousy, some lovers visit the Temple to complain of their torment and unfulfilled desires, a context more reminiscent of the courtly realm.

Notwithstanding the powerful celebration of female fertility that *Venus genetrix* represents, her image in the Temple is explicitly "manmade," produced of a substance like glass, "faire and brickle." This serves as a dramatic contrast to the living vegetation of the earlier image of Venus (the "fruitfull sides" of the "mirtle trees" drop "sweet gum"; ivy, eglantine, and caprifole entwine the trees, which embrace one another of their "owne inclination," 3.6.43–4). Her genitalia are less explicitly female than they are in the Garden, her mysterious androgyny being hidden by a veil: "But sooth it was not sure for womanish shame, / Nor any blemish, which the worke mote blame" (4.10.41). The disclaimer undercuts itself, however, by introducing the concept of shame, which is then projected onto the other figures present, Womanhood and her companions. Even farther removed from the free female sexuality of the Garden, the "beuie of fayre damzels" in the Temple seem particularly concerned with "womanish shame" and the need to prevent flaws in the workmanship of the lady's social image. Although Venus, a goddess and an image of the androgynous Queen Elizabeth, may freely exhibit desire and provoke it in others quite openly, her female devotees must use much more discreet and indirect means to provoke desire, veiling their own desire for a hermaphroditic union with a lover-husband not with a literal veil but with the metaphorical veil of modesty referred to by Puritan divines:

To shew how a modest countenance and womanly shamefastnesse do commend a chaste wife, it is observed that the word Nuptiae, which signifieth the marriage of the woman, doth declare the manner

of her marriage; for it importeth a covering, because the virgins
which should be married, when they came to their husbands, for
modesty and shamefastnesse did cover their faces; as wee reade of
Rebeccah, which so soon as she saw Isaak and knew that hee should
bee her husband, she cast a vaile before her face, shewing that modesty should be learned before marriage, which is the dowry that God
addeth to her portion.[17]

Amoret, a composite of all feminine virtues, including shamefastness, cheerfulness, modesty, and courtesy, must somehow
enact them as well as the more overt sexual drive of both Ven-
uses; she must employ seemingly contradictory behaviors that
will lure and rebuff Scudamour simultaneously. Her response to
Scudamour seems confused or ambiguous precisely because her
lessons conflict—taught to assent unequivocally to sexuality in
the Garden of Adonis, instructed in the Temple to at first demur,
lest she be thought too light, Amoret's ability to love as a woman
is conditioned by conflicting discourses. Somewhat distanced
from the statue of Venus, Amoret is significantly much closer to
Womanhood, in whose lap she sits, encircled by the allegorical
virtues she is to subsume into an all-encompassing representation of feminine love:

> The first of them did seeme of ryper yeares,
> And grauer countenance then all the rest;
> Yet all the rest were eke her equall peares,
> Yet vnto her obayed all the best.
> Her name was *Womanhood*, that she exprest
> By her sad semblant and demeanure wyse:
> For stedfast still her eyes did fixed rest,
> Ne rov'd at randon after gazers guyse,
> Whose luring baytes oftimes doe heedlesse harts entyse.
>
> And next to her sate goodly *Shamefastnesse*,
> Ne euer durst her eyes from ground vpreare,
> Ne euer once did looke vp from her desse,
> As if some blame of euill she did feare,
> That in her cheekes made roses oft appeare.
> And her against sweet *Cherefulnesse* was placed,
> Whose eyes like twinkling stars in euening cleare,
> Were deckt with smyles, that all sad humors chaced,
> And darted forth delights, the which her goodly graced.
>
> And next to her sate sober *Modestie*,
> Holding her hand vpon her gentle hart;

And her against sate comely *Curtesie,*
That vnto euery person knew her part;
And her before was seated ouerthwart
Soft *Silence,* and submisse *Obedience,*
Both linckt together neuer to dispart,
Both gifts of God not gotten but from thence,
Both girlonds of his Saints against their foes offence.

(4.10.49–51)

Scudamour is initially abashed by this imposing array of feminine virtue, which quells, as it is intended to do, his impetuous,
invasive masculinity. He is at first loath to commit the sacrilege
of robbing the Temple of its priestess Amoret, but then consciously reasserts his explicitly gendered masculine erotic role:

Tho shaking off all doubt and shamefast feare,
Which Ladies loue I heard had neuer wonne
Mongst men of worth, I to her stepped neare,
And by the lilly hand her labour'd vp to reare.

(4.10.53)

Amoret's gendered imperative is to retain shamefastness,
whereas Scudamour's, as a would-be "man of worth," is to shake
it off and to defy Womanhood's rebuke of his boldness. Scudamour describes himself as a victorious hunter and martial con-
queror, who "all that while / The pledge of faith, her hand
engaged held, / Like warie Hynd within the weedie soyle, / For
no intreatie would forgoe so glorious spoyle" (4.10.55).

When Amoret pleads to be released with both "tender teares"
and "witching smyles," she should not be censured for sending
double messages. She is, in fact, dutifully imitating the behavior
commended by Guazzo:

For first, to the gravenesse of her wordes, agreeth the sweetnesse of
her voice, & the honestie of her meaning: so that the mindes of the
hearers intangled in those three nets, feele themselves at one instant
to be both mooved with her amiablenesse, & brideled by her honestie. . . . Shee will also in talke cast oft times uppon a man such a
sweete smile, that it were inough to bring him into a fooles Paradise,
but that her verie countenaunce conteineth such continencie in it, as
is sufficient to cut off all fond hope. (*CC,* 115v–116r)

Amoret's education in the Garden and as a priestess of *Venus
genetrix* demands that she respond to love, yet she must exemplify modesty and shamefastness even as she does so. Amoret re-

sides in the liminal area David Miller alludes to in his discussion of *Amoretti* 67, which repeats the motif of the lover laying hold of the shy yet willing deer. The sonnet explores "crossing thresholds: the threshold between courtship and betrothal, between resistance and surrender, between surrender and conquest."[18] A loving but chaste woman, Amoret understands the tenets of courtesy literature only too well and enacts them perfectly.

*   *   *

The feminine qualities enumerated in Castiglione's *The Courtyer,* Guazzo's *The civile Conversation,* and Spenser's Temple of Venus episode demand that women practice an appropriate mean of courteous behavior between the extremes of aggressive forwardness and silent prudishness, as the carefully balanced seating arrangements of the feminine virtues in the Temple suggest (Shamefastnesse sits opposite Cherefulnesse, Modestie sits opposite Curtesie, and Amoret sits at the intersection of these virtues in the center).[19] Fittingly, in *The Faerie Queene*'s second book, which is devoted to temperance, we encounter, with Guyon, exemplars of temperate courtly female behavior in Medina and Alma and blatantly intemperate behavior in Phaedria and Acrasia.[20] These characters serve double duty, representing allegorically the virtues and vices between whom the titular male knight as an Everyman figure must choose and literally the social behaviors to be imitated or avoided by female readers of the text as courtesy literature. Both Alma and Medina are depicted within a courtly context of mixed company, and each is praised for her ability to entertain gentlemen both modestly and chastely. Yet the strategies used by chaste and unchaste women alike differ only in degree, not in kind.

The behavioral mean for courtly women, an unfixed, ideal place situated somewhere between wantonness and utter silence, is exemplified by Medina, a "sober sad, and comely curteous Dame" (2.2.14). The delicacy with which Medina balances these alliterative—and seemingly antithetical—requirements is evident in her hospitable entertainment of Guyon:

> She led him vp into a goodly bowre,
> And comely courted with meet modestie,
> Ne in her speach, ne in her hauiour,
> Was lightnesse seene, or looser vanitie,
> But gratious womanhood, and grauitie.

(2.2.15)

In fact, her behavior recalls Castiglione's exacting description of the courtly woman's conversational manner:

> I saye that for hir that liveth in Court, me thinke there belong[e]th unto hir above all other things, a certaine sweetenesse in language that maye delite, wherby she may gently entertaine all kinde of menne wyth talk worth the hearing and honest, & applyed to the time and place, and to the degree of the person she communeth withal. Accompanying with sober and quiet maners, and with the honesty that must alwayes be a stay to hir dedes, a ready livelinesse of wit, whereby shee may declare hir selfe far wide from all dulnesse: but wyth suche a kinde of goodnesse, that she may bee esteemed no lesse chaste, wyse and courteisc, than pleasaunt, feat conceited and sober: and therefore must shee keepe a certaine meane verye harde, and (in a maner) dirived of contrarie matters, and come just to certaine limits, but not passe them. (sig. N7r)

A "certaine sweetenesse," "a certaine meane," "certaine limits"—Castiglione's mystification of modesty here defies clear interpretation and inevitably sets up some women to fail, as do Medina's two sisters, who cannot tread the fine line between extremes. During the feast, Medina's elder sister Elissa "scould, and frownd with froward countenaunce, / Vnworthy of faire Ladies comely gouernaunce," whereas her younger sister Perissa resembles Phaedria in her excessive frivolity:

> Full of disport, still laughing, loosely light,
> And quite contrary to her sisters kind;
> No measure in her mood, no rule of right,
> But poured out in pleasure and delight.
>
> (2.2.36)

Perissa is also excessive in her consumption of meat and wine and is "of her loue too lauish," a connection frequently made by Vives, who warns women that such idle participation in public entertainments and feasting on rich foods render them vulnerable to attacks on their chastity (as in chapter 8, "Of the orderyng of the body in a virgyn" in *ICW*). That Medina and her sisters are born of different mothers suggests that the women's differing behavior is the "natural" inheritance from their respective mothers (and elides the sire's poor judgment in marrying his first and third wives, Elissa's and Perissa's mothers). Alternatively, the detail could indicate the crucial role of the mother in imbuing her children with dominant standards of conduct. Either way, the two

intemperate sisters are represented as being insufficient in the
art of courtesy; the two "fained cheare, as for the time behoues, /
But could not colour yet so well the troth, / But that their natures
bad appeard in both" (2.2.34). In other words, Medina's sisters
are insufficiently artful.

Guazzo's Anniball further expounds the contemporary feminine behaviors Medina and her sisters represent:

> Yea, shee must not onelie have regard to keepe her tongue, but be-
> sides to accompanie her words, her laughter, her lookes, and behav-
> iour, with such a grave and stately majestie, as beseemeth a
> matrone. . . . Moreover, there are some, who coveting to be counted
> unreasonable honest, frowne so ill favouredlie, and set suche a so-
> lemne and sowre countenaunce on the matter, that they make men
> thinke them rather proude than honest. . . . Yea, and by that coie
> cloude, the bright shining of their beutie and vertue is overcast. (*CC*,
> 115r)

William Guazzo concurs, as he objects to women demonstrating
"daintie coinesse" in attempts to be thought more chaste: "For
they consider not how bountie and curtesie are nothing repugnant to honestie, but rather alwaies accompanie it" (*CC*, 115v).
Left unspecified is how much "bountie" a woman could exhibit
without being judged as too free with her favors. Thomas Salter
also warns against extremes: "For truely, as too muche bold-
nesse (beeyng a thing more conveniente for those that, to reprove
vice, use the partes of divers personages in Comedies and Trage-
dies, then for a modeste or milde maiden) is to bee shonned and
eschewed as a fault infamous: so to the contrary, too muche fear-
fulnesse or shamefastnesse, where it is needelesse, is a pointe of
greate follie" (*MM*, sig. E4v). The trick, of course, is deciding
when a display of extreme shamefastness is "needelesse" and
when necessary, modesty being a highly contextualized virtue
and contingent on the impression made on the observer. Brathwait comments on the specularity and the "tempering" of the
feminine ideal:

> a modest and well *Behaved Woman* may by her frequent or resort
> to *publike* places, conferre no lesse benefit to such as observe her
> *behaviour*, than occasion of profit to her private family, where shee
> is *Overseer*. I have seene some in these places of *publike repaire*,
> expresse such a well-seeming State without Apish formality, as
> every action deserved imitation of such as were in their Company.
> Their Conceits were sweetly tempered without lightnesse; their jests

savory, yet without saltnesse; their discourse free without nicenesse; their answers milde without tartnesse; their smile pleasing, mixt with bashfulnesse; their pace gracefull without too much activeness; their whole posture delightfull with a seemely carelesnesse. These are such mirrors of modesty, patternes of piety, as they would not for a world transgresse the bounds of Civility. (*EG*, 52)

Unlike Guyon, whose denial (or repression) of his sexuality informs a quest that culminates in the orgiastic destruction of the Bower of Bliss,[21] Medina evinces a more truly tempered sexuality. Successfully operating within the demanding liminal space between the worlds of the completely unknowing virgin and the fully aware matron, Medina uses her sexual powers to civilize rather than seduce the knights with whom she comes in contact. This influence on the gentlemen in her castle is apparent when Huddibras and Sansloy erupt into rancorous combat and she intercedes with dishevelled hair and bare breast; while her sisters urge on their lovers, Medina uses "pitthy words and counsell sad" to dissuade them, and eventually they heed her "discrete behests" (2.2.28, 32). She evinces wisdom, a humanist distaste for needless violent confrontation, and rhetorical skill in responding to men as fellow courtiers rather than potential sexual conquests. In contrast, Phaedria reduces all male-female interactions to the merely sexual. When Guyon and Cymochles clash, Phaedria intervenes as Medina has done, baring her breast and cajoling the knights to cease, except that she does so by proposing a transformation of martial encounters into amorous ones.[22] Phaedria, and later the bathing nymphs, function as Acrasian apprentices in trying to short-circuit Guyon's mission by doing "all, that might his constant hart / Withdraw from thought of warlike enterprize" (2.6.25). Medina instead encourages Guyon in his quest by offering him necessary hospitality, inviting him to recount his virtuous adventures so that the entire company might "learne from pleasures poyson to abstaine: / Ill by ensample good doth often gayne" (2.2.45), and capably assuming responsibility for the socialization of the infant Ruddymane.

Alma succeeds Medina as a more fully developed version of the temperate courtly lady, and the sexuality in her house is limited to the conversations in mixed company idealized by Castiglione and Guazzo. Within the parlor of the heart, "A louely beuy of faire Ladies sate, / Courted of many a iolly Paramoure, / The which them did in modest wise amate" (2.9.34). Cupid here is unarmed, hence the modesty of both ladies and men as they "amate," and it is possible that Spenser also intends a pun on "sate" as not only a verb but also an adjective, indicating that the ladies are not lustful but content, or satisfied, with their innocent love games. As David Miller points out, just when we expect to encounter genitalia in the tour of the body, we move instead to "a sublimated image of human sexuality in the parlor of the heart."[23] Alma's liminal status as a maiden ripening into readiness for marriage is explicit in Spenser's description of her as

> a virgin bright;
> That had not yet felt *Cupides* wanton rage,
> Yet was she woo'd of many a gentle knight,
> And many a Lord of noble parentage,
> That sought with her to lincke in marriage:
> For she was faire, as faire mote euer bee,
> And in the flowre now of her freshest age;
> Yet full of grace and goodly modestee,
> That euen heauen reioyced her sweete face to see.
>
> (2.9.18)

The qualifying "yet" in the penultimate line suggests the difficulty of maintaining both beauty and modesty in courtly surroundings, but Alma gracefully meets the challenge, balancing cordiality with sexual restraint as she entertains Guyon and Arthur with "gentle court and gracious delight / . . . with mildnesse virginall, / Shewing her selfe both wise and liberall" (2.9.20). She, like Medina, is adept at modeling ideal femininity as she participates in courtly life. "Shewing her selfe" underscores how assertive such seemingly self-effacing behavior may be.

Phaedria, in contrast, willfully misconstrues the art of "civil conversation" between men and women in the same way that William Guazzo does; he initially understands Anniball's term to mean "amorous incounters" (*CC*, 112r).[24] Phaedria reduces her repertoire of social skills to the overtly sexual. Over and over, Spenser emphasizes her flirtatiousness, her frivolity, her "light behauiour, and loose dalliaunce," and especially her immodest mirth, all of which behaviors indicate wanton sexual standards; according to Vives, women are "more disposed to pleasure and daliaunce" than men (*ICW*, sig. B2r). Theresa Krier observes that Spenser gives "to female characters like Phaedria and the nymphs of the fountain in the Bower of Bliss senses of humor that range from giggling silliness to ironic mockery of Guyon's solemnity";[25] such characterization makes sense in the context of courtesy literature strictures against excessive merriment and indecent humor. Vives advises maidens to avoid laughing, "whiche is a sygne of a very light and dissolute mynde, let hir se that she laughe not unmesurably" (ICW, sig. L4v). Phaedria, however, laughs constantly: .

> Sometimes she sung, as loud as larke in aire,
> Sometimes she laught, that nigh her breth was gone,
> Yet was there not with her else any one,
> That might to her moue cause of meriment:
> Matter of merth enough, though there were none,
> She could deuise, and thousand waies inuent,
> To feede her foolish humour, and vaine iolliment.
>
> (2.6.3)

Even though Phaedria could presumably justify her playfulness as constituting a legitimate attempt to entertain a gentleman companion (an appropriate feminine endeavor, according to Castiglione), her courtesy is still judged to be excessive. The narrator focuses not on her matter (although given her penchant for the sexual double entendre, the numerous merry tales she recounts are probably indecent), but on her manner, her breach of social decorum:

> nothing well they her became;
> For all her words she drownd with laughter vaine,
> And wanted grace in vtt'ring of the same,
> That turned all her pleasance to a scoffing game.
>
> (2.6.6)

Guyon is equally disgusted. He initially tries to be courteous, "But when he saw her toy, and gibe, and geare, / And passe the bonds of modest merimake, / Her dalliance he despisd, and follies did forsake" (2.6.21). Guazzo recommends that instead of such "smiling countenaunces," "wanton glaunces," "yeelding gestures, and other lascivious intising trickes," women should cultivate "a grave looke, a demure countenance, modest gestures, and behaviour meete for an honest woman" (CC, 136r). Castiglione concurs, suggesting that the appropriate response of a courtly lady to wanton conversation, bawdy jokes, or sexual double entendres is neither to join in nor to leave, but to use the occasion as an opportunity to display a carefully constructed feminine modesty:

This woman ought not therefore . . . be so squeimish and make wise to abhorre both the company & the talke (though somewhat of the

wantonnest) if she be present, to get hir thence by & by, for a man
maye lightlye gesse that shee fayned to be so coye to hyde that in
hirselfe which she doubted others might come to the knowledge of:
and such nice fashions are always hateful. Nether ought she again
(to shewe herself free and pleasant) speake wordes of dishonesty,
nor use a certaine familiaritie without measure & bridle, and fashions to make men beleeve that of her, that perhappes is not: but
being present at such kinde of talke, she ought to give the hearing
with a little blushing & shamefastnes. (sig. N7r–v)

An excess of either gaiety or modesty tarnishes the lady's reputation, but to exhibit only "a little" blushing demands exceptional
skill, self-control, and keen awareness of audience. Castiglione's
court lady, according to Jones, "needs a triple consciousness:
she must know how to avoid appearing to be faking prudishness."[26] Phaedria, just as she fails to control her little gondelay
as she rows on the Idle Lake, blithely fails to acknowledge the
imperative of tempering her manners to a mean between excessive mirth and modesty and indirectly illustrates the high level of
performance skill demanded of the respectable female courtier.

*   *   *

Guyon finds a more congenial companion in Shamefastness,
who represents, in contrast to the immodesty of the glittering,
ebullient Phaedria, the potential for excessive feminine restraint
when participating in civil conversation. Although Shamefastness and Prays-desire are often interpreted simply as external-
izations of aspects of the male knights' characters,[27] they should
also be considered in their own right, given their relevance to female readers. Allegorically, a female reader might see herself
entertaining or pursuing glory (Arthur) and temperance
(Guyon); literally, a female reader might look to Shamefastness
and Alma as exemplars. Shamefastness's name, repeated almost
ad nauseam in courtesy literature for women, is reminiscent of
such pronouncements as Edmund Tilney's in his *A briefe and
pleasant discourse of duties in Mariage, called the Flower of
Friendshippe* (1568): "And if so be that there were but one onelye
vertue in a woman, it might well be shamefastnesse."[28] Hamilton
cites Elyot's paraphrase of Aristotle in *The Boke Named the Governour* 1.9 on shamefastness functioning as a bridle and desire
for praise as a spur for youthful gentlemen, yet Spenser's use of
female allegorical figures to represent these qualities reminds
readers that young ladies were also expected to use the bridle

and the spur, to blend the fear of sexual shame with the desire for active virtue.

Since a woman could prove her chastity only by abstaining from action, however, her virtue was more difficult to establish than that of a man who could perform more quantifiable feats in battle. "Well doing," for a woman, was not to do ill, to refrain from any actions that could be misconstrued as unchaste, hence Shamefastness's retiring quality and lack of ease in male company. She dreads sexual slander so much that she experiences obvious discomfort and is reluctant to give Guyon the slightest sign of encouragement, for fear that it might redound to her discredit. Spenser's visual details underscore this: her garment is "Close round about her tuckt with many a plight," as if she is hesitant to expose her body to the possibility of sexual misadventure, and her emblematic bird, which is "as yet ashamd, how rude *Pan* did her dight" (2.9.40), represents not merely reclusiveness but a well-warranted mistrust of male aggressors. Shamefastness clearly fears the sexual ramifications of social converse with men as much as Phaedria openly welcomes them.

Such modesty is laudable to an extent but is criticized when overdone; the narrator's admiration of Shamefastness, who is "modest of demaine" (2.9.40), is clearly qualified by an awareness of her lack of graceful ease in mixed company, marked by her blush ("But that too oft she chaung'd her natiue hew"). As Hamilton observes, "Blushing is a sign of innocence but also shows an awareness of guilt." His subsequent commentary may, however, obscure the gendered implications of the blush for women, which both Spenser and many modern critics seem to equate with sexual shame. The manifestation of Shamefastness in the Temple of Venus "Ne euer durst her eyes from ground vpreare, / Ne euer once did looke vp from her desse, / As if some blame of euill she did feare, / That in her cheekes made roses oft appeare," a shyness that must be tempered by her opposite Cheerfulness.[29] Women must attend both to the ways they look at others and the appearance they present when others look at them. Shamefastness's blush reveals simultaneously her innocence and her sexual awareness of the double entendres employed in her conversation with Guyon (she wishes to avoid converse with him in the sexual sense even as she attempts to converse with him in the civil sense). The erotic connotations of Spenser's description of this activity—"the strong passion mard her modest grace"—points to this dual knowledge and the ease with which a woman could be judged either for having too much modesty or not enough.

Ironically, her frequent blushing has the effect not of deflecting Guyon's attentions away from her, but of increasing them, which is consistent with courtesy literature's commitment to the teaching of the politics of desire. Vives observes, "For whan nature had ordeyned, that our faces shoulde be open and bare of clothes, she gave it the vaille of shamfastnes, where with it should be covered . . . that who so did looke upon it, shuld understand some great vertu to be under that cover: nor no man should see it covered with that vayle, but he should love it" (*ICW*, sig. K1r). Indeed, Shamefastness's appearance is beautified by the blush, but again Spenser uses the terminology of artifice, suggesting that her blush is consciously crafted to adhere to prescribed codes of femininity:

> So long as *Guyon* with her commoned,
> Vnto the ground she cast her modest eye,
> And euer and anone with rosie red
> The bashfull bloud her snowy cheekes did dye,
> That her became, as polisht yuory,
> Which cunning Craftesmans hand hath ouerlayd
> With faire vermilion or pure Castory.

(2.9.41)

She blushes to indicate her sexual honesty, her ostensible lack of sexual guilt and lack even of the desire to encourage sexual attention, and yet in the very act of behaving modestly, she incurs the danger of being thought to blush artfully. This practice is condemned by Richard Brathwait: "Many desire to appeare most to the *eye*, what they are least in *heart*. They have learned artfully to gull the world with apparences; and deceive the time, wherein they are Maskers, with vizards and semblances. These can enforce a smile, to perswade you of their affability; counterfeit a blush, to paint out their modesty" (*EG*, 114). By placing Guyon in the position of aggressor, and accepting the role of the pursued in a reversal of Phaedria's immodest behavior, Shamefastness manages to prove far more enticing to the temperate man. Her sexual self-consciousness is diminished only when Guyon also blushes, giving her the opportunity to try to put him at ease by looking away and dissembling. Only then is truly mutual social conversation achieved: "Thus they awhile with court and goodly game, / Themselues did solace each one with his Dame."

This episode illustrates how problematic the notion of innocent, unwitting, "carelesse" modesty really is.[30] *Can* modesty
ever be careless? To what extent is this a contradiction in terms?
Renaissance courtesy literature, in advocating maidenly blushes, implies that women could, and should, fashion themselves as
modest, as Castiglione's recommendation of "a little" blushing
implies. The preceptor in *Hic Mulier* seems to accept this premise as well, urging women to control the impressions they make
on men by revealing only what is desirable, as the epigraph to
this chapter indicates. Salter repeats advice resembling Castiglione's in its indirect attribution of agency to the woman: "Likewise, where it behoveth her to shewe her vertue, she shall bee
readie, but not to[o] bolde, and by a sodaine blushing, whiche immediately will overspread her lillie cheekes with roseate read,
she shall shewe that she beareth in her breaste a reverente
harte, farre separated from infamous and reprochfull shame"
(*MM*, sig. E4v–F1r). Veils are only necessary in the presence of
others, those who constitute an audience for a woman's performance of modesty. Brathwait's equation of the blush and the veil
further destabilizes the meaning of modesty: "Now, *Gentlewomen*, you are to put on your vailes, and goe into *Company*.
Which (I am perswaded) you cannot enter without a maiden-
blush, a modest tincture" (*EG*, 41).

As Ruth Yeazell points out, "It is a commonplace of the advice
literature that women's modesty is instinctive, but the very existence of the literature testifies to the belief that the 'instinct'
must be elaborately codified and endlessly discussed: woman's
'natural' modesty must be strenuously cultivated, the argument
goes, lest both sexes fall victim to her 'natural' lust." Yeazell focuses on courtesy literature of the eighteenth century, but the
common thematic assumptions are striking—a woman should
exhibit her modesty but at the same time be unconscious of
doing so; modesty "creates love in the very act of restraining it";
the modest woman "occupies a mystified space between . . .
imagined opposites" of "prude" and "coquette"; true modesty
borders on becoming "a mere matter of appearances."[31] Paradoxically, modesty could become a vehicle for self-display or a
tactical advertisement of feminine charms and virtues in attempts to attract rather than rebuff a suitor.[32]

Guazzo seems to legitimize the strategic manipulation of modesty: "And as Goldsmithes sometime cover their ware and jew-
ells with a Glasse, to make them shew the better, so a mayde
under the vaile of modestie, ought to inclose all her other perfec-

tions, to increase the brightnesse of them, and the more forcibly to draw the eyes and the hearts of others, to have her in admiration" (*CC*, 159r–v). (Spenser will use Guazzo's goldsmith image, more ominously, in describing the creation of the False Florimell in 4.5.15: "As guilefull Goldsmith that by secret skill, / With golden foyle doth finely ouer spred / Some baser metall, which commend he will / Vnto the vulgar for good gold insted.") Here modesty is reduced to a veil, one with the intention not of deflecting but attracting attention. Despite Vives's admonition that a woman should "use no feignyng, nor clokyng, eo [*sic*, misprint for to] seme good with al" (*ICW*, sig. J3v) and should "be in dede, as she sheweth demure, humble, sobre, shamefaste, chaste, honest, and vertuous, bothe let hir seme so, and bee so" (sig. J4r), his injunction is undermined by the generic context in which his words appear, a book constituting a systematic program intended to help females refashion themselves into the feminine ideal constructed by the author. The slippage between the modesty the veil represents and the veil itself in the following excerpt from Brathwait reveals how easily one could assume a virtue: "Women in sundry Countryes, when they goe into any *publike* concourse or presse of people, use to weare vayles, to imply that secret inscreened beauty which best becomes a *Woman, Bashfull modesty*. Which habit our owne Nation now in latter yeares hath observed: which, howsoever the intention of the wearer appeare, deserves approvement: because it expresseth in it selfe *Modest shamefastnesse*, a Womans chiefest Ornament" (*EG*, 50).

Even the standard defense against accusations of hypocrisy, that one was to strive to seem virtuous in order that one might become so indeed (as Hamlet urges Gertrude in the closet scene to "Assume a virtue, if you have it not," 3.4.160), fails to establish the integrity of modest behavior, simply because it can never be authenticated definitively. By feigning shamefastness, women could turn ostensible sexual innocence into a seduction technique, as Duessa does in Book 1, and consequently defeat the validity of the sign's significance.[33] Fine lines exist between sincere, unconscious modesty; conscious but genuine modesty (assumed, but with virtuous intent); and calculated modesty (engineered to hide actual unchastity). Jones acknowledges that distinguishing between true and false modesty could indeed be problematic: "Castiglione's comments on the *donna di palazzo* (significantly, she is not called a *cortigiana*/courtesan because the term already connoted a prostitute) illustrate in their syntax a continual vacillation between the spontaneous natural modesty attributed to women and the necessity for artifice."[34] In light of this practice, the early modern usage of "honest" as a synonym for chaste is rather ironic.

Consequently, great skill was required in reading the female blush, as John Lyly reveals in *Euphues and his England*: "if a fayre woman having hearde the suite of a Lover, if she blush at the first brunt, and shew hir bloud in hir face, sheweth a well disposed minde: so as vertuous women I confesse are for to be chosen by the face, not when they blush for the shame of some sinne committed, but for feare she should comit anie, all women shall bee as *Caesar* would have his wife, not onelie free from sinne, but from suspition."[35] This distinction is not always easy to discern. Malecasta's rejection of modesty is blatant and clear-cut:

> Ne reckt she, who her meaning did mistrust;
> For she was giuen all to fleshly lust,
> And poured forth in sensuall delight,
> That all regard of shame she had discust,
> And meet respect of honour put to flight:
> So shamelesse beauty soone becomes a loathly sight.
>
> (3.1.48)

Other women, however, who do attempt to practice modesty can become victims of others misreading even moderate modesty for sexual guilt (in other words, a woman, even when obeying Castiglione's excellent advice, cannot always control others' perceptions of her). The truly "good" woman is inevitably implicated in this deferral of meaning and is thereby deprived of the means to prove herself virtuous, since the signs could be usurped so easily, as Hero's plight in *Much Ado about Nothing* demonstrates. Claudio derisively (and erroneously) glosses Hero's blushing countenance as indicative of sexual knowledge rather than innocence:

> She's but the sign and semblance of her honor.
> Behold how like a maid she blushes here!
> O, what authority and show of truth
> Can cunning sin cover itself withal!
> Comes not that blood as modest evidence
> To witness simple virtue? Would you not swear,
> All you that see her, that she were a maid,
> By these exterior shows? But she is none:

> She knows the heat of a luxurious bed;
> Her blush is guiltiness, not modesty.
>
> (4.1.33–42)[36]

Britomart's blushes operate within the same matrix of sexual innocence, desire, and guilt. When Redcrosse asks her to explain her disguise and quest, she blushes furiously, and proceeds to give an explanation of her knightly persona that attests to outraged modesty (she claims that Artegall has wronged her) rather than to her erotic desire (3.2.5). Her blush in 3.3.20 (compared to that of Aurora when leaving Tithonus's bed) is even more strongly linked to sexual shame and a woman's reluctance to have her sexual desires made public. Britomart experiences such conflicts because of her signification in two different genres: despite her central role as a romance and epic figure, she must also conform to the strictures of courtesy literature as the representative of chastity. When Margaret Thickstun asserts that Britomart does not learn about chaste love through trial and error (as the other knights learn about their virtues) but instead "practices chastity instinctively,"[37] she attests to the degree to which women were supposed to make their chastity *seem* instinctive. To illustrate the ideal response of a young maiden to the marital imperative, Vives refers to Virgil's Lavinia, who simply weeps and blushes passively while her parents arrange her marriage to Turnus. Britomart's circumstances, of course, demand much more assertiveness than did Lavinia's and hence seem to contribute to her genuine dismay and fear that she will be accused of unnatural behavior. Krier notes, "The shock of becoming aware of Artegall launches her into shame over her nascent erotic awareness, impulses she is inclined to hide"; Britomart "is shocked, horrified, and shamed by the discovery of her sexual nature."[38] I would suggest that Britomart is less horrified at the existence of her sexuality than by the way that sexuality may be perceived by others; she may merely be worried that she is violating the social code of maidenly modesty, which calls for women to hide such feelings. Florimell's love for Marinell and her joy at their reconciliation, though equally as strong as his, must be consciously veiled with modesty for similar reasons:

> chearefull signes he shewed outwardly.
> Ne lesse was she in secret hart affected,
> But that she masked it with modestie,
> For feare she should of lightnesse be detected.
>
> (4.12.35)

When Britomart at last encounters Artegall face-to-face, she strives desperately to control her countenance and behavior so she can test the intentions of her suitor and maintain her own reputation for chastity, as Castiglione prudently recommends. Her desire, however, makes this difficult. She is at first flushed with the heat of battle, but the color in her face intensifies once she hears Artegall's name. Her heart leaps,

> And all her vitall powres with motion nimble,
> To succour it, themselues gan there assemble,
> That by the swift recourse of flushing blood
> Right plaine appeard, though she it would dissemble,
> And fayned still her former angry mood,
> Thinking to hide the depth by troubling of the flood.
>
> (4.6.29)

She fights the telltale blush, but Glauce's words inspire yet another blush in stanza 32. Her "modest countenance" successfully serves its purpose in attracting yet restraining Artegall's passion, as Castiglione's Lord Julian recommends; the lady can "shewe him whom she loveth all tokens of love, but [except for] such as may bring into the lovers minde a hope to obtaine of hir any dishonest matter" (sig. Q8v). Artegall's fervor is duly tempered:

> Besides her modest countenance he saw
> So goodly graue, and full of princely aw,
> That it his ranging fancie did refraine,
> And looser thoughts to lawfull bounds withdraw;
> Whereby the passion grew more fierce and faine,
> Like to a stubborne steede whom strong hand would restraine.
>
> (4.6.33)

He lays siege to her heart, and she endeavors to practice the appropriate maidenly response to an honorable man professing love and offering marriage outlined by Castiglione. This involves evasive tactics, such as trying to change the subject or pretending either to misunderstand his intentions or to assume he is joking (sig. Q6v–Q8v). Britomart is too passionate and sincere to excel at such ploys; she simply can't resist Artegall's advances, "How euer she her paynd with womanish art / To hide her wound, that none might it perceiue: / Vaine is the art that seekes it selfe for to deceiue" (4.6.40). The art is "womanish" because courtesy literature holds women far more responsible than men for exercising sexual discretion.

The degree to which Britomart's behavior is constrained by *The Faerie Queene*'s discursive didacticism is evident when her response to finally beholding her long-desired beloved in person is contrasted with that of Claridiana. The foremost lady knight of *The Mirrour of Princely Deedes and Knighthood*, Claridiana travels from her native Trabisond to joust with the Knight of the Sun in defense of her own beauty and to challenge the supremacy of the Princess Lindabrides, whom the knight serves. After an encounter in which *both* use magic spears and exchange mutual blows on the helm (representative of love's wounds), Claridiana responds to her knight's greeting "with a merry and cherefull countenance" and ready words, making no attempt whatsoever to mask her desire and under no generic compulsion to dissemble (Bk. 1, pt. 2, ch. 31, 106v). Spenser's decorousness is also evident in the lack of amorous play between Britomart and Artegall, the short shrift given the consummation of their love in Merlin's prophecy of their heroic progeny, and the indefinite deferral of their marriage. The love modeled in *The Mirrour* is much more overtly erotic. When Claridiana has acquiesced to the Knight of the Sun's request that he serve as her knight, he kneels to kiss her hands "but she in no wise would consent thereunto, but caused him to stand up, and tooke him in hir armes, whereas grew betweene them so great love, that nothing was to separate them but only death, & although these loving words passed betweene them, & seemed that there was no conclusion of anie thing, yet in their heartes there was so strong a knot made, that before it should be undone, it should be greatly lamented" (Bk. 1, pt. 2, ch. 51, 200r). Later in the narrative, the knight embraces Claridiana more fulsomely. After she objects that she wishes to delay consummation of their love until they are married, they exchange vows. Once again he kisses her hands, but

This beeing done, he by little and little beegan to take heart at grasse, and to embolden himselfe, and what with requestes and otherwise (for that the Pallace was solitarie and fit for the purpose) the royall Princesse was overcome and made a wife, the more for hir honour and glorie, and exalting of the two Empires. . . . When the roiall Princesse saw that the knight of the Sunne had accomplished his desire, she was neither wrathfull nor angrie, although it was done partlie against hir will, but as then seeing that there was not any other remedie, shee loved him as hir spouse, and obeyed him as hir husband, and desired him with as much speede as was possible, that the solempnitie of the marriage might bee celebrated, beecause if it should so fall out that shee were with childe, hir errour might not bee seene. (Bk. 1, pt. 3, ch. 50, 249v–250r)

The romance text attempts to portray simultaneously Claridiana's desire and her honor (the consummation is "done partlie against hir will" and although she eventually bears twins, she manages to keep her pregnancy secret from the court of Greece because the children are stolen immediately after birth) but registers no compulsion to present her as an exemplar of chastity, as Spenser's text demonstrates. Britomart, having at last consented "To be his loue, and take him for her Lord, / Till they with mariage meet might finish that accord" (4.6.41), must now work on fashioning herself as a dutiful wife. Displeased at Artegall's leaving her to continue his quest, she endeavors to disguise her feelings and acquiesce in his plans, practicing at least the appearance of submission until it should become "natural" to her.

Spenserian metaphors for female modesty include not only the "veil" of the blush, but also that of the hair. According to 1 Cor. 11:15, "if a woman have long heere, it is a praise unto her: for her heere is given her for a covering,"[39] and the author of *Hic Mulier* alludes to this verse to reiterate gender differences: "The long hayre of a woman is the ornament of her sexe, and bashfull shamefastnesse her chiefe honour: the long haire of a man, the vizard for a theevish or murderous disposition."[40]

Even before Milton described Eve's ringlets as "wanton," Spenser had used the hair of female characters to comment on their moral state. The more sexually continent women control their hair as they do their desires and behavior: Medina dresses her hair "In breaded tramels, that no looser heares / Did out of order stray about her daintie eares" (2.2.15), and Alma's "yellow golden heare / Was trimly wouen, and in tresses wrought, / Ne other tyre she on her head did weare, / But crowned with a garland of sweete Rosiere" (2.9.19). Again adhering to the mean necessitated by the gentlewoman's dual responsibility to Christian modesty and courtly display, Spenser conflates New Testament descriptions of the modest and the immodest woman, especially 1 Pet. 3:3: "Whose [the godly woman's] apparelling let it not be outwarde, as with broyded heere, and golde put about, or in putting on of apparel." Similarly, 1 Tim. 2:9 admonishes that women should "araye them selves in comelie apparel, with shamefastnes & modestie, not with broyded heare, or gold, or pearles, or costly apparel." Christian precepts and courtesy literature call for modesty, yet Castiglione also mandates that female courtiers be beautiful; Spenser's ladies must strive to be both.

Spenser's descriptions of Britomart's veil of long, golden hair suggest an attempt to accommodate the conventions of both romance and courtesy literature. Britomart's abandonment of her armor in Malbecco's castle and loosening of her hair not only mark her as unmistakably feminine but also foreshadow modest submission to her future husband, which may partially explain the reassurance of her companion knights. Britomart's "silken veile" inspires esteem, wonder, even awe and adoration rather than mere sexual admiration and usually works to restore social harmony (see 3.9.20 and 4.1.13).[41] During her encounter with Artegall in 4.6.20, Britomart's hair begins to assume a more overtly sexual significance when it is loosened from its "wonted band," as if to anticipate the relaxation of her virginal control over her body now that she has at last discovered her intended husband.

However, Britomart's loosened hair usually signifies within the realm of "careless" modesty, in sharp contrast to the much more contrived, self-conscious, and therefore immodest "modesty" practiced by less noble women in *The Faerie Queene*. A woman's hair, as well as her blushes, could be used to signify inconclusively or to convey a questionable shamefastness (a notable historical example being Frances Howard's defiantly loose hair at her wedding to Robert Carr on 26 December 1613, an assertion of her virginity and therefore of the Earl of Essex's impotence).[42] Phaedria's sexual looseness is evident when Guyon perceives her "dressing of her heare" on one of the wandering islands; when he ignores her, she leaves "her lockes vndight" and immodestly rows after him. Ironically, Phaedria's loosened hair, which should be the primary sign of feminine modesty, is used as a sexual lure, underscored by the erotically charged description of her little island, which "seemd so sweet and pleasant to the eye, / That it would tempt a man to touchen there" (2.12.14). After unsuccessfully "faining dalliance and wanton sport, / Now throwing forth lewd words immodestly," Phaedria finally retreats when the Palmer chastises her "for being loose and light." Yet Phaedria's seduction attempt merely emphasizes the ironic truth inherent in courtesy literature ideology: modesty can be highly erotic.

Acrasia's nymphs are more successful than the rather heavy-

handed Phaedria in their manipulations of the maidenly blush
and loosened hair to tempt Guyon to sexual sin:

> Then th'one her selfe low ducked in the flood,
> Abasht, that her a straunger did a vise:
> But th'other rather higher did arise,
> And her two lilly paps aloft displayd,
> And all, that might his melting hart entise
> To her delights, she vnto him bewrayd:
> The rest hid vnderneath, him more desirous made.
>
> With that, the other likewise vp arose,
> And her faire lockes, which formerly were bownd
> Vp in one knot, she low adowne did lose:
> Which flowing long and thick, her cloth'd arownd,
> And th'yuorie in golden mantle gownd:
> So that faire spectacle from him was reft,
> Yet that, which reft it, no lesse faire was fownd:
> So hid in lockes and waues from lookers theft,
> Nought but her louely face she for his looking left.
>
> (2.12.66–67)

The nymphs here illustrate that modesty is easily abused; the
courtesy literature discourse can be turned against itself by
women determined to entice men either by being shameless or
by feigning shamefastness. The coy nymph adds yet another
weapon to her arsenal, that of laughing but with a blush, so that
she plays out more deftly and effectively Phaedria's shameless
laughter and sexual gambits. John Davies remarks on such
strategies: "Who so will keepe his Soule, and Body chast / From
Womans haunt, he must him selfe retire; / Yea, though they
seeme religious, and shamefaste: / For, blushing Women most
inflame Desire."[43] This artful modesty proves titillating, since
Guyon has a predilection for shamefast ladies, and he does indeed succumb, at least momentarily, to her well-executed feminine wiles:

> Withall she laughed, and she blusht withall,
> That blushing to her laughter gaue more grace,
> And laughter to her blushing, as did fall:
> Now when they spide the knight to slacke his pace,
> Them to behold, and in his sparkling face
> The secret signes of kindled lust appeare,
> Their wanton meriments they did encreace,

> And to him beckned, to approch more neare,
> And shewd him many sights, that courage cold could reare.
>
> (2.12.68)

The nymphs' constant awareness of the impression they make ("they spide the knight") and their agency ("shewd him many sights") are simply exaggerated manifestations of the courtesy literature dynamic.

Acrasia's use of the veil as an incitement to desire is probably the most egregious example in the poem. She employs, instead of her hair or the blush, a literal veil, yet one that is diaphanous, thus mocking the conventions of modesty. Miller describes Acrasia's technique as effective "alternations of concealment and display or invitation and delay,"[44] a technique articulated in the rose song of 2.12.74:

> the Virgin Rose, how sweetly shee
> Doth first peepe forth with bashfull modestee,
> That fairer seemes, the lesse ye see her may;
> Lo see soone after, how more bold and free
> Her bared bosome she doth broad display.

Acrasia outrages because she refuses to play the role of the innocent maiden, even to seduce; she is much more frank in acknowledging and consciously exploiting her sexuality for her own ends.

Female readers of the Bower of Bliss are, in one sense, expected to practice with Guyon "reason's resistance to erotic impulse,"[45] but courtesy literature's designs upon women include training them to provoke as well as control erotic impulse. The implied quest made by female readers through the world of Book 2 demands a different, more subtle version of Guyon's temperance. They must acknowledge and even use their sexuality but learn to temper it aright. They cannot reject Acrasia as unequivocally as Guyon ultimately does. At the same time that male readers are learning to resist alluring women in the interest of cultivating temperance, female readers are learning to resist *becoming* excessively alluring women, or how to negotiate the social imperative to be alluring but not so alluring that they could be condemned as temptresses. Female readers, unlike Guyon, cannot simply demolish the Bower of Bliss—they must continue to inhabit gardens, palaces, banqueting houses, and other, often sexualized, courtly settings built by Acrasia, but somehow transform the manner of entertainment of male guests there into the modest practice exemplified at Medina's castle and Alma's house.

Spenser's exemplars of modesty and immodesty collapse into one another in a bewildering fashion. The bodies of female figures in Book 2, modest and immodest alike, utilize complexion, hair, and clothing as "veils" that enable them to "dis-cover" their modesty, to use feminine virtue as a means of self-display, to appear to rebuff the viewer's gaze while actually seeking it. In this chapter I have tried to show how courtesy literature and Spenserian romance imply that a lady's beauty and accomplishments will be noticed and rewarded if, paradoxically, she strives to be modest, but also that she faces an ever-present threat of misinterpretation as she maneuvers within the narrow space allowed her between behavioral extremes. Vives's solution for the maiden (simply to avoid company) was hardly feasible for adult gentlewomen of the English court, and throughout *The Faerie Queene* Spenser hints at the sexually mature woman's difficulty in negotiating an honorable reputation. Once a woman had mastered the art of alluring modesty and had attracted a deserving lover, how was she to control the erotic forces she had unleashed? The dutiful female response to this dilemma proposed in *Haec Vir*, "Comeliness shall be then our study, fear our Armor, and modesty our practice," is simply too pat.[46] Even more difficult, how was a lady to prove the sincere strength of her love without transgressing established codes of chaste behavior?

Spenser's text registers awareness of the complications accompanying the translation of ideals into social practice and of the ease with which chastity can be "debased into discretion," the art of seeming chaste.[47] He clearly condemns Duessa and the False Florimell for practicing this technique, but is more ambivalent about assigning culpability to other errant ladies, such as Priscilla and Serena. How *were* female courtiers to negotiate the world of courtship and safely move from the protected castle of the virginal Alma through the open forest with a knowing Serena? In my next chapter, I will concentrate on those sexually awakened women who, unlike Britomart, do not have any physical armor to protect their chastity. As Amoret's fate implies, the feminine education provided in the Garden and the Temple ultimately proves insufficient, even in Spenser's Fairyland, and thus exposes the unreliability of courtesy literature as a genre intended to equip the female courtier.

5

Courtship and the Female Courtier:
The Problem of Chastity

... it is not sufficient to be honest and innocent in deede, if shee doe not likewise avoide all suspition of dishonestie. And if shee looke well into the matter, shee shall finde small difference (in respect of the world) betweene being naught, and being thoughte naught.
—George Pettie, trans. *The civile Conversation of M. Stephen Guazzo* (1586)

Given *The Faerie Queene*'s nature as a work of courtesy literature, one might reasonably expect Spenser to employ the "behavior modification" strategies typical of Renaissance formal attacks and defenses of the female sex, as Linda Woodbridge asserts: "This is Spenser's avowed method in Book III of *The Faerie Queene*, where he encourages chastity in women by the positive example of Britomart, Florimell, Amoret, and Belphoebe, and discourages unchastity by the negative example of the Squire of Dames' fruitless quest for chaste women and of ... the promiscuous Hellenore."[1] Yet this binary classification of female characters is substantially undercut by their participation in multiple genres, each with its own criteria for judging the "good" woman.[2] Certainly Britomart, as the knight of chastity, possesses a practically unassailable reputation, as does her Ariostan prototype, Bradamante. But how were other errant, unwed heroines, lacking the armor of the fiercely constant lady knight, to express simultaneously the sexual desire and sexual restraint demanded of them by the respective generic discourses of romance and courtesy literature? Margaret Thickstun believes that Florimell and Amoret possess a type of "moral immunity" against accusations of errancy. Traversing Fairyland far from court in response to their erotic desires (implying some degree of transgression of social codes for good women), these two "do

not incur as much censure for their attractiveness and its consequences as Britomart would, even though she is better equipped
to defend herself. Their obvious helplessness and deference to
male defense and assistance play into accepted ideals of womanhood so that, as long as they continue to shriek and run, no one
will ask them what they were doing out alone."[3] Yet Amoret and
Florimell, despite their shrieking and running, are occasionally
caught, suggesting that the distinction between these chaste
women and their immoral counterparts is perhaps less unequivocal than Woodbridge and Thickstun imply, and that internal
contradictions and inconsistencies destabilize the text's formula-
tion of "good" versus "bad" women.

Spenser's descriptions of innocent, loving ladies caught in
morally compromising situations are marked by subtle ambiguities that manage both to condone and to condemn female behavior, thus rendering any seemingly straightforward interpretation
of *The Faerie Queene*'s stance on female chastity problematic.
Suspended between the moralistic codes of courtesy literature
and the easygoing conventions of the romance, female characters and readers alike are never certain how their behavior will
be, or should be, construed. Even when characters are situated
in an unmistakable romance world, they are constantly pres-
sured by the strict sexual standards formulated in courtesy literature and by a political climate in which a woman's sexual
integrity is largely a matter of public construction and reconstruction. This tension helps to explain Chrysogone's oddly dis-
junctive fear of dishonor when she has been impregnated by the
sun. She is described in 3.6.10 as "conceiving" shame even as she
conceives her children, although she is utterly guiltless of any
unchaste behavior. Serena is perhaps the most conflicted of all
such characters, in that she exhibits full awareness of her indiscretion but is unable to escape the consequences of her sexuality, try as she might to enact the hermit's advice. These female
characters are understandably a bit skittish, given the pitfalls
confronting women as they gingerly tread the intricate maze of
courtship.

This chapter, then, will be devoted to an exploration of the dynamic of chastity as cultural performance and the dilemma be-
setting early modern Englishwomen who needed to display their
chastity as virgins even as they sought to contract eligible marriage alliances. Ironically, what should be a most private virtue
is insistently made public in Spenser's poem. Drawing examples
from Books 4, 5, and 6 (traditionally considered to treat the "pub-

lic" virtues as contrasted with the "private" virtues of the first
three books), I will consider the process by which several of
Spenser's ladies first forfeit (willingly or otherwise), and then
struggle to reconstruct, their sexual honor.[4] This process, informed by the strictures of courtesy literature, is particularly
pronounced in Book 6, Spenser's legend of courtesy.

*   *   *

After hearing Lord Julian's description of the courtly lady in
Castiglione's *The Courtyer*, the misogynistic Gaspar jokes, "I
wonder then . . . since you give wome[n] both letters, & stayed-
nesse, and noblenesse of courage, and temperaunce, ye will not
have them also to beare rule in Cities, and to make lawes, and to
leade armies and men to stand spinning in the kitchin." Julian
then hedges, saying, "I have not appointed them these offices,
bycause I fashion a waityng Gentlewoman of the Court, not a
Queene" (sig. O1v). Spenser sets no such limitations on the
scope of his poem and simultaneously fashions both a queen and
courtly gentlewomen, which blurs the distinctions between royal
and nonroyal, between the quintessentially virginal and the (potentially) sexually experienced. As Spenser's preeminent exemplars of chastity, Belphoebe and Britomart neatly embody
William Baldwin's definition of the virtue in *A treatise of morall
phylosophie* (1547): "Chastitie and puritie of life consisteth
eyther in sincere virginitie, or in faithfull matrimonie."[5] Spenser
does single out both Belphoebe's chastity and Britomart's loyalty
in love as worthy of imitation by all ladies, but the majority of
Spenser's female characters are vulnerable to physical and verbal abuse. They are significantly less free than the warrior Britomart to violate sexual codes, to play with gender reversal, and to
exhibit sexual assertiveness.

As courtly ladies, not lady knights, they are constrained by
courtesy literature's assumptions about chaste female behavior,
and their sexual virtue is constantly open to question. Vives's introduction to *The Instruction of a christen woman* implies that
women should be judged solely on their chastity:

> Moreover though the preceptes for men be innumerable: women yet
> maie be enformed with fewe wordes. For men must be occupied
> bothe at home and forthe abrode, both in their own matters & for the
> com[m]o[n] weale. Therfore it can not be declared in few bokes but
> in many and long, how thei shal handle them self in so many and di-
> vers thynges. As for a woman hath no charge to se to, but hir hones-

tee and chastitee. Wherfore whan she is infourmed of that, she is sufficiently appoincted. (sig. A3r)

A woman, according to Vives, should go into society very little; even when accompanied by family members, she experiences "extreme peryl of hir beautie, honestie, demurenes, witte, shamfastnes, and vertue" (sig. L2r). Ruth Kelso's list of the qualities English and continental writers of courtesy literature praised most frequently as constituting perfection for women includes beauty, humility, sweetness, simplicity, peaceableness, kindness, piety, temperance, obedience, and patience. However, chastity is emphasized above all other virtues.[6] Chastity came to be construed rather freely, being used to describe feminine virtue in general terms, but the underlying sexual implications were omnipresent.

Chastity was the virtue most closely identified with the feminine gender, just as courage (or sometimes justice) was with the masculine, a pairing implied by the description of Sclaunder's victims: "Ne euer Knight so bold, ne euer Dame / So chast and loyall liu'd, but she would striue / With forged cause them falsely to defame" (4.8.25). This gendering of honor and public reputation is consistent with other Renaissance works. Torquato Tasso's *Discorso della virtù feminile e donnesca* (1582) designates chastity as the dominant virtue for women and courage for men, although both sexes were expected to display, to a lesser degree, the virtues of the other. The primary vice for each sex was, correspondingly, lack of chastity for women and cowardice for men; the most "acceptable" vice was the antithesis of the opposite sex's dominant virtue (men were most excused for lack of chastity and women for cowardice or timidity).[7]

Given that female honor and shame were based almost exclusively on this one quality, some women (not surprisingly) strove merely to maintain the appearance and not the substance of chastity, thus creating a paradox similar to that of a woman's blushing at will as she practiced the art of modesty. How, then, is a reader of a woman's character to distinguish between the chastity maintained out of fear of getting caught and the more honorable desire either to remain a virgin or to remain true to only one lover? Spenser addresses this hermeneutic impasse in the Squire of Dames's predicament; what seems at first to be an extremely cynical view of female virtue is actually a commentary on the subjective nature of such moral judgments. In one year the Squire finds hundreds of women willing to have him "serve" them and who thank him for his "good partes," whereas in his search for the same number to refuse him and therefore "abide for euer chast and sound" (3.7.56), only one damsel, who is of low degree, wholeheartedly rejects his advances. She embraces chastity for its own sake; the others refuse him for want of occasion or fear of shame. Or at least according to the Squire. These women are never allowed to speak for themselves, and as such the Squire's assessment of their motives may simply reflect both his assumptions about women as he interprets their responses and his desire to impress Satyrane with the number of his conquests. The narrator mitigates the harshness of the Squire's dismissal of female chastity with a more sympathetic commentary in 3.8.44, which asserts that the Squire of Dames's "long discourse of his aduentures vaine . . . himselfe, then Ladies more defames." Seduction obviously involves a seducer; if read with an eye sympathetic to women, the Squire's morals and substantial inconstancy to Claribell seem more offensive than the women's responsiveness to his overtures. We have no way of knowing what has "actually" transpired between the Squire and his purported conquests. The passage provides no absolute judgment about the sexual appetites of women, but instead attests to the ease with which their reputations can be manipulated.

Castiglione's discussion of women's "sincere" chastity is similarly problematic. Lord Cesar asserts that the bridle to women's incontinence "is the zeale of true vertue, and the desire of good name" and not simply fear of shame, adducing several examples of female virtue (sig. P7v). These stories of women who preferred death to defloration provide the matter of much Elizabethan courtly fiction and also constitute a subtext for such Spenserian passages as the defense of Florimell's contested feminine honor:

> Eternall thraldome was to her more liefe,
> Then losse of chastitie, or chaunge of loue:
> Die had she rather in tormenting griefe,
> Then any should of falsenesse her reproue,
> Or loosenesse, that she lightly did remoue.
>
> (3.8.42)

Florimell remains faithful to Marinell despite Proteus's entreaties, symbolized by the waves pounding on her prison of rock. She thus is at one with the faithful women who resist sexual temptation, who, in Cesar's words, are "stiffe in their infinit steedinesse, more than the rockes, against the surges of the sea" (sig. Q5r).

The narrator wants to enroll Florimell's deeds in the hearts of "euery honourable Dame" so that they can emulate her virtue and receive like fame, but if they do so, they will also have to suffer some degree of infamy as well. Women attempting to imitate Florimell will inevitably be rendered suspect, because they cannot prove their chastity, or their ability to say no, unless they find (or place) themselves in a morally compromising situation. In addition, the more beautiful a woman is, the more she is considered to be predisposed to sexual guilt. Guazzo's Anniball alleges that "bewtie breedeth temptation, temptation dishonour: for it is a matter almost impossible, and sieldome seene, that those two great enimies, bewtie, & honestie agree together. . . . And though it fall out often that bewtie & honestie are joyned togither, yet it falleth out sieldome, but that exquisite bewtie is had in suspition" (*CC*, 124v–125r; Hamlet's condemnation of Ophelia in the nunnery scene—"are you honest? . . . . Are you fair?" (3.1.102, 104)— rests on similar assumptions). Several recent critical works have explored this notion that woman's beauty renders her complicitous in her own rape; Ann Rosalind Jones, for example, provides a gloss of the attitude expressed by Guazzo: "the lady must be beautiful enough to attract men, but alert to the possibility that she will be criticized for doing it too well. She must look seductive, but she must be seen not to be seduced."[8]

Guazzo concludes that women should strive to be beautiful according to "the mean," so that they might escape unwanted attentions while still retaining enough desirability in men's eyes to be pursued as a marriage partner, a very difficult balance to achieve. (This is the predicament of Priscilla and Serena, who reveal their charms only to their lovers but then are unfortunately desired by other men as well.) Valued in society according to their ability to attract men sexually and yet held responsible for the effects of their provocation, women were subject to calumny on a grand scale. Master Anniball's confident assertion that "Honest women flie in deede those which follow them dishonestly. Yea, and the unhonest flie too, though they suffer themselves soone to be overtaken" (*CC*, 111v) is a catch-22—if good women happen to be caught, they are automatically tainted with dishonesty.

This paradox underlies Spenser's description of Amoret escaping from Lust; her pace is "More swift then *Myrrh*' or *Daphne* in her race, / Or any of the Thracian Nimphes in saluage chase" (4.7.22). None of these mythical characters provide true parallels to Amoret's situation (Myrrha, clearly guilty of sexual sin in committing incest with her father Cinyras, flees his wrath; Daphne flees her lover Apollo's lust and remains adamantly virginal; the Thracian nymphs are amazons accompanying Camilla in battle), yet these allusions inevitably color the reader's perception of Amoret's chastity. Spenser uses an almost identical comparison to describe Florimell's plight:

> Not halfe so fast the wicked *Myrrha* fled
> From dread of her reuenging fathers hond:
> Nor halfe so fast to saue her maidenhed,
> Fled fearefull *Daphne* on th' *Aegaean* strond,
> As *Florimell* fled. . . .

(3.7.26)

Not simply a convenient, standardized formula for "she ran quickly," these allusions are suited to their context in the Spenserian narrative. Belphoebe's speed when pursuing Lust, for example, is compared unambiguously to that of Diana's when avenging her mother's honor (4.7.30). The peculiar conjunction of allusions in the descriptions of Amoret and Florimell may speak to the plight of the chastely loving woman whose experience cannot be neatly categorized as that of either virgin or whore, or, rather, of the living but guilty or virtuous but dead woman of courtesy literature. Amoret desires to establish a mean between the two, but ultimately is prevented from doing so. She is not necessarily guilty of sexual surrender and Myrrha-like lasciviousness but she understandably seems to prefer the consummation of her love for Scudamour to being transformed, like Daphne, into a tree.

Amoret's and Florimell's liminal status is remarkably relevant to Spenser's female contemporaries, given the prevailing conditions at the Elizabethan court. Although "old" historicism is currently an unfashionable mode of literary criticism, Wolfgang Iser's distinction between "participants" (contemporary readers) and "observers" (later readers) is particularly apposite to an analysis of Spenser's "errant" female courtiers that accepts as subtexts not only conduct manuals but also the experiences of Elizabeth's ladies-in-waiting.[9] The tenets of courtesy literature cannot be said to describe the actual sexual practices of the women to whom they were addressed, and a few aristocratic Englishwomen at court (such as Penelope Devereux Rich) may have enjoyed a greater degree of sexual freedom than others of their sex, but chastity (or at least the appearance thereof) was nevertheless demanded of all female courtiers.[10]

Becoming (and remaining) a lady-in-waiting, which provided women with prestige, power in the form of access to the queen, and opportunities to form advantageous marital alliances at court, demanded an apparent dedication to chastity. Men were, therefore, not the only ones to adopt fictional personas in the competition for evanescent royal favors. While male courtiers, in the arena of Accession Day tourneys, disguised themselves as Elizabeth's devoted knights vying for their "lady's" love or to defend her beauty and honor, female courtiers constructed themselves as chaste, innocent maidens to achieve similar ends. Elizabeth and Anne Russell, for example, made a bid for positions as maids of honor in a staged scene resembling the setting of Pastorella's attendant "louely lasses" in 6.9.8. Visiting Lady Russell at Bisham in 1592, the queen encountered the two girls dressed as shepherdesses and sewing samplers, which depicted the "follies of the Gods, who became beastes, for their affections" and the "honour of Virgins who became Goddesses, for their chastity."[11] Once ensconced at court, female courtiers, according to Sir John Harington's recollection, practiced prevarication: the queen "did oft aske the Ladies around hir chamber, If they lovede to thinke of marriage? And the wise ones did conceal well their liking hereto, as knowing the Queenes judgment in this matter."[12] Elizabeth's oft-noted penchant for dressing her ladies in white and silver to signify her purity as a reincarnated Diana constrained her female courtiers to play the role of virginal attendant nymphs, whether they found the pose congenial or not. If not balanced carefully, the inevitable tensions between the role played and the sexual desires of the women could result in political disaster, given Elizabeth's notable touchiness about the conditions under which her ladies contracted marriage. Whether one attributes her volatile responses and occasional resentment to jealousy of her ladies' comparative sexual freedom, or simply to a prudent desire to exercise control over any noble alliance that might redistribute factional powers, the virgin queen could be easily offended by the romantic assertiveness of her maids of honor.[13]

Despite Elizabeth's apparent preference that her maids indeed remain maids, many of them did marry. Thirteen earls and five barons chose to marry Elizabethan maids of honor.[14] More than a few were involved in clandestine affairs, some of which led to secret marriages, social scandals, and, frequently, political retribution. As Maureen Quilligan points out, Elizabeth had difficulty controlling "the traffic in women in her own court."[15] The

Sidney family succeeded in evading the queen's meddling in their marriage negotiations, notably those of Robert Sidney to Barbara Gamage and of Philip Sidney to Frances Walsingham. However, the Earl of Essex's secret marriage to Frances after she was widowed was revealed when her pregnancy could not be disguised. She thus became an unofficial exile, because Essex tried to appease the queen by having his wife live "very retired in her mother's house" away from court.[16] Catherine Grey had earlier in Elizabeth's reign indulged in a clandestine romance, resulting in her marriage to Edward Seymour in 1560. They were both sequestered in the Tower, where she bore a son (followed by another son in subsequent years). This marriage did, according to Curt Breight, create a genuine threat to the stability of Elizabeth's government, in that it encouraged machinations on the part of Seymour, the Earl of Hertford, to press his claim to the succession. He may have tried to arrange a marriage between Arabella Stuart and his grandson William, the eldest son of Lord Beauchamp, in 1602–1603 (in order to join the Suffolk with the Stuart lines), but Arabella was arrested in time to prevent the event. Resentful of this interference, she refused to participate in Elizabeth's funeral. Arabella and William finally did marry secretly in 1610; they were imprisoned, and after a daring escape Arabella was returned to the Tower. She died there in 1615.[17]

Catherine Grey's sister Mary also outraged the queen by marrying not only secretly but also beneath her station; in 1565 she married Thomas Keys, who was consequently placed in the Fleet Prison, while Mary was shipped off to be kept under surveillance by a succession of various nobles. Mary Shelton, another one of Elizabeth's maids, had her finger broken by Elizabeth who handled her roughly after discovering Mary's secret marriage to James Scudamore. Thomas Perrot and Lady Dorothy Devereux also married secretly, and the third Earl of Southampton, Henry Wriothesley, was forced to marry Elizabeth Vernon when she became pregnant.[18] The pregnant Mary Fitton was dismissed from court in 1601 following her affair with the Earl of Pembroke; Elizabeth had rebuked Fitton during the masque celebrating the marriage of Anne Russell and Henry Somerset by responding, when Fitton, as Affection, asked her mistress to join the dance, "Affection is false."[19] Perhaps the most famous sexual intrigue of Spenser's day was the affair between Sir Walter Raleigh and Elizabeth Throckmorton. After marrying Raleigh secretly and bearing his child at her brother Arthur's house, Elizabeth returned to court to assume her former position as a maid of honor but was found out and imprisoned (an event I will discuss at greater length in relation to the character of Serena). Certain of Spenser's romance motifs, such as the secret love match and imprisonment of Claribell and Sir Bellamoure in Book 6, thus may be read as not only serving generic demands but also possessing immediate resonance for those readers familiar with the risks of contracting imprudent marriages.

Sexual dissimulation must therefore have become a necessary accomplishment for ladies of the court, who were forced to negotiate a dangerous space between the chastity imposed by the queen and the romantic involvement motivated not only by their own desire but also the broader sociosexual and economic mandate that most women marry. Such dissimulation would taint all love affairs, no matter how virtuous, with the stigma of the illicit, and Guazzo's rather cynical assessment of female behavior, which serves as the epigraph to this chapter, must have been fully comprehensible to the female readers of Elizabeth's court. The "small difference (in respect of the world) betweene being naught, and being thoughte naught" (CC, 135r) leaves the chaste woman in the limbo of never being able to distinguish herself definitively from the False Florimells of the world. As Castiglione notes, all a woman can do is devote her energies to forestalling malicious misrepresentations of her conduct: "She ought also to be more circumspect & to take better heed that shee give no occasion to be yll reported of, & so to behave hirselfe, that she be not only not spotted w[ith] any fault, but not so much as w[ith] suspition. Bycause a woman hath not so many wayes to defende hyr selfe from slanderous reportes, as hath a man" (sig. N7r). Bernard urges men, especially in their playing of "Merie Prancks" and joking, to "have respect and reverence, as well in thys, as in all other things, to women, and especially where the stayning of their honestie shal consist" (sig. M8r). Gaspar objects to this favoritism, but Bernard responds that jokes affect women more than they do men: "And that bycause wee our selves have established for a law, that in us wanton life is no vice, nor default, nor any slaunder, and in women it is so greate a reproch and shame, that shee that hath once an ill name, whether the reporte that goeth of hir be true or false, hath lost hir credite for ever" (sig. M8v). Jacques Du Bosc reiterates this advice in his chapter entitled "Of Reputation": "And notwithstanding, since it is not enough to be vertuous, and that we must perswade it, they should beware of apparances, and take away the pretext from slanderers, who make the guilty when they cannot find them. . . .

Verily wee are obliged to do all we can, to take away the subject of ill tongues, and to avoyd scandall: But the wisest, yea, and the most vertuous, labour herein sometimes to no purpose: For do they what they can, or cannot do, there is no infallible rule or meanes, to save ones Reputation; and since it depends so upon the opinion of others, there is more fortune then prudence" (*CW*, sig. N1v–N2r).

Barbara Lewalski has suggested that Lady Mary Wroth's *Urania* revises romance conventions "to explore female rather than male heroism, the challenges of love rather than of war. There are not Britomarts or Bradamantes; heroism for women from shepherdesses to queens involves attaining personal integrity and agency, especially in regard to love, amid the social and psychological constraints of a patriarchal society."[20] Spenser may have to some degree anticipated such concerns in his treatment of Amoret, Priscilla, and Serena, whose stories could have proved even more compelling for early female readers than those of the more exotic Britomart and Belphoebe. While certainly not the protofeminist Wroth seems to have been, Spenser does at least acknowledge the tenuousness of the gentlewoman's position. If a lady is even pursued by a lustful man, for example, she is considered to some extent culpable, and her purity is inevitably sullied. It is no wonder, then, that many of Spenser's ladies do battle not with actual opponents, as their male knights do, but instead with a nebulous enemy, social slander, their paramount concern being their sexual reputation.

*   *   *

The trials of Amoret, who has been reared with Pleasure for a companion in the sexual landscape of the Garden of Adonis, but who has also pledged herself a vassal to Britomart, or chastity, are intensified by the suspiciousness with which society regards beautiful women. Caught between the chivalric romance code that requires her to show courtesy to her defender and conduct literature's mandate that she avoid all appearance of compromising sexual behavior, while also conscious of her position as a virgin wife, Amoret inevitably worries that her reputation will suffer when traveling with Britomart. Amoret assumes Britomart to be a male knight, and with good reason—Britomart, "for to hide her fained sex the better" (4.1.7), adopts the behavior of a lustful man:

> For *Amoret* right fearefull was and faint,
> Lest she with blame her honor should attaint,

That euerie word did tremble as she spake,
And euerie looke was coy, and wondrous quaint,
And euerie limbe that touched her did quake:
Yet could she not but curteous countenance to her make.

For well she wist, as true it was indeed,
That her liues Lord and patrone of her health
Right well deserued as his duefull meed,
Her loue, her seruice, and her vtmost wealth.
All is his iustly, that all freely dealth:
Nathlesse her honor dearer then her life,
She sought to saue, as thing reseru'd from stealth;
Die had she leuer with Enchanters knife,
Then to be false in loue, profest a virgine wife.

(4.1.5–6)

Amoret here echoes the common theme of courtesy literature exemplars—better dead than sullied—and she has cause to worry. Once assured that Britomart is in fact a woman, Amoret freely shares her companion's bed, where they exchange accounts of their love quests and pity each other (4.1.16), yet this innocent companionship results in Amoret's vilification by Ate, who maliciously reports to Scudamour that his wife has transferred her affections to another "with whom now she goth / In louely wise, and sleepes, and sports, and playes": "I saw him haue your *Amoret* at will, / I saw him kisse, I saw him her embrace, / I saw him sleepe with her all night his fill" (4.1.49).[21] The growing but misunderstood friendship of Britomart and Amoret, who embody militant chastity and passionate sexual love, respectively, suggests that the two are actually compatible, but that society continues to view them as categorically opposed and assumes that a woman cannot embody both qualities simultaneously.

As Castiglione notes, slandering worthy gentlewomen "is a kinde of Courtiers trade" (sig. Cc2v, 1588 ed.), and Sclaunder, who is harsher even than Ate, is an adept. Traveling with Arthur in 4.9.18, Amoret continues to demonstrate concern about her honor ("now in feare of shame she more did stond"). Spenser manages to defend Amoret and Aemylia, but only at the cost of reproving his contemporary audience:

Here well I weene, when as these rimes be red
With misregard, that some rash witted wight,
Whose looser thought will lightly be misled,
These gentle Ladies will misdeeme too light,

> For thus conuersing with this noble Knight;
> Sith now of dayes such temperance is rare.[22]

(4.8.29)

Calidore's confident assurance when traveling in mixed company ("Fearelesse, who ought did thinke, or ought did say, / Sith his own thought he knew most cleare from wite," 6.3.16) is simply unavailable to Amoret. Whether she actually is or is not sexually pure is beside the point. Amoret's and Aemylia's accuser, the hag who is the "slaunder of her sexe," dramatizes the no-win situation inherent in Vives's warning to young women in his *Instruction*:

> For nothyng is more tender, than is the fame and estimacio[n] of women, nor nothinge more in daunger of wronge: in so much that it hath be sayde, and not without a cause, to hange by a cobweb, because those thynges, that I have rehersed, be required perfette in a woman: and folkes judgementes bee dangerous to please, and suspiceous . . . if a sklaunder ones take holde in a maydes name by folkes opinion, it is in a maner everlastynge, nor can not be wasshed awaie without great tokens and shewes of chastitee and wisedome. If thou talke littel in company, folkes thynke thou canste [knowest] but littell good: if thou speake muche, they recken the lyght: if thou speake uncunnyngly, they count the dul witted: if thou speake cunnyngly, thou shalte be called a shrewe: if thou answere not quickly, thou shalte be called proude, or yl brought up: if thou answere [readily], they shall saie thou wylte be sone overcomen, if thou sitte with demure countenaunce thou arte called a dissembler: if thou make muche movynge, they will call the foolyshe: if thou loke on any syde, than will they saie, thy mynde is there: if thou laugh whan any man laugheth though thou do it not a purpose, streyght they will say thou haste a fantasye unto the man and his saiyng, and that it were no great maistry to wynne the. . . . How muche were it better to abyde at home, than go forth and here so many judgementes, and so dyvers upou [*sic*] the, and be in so many jeopardies? (*ICW*, sig. L2r–v)

In other words, it is the interpretation of the event or behavior, not the behavior itself, that determines the status of the woman's reputation. The locus of control is removed from the woman to her audience.

Sclaunder purportedly attacks only guiltless people—"Her nature is *all goodnesse* to abuse, / And *causelesse* crimes continually to frame, / With which she *guiltlesse* persons may accuse, / And steale away the crowne of their good name" (4.8.25, my emphasis)—and yet most critics have attributed to Amoret some degree of culpability in becoming estranged from Britomart and subsequently being attacked by Lust. Spenser's text makes the extent of her guilt difficult to assess in that his description of the incident is riddled with contradictions. Amoret is presented in 4.7.2 as a hapless victim of the violent forces found in the forest, yet her decision to alight to rest there because she and Britomart are weary of the way and of warlike exercise can be construed as signaling a lack of moral vigilance. Hesitant to ascribe this flaw to Britomart, who explicitly represents chastity, most critics assume that of the two Amoret is the more culpable. In 4.7.4, Spenser again uses ambiguous language in attributing a motive to Amoret, who, "of nought affeard, / Walkt through the wood, for pleasure, or for need." "Of nought affeard" could attest either to her utter innocence or to her foolish lack of discretion. Hamilton notes that "need" could be a euphemism for Amoret's relieving herself but then suggests that she "exposes herself to rape under some inner compulsion." This imputation follows from Britomart's alternative account in the previous canto, the diction of which is charged with innuendo: Britomart thought Amoret "wandred was, or gone astray." The connotations are clear. Even though Amoret is described as "vnawares" when the beast approaches, she can still be condemned for her response: "Feebly she shriekt, but so feebly indeed, / That Britomart heard not the shrilling sound"—lines that Hamilton takes to mean "she does not want to, or cannot" arouse Britomart. The hapless Amoret suffers blows from Timias, or Honor, as Lust uses her for a buckler, and her silken garments become stained with his coal-black blood. The fact that Honor is trying to defend her and that she is stained with Lust's blood rather than her own suggests that the marks may signify the blackening of her reputation rather than the act of intercourse, but the phallic implications of the scene are too pronounced to ignore altogether.

Aemylia seems even more culpable than Amoret and more firmly situated in the traditions of courtly fiction and courtesy literature than in those of allegorical romance, given her placement in a "realistic" social and familial context. Yet her story is also characterized by contradictions arising from the pitting of faithfulness in love against discretion. Aemylia claims that her father, "who me too dearely well did loue," had refused his consent to her marriage, compelling her to run away. (Her "fixed mind," 4.7.16, which Hamilton glosses as "stubborn rather than constant," must presumably differ from Amoret's and Britomart's admirable constancy by virtue of the unequal social posi-

tions of the lovers and the textual presence of a disapproving
authority figure.) Whereas Amoret's motive for entering the forest is highly ambiguous, Aemylia intentionally arranges to meet
her lover in the grove, to which she "boldly" came upon her "feeble" feet (4.7.17). Aemylia's self-characterization here as she tells
her story to Amoret speaks to her conflicting desires to appear
brave and loving while at the same time reluctant, modest, and
chaste. Concern for her lover, however, prevents Aemylia from
maintaining this precarious balance; when she sees her lover's
friend Placidas, "All mindlesse of her wonted modestie, / She to
him ran, and him with streight embras / Enfolding said, And liues
yet *Amyas*?" (4.8.63). The happy ending to her story and also that
of Poeana (whose "lewd loues and lust intemperate" are eventually reformed when she is matched with Placidas, so much so
"That all men much admyrde her change, and spake her praise")
suggests that feminine honor is subject to constant reinterpreta-
tion and is rarely fixed.

Less fortunate than Aemylia, Priscilla is brought to the brink
of social ruin by her clandestine assignation with Aladine. In a
"couert glade / Within a wood," Priscilla shares with her knight
the "ioyous iolliment / Of their franke loues, free from all gealous
spyes" (6.2.16)—that is, until another pair happens upon them,
and the knight, "fierce and whot," desires Priscilla's "louely
courtesyes" for himself and attacks Aladine. When Calidore
comes upon them, Priscilla assumes a defensive posture, which
reveals her desire both to prove her constant love for Aladine, to
whom she is "for euer bound," and to maintain her reputation. As
she weeps and wipes the blood from Aladine's wounds, Priscilla
protests that they had been "Ioying together in *vnblam'd* delight" (my emphasis). Yet when the private affair becomes public,
she will indeed be blamed, and she grieves not only for the wound
Aladine has suffered but also for the metaphorical wound her
reputation, both social and sexual, will sustain. The lustful knight
has left them both "nigh dead," Aladine mortified by a physical
wound and Priscilla by shame.

Her care continues to be divided between satisfying the conflicting demands of love service and social appearance: "that
faire Lady would be cheard for nought, / But sigh'd and sorrow'd
for her louer deare, / And inly did afflict her pensiue thought, /
With thinking to what case her name should now be brought"
(6.3.6). Just as she was earlier forced to resort to subterfuge to
act on her love, so now she must resort to similar tactics to maintain her honor: she "gan t'aduize, / How great a hazard she at

earst had made / Of her good fame, and further gan deuize, / How she the blame might salue with coloured disguize." As she grieves for Aladine's pain, so he grieves for hers. They both worry about how to "saue whole her hazarded estate" and turn to Calidore, who skilifully manages to save Priscilla's honor without sullying his own. Calidore presents

> The fearefull Lady to her father deare,
> Most perfect pure, and guiltlesse innocent
> Of blame, as he did on his Knighthood sweare,
> Since first he saw her, and did free from feare
> Of a discourteous Knight, who her had reft,
> And by outragious force away did beare.
>
> (6.3.18)

Calidore's defense of Priscilla validates the lady's romance quest for love over the preservation of her honor, but he must equivocate to do so, and her escape is a narrow one indeed. The lady's reconstruction of honor is accomplished not by her own action but by the testimony of a male knight to a patriarch. She can participate in but not completely control her own recuperation. As Cavanagh observes, "chastity results from societal affirmation, not from physical integrity."[23]

Serena can also be accused of willful wandering. When Calepine shifts his attention away from her to Calidore, Serena apparently continues to act on the sensual desires that brought her to the wood in the first place:

> The faire *Serena* (so his Lady hight)
> Allur'd with myldnesse of the gentle wether,
> And pleasaunce of the place, the which was dight
> With diuers flowres distinct with rare delight,
> Wandred about the fields, as liking led
> Her wauering lust after her wandring sight,
> To make a garland to adorne her hed,
> Without suspect of ill or daungers hidden dred.
>
> (6.3.23)

The qualification of the final line, attesting to her innocence, fails to counteract the impression created by the accretion of loaded diction scattered throughout the stanza ("allur'd," "wandred," "wauering lust"). The Blatant Beast catches Serena "vnaware," as Lust does with Amoret, suggesting her innocence, but again she is stigmatized by Spenser's word choice: the creature

"Caught her thus loosely wandring here and there, / And in his wide great mouth away her bare." The adverb "loosely" could modify either the way he caught her up or, more pejoratively, describe the quality of her wandering. Spenser here literalizes the act of bandying a lady's name around in public, but she cannot be exonerated from some of the shame. Her wounds prevent her from riding, and Calepine holds her in place while guiding the horse, which suggests that she has relinquished the control of her concupiscible appetites to her lover.

Serena fares much worse than Priscilla in terms of the reconstruction of her honor. Her persistent *lack* of serenity derives from her literary entrapment. She has imagined herself to be acting within the generic conventions of the romance, yet Calidore, as the knight of courtesy, has brought with him into the grove (however unintentionally) the conventions of the public world. In 6.3.20, Calepine and Serena are situated "In couert shade" so that Calepine might "solace with his Lady in delight." In earlier books, lovers engaged in similar activities in suitable allegorical settings such as the Garden of Adonis and the Temple of Venus were protected by tutelary goddesses, but now we see them in a world much less overtly allegorical and one subject to intrusions of social judgment. Calepine thinks himself "far from enuious eyes that mote him spight," yet even Calidore's unspiteful eyes serve to disrupt the sexual idyll. Serena is "full faire to see, / And courteous withall," but the sexual courtesies granted by the romance mistress are fundamentally opposed to the feminine chastity and restraint prescribed by courtesy literature.

When Serena is attacked by the beast and cries for help, the knights start up "like men dismayde" and run to rescue "the distressed mayde."[24] The Blatant Beast carries Serena far into the woods "For to haue spoyled her," suggesting both physical rape and the spoiling of her sexual reputation. Her final degradation is to be "All in gore bloud there tumbled on the ground, / Hauing both sides through grypt with griesly wound." Serena, unlike Amoret, is stained with her *own* blood, and thus provides an unromanticized version of the pastoral idyll that "spoils" a woman of her virginity and spots her reputation. "Tumbled," as used in *Hamlet* 4.5.62, suggests a sexual encounter, as does Claribell's similar wounding in 6.12.4 and subsequent pregnancy: her "sides before with secret wound / Of loue to *Bellamoure* empierced were." Book 6, characterized by an unresolved tension between the literary topoi of pastoral romance and the social codes of sixteenth-century England, is less delightful and restorative than it might at first seem.

The ease with which pastoral could be employed to comment wittily on contemporary social affairs is revealed in an account of the discovery of Sir Walter Raleigh's and Elizabeth Throckmorton's sexual indiscretion:

> S.W.R., as it seemeth, have been too inward with one of Her Majesty's maids. All think the Tower will be his dwelling, like hermit poor in pensive place, where he may spend his endless days in doubt. It is affirmed that they are married; but the queen is most fiercely incensed, and, as the bruit goes, threateneth the most bitter punishment to both the offenders. . . . All is alarm and confusion at this discovery of the discoverer, and not indeed of a new continent, but of a new incontinent.[25]

Serena and Timias do, in fact, spend time in a hermitage, and the parallels between Raleigh, Timias, and Calepine, Throckmorton and Serena are many. The Raleigh/Timias link is particularly pronounced in the 1596 edition of the poem; Calepine figures the personal aspect of Raleigh's life, his roles as gentleman and Throckmorton's lover, and Timias the public aspect, the avowed lover of Elizabeth/Belphoebe and the recipient of shame.[26] The carpe diem motif evoked in Spenser's description of Serena's "wandering" to pick flowers for a garland, as well as Serena's name, also appear in a lyric poem attributed to Sir Walter Raleigh, "To his Love when hee had obtained Her":

> Now Serena bee not coy;
> Since we freely may enjoy
> Sweete imbraces: such delights,
> As will shorten tedious nightes.
>
> . . . .
> So fraile is all thinges as wee see,
> So subject vnto conquering Time.
> Then gather Flowers in theire prime. . . .[27]

Without assuming that the Raleigh/Throckmorton parallel exhausts the meaning of the Calepine/Serena/Timias episode of 6.3–5, I would like to read it in light of Raleigh's and Throckmorton's experience at court. They certainly seem to have read Spenser's poem this way, and characters in Lady Mary Wroth's *Urania* were similarly linked to particular Jacobean courtiers.[28] Eugene Kintgen notes in his study of Tudor reading practices that "sensitivity to the parallels between historical or fictional and contemporary situations was constantly stressed in both secular and religious instruction, and it would have been the exception rather than the rule for someone to have escaped internalizing it."[29]

Elizabeth Throckmorton had become a maid of honor in 1584 at the age of twenty. She and Raleigh fell in love in the early 1590s; she conceived a child, and the couple married secretly. Throckmorton's brother Arthur notes in his diary that he first learned of their marriage on 19 November 1591. Elizabeth turned to Arthur for help, removing to his house on 28 February to begin her lying-in. While Raleigh was away preparing a naval expedition, she bore a son on 29 March 1592. The child was baptized Damerei on 10 April and sent out to a wet nurse while Elizabeth returned to court on 27 April. Neither Raleigh nor Elizabeth apologized to the queen or attempted to conciliate her, and the couple, once found out, were placed under house arrest in late May or early June and imprisoned in the Tower in August.[30] The lack of hospitality shown Calepine and Serena by Turpine may allude to the malicious pleasure some members of the "civilized" court took in the couple's downfall. Although the salvage man contrives to cure Calepine, he cannot heal Serena, whose wound is "inwardly vnsound" (6.4.16), reflecting the double standard operative at the Elizabethan court: a lady's reputation and position were usually more fragile than her knight's. Raleigh, as a matter of fact, spent only five weeks in the Tower before being released to salvage for the queen the goods from the captured ship *Madre de Dios* in the west country. Throckmorton, however, was not released until the end of the year, in late December, and this bespeaks not only her political dispensability but also, according to A. L. Rowse, her greater offense. She had returned to court, boldly reassuming the now-inappropriate role of a virginal maid of honor, and thus challenged the queen's strict rules.[31] Elizabeth was never allowed to return to court, although Raleigh did so after five years of exile.

One wonders if the couple would have been treated less harshly had Elizabeth not borne a child. While a man's sexual activity is marked by no visible sign, pregnancy provides indisputable evidence of a woman's. As Constance Jordan wryly observes, "Her body can and commonly does signify that she is sexually active whether or not she wishes the fact to be known. Maternity, unlike paternity, is not a discretionary matter."[32] Serena's wounds from the Blatant Beast seem far more serious

than those inflicted on Amoret by Lust and Timias, so much so
that some connection to the baby that mysteriously appears out
of nowhere seems likely. Serena has, of course, engaged with Calepine in "loues delight" (6.3.21), and later, having been savaged
by the Blatant Beast, she is left "All in gore bloud there tumbled
on the ground, / Hauing both sides through grypt with griesly
wound" (6.3.27). In describing Serena's wound as "inwardly vnsound," Spenser's language signifies more than the double standard; although both Serena and Calepine have been "wounded"
as a result of their sexual indiscretion, her wound, unlike his,
"fructifies," suggesting pregnancy. The sudden appearance in
6.4.17 of "A cruell Beare, the which an infant bore / Betwixt his
bloodie iawes, besprinckled all with gore," which startles not only
Calepine but also the reader, may register more logically in the
narrative than one might initially surmise. The blood on the
bear's jaws could derive either from the bear's previous victim
or, as A. C. Hamilton points out and I am arguing, from the baby's
extremely recent birth, particularly as the word "gore" is used
both to describe Serena's bleeding and the blood covering the
baby. Given the baby episode's interpolation in the Serena/Calep-
ine narrative, the Shepherd's hunch upon discovering the aban-
doned Perdita in Shakespeare's *The Winter's Tale* seems
apposite: "A pretty one, a very pretty one: sure some scape.
Though I am not bookish, yet I can read waiting-gentlewoman in
the scape. This has been some stair-work, some trunk-work,
some behind-door-work. They were warmer that got this than
the poor thing is here" (3.3.71–6). The graphic *blason* highlighting Serena's upreared belly on the cannibals' altar leads James
Nohrnberg to observe, "Serena almost seems to be pregnant",[33]
even though the baby has departed the narrative by this point,
Serena still bears the shame of the pregnancy. Although the discovery of an infant in the wilderness is a standard feature of
Greek romance, the incident occurs in the book devoted to courtesy, and thus suggests as well the consequences of producing a
child out of wedlock, particularly under circumstances that vio-
lated so flagrantly the queen's desires. Serena's plight revises
the typical romance topos of the abandonment and eventual recovery of an infant, such as that informing the story of Claribell,
Bellamour, and Pastorella, and situates childbirth in a context of
female shame and recuperation.

Suffering from her multiple wounds (those of love and of the
social shame associated with the bite of the Blatant Beast), Serena's pain is described in terms evocative of childbirth:

   Vpon the ground her selfe she fiercely threw,
   Regardlesse of her wounds, yet bleeding rife,
   That with their bloud did all the flore imbrew,
   As if her breast new launcht with murdrous knife,
   Would streight dislodge the wretched wearie life.
   There she long groueling, and deepe groning lay,
   As if her vitall powers were at strife
   With stronger death, and feared their decay,
   Such were this Ladies pangs and dolorous assay.

                (6.5.5)

The copious bleeding, "long groueling," "deepe groning," and "pangs" point simultaneously to the throes of death and of labor. Renato Poggioli contends that "the pastoral ignores openly . . . the realities of childbearing," but this passage suggests otherwise.[34] (Although the bear episode in canto 4 immediately precedes Serena's travail in canto 5, the narrative logic of Spenserian allegory need not be temporally sequential. Britomart wounds Marinell in 3.4, which instigates Florimell's flight, yet Britomart, Arthur, and Guyon have already seen her in motion in 3.1.)

 Serena's abrupt and isolated experience of childbirth reveals her alienation from the highly ritualized process of early modern English childbirth, which progressed from the woman's appointment of several friends to attend her, to the lying-in, birth, and childbed privilege (roughly a month), and finally to the churching ceremony that signaled the "purified" woman's reintegration into society and her readiness to resume normal domestic duties. According to historian Adrian Wilson, "the social space of the birth . . . was a collective female space, constituted on the one hand by the presence of gossips and midwife, and on the other hand by the absence of men."[35] Denied a female midwife, Serena's baby is delivered to its father by a bear.

 The appearance of a bear in the Spenserian (and also the Shakespearean) romance serves not only to signify brute sexual desire but also, and more emphatically, to defer, displace, or avenge the shame imposed on the slandered woman. Unlike Hermione, Serena actually is guilty of sexual indiscretion. Spenser's allegory, however, serves to distance her from accountability as a mother, even as it suggests that the consequences for female lovers are much harsher than for their male counterparts.[36] Serena is constructed primarily as a lover rather than as a mother; her childbirth experience is the cause of social shame and public scandal rather than private joy. Her role at the Elizabethan court as one of "Diana's nymphs" suggests another ursine connection, the Ovidian analogue of Callisto's shame and subsequent metamorphosis. A "knight of *Phebes* troope" (and indeed the goddess's favorite), Callisto is raped by Jove, who has initially assumed the guise of Diana. Callisto's pregnancy is revealed nine months later when Diana invites her nymphs to bathe with her, and the goddess banishes her in anger. After Callisto bears Arcas, jealous Juno has the evidence she needs ("was there, arrant strumpet thou, none other shift to finde, / But that thou needes must be with barne, that all the world must see / My husbandes open shame and thine in doing wrong to mee?") and spitefully turns Callisto into a bear. Spenser's readers may have found Ovid's commentary strikingly apt; the Golding translation notes the instability of favored status at court ("but favor never lasteth long") and claims that because Diana is still a virgin, she misses the "thousand tokens . . . By which the Nymphes themselves (men say) hir fault did well espie," a reminder that female courtiers were subject to constant surveillance, that of their peers as well as of their queen. Any misstep could fuel courtly gossip or, worse, be used by one's enemies among Elizabeth's attendants to diminish one's position. Callisto's clothes "were pluckt away," either by Diana or by her nymphs, who may act from spite, given Callisto's earlier favored status (after her rape she no longer "preases . . . to bee / The foremost of the companie, as when she erst was free").[37]

Serena's link with the bear goes beyond the Callisto myth, however, to encompass early modern assumptions about the parallels between bears and women, particularly mothers. Bears, both male and female, were considered notoriously lustful. However, Edward Topsell's description of ursine sexual practices in *The Historie of Foure-footed Beastes* (1607) particularly emphasizes female insatiability: "A Beare is of a most venereous and lustfull disposition, for night and day the females with most ardent inflamed desires, doe provoke the males to copulation, and for this cause at that time they are most fierce and angry."[38] The manner of the bear's copulation is "like to a mans"; also "like to a mans" is its fertility cycle, which includes a period of hibernation following conception and birth (a rough parallel to the woman's lying-in period).[39] Topsell contends that female bears carry their young for about a month, "for wild beasts doe not couple themselves being with young . . . and the beares being (as is already said) verie lustfull, to the intent that they may no longer want the company of their males, do violently cast their whelps and so presently after delivery, do after the maner of conies betake themselves to their lust, & norishing their yong ones both togither" (37). (Unlike bears, the sexual practice of early modern women immediately following childbirth seems to have been abstention during the period of privilege.) After she has littered, "the old beare dailye keepeth [the cub(s)] close to her brest . . . till they be thirty daies old; at what time they come abroad, being in the beginning of May" (38). Both in the Spenserian and the Shakespearean text, the liminal figure of the bear appears in conjunction with the "delivery" of a child and marks the transition from winter to spring; the bear's emergence from hibernation was associated with Candlemas, the Feast of the Purification of the Virgin Mary on 2 February, which makes the bear a logical choice for allegorical representation of women's sexual shame and recuperation of that shame.[40] The multiple meanings of the bear image thus suggest numerous ways to read Serena: natural history marks her as inherently lustful; the Callisto myth marks her as socially alienated as a result of her defloration and ashamed of transgressing courtly behavioral codes; the association with the Virgin Mary (a woman initially condemned for illicit sexual conduct and then rehabilitated as an icon of virtue) marks her as capable of purification.

Most of the bears featured in Renaissance romances and plays were female: the hero of the popular anonymous play *Mucedorus* (1598) rescues Princess Amadine by killing a she-bear, and the bear pursuing Pamela in Sidney's *Arcadia* is also female. Defeating a female bear might have provided more prestige than defeating a male bear, given that female bears were considered more fierce. Aristotle's *Historia Animalium* claims that the "females of all animals are less violent in their passions than the males, except the female bear and pardalis, for the female of these appears more courageous than the male."[41] Part of Satyrane's training in ferocity entails tearing the she-bear's whelps from her teats (1.6.24), and Morocco boasts in *The Merchant of Venice* 2.1.29 of plucking "the young sucking cubs from the she-bear" (hence, in *The Winter's Tale*, Perdita's being torn from her mother's breast with "The innocent milk in it [*sic*] most innocent mouth," 3.2.100). Topsell adds biblical precedent in his summary of popular bear lore: "Great is the fiercenes of a beare, as appeareth by holie scripture *Osee* [Hosea] 13. *I will meet them as a beare robbed of her whelpes* (saith the Lorde) *and will teare in pieces their froward heart. And Chusai* telleth *Absalon.* 2

Sam. 17. *Thou knowest that thy father and the men that bee with him be most valiant and fierce like a shee beare robbed of her Whelpes*: for a shee beare is more couragious then a male" (43).

Serena, however, demonstrates none of this fierceness. Her maternity is rendered obliquely, the Spenserian text both pointing to and obscuring her childbirth experience, both condemning and exonerating her. The nuances of Spenser's depiction of Serena become clearer when contrasted with that of her romance counterpart Hermione. Like Serena, Hermione is vulnerable to sexual shame (although with much less cause). Leontes casts slur after slur on Hermione's chastity: "My wife is slippery," "My wife's a [hobby]-horse, deserves a name / As rank as any flax-wench that puts to / Before her troth-plight" (1.2.273, 276–78), "Were my wive's liver / Infected as her life, she would not live / The running of one glass" (1.2.304–6), and so on. Leontes determines that the "bastard" Perdita be put out to die. Yet the abandonment of Perdita, unlike that of the Spenserian baby, is juxtaposed with an assertive maternal presence. As Antigonus takes leave of the child, he recounts his disquieting apparition of Hermione, who claims the power to name her baby.[42] Just as Antigonus has denied Hermione her daughter, she threatens him with the loss of Paulina and, by implication, his own three daughters.[43] Having initially appeared in Antigonus's vision as weeping and "gasping to begin some speech," Hermione's words and demeanor become increasingly vengeful, and she vanishes amidst loud shrieks that anticipate the "savage clamor" marking the bear's ferocious entrance in 3.3. The two halves of the play each end with a dramatic shock: the appearance of the bear and the statue that comes to life.[44] Structurally, then, Hermione is equated with the bear that wreaks vengeance on Antigonus for daring to think that Perdita is indeed the daughter of Polixenes, and she is further associated with the bear by means of her being the Emperor of Russia's daughter (an alteration of the *Pandosto* source, in which Egistus, the Polixenes figure, not the Leontes-Pandosto character, is married to the Russian princess).[45]

Antigonus clearly expresses his belief that the child is Polixenes' in 3.3.41–46 and had hinted at it earlier when he warned Leontes that rejecting the child would cause "three great ones [to] suffer, / Yourself, your queen, your son" (2.1.128–29). This caution only reinforces Leontes' suspicions that the child is not part of his family, in that Antigonus fails to mention the jeopardized honor of the unborn child. As if to reprove her husband's too-ready complicity with the king, Paulina later argues for "the sacred honor" of the *entire* royal family ("himself, his queen's, / His hopeful son's, his babe's," 2.3.85–86), which has been questioned by Leontes. When Leontes brutally refuses to acknowledge the "brat," whom he first plans to burn and then merely expose in some desert place "Where chance may nurse or end it," Antigonus prays, "Some powerful spirit instruct the kites and ravens / To be thy nurses! Wolves and bears, they say, / Casting their savageness aside, have done / Like offices of pity" (2.3.186–89). Ironically, Antigonus lacks the pity commonly attributed to bears ("it is received in many Nations, that children have bene Nursed by beares," Topsell, 41), and he thus deserves to be killed by the wild beast "which spares the innocent child, but destroys the corrupted agent of tyranny."[46] Unlike the heroic Calepine, whose heart is pierced with pity for the baby and therefore runs "with zealous haste, / To rescue th' infant," Antigonus is characterized as a courtier completely out of his element when in the pastoral realm and as abjectly helpless to resist the enraged bear/mother.

Given the preponderance of female bears in romance literature, why, then, does Spenser's text run counter to tradition and gender the bear male? Doing so downplays Serena's identity as a mother, and it also deflects some of her culpability onto Calepine, who must confront in the bear and the baby both the nature and the result of his own sexual appetite. His encounter with the bear as he carelessly takes a stroll reenacts Serena's with the Blatant Beast when she chose to "wander."[47] Calepine also seems culpable in his decision to amuse himself by taking a walk when Serena remains in great pain. One might read this action as Calepine's vain attempt to dissociate himself from scandal, as Raleigh did on 10 March 1592, desperately responding to Sir Robert Cecil's queries with evasion and denial: "I mean not to cume away, as they say I will, for feare of a marriage, and I know not what. If any such thing ware, I would have imparted it unto yourself before any man livinge; and, therefore, I pray believe it not, and I beseich you to suppress, what you can, any such mallicious report. For I protest before God, ther is none, on the face of the yearth, that I would be fastned unto."[48] Just as Calepine is absent during Serena's agonizing pains, so Raleigh was absent from Throckmorton when Damerei was born. Spenser could simply be aiming at humor in his description of Calepine's discomfort as he wanders in vain trying to find his way out of the wood, while "euermore his louely litle spoile / Crying for food, did greatly him offend," but Calepine reveals a strange ambivalence toward the baby. He risks his life to save it from the bear, he tenderly checks to see if the infant (a boy, like the Raleighs' Damerei) is hurt, yet is distressed by its presence and is extremely eager to distance himself from it.

Yet Spenser's ambiguous (and circumspect) representation of his disgraced friend and patron also restores him to heroic status. Typically, romance heroes rescued their ladies from bears; here, of course, Calepine rescues a baby, but he might at the same time be assisting in the "delivery" of Serena, especially given one of the medicinal properties of the bear recounted by Topsell: "if a woman bee in sore travile of child-birth, let a *stone* or arrow which hath killed a man, *a beare* or a bore, be throwne ouer the house wherein the Woman is, and she shall be eased of her paine" (43; my emphasis—Calepine uses a stone to choke the bear). The parallel of the bear carrying the infant between bloody jaws and the Blatant Beast carrying the bleeding Serena suggests that in rescuing the child the unarmed Calepine somehow also assists his lady. The transition from 6.4 to 6.5 is marked by Calepine throwing himself in anguish on the ground in his despair over losing Serena, an action then mirrored by Serena when the salvage man is unable to locate Calepine. This textual doubling emphasizes the depth of the couple's love rather than their indiscretion, and certainly the distancing of the infant from Serena serves to protect her from unequivocal shame.

The appearance of Matilde, the wife of Sir Bruin (Spenser indulges here in elaborate wordplay on "bears," "barren," "bearing," etc.), relieves Calepine and further mitigates Serena's sexual guilt. In contrast to Serena, Matilde suffers sexually derived shame not because of bearing a child but because she has *failed* to do so. According to 1 Tim. 2:5, women were "saved" through childbearing; this was true in a social as well as a spiritual sense for women among the landed elite. This group, in fact, experienced "a mean level of childlessness of almost 19 per cent" between 1590 and 1740,[49] and several of Spenser's female contemporaries, like Matilde, probably experienced despair at their inability to present their husbands with an heir. Margaret Dakins Hoby, for example, describes fasting and "begging of the Lord that blissinge wch yet I want."[50] Men, too, recorded their disappointment and concern when their wives failed to conceive, which suggests that the emotional pressure placed on barren women, intentional or not, must have been intense. Some of Matilde's dejection certainly seems to stem from the blame imposed upon her by her husband.

However, Matilde does not condemn herself for barrenness.

She first blames the heavens, which "Haue not vouchsaft to graunt vnto vs *twaine*/ The gladfull blessing of posteritie" (6.4.31, my emphasis). Here she seems to assert the reciprocity of their infertility, and her complaint about "The good Sir *Bruin*, growing farre in yeares; / Who thinkes from me his sorrow all doth rize" (6.4.33) may imply that his age could be more to blame than her womb. Happy to be of service, the courteous (and immensely grateful) Calepine relinquishes the boy to his eager foster mother, whose name, Hamilton points out, alludes to Tasso's Matilda, who reared Rinaldo, and to Merlin's mother. Making explicit the parallel between her nurturing office and that of the mother bear, who, it was popularly assumed, licked her cubs into shape after they had been expelled from the womb ("a little congealed blood like a lumpe of flesh, which afterwarde the old one frameth with her tongue to her owne likenes," Topsell, 37),[51] Calepine attests to her power over the child's character,

> in which ye may enchace
> What euer formes ye list thereto apply,
> Being now soft and fit them to embrace;
> Whether ye list him traine in cheualry,
> Or noursle vp in lore of learn'd Philosophy.
>
> (6.4.35)

Perhaps more importantly, Matilde shapes not only the child, but also Sir Bruin's perception: "she so wisely did, / And with her husband vnder hand so wrought, / That when that infant vnto him she brought, / She made him thinke it surely was his owne" (6.4.38). Leaving her methods to conjecture, the text hints at a benign female duplicity and power ("vnder hand"). The ultimate effect of this transference of the baby from (presumably) Serena to the bear to Calepine to Matilde to Sir Bruin serves to deflect shame away from the two women and onto the blissfully ignorant, semi-cuckolded Sir Bruin. Matilde's determination to convince Bruin that the baby is his own is a deceitful act that, like Calidore's selective defense of Priscilla, is a concession to the preservation of feminine honor. In fact, Serena's disgrace proves to be the means of obliterating Matilde's disgrace—the plot momentarily shifts its focus from a woman trying to prevent the public from knowing that she has borne a child to a woman trying to convince the public that she has done so.

The sexual shame associated with childbirth suffered by Serena (and Hermione) profoundly alters the nature of their social relationships. Although Matilde's honor is, presumably, fully restored (she leaves the stigma of barrenness behind her in the woods), Serena's recovery from disgrace is never completely accomplished. Furthermore, she knows nothing of the female companionship experienced by those women among Spenser's readership who gave birth.[52] With only the bear and the salvage man to act as midwife—"He reared her vp from the bloudie ground, / And sought by all the meanes, that he could best / Her to recure out of that stony swound, / And staunch the bleeding of her dreary wound"—and as solicitous surrogate "husband,"[53] Serena decides to "wend abrode, though feeble and forlorne" (or, as Hermione complains of her own enforced movement, before she has recovered "strength of limit"). After the baby has been given to Matilde, Serena moves toward partial recovery. Arthur conducts her, along with the wounded Timias, to the hermit's chapel, which, with its ivy-decked roof, "Seem'd like a groue," a suitable holy counterpart to the sexually tainted groves where Serena and Timias sustained their initial wounds. These are "now much more increast, / For want of taking heede vnto the same." As the hermit explores the wounds, he finds that

> they had festred priuily,
> And ranckling inward with vnruly stounds,
> The inner parts now gan to putrify,
> That quite they seem'd past helpe of surgery,
> And rather needed to be disciplinde
> With holesome reede of sad sobriety,
> To rule the stubborne rage of passion blinde.
>
> (6.6.5)

The hermit "the art of words knew wondrous well," which suggests that his "holesome reede" serves as an analogue of Spenser's advice to the gentle readers of his poetic courtesy literature. Yet the message to female readers is by no means unambiguous. His advice seems to resemble that of Vives in *The Instruction of a christen woman*:

> First learne your outward sences to refraine
> From things, that stirre vp fraile affection;
> Your eies, your eares, your tongue, your talk restraine
> From that they most affect, and in due termes containe.
> . . . .
>   auoide the occasion of the ill:
> For when the cause, whence euill doth arize,

> Remoued is, th'effect surceaseth still.
> Abstaine from pleasure, and restraine your will,
> Subdue desire, and bridle loose delight,
> Vse scanted diet, and forbeare your fill,
> Shun secresie, and talke in open sight:
> So shall you soone repaire your present euill plight.
>
> (6.6.7; 14)

The hermit addresses Timias as well as Serena, which implies some awareness that the double standard for male and female behavior is injust. The hermit's advice is, however, oddly ineffectual, as if Spenser might be doubting the efficacy of his own work, or his audience's willingness to comply. Timias lapses back into his characteristically rash defense of damsels in distress, and the hermit's lecture proves an insufficient churching ceremony, the ritual that marked a woman's "purification" (a residual, Catholic notion) and her reintegration into society (the preferred Protestant interpretation). The hermit's inadequately performed churching ceremony is soon upstaged by its antithesis, the cannibal ritual during which Serena is stripped and laid *on* the altar rather than kneeling, veiled, *at* the altar.

Serena's ensuing encounters with Mirabella and the cannibals suggest that she either fails to negotiate the maze of feminine honor with sufficient care or that the world beyond the hermit's cell is simply unable to reconcile active female sexuality with honor. Whipped by Disdain and Scorn, Mirabella has committed the crime of withholding herself from men to an extreme; she is punished for not accepting and returning their love, whereas Serena may not have restrained herself sufficiently, highlighting the delicate (or rather, impossible) balance the lady was expected to maintain in dispensing her romantic favors.[54] The narrator pointedly warns female readers not to overdo their chaste reluctance:

> Ye gentle Ladies, in whose soueraine powre
> Loue hath the glory of his kingdome left,
> And th'hearts of men, as your eternall dowre,
> In yron chaines, of liberty bereft,
> Deliuered hath into your hands by gift;
> Be well aware, how ye the same doe vse,
> That pride doe not to tyranny you lift;
> Least if men you of cruelty accuse,
> He from you take that chiefedome, which ye doe
>   abuse.

And as ye soft and tender are by kynde,
Adornd with goodly gifts of beauties grace,
So be ye soft and tender eeke in mynde;
But cruelty and hardnesse from you chace,
That all your other praises will deface,
And from you turne the loue of men to hate.
Ensample take of *Mirabellaes* case,
Who from the high degree of happy state,
Fell into wretched woes, which she repented late.[55]

(6.8.1–2)

Yet Serena, with "soft and tender" mind, has yielded to Calepine and has suffered as a consequence. By advocating female sexual generosity in his authorial intrusion and contradicting rather than underscoring the hermit's advice to Serena, Spenser seems to sympathize with a woman's tendency to err on the side of passion rather than of caution. However, Serena's encounter with Mirabella serves to undermine the hermit's seemingly straightforward injunction to abstain from romantic entanglements and to heighten Serena's fears of committing social indiscretions rather than to assuage them.

Serena has been so sensitized to sexual shame that she flees when she sees Mirabella, "afeard / Of villany to be to her inferd: / So fresh the image of her former dread, / Yet dwelling in her eye, to her appeard" (6.8.31). Eve Rachele Sanders views Serena as a female reader of courtesy literature who has learned to apply Mirabella's disgrace to herself.[56] Yet even as she defines herself in opposition to Mirabella and behaves with apparent circumspection by fleeing the contagious presence of the "evil" female exemplar, Serena places herself in an extremely vulnerable sexual position. Serena only alights from her horse when she sees "nought, / Which doubt of daunger to her offer mought," but her vigilance is rewarded by being attacked by cannibals.

Although she is rescued from death by Calepine, Serena's honor has sustained a significant blow. She ends where she began—with Calepine in the compromising setting of a forest grove. Now, however, her position is much more degraded and physically vulnerable than it was when she was first introduced. Alienated from her lover (whom she fails to recognize in the dark) and from her own body, Serena's shame in being naked recalls the postlapsarian Eve, who also suffers transformation from a carefree pastoral-romance lover into a sexual temptress in a fallen, condemned world.[57] Spenser's text points insistently to women's difficulties in reconciling sexual desire with the protection of her person and her honor, and Serena seems more confused than ever about the womanly role she is supposed to enact:

> So inward shame of her vncomely case
> She did conceiue, through care of womanhood,
> That though the night did couer her disgrace,
> Yet she in so vnwomanly a mood,
> Would not bewray the state in which she stood.
>
> (6.8.51)

Hamilton describes Serena as being "withdrawn, ungrateful, and unloving," an unhappy state deriving from her "conceiving" first a child, then shame that is never fully erased. Serena's experience, as well as that of most of the other heroines discussed in this chapter, seems to suggest that the "care of womanhood" involves a constant attention to the construction of feminine honor and devotion to concealment of female sexuality and its effects, a sobering corrective to the sexual freedom enjoyed in Book 3's Garden of Adonis.

Hermione's social relationships are also radically recalibrated, yet in contrast to Serena, her disrupted childbirth rites are finally completed. Her initial woman's month having been brutally interrupted, she goes on to experience an extended, sixteen-year period of liminality and "lying-in" accompanied, the text implies, only by women. The effects of this may be seen in the statue scene: she speaks lovingly to her daughter, whom Paulina refers to as "our" Perdita, but embraces her husband in silence. Countering the earlier trial scene, a public ritual of shaming rather than of purification, the statue scene reenacts not only the delayed churching ceremony, complete with gossips and veil, but also the birth.[58] The "midwife" Paulina at last delivers Perdita to her chaste mother, thus reversing the earlier delivery of Perdita into the hands of the Shepherd, overseen by a savage bear and a sexually suspect Hermione.

Spenser's and Shakespeare's bears are, finally, multivalent creatures associated with women's sexual appetite and the act of generation. Nevertheless, they exercise a certain rough justice and represent the means by which female characters achieve a limited or temporary recuperation of their social reputation. These depictions of the "pleasing punishment that women bear" (*Comedy of Errors*, 1.1.46), by combining a traditional ro-

mance topos with allusions to contemporary social practice, acknowledge the difficulty, and often the cost, of diffusing the
sexual shame associated with childbearing.

The public construction of female chastity is nowhere more evident than at the two tournaments featuring Florimell's cestus
as the prize. The "precious relicke" is stored in an ark of gold
that "bad eyes might it not prophane"; it is "A gorgeous girdle,
curiously embost / With pearle and precious stone, worth many
a marke" (4.4.15), a description suggesting the "jewel" of virginity as well as the prizes typically awarded at Elizabethan and Jacobean tournaments.[59] For the symbolism of the cestus Spenser
draws on classical epic and Renaissance epic romance, but he
revises the Homeric description equating the cestus with Venus's beauty, seductiveness, and sexual passion so that it also
represents the virtue of chastity, or sexual restraint. Tasso's use
of the girdle or zone motif to represent Armida's sexual desires
in *Gerusalemme Liberata* 16.24–25 is much closer to the Homeric source in tone, emphasizing female sexuality as a temptation and its negative effect on the hero rather than sexuality as a
potential virtue that, when properly directed, could bring honor
to a heroine.

Spenser explicitly reinvokes the cestus myth in such a way as
to connect sexual pleasure with marriage, as Erasmus had done
earlier in his 1523 colloquy "Marriage." Eulalia, in the process of
advising Xanthippe to be agreeable to her husband, refers to
Venus as the "patroness of married love" and owner of a girdle
that arouses love. According to Eulalia's moral gloss, the myth
"teaches that a wife must take every precaution to be pleasing to
her husband in sexual relations, in order that married love may
be rekindled and renewed and any annoyance or boredom driven
out of mind."[60] The cestus is a highly allusive symbol, recalling
not only the Venus myth but also the tradition treating the Virgin's belt as a relic of fertility;[61] the legend of Hercules claiming
the girdle of the amazon Hippolyta and its Renaissance interpretation as signifying the triumph of virtue over lust; and the tradition of the husband unloosing his bride's cestus to release her
from virginity on the wedding night, a tradition Sir Thomas Elyot
refers to in the story of Titus and Gysippus: "the custome is, that,
notwithstanding anye ceremonie done at the time of the Spousi-
alles, the mariage notwithstandinge is not confirmed, untill at
night, that the husband putteth a ring on the finger of his wife,
and unloseth hir girdell. . . . [and] undoe hir gyrdel of virginitie."[62]

Erasmus's emphasis, however, is on the husband's sexual pleasure and the good wife's dutiful compliance.

Spenser hints at a similar conduct-manual meaning in the implicit parallel between wife and horse at Florimell's marriage
tournament. Significantly, Guyon's "Golden Bridle," his horse
Brigadore, is restored at the same time that Florimell's golden
girdle is restored to her. This provides a moment of comic relief,
but it also bears on one of the tournament's central concerns:
control of female sexuality within marriage. The Greek romance
motif of recognition of a long-lost love is here applied to Guyon's
horse, with whom he is joyously reunited once the telltale birth-
mark is identified. (Guyon recalls "Within his mouth a blacke
spot doth appeare, / Shapt like a horses shoe" just as Pastorella
will later be identified by the rose on her breast.) The joint restoration of Brigadore to Guyon and Florimell to Marinell suggests
a play on the woman's experience of the "bridal" as a time to direct her sexual desire toward her husband but otherwise "bridle" her passions, just as Brigadore breaks his bands and frisks
with pleasure, but only in the company of his master. William
Whately makes the comparison more overtly in a 1617 wedding
sermon entitled *A Bride Bush*: the good wife "submits her-selfe
with quietness, cheerfully, even as a well-broken horse turns at
the least turning, stands at the least check of the riders bridle,
readily going and standing as he wishes that sits upon his
backe."[63] Vulcan's original intention in fashioning the girdle, "to
bind lasciuious desire, / And loose affections streightly to res-
traine," after his wife has been initiated into the pleasures of the
marriage bed, suggests that all women have rampant sexual desires in need of restraint.

The translation of the cestus into such quotidian terms reflects
Spenser's technique of moving with ease among genres in an effort to reconcile romance and courtesy literature and create a
synthesis of chastity and marital love. Yet although Guyon's chivalric honor is unambiguously restored along with his *cheval*, the
restoration of Florimell's honor is less certain. Equated with the
jewel of a woman's virginity, the cestus also possesses magical
properties that presumably assist the owner to practice chastity.
This characteristic, however, blurs the degree of agency attributed to both wearer and girdle:

> That girdle gaue the vertue of chast loue,
> And wiuehood true, to all that did it beare;
> But whosoeuer contrarie doth proue,

> Might not the same about her middle weare,
> But it would loose, or else a sunder teare.
> Whilome it was (as Faeries wont report)
> Dame *Venus* girdle, by her steemed deare,
> What time she vsd to liue in wiuely sort;
> But layd aside, when so she vsd her looser sport.
>
> (4.5.3)

To what extent does the cestus impart the virtue, and to what extent must the wearer will herself to be chaste in order to wear the cestus? Where is female chastity ultimately to be located: in the woman, in some external control symbolized by the cestus, or merely in the perception of the beholder? The meaning of the cestus is notoriously unstable; it functions as a symbol of shame as well as of honor.

Despite the narrator's unmistakably didactic intent, indicated in the inexpressibility topos of 5.3.3 ("To tell the glorie of the feast that day . . . / Were worke fit for an Herauld, not for me: / But for so much as to my lot here lights, / That with this present treatise doth agree, / True vertue to aduance, shall here recounted bee"), the cause of "true vertue" is not especially well served in either tournament. Spenser transforms the chivalric romance tradition pairing the most beautiful woman with the most valorous man ("And of them all she that is fayrest found, / Shall haue that golden girdle for reward, / And of those Knights who is most stout on ground, / Shal to that fairest Ladie be prefard") into a chastity contest. In 4.5.1, he inserts an unusual criterion: she "That fairest is and from her faith will neuer swerue" should win the golden girdle. Yet several of the ladies elevate the importance of beauty over virtue and desire to win the girdle "for glorie vaine, / And not for vertuous vse, which some doe tell / That glorious belt did in it selfe containe, / Which Ladies ought to loue, and seeke for to obtaine."

By staging a showdown between Amoret and the palpably unchaste False Florimell, Spenser attempts to reaffirm Amoret's purity, but the outcome of the tournament precludes any certainty about her preeminence in the public eye as both the most beautiful and most chaste. The False Florimell's beauty serves to distort and unsettle previous judgments: "For all afore that seemed fayre and bright, / Now base and contemptible did appeare, / Compar'd to her, that shone as Phebes light, / Amongst the lesser starres in euening cleare" (4.5.14). The False Florimell is compared, ironically, to the chaste moon, but any semblance of chastity she manages to convey is belied by the fact that the girdle will not stay on her waist. As often as she fastens it around her, it "disclos'd," suggesting not only the literal loosening but also the act of disclosure, of communicating the wearer's lack of chastity. Even when given such an obvious sign, most of the male judges prefer to redefine chastity and the terms of the contest to justify their preference for the False Florimell. Contrary to expectations, Amoret does not win the contest unequivocally, a result that underscores the theatrical nature of chastity.

The False Florimell constitutes a threat to Florimell's honor as well. The witch's masterpiece confuses not only the crowd but also the bridegroom; Florimell's shame at Braggadocchio's slight is intensified by her husband's reaction. Dumbfounded, Marinell "long astonisht stood, ne ought he sayd, / Ne ought he did, but with fast fixed eies / He gazed still vpon that snowy mayd" (5.3.18). The beautifully chaste and the beautifully unchaste are initially indistinguishable. The confusion perhaps derives from Florimell's not unproblematic relation to the cestus. She is described as treasuring the cestus, understanding it to represent her honor ("That goodly belt was *Cestus* hight by name, / And as her life by her esteemed deare," 4.5.6), yet Florimell abandons the cestus when, ironically, trying her utmost to preserve her virginity. Although Hamilton's suggestion that she has lost her maidenhead (Satyrane discovers the cestus when the hyena is devouring her palfrey) seems a bit extreme, certainly the state of the golden girdle, "Distaynd with durt and bloud" (3.8.49), connotes some degree of defilement. Far from providing visible proof of sexual abstinence (as pregnancy provides undeniable proof of sexual activity), the cestus fails to resolve the interpretive dilemma presented by the errant romance lady.

Artegall finally sets the two Florimells side by side, "Of both their beauties to make paragone, / And triall, whether should the honor get," and Florimell triumphs, but perhaps only because of her superior show of femininity. She is an attentive reader of courtesy literature, one who is

> Adorn'd with honor and all comely grace:
> Whereto her bashfull shamefastnesse ywrought
> A great increase in her faire blushing face;
> As roses did with lillies interlace.

For of those words, the which that boaster threw,
She inly yet conceiued great disgrace.

(5.3.23)

At last the impostor vanishes, leaving behind "th'emptie girdle, which about her wast was wrought." Yet how is it that the girdle has remained around the False Florimell's waist long enough to cause such confusion, when earlier it invariably loosened and fell off? How, in fact, has the False Florimell come to be in possession of the girdle, a fact that seems to contradict the properties of the cestus? Presumably it should not have remained around the False Florimell's waist:

> Full many Ladies often had assayd,
> About their middles that faire belt to knit;
> And many a one suppos'd to be a mayd:
> Yet it to none of all their loynes would fit,
> Till *Florimell* about her fastned it.
> Such power it had, that to no womans wast
> By any skill or labour it would sit,
> Vnlesse that she were continent and chast,
> But it would lose or breake, that many had disgrast.

(5.3.28)

This ambiguity about the authenticity or consistency of the cestus's virtues inevitably detracts from Florimell's vindication. The False Florimell has left the girdle "empty" in that its meaning has been distorted, or at least open to question. Readers have been left similarly uncertain about the moral status of Spenser's other errant heroines, female exemplars of chastity whose ability to combine virtue and sexual desire is simultaneously affirmed and denied. Amoret's, Serena's, and Florimell's sexual virtue is constantly interrogated and judged, interpreted and reinterpreted—by themselves, by other characters, by readers—and Spenser's text defers any definitive defense or condemnation. In creating such a Protean text, Spenser enables his royal and non-royal female readers alike to lay claim to the poem. In addition, the slippage that occurs between genres forces readers to question the validity of a variety of discourses that present conflicting constructions of feminine virtue. A similar instability marks Spenser's depiction of the piety practiced by female readers, the focus of my final chapter.

6

Chaste but Not Silent:
Reading and Female Piety

> Neither a vertuous mother ought to refuse lerninge on the boke, but nowe and than study and rede holy and wyse mens bokes, and though she do it not for hir owne sake, at the leaste wyse for hir children, that shee maie teache them, and make them good.
>
> —Juan Luis Vives, *The Instruction of a christen woman*

> *Timothy* was nourished up in Godlines by his Mother and Grandmother, godly nursses, therefore he followed the doctrine of godlines continually.
>
> —William Kempe, *The Education of children in learning* (1588)

The ornamental head- and foot-pieces used in Thomas Bentley's *The Monument of Matrones* (1582) were also used in the 1609 and 1611 folio editions of Spenser's *Faerie Queene*.[1] Yet the texts are linked substantively as well as visually, both attempting to inscribe piety in their female readers. My final chapter explores how the various devotional discourses women read (and were read by) may have informed early modern readings of Book 1, Spenser's legend of holiness. Drawing on residual Catholic narratives of saints' lives as well as John Foxe's accounts of pious women martyrs in his *Actes and Monuments* (1563), Spenser promotes a Protestant female heroic ideal by rendering Una not only as a chivalric romance lady but also as the godly wife celebrated by religious apologists. Moreover, the extensive process of the Redcrosse Knight's sanctification is largely overseen by nurturing maternal figures who function as teachers as well as readers in ways consistent with the prescriptions found in didactic literature of the period. In fact, the preponderance of spiritual authorities in Book 1—Una, Fidelia, Speranza, Charissa, and Mercie—are female. Multiple allegorical meanings have been

218

suggested for these characters. Charissa, for example, can be read politically as another image of Elizabeth I (described by John Jewel as "the only nurse and mother" of the English church), iconographically as an image of *caritas*, and theologically as the Church, wisdom, or word of God (the Church, according to Leonard Wright, "hath nursed you with her breasts, and brought you up in the knowledge of the truth").[2]

Here, however, I want to read Spenser's sacred and profane images of "mother church" in the context of sixteenth- and early seventeenth-century arguments that godly women should nurture their children both physically, by breast-feeding, and metaphorically, by catechizing and teaching.[3] Both Catholic humanists and Protestant reformers urged women to assume responsibility for the spiritual education of their children, and as Juan Luis Vives observes in *The Instruction of a christen woman*, the extent of a mother's influence over her family could be considerable: the babe "takethe hir firste condycions and informacion of mynde, bye suche as shee hereth or seeth by hir mother. Therfore it lyethe more in the mother, than men wene, to make the condicions of the chyldren. For she maie make them whether she wyl, very good, or verye badde" (sig. Ff4v).[4] English church history bears this out—some of the most zealous Protestants and Catholic recusants were women, who promulgated their views, whether orthodox or heretical, through domestic authority.

Spenser's depiction of holy and unholy women in Book 1 exhibits a similar awareness of their power to further or hinder the work of the English Reformation and may even have been intended to inculcate Protestant piety in female readers. Yet, because both error and truth are allegorized in terms of maternal nurture, Spenser's treatment of his female figures also registers a more general ambivalence about women's authoritative role in the process of religious education and socialization, regardless of doctrinal position. In *A view of the state of Ireland* (1633), Spenser clearly articulates his concern about the potent linguistic and spiritual influence of Irish mothers: "the Childe that suckethe the milke of the nurse muste of necessitye learne his firste speache of her . . . . Comonlye the Childe takethe moste of his nature of the mother besides speache manners inclynacion. . . . what they receave once from them they will hardelye ever after forgoe."[5] Book 1 of *The Faerie Queene* explores in particular the problematic relationship of women to the word of God and the paradox that they might, in the process of humbly fulfilling their religious obligations, exercise excessive authority. The following discussion, then, will consider the ways in which Spenser not only valorizes female devotion but also undercuts or displaces the power he seems to celebrate. After providing a brief overview of early modern English attitudes toward the role literacy played in the practice of female spirituality, I will examine the ways women in Book 1 function as religious guides of both husbands and children, focusing in particular on Spenserian "wet nurses," those characters who literally dispense the "milke of the worde" (primarily Error and Charissa), and then on Redcrosse's "dry" nurses (Una, Fidelia, and Mercie). When describing good mothers as well as bad, however, the text seeks to contain the volatile interaction of women with the word as they perform their catechetical duties.

*   *   *

Sixteenth-century humanist educational reforms and the Protestant call for popular access to God's word generated numerous debates about the implications of women's literacy. Catholic and Protestant reformers alike recommended that women be encouraged to read for religious self-edification. Devotional works such as *The Monument of Matrones* specifically addressed female readers (according to Bentley, it was "more proper and peculiar for the private use of women than hertofore hath beene set out by anie") and urged them to emulate biblical models such as the virtuous woman of Proverbs 31, the five wise virgins of Matthew 25, and the woman clothed with the sun in Revelation.[6] John King notes that these biblical women served as "generic types symbolizing the literacy and pious devotion appropriate to all womankind."[7]

Reading the Bible was not universally promoted for women, however, and lower-class women were excluded particularly. In an attempt to control potentially subversive interpretations, the 1543 Parliamentary Act for the Advancement of True Religion and for the Abolishment of the Contrary prohibited the Bible "to all women, artificers, prentices, journeymen, servingmen, yeomen, husbandmen, and labourers." Gentlemen and gentlewomen were, however, permitted "to read and peruse, to their edifying, so that they did it quietly, without arguing, discussing, or expounding upon the Scripture."[8] Spenser's poem is consistent with this class distinction; those women in Book 1 who are praised most for their appropriation of biblical precepts are of high social standing—Una is the daughter of a king, and Caelia's daughters are gentlewomen of an elevated though unspecified social rank. Even works praising women's devotion suggested that their understanding of what they read would be subject to ecclesiastical authority. Emblematic of women's relation to the word, a woodcut in the 1570 edition of *Actes and Monuments* depicts a little boy, hobbyhorse in hand (a youthful Christian warrior-knight in training?), being led by a woman into a church where three women read the Bible, but *below* the pulpit where the minister is preaching.[9]

Proponents of female literacy also argued that it enabled women to provide their children and female servants with necessary instruction in the "mother" tongue. Vives urges, "lette hir learne for hir selfe alone and hir yonge childrene, or hir systers in our lorde" (sig. D1r) and elsewhere admonishes:

> if the mother can skyll of lernynge, let hir teache hir little children hir selfe, that they maie have all one, bothe for their mothers, their nourise, and their teacher. . . . Neither a vertuous mother ought to refuse lerninge on the boke, but nowe and than study and rede holy and wyse mens bokes, and though she do it not for hir owne sake, at the leaste wyse for hir children, that shee maie teache them, and make them good. (sig. Ff4v)

Studying "wyse mens bokes" would presumably ensure a safe transmission of doctrine from man to child without extensive, contaminating female mediation, and translation of religious texts was one of the most acceptable forms a woman's venturing into print could take.[10] Illustrating the way female literacy was co-opted by a domestic agenda is the epigram concluding Holland's translation of Plutarch's "Education of Children," which describes Eurydice of Hierapolis's maternal devotion:

For when her children were well growen: good ancient Lady shee,
And carefull mother tooke the paines to learne the A. B. C.
And in good letters did so far proceed, that in the end
She taught them those sage lessons which they might comprehend.[11]

Protestant divines as well as Catholic humanists advised that women should actively participate in the religious education of children. As Bentley comments, "It is the mothers office, as well as the fathers to instruct hir children with preceptes & good doctrine."[12] One of the most extended explanations of the efficacy of "mothers peculiar care in nurturing young children" is provided by William Gouge:

... let mothers especially note this point of *timely nurture*, as a point in peculiar appertaining to them. . . . Oft doth *Salomon* warne children not to forsake *their mothers teaching*. Whereby he implieth that mothers should teach their children especially while they are young: which duty so belongeth to a mother, as *Salomon* laieth the blame, and shame of the neglect thereof upon her: on the other side the honour of well nurturing children redoundeth especially to the mother. To this purpose is it, that the particular names of the mothers of the kings are recorded in Scripture: intimating thereby that mothers were a maine cause of the piety, or impiety of such children. *Salomon* and *Absolom* had both one father, but divers mothers. May we not well thinke that *Salomons* mothers care to instruct him was an especiall meanes of his piety: and that *Absoloms* mothers neglect of this duty, was some cause of his impiety? . . . Home-experience confirmeth as much: for if father and mother be of divers religions, most of the children will follow the mother. . . . Her precepts therefore and practise in that respect are best heeded by the children, and she hath the best opportunity to perswade them to what she liketh best: so as what they learne in their younger yeares, commonly they learne of their mothers: and that which then they learne, for the most part sticketh most close unto them, and is longest retained by them.[13]

Although he goes on to note that fathers share the responsibility of teaching young children, he devotes only a very brief paragraph to this topic, perhaps because it did not require arguing; the lengthier discussion of the role of mothers suggests that it needed more extensive justification. The Geneva Bible gloss on Deuteronomy 21:18 ("it is the mothers duetie also to instruct her children") bespeaks a similar necessity.

Extant records of Renaissance Englishwomen's reading suggest that much of it (whether readers were Catholic, Anglican, or "Puritan") was put to the devotional and instructional uses prescribed by moralists. Anne Clifford, for example, read the Bible or heard it read often, in addition to such works as Augustine's *City of God*, "Parson's resolutions," and "Mr *Saragol's* Book of the Supplication of the Saints."[14] Much of this reading was communal, and it prepared women to supervise the spiritual education of younger members of the household, as Lady Margaret Hoby did, although she had no children of her own. Hoby records reading the Bible to a Mrs. Ormston as well as reading to her "workwemen," her mother, and a sick maid. On several occasions, she "read of the book of marters" and heard it read aloud by one of her maids while she worked. Hoby's duty took her beyond her immediate household; she notes that she "reed and talked with a yonge papest maide," presumably with the intention of converting her.[15] The "religious course" of Hoby's life in both "publike and private callings" was noted on her death monument, as was her commitment to "propagatinge his holy word in all places where she had power."[16]

Hoby's proselytizing zeal was not atypical; in fact, women seem to have played significant roles not only in keeping Catholicism alive (practiced covertly within households, it depended a great deal on the support of recusant women)[17] but also in furthering reform movements throughout the century. For example, women served as active religious agents in the proliferation of early sixteenth-century Lollardy. Claire Cross suggests that "considerably more women than the churchmen suspected acquired the ability to read in order to peruse lollard books. . . . As mothers and grandmothers they had unique authority over impressionable children and far more women than have been recorded may have been responsible for helping educate succeeding generations in heresy."[18] Anglican apologist Richard Hooker acknowledged women's spiritual efficacy and enthusiasm in serving "as instruments and helps in the cause"; he notes that Calvinistic ministers encouraged female proselytes, because "Apter they are through the eagerness of their affection, that maketh them which way soever they take, diligent in drawing their husbands, children, servants, friends and allies the same way."[19] Once firmly established in the latter part of the sixteenth century, however, the reformed church became less tolerant of women's spiritual assertiveness.[20] Given the inherent conflict between the theological equality of male and female souls promised in Gal. 3:28 and the practice of faith in a patriarchal society, *The Faerie Queene*'s contradictory messages extolling and decrying women's catechetical power are perhaps to be expected.

Although some opportunities for female autonomy and leadership were curtailed by the dissolution of religious communities during the 1530s, women were still able to maintain supportive networks and form smaller female communities within individual households. Many aristocratic women exercised significant control over the spiritual as well as material governance of their estates. The House of Holiness, a notably feminine domain, is a fictional analogue for various aspects of these households and communities. The porter Humility, the franklin Zele, the squire Reuerence, and the groom Obedience are all male, but they

serve Caelia, "the Ladie of the place" (1.10.8), as subordinates.
The ancient house is

> Renowmd throughout the world for sacred lore,
> And pure vnspotted life: so well they say
> It gouernd was, and guided euermore,
> Through wisedome of a matrone graue and hore.
>
> (1.10.3)

Caelia's epithet as "matrone sage" (1.10.11), her hospitality, and
her charitable acts demonstrate her adherence to the Pauline requirements for the exemplary pious woman: she will be "wel reported of for good workes: if she have nourished her childre[n],
if she have lodged the stra[n]gers, if she have washed the Saintes
fete, if she have ministred unto them which were in adversitie, if
she were co[n]tinually give[n] unto everie good worke" (1 Tim.
5:10). Significantly, like Una (and most of the other women in
Book 1), Caelia is quite verbal, launching into a veritable homily
on humanity's errant ways (1.10.10) when the travelers arrive.

Caelia's religious zeal has not prevented her from doing her
worldly duty by her daughters in arranging suitable marriages
for each of them (*"Fidelia* and *Speranza* virgins were, / Though
spousd, yet wanting wedlocks solemnize; / But faire *Charissa* to
a louely fere / Was lincked, and by him had many pledges dere,"
1.10.4). Most importantly, however, Caelia is praised for her careful religious training of her daughters, who have been "well
vpbrought / In goodly thewes, and godly exercise" and are "most
sober, chast, and wise." Their glad reception of Una contrasts
markedly with the irreverence and lack of hospitality shown her
when she visits the unholy house of the mother-daughter duo
Corceca and Abessa in canto 3.

Although Caelia and her daughters will take or have taken husbands (thus distinguishing this Protestant community from its
Catholic counterparts), male authority is conspicuously absent—
Caelia is either a widow or symbolically married to Christ (as
Hamilton suggests), Charissa's husband never appears, and Fidelia and Speranza are promised but not yet married. Protestant
divines such as William Gouge, John Dod, and Robert Cleaver
concede that women may take charge of household devotions if
their husbands are unable to do so. Gouge explains that a wife
can pray, read, teach, and otherwise assume devotional responsibilities "when her husband is absent, or negligent and carelesse, and will not himselfe doe them; or it may be, is not able to

doe them" (DD, 260). The inhabitants of the House of Holiness, then, observe contemporary behavioral guidelines and are technically subject to their absent husbands, but their unmediated relationship with God and their cooperative female community effectively undercut the standard Protestant model for household religious governance, which is based on a single male authority.

Caelia's attention to her daughters' education resembles that of the many early modern mothers who took their catechetical duties very seriously. When attesting to their own spiritual nurture, two women diarists sound no less hagiographic in their descriptions of their mothers than Spenser does in describing Caelia. Grace Sharington Mildmay recalls the high moral standards of both her parents, but particularly praises her female models—her governess, her grandmother, and especially her mother:

> My reverend mother Lady Sharington . . . was as an angel of God unto me when she first put me in mind of Christ Jesus and examined me in my tender age what were my thoughts when I was alone. And therewithall, instructed me continually, when I was alone to remember God, to call upon him. . . .

> All my mother's counsels have I laid up in my mind, almost these fifty years. . . . Mine own mother gave me a good example herein, for every morning she would withdraw herself alone and spend an hour in meditation and prayers to God, with her face all blubbered with tears. . . . My grandmother, the mother of my mother, was . . . also a godly and religious woman. She delighted in the word of God and spent much time therein all her days. . . . The same God which my mother was so diligent and careful to plant in my heart hath never forsaken me from my childhood unto this day.[21]

By recording these reflections in order to instruct her daughter, Mary, and Mary's children, Lady Mildmay herself enacts the mother's role of spiritual guide.

Anne Clifford also comments gratefully on the devoted instruction given her by her mother, Margaret Russell, the Countess of Cumberland (one of the dedicatees of Spenser's Fowre Hymnes). Anne is described in an inscription on a family portrait at Appleby Castle as being "blessed by the education and tender care of a most affectionate deare and excellent Moother, who brought hir up in as much Religion, goodnes, and knowledg, as hir seakts and yeares weare capabell of." Late in life Anne proclaimed that she had been "bourne, bred and educated (in the Church of England) by my blessed mother."[22] Self-proclaimed daughter Aemilia Lanyer also pays tribute to the countess as the spiritual leader of the female community at Cookeham in *Salve Deus Rex Judaeorum*. Utilizing the common trope of mother/teacher-as-nurse, Elizabeth Cary's daughter also praises her mother's devotion: "nor was her care of her children less [than care for ordering the household], to whom she was so much a mother that she nursed them all herself, but only her eldest son (whom her father took from her to live with him from his birth), and she taught 3 or 4 of the eldest."[23] The tenets set forth in devotional literature and Spenser's poem guided many other aristocratic women of the late sixteenth and early seventeenth century. Lady Anne Bacon, for example, provided her sons with moral instruction through numerous letters written throughout her lifetime; Lettice, Lady Falkland catechized her maids daily; and Anne Fitzwilliam "took the most care of the educatyon" of her two sons and three daughters.[24]

The role of spiritual guide thus seems to have been embraced enthusiastically by many early modern Englishwomen, perhaps because this was one area in which they could openly excel.[25] Robert Cleaver, in *A Godlie Forme of Householde Government* (1598), which is dedicated not only to several men but "also to their religious and vertuous wives," certainly confirms this: "if at this day a due survey shuld bee taken of all men and women throughout her Majesties dominions, . . . there would bee found in number moe women that are faithful, religious and vertuous, then men."[26] Cleaver's remarks were not atypical. Puritan Daniel Rogers proclaims in *Matrimoniall Honour* (1642) that "the Lord hath gifted and graced many women above some men, especially with holy affections."[27] Providing a rationale for women's propensity for piety, Richard Sibbes explains: "For the most part women have sweet affections to religion, and therein they oft goe beyond men. The reason is, Religion is especially seated in the affections: and they have sweet and strong affections. Likewise they are subject to weakenesse, and God delights to shew his *strength in weaknesse*. And thirdly, especially Child bearing-women, bring others into this life with danger of their own, therefore they are forced to a nearer communion with *God*, because so many children as they bring forth, they are in perill of their lives."[28] A less-flattering rationale, summarized by Maclean, claimed that women lacked "meditative powers (*contemplationis defectus*) which ma[de] them, with rustics and the simple-minded, well suited to devoutness, but ill suited to intellectual disciplines."[29] Such generalizations about women's piety (antici-pating Victorian sensibilities) may have been a projection, as seems to be the case with Vives's judgment ("The devocion of holy thynges moste agreeth for women. Therfore it is a farre worse syght of a woman, that aborreth devocion" (ICW, sig. K1v).[30]

Attesting to the ability of women to surpass men in the spiri-tual arena were the Catholic and Protestant accounts of female martyrs popular during the period. John King suggests that Spenser "fashioned a distinctively Protestant version of the saint's life in Book 1 of The Faerie Queene; he rejects many ele-ments in medieval lives of saints, notably those in The Golden Legend, which Protestants regarded as superstitious."[31] King may have been referring primarily to Redcrosse rather than to Una, whose participation in the discourse of the virgin martyr-saint serves as a corrective to the morally suspect errancy of the romance lady but foregrounds the suspect freedom character-istic of women members of the early church. The Protestant version of saints' lives was, of course, John Foxe's Actes and Monuments, which was highly recommended reading for women.[32]

Rather than merely assisting in the formation of St. George, Una demonstrates the ability of women to become saints in their own right and is thus reminiscent of holy wandering women, in particular St. Thecla, whose exploits are recorded in the New Testament Apocryphal Acts of Paul and Thecla.[33] After her con-version, the innocent Thecla seeks Paul "as a lamb in the wilder-ness," a figure Spenser also employs as he describes Una being accompanied by a "milke white lambe" ("So pure an innocent, as that same lambe, / She was in life and euery vertuous lore," 1.1.5).[34] Despite her purity (or perhaps because of it), Thecla, like Una, is subjected to sexual assault. As a punishment for resisting the advances of Alexander in Antioch she is condemned to do battle with wild animals, but when she is bound to a fierce lioness prior to the event, the lioness licks her feet. Similarly, Una's lion "kist her wearie feet, / And lickt her lilly hands with fawning tong" (1.3.6). When Thecla is finally placed in the arena with rag-ing lions and bears, the lioness first lies down at her feet and then kills a bear who is attacking the saintly lady. The lioness also kills a violent lion, even though she dies in the attempt, just as Una's lion sacrifices himself in defending her against the assault of Sansloy (1.3.42).

Desirous of baptism, Thecla throws herself into a pool full of sharks, but they are struck dead while she is surrounded by a cloud of fire. The cloud protects her body against physical violence and her nakedness from the viewers' curious gaze in a triumphant conjunction of spiritual power and feminine modesty. Like Thecla, Una strives to keep her body inviolate and hidden (especially her face), and yet reveal enough of her truth and beauty so that she can work the conversion of others, especially the satyrs. The nymphs resent Una for this beauty, whereas Thecla's story emphasizes female solidarity: Thecla is defended not by a lion but by a lioness, those specifically identified as taking Thecla's part in the battle and cheering at her deliverance are the women in the crowd, and she is adopted as a daughter by a woman whose servants Thecla then converts. Later she resorts to male disguise in order to pursue Paul and his teaching, but Una never compromises her femininity to this extent.

The travels and travails of Thecla and other virgin saints served to illustrate the admirable qualities of piety, zeal, and purity, but their rejection of male authority within the domestic realm, implicit in their dedication to virginity, could prove threatening in a culture that constructed femininity as passive and submissive. Thecla's pagan parents consider Paul a sorcerer who has enchanted their daughter with erotic charms (always a useful explanation for inexplicable female behavior, or autonomous decisions that fail to conform to social expectations for young women; Brabantio resorts to the same theory to explain Desdemona's love for Othello).[35] As Richard Halpern notes in a slightly different context, wandering virgins tread a thin line between virtuous conformity and resistance to or subversion of societal norms: "Amazons and the nymphs of Diana also withold [*sic*] their sexuality in ways that make them independent, strange, and frightening to men. All of these figures mark the point at which virginity ceases to denote submission and begins to denote revolt, at which purification becomes danger. In all of these cases, moreover, active virginity is marked by wandering."[36] The threat Thecla's wandering represented (she was, in fact, condemned to be burned as an example to the young women in her city who might refuse marriage in order to devote themselves more fully to Christianity, but she was ultimately released) was gradually softened as she came to be revered for a more domesticated, less militant type of chastity. Troubled wives came to visit her shrine for help with their concerns about marriage, lovemaking, and fertility: "Outside the shrine, Thecla, the wild virgin girl bewitched by the message of Paul, could now be invoked, on her feast day, to give her blessing to an orderly hierarchy, in which every category of woman was expected to strive to maintain the purity appropriate to her state."[37]

Una is, on the surface, less of a threat to gender distinctions than Thecla, in that Spenser downplays the element of female solidarity in her story. Una acts as a docile, submissive daughter when restored to her parents, and unlike Thecla, who rejects her destined husband Thamyris to follow Paul, Una actively seeks marriage in the person of her soon-to-be betrothed, Redcrosse. In addition to her significance in the spiritual allegory as Ecclesia, the true spouse of Christ, the woman clothed with the sun in Revelation, and the bride searching for her husband in the Song of Songs, Una represents the virtuous Protestant wife. Setting an example for female readers in her solicitude for Redcrosse, Una nobly fulfills the third cause for matrimony listed in the 1559 Book of Common Prayer: "the mutual society, help, and comfort, that the one ought to have of the other, both in prosperity and adversity."[38]

Una fulfills in almost every respect the marriage prayer that the bride "may be [as] loving and amiable to her husband as Rachel, wise as Rebecca, faithful and obedient as Sarah, and in all quietness, sobriety, and peace be a follower of holy and godly matrons"[39] (with the possible exception of quietness). As Redcrosse's spiritual guide, Una must constantly teach him the tenets of a godly life, and her inner power and strength constantly threaten to diminish, or certainly qualify, his heroic stature as the knight of holiness.[40] Una achieves a precarious balance of wifely submission and strong leadership, but not without drawing attention to the autonomy exercised by women who read and taught God's word to their servants and children. Having successfully worked to redeem the soul of the man who must physically redeem her parents, Una is left silenced at the end of Book 1, awaiting the opportunity to resume her role as teacher and nurse in the rearing of godly children.

* * *

In the late sixteenth century, the term "to nurse" could be used in a general sense to indicate fostering or cherishing; often, the "wet" nurse, hired specifically to suckle a baby, was distinguished from the "dry" nurse, who was charged with the overall supervision of one or more children. New Testament nursing metaphors incorporate both senses of the word. A verse in Peter urges, "As new borne babes desire the syncere milke of the worde, that ye maye growe thereby" (1 Pet. 2:2), and Paul reminds the Thessalonians, "we were gentle among you, even as a nource cherisheth her children" (1 Thess. 2:7). Clearly not gender specific, these metaphors could be appropriated by anyone formally charged with the spiritual instruction of others, including male heads of households, ecclesiastics, or the monarch (James I referred to himself as the "nurse-father" of the English church, and the Geneva Bible gloss on 1 Thess. 2:7 likens apostolic service to that of the "tender mother which nourceth her children, and thinketh no office to vile for her childre[n]s sake"). Mothers were, however, singled out for the task of caring for the very young, and the metaphorical significance of the nursing image was often conflated with the literal practice in sixteenth- and early seventeenth-century descriptions of virtuous mothers. (Allegorical and literal readings of literary exemplars were often coterminous. Despite Bentley's note on Gomer's daughter Loruhamah in Hosea 1—"reade this mistically"—he proceeds to treat her as a negative exemplar of condemned sexual behavior.)[41]

Whether the decision to put infants from aristocratic families out to nurse was made by husbands or wives or both, it conflicted with the ideological imperative, promulgated by moralists throughout the period, that women should nurse their own children.[42] These authors reaffirmed the classical notion that a woman imparted, along with her milk, her own character to a nursing child. Sir Thomas Elyot refers to this notion in *The Boke Named the Governour*: "First they, unto whome the bringing up of such children apperteineth, they ought against the time as their mother shall bee of them delyvered, to be sure of a nourse, which should be of no servile condition, or vyce notable. For as some auntient writers do suppose, oftentimes the childe sucketh the vyce of his nourse, with the milke of hir pap."[43] Vives contends that "we sucke out of our mothers teate togither with the milk not only love but also condicions & disposicions" (*ICW*, sig. B1v). Sir Thomas More pointedly describes Utopian women as eager to suckle their children and even valorizes nursing over giving birth:

> Babies are always breast-fed by their mothers, except when death or illness makes this impossible, in which case the Styward's wife takes immediate steps to find a wet-nurse. This presents no problem, for any woman who's in a position to do so will be only too glad to volunteer for the job. You see, such acts of mercy are universally admired, and the child itself will always regard her as its real mother.[44]

More's friend Erasmus devoted an entire colloquy to the subject. In "The New Mother" (1526), Erasmus's persona Eutrapelus urges Fabulla, who has sent out her newborn son to be nursed, to fulfill her Christian duty by feeding the child herself.[45] Expounding on the promise in 1 Tim. 2:15 that women will be saved through childbearing, Eutrapelus argues, "You haven't fulfilled the duty of a childbearer unless you've first formed the delicate little body of your son, then fashioned his equally pliable mind through good education." Thoroughly convinced, Fabulla enlists his help in trying to persuade her husband and parents that she indeed should feed the child. Fabulla's need to persuade her husband suggests that much of the criticism of vain or selfish non-nursing women might have been better directed to their husbands.[46] Gouge admits that "husbands for the most part are the cause that their wives nurse not their owne children" (DD, 518).

As a consequence of the desire of aristocratic parents for as many children as possible and the assumption that sexual intercourse tainted breast milk, many babies were put out to nurse. However, some husbands seem to have discouraged their wives from breast-feeding out of solicitude because it caused extreme discomfort; others (although the literature usually blames the women for such selfish concerns) may have wished to avoid domestic inconvenience and alterations to the female figure.[47] In Guazzo's *civile Conversation*, Anniball complains that "women at this daie are so curious of their comlinesse, or rather of their vanitie, that they hadde rather pervert the nature of their Children, then chaunge the fourme of their firme, harde, and round pappes" (143r–v). That women may not have been as vain as this censure implies and may instead have faced considerable male opposition to breast-feeding is made evident by the example of Anne Fitton Newdigate, whose first child was born in 1598. Her father wrote that he was "sory that yoʳ self will needs nurse her." Sir William Knollys, who stood as godparent, expressed similar negative sentiments, and a letter from Anne's mother hints at opposition from her son-in-law: "I have sent you a nourse's rewarde xˡˡ to by you a certle for my doughter [granddaughter]. . . . I longe to heer how all thinges abowte your new Charge goeth, for I parswaed myself that my sonne Newdygat wyll not go backe wᵗh hys worde. I pray God send you well to doe wᵗh it."[48] Elizabeth Cary intended even to nurse her prematurely born granddaughter along with her own child who had not yet been weaned, but the baby died.[49]

Later in the century numerous Protestant writers continued

to advocate that mothers nurse their own children and used willingness to nurse as a barometer of a woman's spiritual devotion. Anglican bishop Jeremy Taylor, for example, considers nursing as "the first, and most natural, and necessary instance of piety which mothers can show to their babes; a duty, from which nothing will excuse, but a disability, sickness, danger, or public necessity."[50] Writing in 1591, Henry Smith argues in *A Preparative to Mariage* that the "first dutie [of parents to children] is the mother's, that is to nurse her child at her owne breast, as Sara did Isaak."[51] Robert Cleaver concurs: "Amongst the particular duties that a Christian wife ought to performe in her familie, this is one: namely, that it belongeth to her to nurse her owne children, which to omit, and to put them forth to nursing, is both against the law of nature, and also against the will of God."[52] Catchily articulating the sentiment in rhyme, Thomas Tusser asserts: "Good huswives take paine, and doo count it good lucke, / to make their owne brest, their owne child to give suck."[53]

Piety may indeed have moved several women, even wealthy ones, to nurse their children; one in particular, Elizabeth Knyvet Clinton, Countess of Lincoln, recorded her regret that she had not nursed her sixteen children (few of whom survived) and addressed her treatise on the subject, *The countesse of Lincolnes nurserie* (1622) to her daughter-in-law Briget, who had chosen to do so. Clinton resembles the male moralists in interpreting the act of maternal nursing as a sign of female holiness, remarking that her contemporaries do not follow the Old Testament Sarah's example of nursing because they "want [lack] her virtue and piety"; later, Clinton claims that giving suck "is numbered as the first of the good works for which godly women should be well reported of." Yet Clinton's rhetoric is more personally inflected than that of male preachers; her peroration valorizes nursing as a devotional exercise and provides guidance for spiritual meditation, so that the mother, as well as the child, could benefit: "Think again how your babe crying for your breast, sucking heartily the milk out of it, and growing by it, is the Lord's own instruction, every hour, and every day, that you are suckling it, instructing you to show that you are his new-born babes, by your earnest desire after his word, and the sincere doctrine thereof, and by your daily growing in grace and goodness thereby."[54] Grace Sharington Mildmay also emphasizes the mother's spiritual profit as well as the child's: "it is a matter of great importance to bring up children unto God . . . and in the exercise of that teaching we

teach and instruct ourselves unto the same end, which is life everlasting."[55]

In the act of suckling their children, women could view themselves simultaneously as active, nurturing agents and as ingenu-
ous recipients of God's grace and word. When reading *The
Faerie Queene*, therefore, women might have found apt fictional
analogues in both Charissa and Redcrosse. The scriptural metaphor of nursing thus became for women far more than a metaphor; it became a means of asserting their spiritual self-worth
and authority, although it may also have subjected them more
fully to a limiting division of domestic labor. John Dod and Robert Cleaver describe nursing and teaching as inextricable in
their description of Timothy's mother Eunice:

> And this dutie the holy Ghost commandeth *Ep. 6, 4. Nurse them up
> in instruction and the feare of the Lord.* And this *Timothies* mother
> did put in practice. For, it is noted of her, that shee instructed *Timo-
> thie* in the scriptures from a childe, and that was a cause, why he was
> so holy a man: she was a Nurse to his soule, as well, as to his bodie,
> and gave him milke out of the breasts of the scripture so soon as he
> had done sucking her owne breasts. So that, as he waxed strong in
> naturall life, so also did he grow in knowledge and grace: and there-
> fore he became so excellent a man, and so worthie a preacher, and
> member of the Church, because his mother fed his soule, as well his
> bodie.[56]

Dod and Cleaver conspicuously omit the beginning of the verse
from Eph. 6:4 ("And ye, fathers, provoke not your childre[n] to
wrath: but bring them up in instruction and information of the
Lord") in their eagerness to promote the ideal of the nursing
mother. A visual emblem of this ideal, the memorial portrait of
Sir Henry Unton's life painted in 1596, depicts his mother, Lady
Anne Seymour, Countess of Warwick, seated with her child in her
arms. (Lady Anne was the daughter of Lord Edward Seymour,
the Lord Protector, and wife first of John Dudley, Earl of Warwick, then of Sir Edward Unton.) Although a nurse and two attendant gentlewomen are present, Lady Anne is positioned as
dispenser not only of noble blood (a large coat of arms is placed
above her head) and breast milk (her right breast seems to be
exposed) but also of learning and moral fortitude—Anne had received a humanist education, was tutored for three years by
Thomas Cranmer, and engaged in correspondence with Calvin.
A sermon preached at Farington in Berkshire, the seventeene

of Februarie 1587 (1591) characterizes her as a "noble lady, a faithful wife, a virtuous woman, and a godly widow."[57]

Spenser, however, represents the implicit dangers of entrusting children's souls to their mother's training by beginning his epic with the monstrous image of an anti-nurse, thus drawing attention to the assumption underlying the above admonitions: that the mother is, in fact, morally pure and possesses the spiritual truth that is to be imbibed by the child along with the breast milk. Initially, the encounter with Error, sought out by the foolhardy Redcrosse, seems to reverse gendered notions of spiritual errancy; women were assumed to be more easily led astray and susceptible to false prophets than were men. (For example, Hooker refers to the women supporting Calvinist preachers as "propense and inclinable to holiness" but as possessing "judgements . . . commonly weakest by reason of their sex.")[58] Una's cautiousness at the mouth of Error's cave ("the perill of this place / I better wot then you," 1.1.13) establishes the nurse's moral superiority. However, the encounter also suggests some ambivalence about acknowledging women as powerful agents of socialization who transmit to their children not only life but also fundamental elements of language, culture, and religion. The monster's body is ambiguously described as "Halfe like a serpent horribly displaide, / But th'other halfe did womans shape retaine, / Most lothsom, filthie, foule, and full of vile disdaine" (1.1.14). Loathsomeness seems to inhere not only in the creature's duplicitous, hybrid nature but also in "womans shape," which is the immediate antecedent of the string of pejorative adjectives. The orality of the encounter renders it not only particularly graphic (always a big hit in the classroom) but also allegorically significant in that it emphasizes Error's breasts and mouth, the orifices that impart the sustaining milk of the word or the poison of error. The fluids that emanate from Error are all perverted images of the natural and nourishing maternal body. Instead of being sustained by milk, her thousand young ones suck first on her poisonous dugs and then on the "cole black bloud" that gushes forth from her headless body, only to burst: "well worthy end / Of such as drunke her life, the which them nurst" (1.1.26). Error illustrates the abuse of the mother's power to shape her children morally. She nurses them daily (as the mother was to catechize her children daily), but with poison, thus instilling tainted religion in their souls, and she dies in a grotesque imitation of the good mother's self-sacrifice.[59]

Corrupt liquid flows not only from Error's breasts and decapi-
tated trunk but also from her mouth in the form of vomit:

> Therewith she spewd out of her filthy maw
> A floud of poyson horrible and blacke,
> Full of great lumpes of flesh and gobbets raw,
> Which stunck so vildly, that it forst him slacke
> His grasping hold, and from her turne him backe:
> Her vomit full of bookes and papers was,
> With loathly frogs and toades, which eyes did lacke,
> And creeping sought way in the weedy gras:
> Her filthy parbreake all the place defiled has.

(1.1.20)

Just as Redcrosse has not yet learned to "read, mark, learn, and
inwardly digest" the truth, so Error has failed to properly digest
the books and papers she has "read," or she may have per-
versely chosen to ingest heretical material, which taints her milk
and offspring as well as her own spirit.[60] Error's mouth and
speech are pointedly depicted as corrupt. When first threatened
by Redcrosse, she "loudly gan to bray," and her young, to escape
the light of his armor, crawl into her "wide" mouth, connoting
verbal transgression. Distinguishing among Error's orifices is as
difficult for the reader as for her young; in a perverted birthing
image, she "poured forth out of her hellish sinke / Her fruitfull
cursed spawne of serpents small"—womb, mouth, and possibly
anus are conflated—and the horror of woman's generating error
through writing may be suggested by her brood being "fowle, and
blacke as inke." Despite the vileness of the image, the text then
seems simultaneously to deny consequence to these errors by
comparing them merely to troublesome gnats (1.1.23). The good
nurse's voice urges the silencing of the bad—Una, observing her
knight trapped in Error's train, advises him to strangle the monster, so he "grypt her gorge" and thus eventually gains control
over her various means of indoctrination. Error thus serves as a
frontispiece not only for Redcrosse's quest for exegetical skill but
also as a specifically gendered illustration of the dangerous results of (corrupt) women reading and dispensing (corrupt) spiritual doctrine.[61]

Duessa, although a less obvious anti-nurse than Error, is also
a purveyor of corrupt teachings, allegorized as liquid suste-
nance. (Cleaver uses the same metaphor of drink when holding
up Timothy's godly mother and grandmother as exemplary
teachers: "Shee may also poure good licour in to their tender

vessels, the savour whereof, shall sticke in them a long while after: I meane, they may sowe in their mindes, the seedes of religion and godlinesse.")[62] In Duessa's presence Redcrosse drinks from the lethargy-inducing fountain that weakens him for his battle with Orgoglio. In contrast, Una's ceaseless prayers and constant watchfulness in canto 11 are coterminous with his saving fall into the well of life, which enables him to slay the dragon. During the battle with Arthur and Timias, Duessa makes use of her golden cup, which brims not with life-giving milk but is "replete with magick artes; / Death and despeyre did many thereof sup, / And secret poyson through their inner parts, / Th'eternall bale of heauie wounded harts" (1.8.14). Corrupt female speech accompanies the administration of the cup ("Which after charmes and some enchauntments said, / She lightly sprinkled on his [Timias's] weaker parts"), carrying gendered as well as eucharistic overtones. The virtuous analogue is Fidelia, who also bears a golden cup (filled with the healing powers of wine, water, and the serpent) and cures Redcrosse's soul with her verbal instruction. When Fradubio describes Duessa as a "filthy foule old woman," he makes no mention of her breasts, speculating instead on the vileness of her nether parts. Yet when Una orders Duessa stripped, her inadequacy as a spiritual nurse is clearly exposed: "Her dried dugs, like bladders lacking wind, / Hong downe, and filthy matter from them weld" (1.8.47).

Providing a necessary corrective to Duessa's deceit and harmful power over Redcrosse, Charissa displays her fruitful body openly: her "necke and breasts were euer open bare, / That ay thereof her babes might sucke their fill" (1.10.30). Duessa's rich headdress ("And like a *Persian* mitre on her hed / She wore, with crownes and owches garnished, / The which her lauish louers to her gaue"), suggesting her whorish nature, resembles Charissa's attire, except that the chaste Charissa's jewels are described as priceless: "And on her head she wore a tyre of gold, / Adornd with gemmes and owches wondrous faire, / Whose passing price vneath was to be told."[63] Within Book 1's nexus of female bodies/nurses, Charissa inhabits a central place between the virginal Una and whorish Duessa as an exemplary wife and mother ("Full of great loue, but *Cupids* wanton snare / As hell she hated, chast in worke and will").[64]

Charissa is recovering from childbirth while Redcrosse undergoes regenerative tutelage by Fidelia and Speranza, implying that the knight constitutes Charissa's latest child.[65] In response to Una's inquiries about the missing Charissa, her sisters explain that she is neither ill nor busy,

> but forth she may not come:
> For she of late is lightned of her wombe,
> And hath encreast the world with one sonne more,
> That her to see should be but troublesome.
>
> (1.10.16)

Once "woxen strong," however, Charissa emerges to provide her young ones with milk and Redcrosse with spiritual truth. That Redcrosse is educated in stages and by different women under Una's and Charissa's supervision illustrates their attention to what and how much Redcrosse should be fed—exemplifying Gouge's caution that "in giving this spirituall food, parents [should] deale with their children, as skilfull nurses and mothers doe in feeding infants: they will not at once cram more into their mouthes, then their stomach is able to digest, but they will rather oft feed them with a little" (*DD*, 540).

Having presumed too much on his spiritual strength and failed, the Redcrosse knight provides a speaking picture of Heb. 5:12: "For when . . . ye oght to be teachers, yet have ye nede againe y^t we teach you the first principles of the worde of God: and are become suche as have nede of milke, and not of strong meat." The "first principles of the worde of God" are the subject of Charissa's instruction:

> And taking by the hand that Faeries sonne,
> Gan him instruct in euery good behest,
> Of loue, and righteousnesse, and well to donne,
> And wrath, and hatred warely to shonne,
> That drew on men Gods hatred, and his wrath,
> And many soules in dolours had fordonne:
> In which when him she well instructed hath,
> From thence to heauen she teacheth him the ready path.
>
> (1.10.33)

The most exemplary of Book 1's nurses in her combination of feeding and teaching, Charissa's duties are nevertheless limited. Once weaned, her charges will seek other teachers:

> A multitude of babes about her hong,
> Playing their sports, that ioyd her to behold,

> Whom still she fed, whiles they were weake and young,
> But thrust them forth still, as they wexed old.

$$(1.10.31)$$

Her instruction of Redcrosse occurs within a domesticated space and takes the form of an elementary catechism, models of which were readily accessible in Bentley's *The Monument of Matrones*. More problematic, however, is the catechizing that borders on preaching practiced by Redcrosse's "dry" nurses Una and Fidelia.

*   *   *

Like Charissa, Una is a strikingly maternal figure, constant in her love and fervent in her efforts to teach the satyrs, Satyrane, and especially Redcrosse "Trew sacred lore," as good mothers were enjoined to do. John King has described Una as a "catechetical figure" who "never carries a Bible, but . . . characteristically voices proverbs and admonitions drawn from the scriptures."[66] Certainly one of the most vocal female figures in *The Faerie Queene*, Una emits "thrilling shriekes," "shrieking cryes," and "loud plaints" to bring the satyrs to her rescue (1.6.6), but soon employs her voice to higher purpose:

> During which time her gentle wit she plyes,
> To teach them truth, which worshipt her in vaine,
> And made her th'Image of Idolatryes;
> But when their bootlesse zeale she did restraine
> From her own worship, they her Asse would
>   worship fayn.

$$(1.6.19)$$

Unlike Charissa, Una instructs her charges in public. Even so, she never transgresses the code established by John Whitgift in his printed disputation with Thomas Cartwright during the 1570s *Admonition* controversy. Cartwright had registered some consternation over Whitgift's assertion that "women may instruct their families, yea, and they may speak also in the congregation in time of necessity, if there be none else there that can or will preach Christ." Yet despite Whitgift's seeming validation of women's voices ("Women were the first that preached Christ's resurrection; a woman was the first that preached Christ in Samaria"), he and Cartwright essentially agreed that women should not be allowed to preach within the Church of England, as Whitgift was careful to qualify his definition of "necessity": "there is no such necessity in this church (God be thanked). . . . [women should preach only in] such places where all be infidels, where they have neither heard of Christ, nor have his word, neither yet any other means to come by the knowledge of the same; which is nowhere in this church."[67] Seen in this light, the satyrs would certainly qualify as infidels ignorant of God's word and thus merit Una's care. Scripture contradicts itself on the subject of women's preaching, as pointed out by Esther Gilman Richey, who cites Joel 2.28's authorization of women's voices ("And afterwarde wil I power out my Spirit upon all flesh: and your sonnes and your daughters shal prophecie") along with Paul's prohibition of women's speech in 1 Tim. 2.11–12: "Let the woman learne in silence with all subjection. I permit not a woman to teache, nether to usurpe autoritie over the man, but to be in silence."[68] Mulcaster weighs in with Paul on this issue, explaining with somewhat heavy-handed humor that he doesn't mean to give women bars to plead at even though they study law or urinals to look at even though they study physic, "nor pulpittes to preach in, to utter their *Divinitie*: though by learning of some language, they can talke of the lining [*sic*]: and for direction of their life, they must be afforded some, though not as preachers and leaders: yet as honest perfourmers, and vertuous livers."[69] The line between "honest perfourmers" and "preachers" was thin, however; Foxe's narratives testify to the verbal defiance of numerous women whose faith was threatened.

Despite her verbal assertiveness, Una remains a zealously devout but modest female, teaching rather than preaching. Although her veil has been torn off by Sansloy and her beauty first inspires the satyrs to worship her, she seems to have resumed her veil by the time she is discovered teaching in 1.6.30 (Satyrane mentions her "straunge habiliment" and responds to her words, wisdom, and deeds rather than her beauty); her veil may even obliquely allude to the sign of submission called for in 1 Cor. 11:5 ("But everie woman that prayeth or prophecieth bareheaded, dishonoreth her head"). Una's wit is "gentle," and the satyrs, though potentially lustful and certainly pagan, are rendered exceedingly childlike by their naïveté. Any hint of overweening authority present in her verbal initiative is safely contained, because of the isolation and domestication of the satyr society and the text's ultimate denial of the efficacy of her words—Una fails to achieve mass conversion among the satyrs.

More immediately receptive than the satyrs as a catechumen is Satyrane, who was deprived of a mother's nurture in childhood, having been "noursled vp in life and manners wilde, / Emongst wild beasts and woods, from lawes of men exilde" (1.6.23). His mother, Thyamis, had sought her truant spouse in the woods (a profane parallel to the wanderings of Una and the bride in the Song of Solomon, who also seek lost mates), was repeatedly raped by a satyr, and eventually bore his child, after which she was sent back home while he took charge of the young boy.[70] Spenser emphasizes the limitations of Satyrane's paternal, sylvan education: "For all he taught the tender ymp, was but / To banish cowardize and bastard feare." Satyrane may be able to tame lions, bears, and bulls (indicating, perhaps, a certain control over his own animal nature), but he lacks knowledge of God. Thyamis tries to be a good mother, returning to the forest to seek her son. Although daunted when she finds him stealing lion's whelps, she nevertheless asks him, for love of her, to leave off such dangerous activity, albeit in amusingly ineffectual fashion: "Go find some other play-fellowes, mine own sweet boy" (1.6.28). Yet such a maternal appeal, unless it is grounded in early physical and spiritual nurture, is useless, and Satyrane's filial duty is paid instead to the satyr who reared him. On a visit to his father, he discovers Una "Teaching the Satyres, which her sat around, / Trew sacred lore, which from her sweet lips did redound" (1.6.30). Her voice (recalling the good woman of Prov. 31:26, who "openeth her mouth with wisdome") makes more of an impression on Satyrane than did his mother's "womanish words":

> He wondred at her wisedome heauenly rare,
> Whose like in womens wit he neuer knew;
> And when her curteous deeds he did compare,
> Gan her admire, and her sad sorrowes rew,
>
> . . . .
> Thenceforth he kept her goodly company,
> And learnd her discipline of faith and veritie.

(1.6.31)

Una thus provides the devoted maternal teaching of which he has been deprived.

Most of Una's maternal care, however, is lavished on Redcrosse, who often seems as much her child as her destined husband, and he acknowledges his reliance on her strength when confronted with the false Una's incongruous frailty: "Why Dame (quoth he) what hath ye thus dismayd? / What frayes ye, that were wont to comfort me affrayd?" (1.1.52). Such a dynamic might not have been out of the ordinary, given, for example, Clinton's observation that "a good wife is called her husband's nurse."[71] Cleaver concedes, "This is allowable, that she [a wife] may in modest sort shew her minde, and a wise husband will not disdaine to heare her advise, and follow it also, if it bee good."[72] Una constantly strives to teach her knight spiritual truths, thus embodying the Geneva Bible gloss on Prov. 31:26: "Her tongue is as a boke whereby one might learne manie good things: for she deliteth to talke of the worde of God." Redcrosse, however, frequently ignores Una's aphoristic counsel, and the deferred instructional dynamic of their relationship resembles that described by Vives: "I wold she [the mother] shoulde have some holy saiynges and preceptes of livinge commenly in use, whiche herde dyvers tymes, shall at the laste abyde in the childrens remembraunce, though thei geve no hede unto them" (ICW, sig. Gg1v).[73] That holiness should be represented by a youthful, untried, and childlike knight and a "weak" woman would not have surprised Richard Sibbes, who likens the founding of the Christian Church in Macedonia by Lydia to the furthering of the Reformation in England by Edward VI and Elizabeth I, a boy child and a woman.[74]

Redcrosse's long delay in embracing her truth highlights Una's devotion, patience, and wisdom, but much of the time her words seem to have no immediate effect. However, Una employs scriptural rhetoric skillfully in her attempt to win Redcrosse from the clutches of Despair. Concerned with both the physical and spiritual status of her knight, Una is well aware of his vulnerability even before they encounter Trevisan in 1.9.21. As William Gouge notes, husbands and wives are to keep each other from sin, as Una does when intervening between Redcrosse and Despair: "For the better effecting of this dutie, husbands and wives must be watchfull over one another, and observe what sinnes either of them are given unto, or what occasions are offered to draw either of them into sinne" (DD, 241). Redcrosse's temptation thus occurs within the providential context of Una's care; she will not allow him to be tempted beyond what he can bear. Redcrosse moves from rejecting Despair's words as "idle speach" to marveling at his "suddeine wit," but Una combats the effects of Despair's "charmed speeches" and "subtill tongue" with her own rhetorical strategies and decisive, almost violent action. When Una sees Redcrosse take up the knife, she scolds him in a manner characteristic both of an imperious romance lady and an overtaxed mother:

Out of his hand she snacht the cursed knife,
And threw it to the ground, enraged rife,
And to him said, Fie, fie, faint harted knight,
What meanest thou by this reprochfull strife?
Is this the battell, which thou vauntst to fight
With that fire-mouthed Dragon, horrible and bright?

(1.9.52)

Here Una acts on the obligation of a Christian helpmate to encourage, even admonish, her spouse in godly behavior. Smith observes: "if they [good wives] see them [husbands] minded to do
any evill, they should stay them, like the wife of Pilate, which
counselled her husband not to condemne Christ." Elsewhere
Smith notes that the wife should help her husband "sometime
with her strength, and sometime with her counsell; for sometime
as God confoundeth the wise by the foolish, and the strong by the
weake; so he teacheth the wise by the foolish."[75] Initially using
the rhetoric of romance to sting Redcrosse's manly pride, Una
then shifts effectively into theological discourse, reminding him
of God's grace by recalling texts from Romans, Ephesians, and
Colossians. Taking control of Redcrosse's peregrinations more
definitely than she has yet done, Una commands, "Arise, Sir
knight arise, and leaue this cursed place," and, perhaps for the
first time, he obeys her immediately.

Una's authority and decisiveness, however, may derive from
her own struggle with despair in 1.7 and the example provided
her by Arthur, whose "goodly reason, and well guided speach"
(in the form of a stichomythic, catechetical exchange in stanza
41) helped restore her faith. The ordering of these episodes reinforces the domestic chain of command outlined in sermon literature: the woman is to learn from her husband, minister, or other
male authority figure and then in turn instruct her children and
servants. Una never gratuitously infringes on male spiritual pre-
rogatives or seeks power in her own right but, balancing her
"hartie words" with a "modest manner" (1.11.1), devotes herself
almost exclusively to the interests of her captive parents and her
child-husband knight.

Like Una, Fidelia strives to teach Redcrosse "celestiall discipline" and soon opens "his dull eyes, that light mote in them
shine." The task of teaching him to read within the "school-
house" of her own home seems to reinscribe the tenets of domestic piety. Yet Fidelia does more than teach. She

heauenly documents thereout did preach,
That weaker wit of man could neuer reach,

> Of God, of grace, of iustice, of free will,
> That wonder was to heare her goodly speach.
>
> (1.10.19)

Although she does not violate the Pauline proscription of 1 Cor. 14:34 ("Let your women kepe silence in the Churches: for it is not permitted unto the[m] to speake"), the power of her sacred oratory to subvert the cosmic order calls into question such culturally limited prohibitions:

> And when she list poure out her larger spright,
> She would commaund the hastie Sunne to stay,
> Or backward turne his course from heauens hight;
> Sometimes great hostes of men she could dismay,
> Dry-shod to passe, she parts the flouds in tway;
> And eke huge mountaines from their natiue seat
> She would commaund, themselues to beare away,
> And throw in raging sea with roaring threat.
> Almightie God her gaue such powre, and puissance great.
>
> (1.10.20)

Unexceptionable when interpreted allegorically, this stanza becomes much more radical when read literally, in light of the number of nonconformist women whose faith did lead them to preach publicly. Just as Bathsheba, Lois, and Eunice were touted as exemplary mothers and speakers, so negative biblical exemplars were used to discourage transgressive female speech acts. Leonard Wright, in *A Patterne for Pastors*, claims to blush for the "unshamefast boldnes" of women preachers and cautions that "women are . . . not to imitate their grandmother Eve in usurping the office of teaching, neither the exa[m]ple of their sister Miriam, in grudging against Moses, neither such proud Jesabels as boldly dare usurpe the name of a Prophetisse to deceive the servantes of God."[76] The final line of stanza 20 ("Almightie God her gaue such powre") may serve as a means of containing the autonomy exercised by Fidelia in the first line ("when she list"). Alternatively, it may suggest unsettlingly that women are apt vehicles for God's inspired message and thus undermine the exclusion of women from sixteenth-century pulpits. Calvin considered women's preaching as a theological "matter indifferent," and Whitgift conceded that women could preach if "they be extraordinarily called thereunto, and have certain and sure signs of their calling," although neither encouraged such practice.[77] Fidelia's "puissance great" might be immediately contained by

Spenser's allegorical design, but her action resonates prophetically.

After learning the lessons of Fidelia, Speranza, and Charissa,
the Redcrosse knight is entrusted to his last female nurse, the
wise and sober matron Mercie. Like Charissa, Mercie also leads
Redcrosse by the hand, guiding the faltering but now upright and
regenerate soul, and during their stay with the beadmen, "in
euery good behest / And godly worke of Almes and charitee / She
him instructed with great industree" (1.10.45). Redcrosse, having
been taught to care for his own soul, is now taught responsibility
for society at large and begins to move further away from the
domestic world of the female-dominated House of Holiness. His
last spiritual guide, Contemplation, is, significantly, male, thus
reinscribing within the text the common educational practice
(for boys) of replacing female tutelage with male when the child
had sufficiently matured.

Several moralists emphasize the youth of the children the
mother is to instruct and assign to the father the instruction of
older children, especially boys. After outlining the husband's duties, for example, Gouge addresses the wife's "lesse[r], but very
needfull matters, as nourishing and instructing children when
they are young" (*DD*, 259), and Cleaver concurs, claiming that
the wife, or "fellowe-helper," can "do much good, in framing the
tender yeares of their children unto good, while they bee under
their hands, for even as a childe cockered, and made a wanton by
the mother, wil be more untractable, when the father shal seeke
to bend him to good: so on the other side, a child wisely trained
up by the mother in the young yeares, will bee the easilier
brought to goodnesse, by the Fathers godly care."[78] Erasmus, in
"The New Mother," suggests the same division of labor: "This
time too will come some day, if God will, when you must send the
boy from home to learn his letters—and harder lessons, which
are the father's responsibility rather than the mother's. Now his
tender age should be cherished."[79] According to Sir Thomas
Elyot, the usual age at which boys were to be weaned from female authority (and protected from potential temptation) was
about seven:

> After a childe is come to seven yeares of age, I holde it expedient,
> that he be taken from the company of women: saving that he may
> have one yeare or two at the moste, an aunciente and sadde matrone
> attendinge on him in his chamber, which shall not have anye young
> woman in hir companye: For though there be no perill of offence in

that tender and innocent age, yet in some children Nature is more prone to vice then to vertue. . . . Wherefore to eschue that daunger, the most sure counsaile is, to withdrawe him from al company of women, and to assigne unto him a tutor, which shoulde bee an auncient and worshipfull man.[80]

Although Elyot urges that aristocratic women provide the rudimentary literacy and spiritual instruction of boys in their mother tongue, he expects male tutors to initiate boys into the mysteries of Latin and Greek, in what Walter Ong terms a "Renaissance puberty rite."[81] Elyot expresses high expectations (and some patronizing blame) in detailing the process of language acquisition:

It shalbe expedient, that a noble mannes sonne, in his infancye, have with him continuallye, onelye suche as maye accustome him by little and little, to speake pure and elegant Latin. Semblablye the nourises and other woemen about him, if it be possible, to doe the same: or at the leaste waye, that they speake no English, but that which is cleane, polite, perfectly, and articularly pronounced, omytting no letter or sillable, as folishe women oftentimes do of a wantonnesse, where by divers Noble menne, and Gentlemennes children (as I do at this day know) have attained corrupt and foule pronunciation.[82]

Read in the context of this social practice, we can account for the conspicuous shift in Redcrosse's mentors from female to male. The godly matron Mercie in Spenser's allegorical exemplum resembles the grave and virtuous dry nurse Elyot acknowledges as a necessary participant in the early instruction of the young governor. Such a nurse serves as a transitional authority figure, as the male child moves from the female realm of the nursery (represented by Charissa) into the male realm of humanist scholarship or "higher" learning (represented by Contemplation). Fidelia having furnished Redcrosse with the basic spiritual literacy required to read "her sacred Booke," Contemplation, the wise hermit of chivalric romance doubling as learned humanist tutor, challenges the knight to practice a more sophisticated faith. Significantly, Una and Charissa do not reveal to Redcrosse his true identity as Saint George. The task of formally placing the knight within the political and religious order is given to the venerable, male Contemplation.

A similar displacement of the nursing mother appears much earlier in Spenser's text. According to the brief account of his upbringing, Arthur—the knight who most fully embodies all public and private virtues—received no maternal care of the kind given

Redcrosse; in fact, he was not even weaned when taken from his mother to receive an all-male education ("For all so soone as life did me admit / Into this world, and shewed heauens light, / From mothers pap I taken was vnfit," 1.9.3). Timon, a wise and experienced fairy knight, played both mother and father when he provided Arthur not only with martial training but also spiritual instruction ("There all my dayes he traind me vp in vertuous lore," 1.9.4). Arthur's education was then augmented by Merlin, who "had charge my discipline to frame, / And Tutours nouriture to ouersee" (1.9.5).

Nevertheless, women's spiritual influence over their children certainly did not abruptly end when their direct supervision of those children ceased. Mercie does lead Redcrosse away from the female House of Holiness to the male community of the beadmen, and yet during his stay there she continues as his governess. Contemplation expresses great reverence for Mercie, is eager to do her bidding, and in fact acts in obedience to her instructions, so that some ambivalence exists about who is technically in charge of the knight's training and the degree to which Mercie has actually relinquished her control of Redcrosse's instruction. Although Redcrosse explicitly thanks only Contemplation for guiding him to heaven, much of the credit belongs to the knight's holy surrogate mothers who have worked tirelessly so that Redcrosse might be worthy of his name. Batty's comment on the "wonderful effectual" nature of maternal discipline seems particularly relevant to Redcrosse's visionary experience, when he embraces more consciously his red cross and yearns to enter the heavenly Jerusalem: "Mothers suckle & nourish your own children, love them, cherish them, & pray for them . . . ; admonish them that they may rather take the Crosse of our Lorde Jesu Christ & followe him, than love this vaine and transitorie life."[83]

How might Spenser's female contemporaries have interpreted his legend of holiness? Some women, viewing themselves as warfaring Christians, may have likened themselves to Redcrosse. Anne Askew, for example, in a ballad composed while she was imprisoned in Newgate, boldly claims:

> Lyke as the armed knyght
> Appoynted to the fielde
> With thys world wyll I fyght
> And fayth shall be my shielde.[84]

Askew is depicted carrying a Bible and confronting the papacy in the form of a dragon in a woodcut on the title page of *The first examinacyon of Anne Askew* (1546); this spiritual everywoman, denied the spear available to Redcrosse, uses her reading as a potent weapon. Less literally embattled, Mildmay also employed the metaphor, recording in her extensive spiritual meditations that faith served as her "armour."[85] Women readily appropriated for themselves the martial imagery of Eph. 6:11–17, as Brathwait encourages them to do (albeit feminizing and demilitarizing it, and thereby limiting the possibility of its subversive use): "Her *head-tyre* puts her in minde of the *helmet of salvation*; her *stomacher*, of the *brest-plate of righteousnesse*; her *partlet*, of the *shield of faith*; her very *shooes*, of the *sandals of peace*. In this Tabernacle of earth, shee is every day nearer her port of rest" (*EG*, 200).

Yet without denying the allegorical primacy of Spenser's representation of sanctification in Redcrosse's struggles, we might also acknowledge that another "norm" of holiness is manifested in the actions of Una and the female inhabitants of the House of Holiness, a norm for pious women consistent with that articulated in the early modern English discourse of the holy mother. The type of holiness Una embodies differs qualitatively from that being learned by Redcrosse; the faith she practices is not that of the newly regenerate soul but that of the mature godly woman. Equated with heavenly grace and the "stedfast truth" whose "loue is firme, her care continuall," and committed to imparting that truth to those in her care, Una serves as the ideal Christian mother. Even the amusing detail of the mother worried about her foolhardy child venturing too near the dragon's corpse (1.12.11) recalls the maternal watchfulness first evident in Una's care for Redcrosse in his contest with Error, a watchfulness that pervades the book.

Adrienne Rich has argued that "Patriarchal monotheism . . . stripped the universe of female divinity, and permitted women to be sanctified, as if by an unholy irony, only and exclusively as mother . . . or as the daughter of a divine father."[86] Yet Spenser's female readers may have readily embraced the nurturing role assigned them, seeing in it an opportunity to exercise a degree of authority and to purify their own souls. Certainly less sensational than the tortured testimony of a martyr such as Anne Askew and less theatrical than Elizabeth's public demonstrations of devotion, the spiritual influence exerted by numerous women over the souls of their family members nevertheless affected the profound religious conflicts and changes of the sixteenth century. Readers of *The Faerie Queene*, therefore, might well have seen

embodied in the holy women of Book 1 more than mere allegorical counters reflecting the gendered idiosyncracies of Latin
grammar. They may have seen, in fact, the cultural ideal of the
pious, faithful woman and, in her foil Error, the dangers inherent
within that ideal.

Afterword

A painting known as *Elizabeth and the Three Goddesses* or *The Judgment of Paris*, dated 1569 and ascribed variously to Hans Eworth, Lucas de Heere, or Joris Hoefnagel, provides a visual metaphor for the approach I have tried to take in my reading of Spenser's *Faerie Queene*. A stately Elizabeth emerges from an archway on the left, carrying the orb and scepter; on the right, Juno, Pallas, and Venus observe and respond in varying ways to the woman who will clearly win—indeed, already has won—the coveted prize, because she combines in one person the attributes associated with the three goddesses. The work has traditionally been read as a complimentary portrait of Elizabeth, one that may allegorically encourage her to marry. And yet the rather unusual composition allows for another reading, one that looks to the margin of the painting where two of Elizabeth's ladies face each other as they enter the scene immediately behind their mistress. Engaged in the business of carrying her train or in sharing the latest court gossip, they seem to have no awareness of the goddesses' presence. However, tension is created by the confrontation of the two balanced groups of three, the tightly clustered Elizabethan women juxtaposed with the more loosely spaced classical goddesses. What interrelationships exist between the two ladies and the goddesses, or Elizabeth, or the viewer? After all, they, as well as Elizabeth, possess some of the power, wisdom, and beauty represented by the goddesses, and, given that Elizabeth never did marry, their connection to the small figure of Cupid who grasps his mother's knees can be considered as great, or greater, than their queen's.[1]

In my reading of Spenser's epic romance, I have tried to adopt a perspective that addresses the textual presence of gentlewomen such as the ones portrayed in the 1569 painting. Mary Ellen Lamb has suggested that one of Spenser's literary successors, Mary Wroth, depicts romance as "an accurate record of cultural codes painfully lived out in the lives" of her female characters and readers.[2] I have been arguing that Spenser's text may have functioned similarly. His inclusion of numerous female exemplars would suggest an awareness of the social roles played by women and of the romance's usefulness as a means of female self-fashioning. Yet his conflation of discourses, particularly those of the romance and of courtesy literature, prevents any single interpretation of these characters. In fact, Spenser's poem allows for a variety of responses from female readers, which range from conventional "better meanings" to genuinely subversive readings. Women are clearly being fashioned as the "subjects" of these texts but are also being allowed extensive liberty to fashion the text in return.

The Elizabethan *Judgment of Paris* is unusual in that it includes no figure of Paris, no authority to indicate the victor with a gesture; Elizabeth's supremacy resides primarily in the eyes of the politically astute beholder. The painting does not preclude alternative readings, such as one that might be constructed by the lover of one of the ladies following Queen Elizabeth, or by the lady herself, and neither does *The Faerie Queene*. The meanings of both poem and painting depend on choices made by readers who might have shared certain assumptions about feminine virtue but whose sociosexual positioning may have led them to adduce very different interpretations. The three goddesses present Paris with a relatively straightforward task, choosing the most beautiful, whereas the first female readers of the painting and of Spenser's poem were confronted with a more complex task: deciding when to remain in the queen's shadow and when to step forth in their own right.

Notes

Introduction

1. Sir John Harington, *Nugae Antiquae*, ed. Henry Harington, 3 vols. (London: J. Dodsley, 1779), 1:iii; 2:15–16.

2. See, for example, Sir Thomas Elyot, *The Defence of Good Women* (1540); George Pettie, *A Petite Pallace of Pettie his pleasure* (1576); John Lyly, *Euphues and his England* (1581); Barnabe Rich, *Riche his farewell to militarie profession* (1581); and Robert Greene, *Mamillia. A mirrour or looking-glasse for the ladies of Englande* (1583). Thomas Nashe's castigation of Greene can be found in *The Anatomie of Absurditie* (1589), sig. A2v. London is the place of publication of all texts cited throughout unless otherwise noted.

3. Linda Woodbridge, *Women and the English Renaissance: Literature and the Nature of Womankind, 1540–1620* (Urbana: University of Illinois Press, 1984), 120.

4. Suzanne W. Hull, *Chaste, Silent and Obedient: English Books for Women 1475–1640* (San Marino: The Huntington Library, 1982), ix–x, 71, 15.

5. Lady Newdigate-Newdegate, *Gossip from a Muniment Room Being Passages in the Lives of Anne and Mary Fytton 1574 to 1618* (London: David Nutt, 1897), 127–28. Stanford's verses, found in Cambridge University MS. D.d.V.75. Fol. 19, are reprinted in William Wells, ed. *Spenser Allusions in the Sixteenth and Seventeenth Centuries* (Chapel Hill: University of North Carolina Press, 1972), 124.

6. Gibson, *A Womans Woorth* (1599), sig. A7r.

7. Gibson, sig. A4r (misnumbered A2); A5r. Henry Lok's *Ecclesiastes* (1597) also contains a lengthy series of dedicatory sonnets to women: the Marquess of Northampton, the Countesses of Derby, Cumberland, Warwick, Pembroke, and Essex, the Ladies Scroop, Rich, and Hunsdon, Elizabeth and Anne Russell, Elizabeth Bridges, the Ladies Southwell, Cecil, Hobbye, Layton, Woollie, and Carey, a mysterious Lady D, Mistress E. Bowes, and finally (and inclusively) the "Honorable Ladies and Gentlewomen, attendants in the Court." He might well have omitted the final sonnet in the sequence, having already provided a very thorough list of attendant ladies.

8. Maureen Quilligan also notes Spenser's "distinctly double-gendered readership" in *Milton's Spenser: The Politics of Reading* (Ithaca: Cornell University Press, 1983), 38, 181.

9. See, respectively, E. C. Wilson, *England's Eliza*, Harvard Studies in English, 20 (1939; reprint, London: Frank Cass, 1966); Frances Yates, *Astraea: The Imperial Theme in the Sixteenth Century* (1975; reprint, London: Routledge and Kegan Paul, 1985); Thomas P. Roche, Jr., *The Kindly Flame: A Study of the Third and Fourth Books of Spenser's "Faerie Queene"* (Princeton: Princeton University Press, 1964); Thomas H. Cain, *Praise in "The Faerie Queene"* (Lin-

251

coln: University of Nebraska Press, 1978); Robin Headlam Wells, *Spenser's "Faerie Queene" and the Cult of Elizabeth* (London: Croom Helm, 1983).

10. See, for example, Catherine Bates, *The Rhetoric of Courtship in Elizabethan Language and Literature* (Cambridge: Cambridge University Press, 1992); Philippa Berry, *Of Chastity and Power: Elizabethan Literature and the Unmarried Queen* (London: Routledge, 1989); Susan Frye, *Elizabeth I: The Competition for Representation* (New York: Oxford University Press, 1993); Stephen Greenblatt, *Renaissance Self-Fashioning* (Chicago: University of Chicago Press, 1980); Mary Ellen Lamb, "Gloriana, Acrasia, and the House of Busirane: Gendered Fictions in *The Faerie Queene* as Fairy Tale," in *Worldmaking Spenser: Explorations in the Early Modern Age,* ed. Patrick Cheney and Lauren Silberman (Lexington: University Press of Kentucky, 2000), 81–100; Louis Montrose, "The Elizabethan Subject and the Spenserian Text," in *Literary Theory/Renaissance Texts,* ed. Patricia Parker and David Quint (Baltimore: Johns Hopkins University Press, 1986), 303–40; Quilligan, *Milton's Spenser;* Mary Villeponteaux, "Displacing Feminine Authority in *The Faerie Queene,*" *Studies in English Literature* 35 (1995): 53–67; Julia M. Walker, "Spenser's Elizabeth Portrait and the Fiction of Dynastic Epic," *Modern Philology* 90.2 (November 1992): 172–99; Julia M. Walker, *Medusa's Mirrors: Spenser, Shakespeare, Milton, and the Metamorphosis of the Female Self* (Newark: University of Delaware Press, 1998); Susanne Lindgren Wofford, *The Choice of Achilles: The Ideology of Figure in the Epic* (Stanford: Stanford University Press, 1992), especially 241–42. John Watkins' *The Specter of Dido: Spenser and Virgilian Epic* (New Haven: Yale University Press, 1995), provides a useful reading of the female figures in Book 2 but still reads Medina and Alma as "surrogates of the Virgin Queen" (8). On the "other" queen in the poem, see Richard A. McCabe, "The Masks of Duessa: Spenser, Mary Queen of Scots, and James VI," *English Literary Renaissance* 17.2 (Spring 1987): 224–42.

11. Marie H. Buncombe, "Faire Florimell as Faire Game: The Virtuous, Unmarried Woman in *The Faerie Queene* and *The Courtier,*" *College Language Association Journal* 28 (1984): 164–75, reads Florimell as a representative female courtier, in combination with her allegorical, neoplatonic significance, but does not address interpretive issues. Mihoko Suzuki registers greater awareness of female readers in her study *Metamorphoses of Helen: Authority, Difference, and the Epic* (Ithaca: Cornell University Press, 1989), 1–2, but her Spenser chapter deals primarily with Britomart and Elizabeth, and her focus on classical epic and the possibility of female heroism necessarily defines heroism in public, traditionally masculine and martial terms, whereas I explore the less obvious female heroism encoded in the courtesy and romance literature of the period. The study that most resembles mine in its attention to the poem's engagement with early modern women's experience is Sheila T. Cavanagh's *Wanton Eyes and Chaste Desires: Female Sexuality in "The Faerie Queene"* (Bloomington: Indiana University Press, 1994). Unlike Cavanagh, however, who asserts that "Spenser's awareness of a 'double-gendered readership' seems to be fundamentally restricted" and that the poem "shows little recognition that male and female readers might bring different perspectives and presuppositions to the text" (3), I emphasize the potential agency of women readers of Spenser's poem rather than the oppressive nature of the poem itself. Our studies are therefore complementary in that they point to the balance described by Robert Darnton: "The history of reading will have to take account of the ways that texts constrain readers as well as the ways that readers take liberties with

texts" ("What Is the History of Books?" in *The Kiss of Lamourette: Reflections in Cultural History* [New York and London: W. W. Norton and Co., 1990], 132).

12. On the attire of maids of honor, see Jane Ashelford, *Dress in the Age of Elizabeth I* (London: Batsford, 1988), 138. References to Spenser's *Faerie Queene* are taken from *Spenser's "Faerie Queene,"* ed. J. C. Smith (Oxford: Clarendon Press, 1909) and will be cited parenthetically in the text, as will glosses from *The Faerie Queene*, ed. A. C. Hamilton (London: Longman, 1977). Although I have not altered the spelling in the Spenser quotations, I have modernized the use of i/j and u/v in other early modern texts.

13. David Miller, *The Poem's Two Bodies: The Poetics of the 1590 "Faerie Queene"* (Princeton: Princeton University Press, 1988), 56–60; Carol Stillman, "Politics, Precedence, and the Order of the Dedicatory Sonnets in *The Faerie Queene," Spenser Studies* 5 (1984): 145.

14. Susanne Woods, "Women at the Margins in Spenser and Lanyer," in *Worldmaking Spenser*, 107–108.

15. *The Yale Edition of the Shorter Poems of Edmund Spenser*, ed. William A. Oram et al. (New Haven: Yale University Press, 1989), 231, 544. See Margaret Hannay, *Philip's Phoenix: Mary Sidney, Countess of Pembroke* (New York: Oxford University Press, 1990), 112, 79–80, and Mary Ellen Lamb, "The Countess of Pembroke's Patronage," *English Literary Renaissance* 12.2 (Spring 1982): 175.

16. Kathy Lynn Emerson, *Wives and Daughters: The Women of Sixteenth Century England* (New York: The Whitston Publishing Company, 1984), 210; French R. Fogle, " 'Such a Rural Queen': The Countess Dowager of Derby as Patron," in *Patronage in Late Renaissance England*, ed. French R. Fogle and Louis A. Knafla (Los Angeles: William Andrews Clark Memorial Library, 1983), 9.

17. Her daughter, another Elizabeth Carey (the wife of Sir Thomas Berkeley), also received literary dedications, among them one from Nashe, who, in *The Terrors of the night Or, A Discourse of Apparitions* (1594), praises the younger Elizabeth for her wit, temperance, and piety and for being a "worthie Daughter" of "so worthie a Mother; borrowing (as another *Phoebe*, from her bright Sunne-like resplendaunce) the orient beames of [her] radiaunce."

18. See Ronald Bond, introduction, *Muiopotmos*, in *Shorter Poems*, 407–11; the dedication is reprinted on p. 412.

19. Percy W. Long argues, romantically but implausibly, for an "intimately personal and gallant" relationship, the lady being adopted as Spenser's courtly "mistress" ("Spenser and Lady Carey," *Modern Language Review* 3.3 [April 1908]: 257).

20. Maureen Quilligan, *The Language of Allegory: Defining the Genre* (Ithaca: Cornell University Press, 1979), 226, describes the reader of allegory as being highly participatory: "If he is something of a voyeur in relationship to orthodox narrative organized along the lines of verisimilitude, then he [or she] is the central character in an allegory. The narrative may be said to 'read' him." Spenser's genre, the allegorized epic romance, virtually demands that women play an active and self-conscious role in reading the text. See also Susanne Woods, "Spenser and the Problem of Women's Rule," *Huntington Library Quarterly* 48 (1985): 150, on Spenser's "poetics of choice."

21. See Fogle, passim.

22. See Jon A. Quitslund, "Spenser and the Patronesses of the *Fowre Hymnes*: 'Ornaments of All True Love and Beautie,' " in *Silent But for the*

Word: Tudor Women as Patrons, Translators, and Writers of Religious Works, ed. Margaret P. Hannay (Kent, OH: Kent State University Press, 1985), 185, 192.

23. Spenser, *Shorter Poems*, 223–24.

24. Caroline Lucas, in *Writing for Women: The Example of Woman as Reader in Elizabethan Romance* (Milton Keynes: Open University Press, 1989), which came to my attention after I had formulated my own thesis, argues a similar point in relation to the prose romances of Pettie, Greene, Rich, and Sidney, which offer the female reader "a variety of often inconsistent, self-contradictory and self-destructive roles to play; crucially, she can refuse to adopt them, becoming, in Judith Fetterley's term, a 'resisting reader' " (2). See also Roberta L. Krueger, *Women Readers and the Ideology of Gender in Old French Verse Romance* (Cambridge: Cambridge University Press, 1993), 17, on female readership as "the simultaneous site of cultural construction and resistance."

25. See, for example, Anthony Grafton, "Renaissance Readers and Ancient Texts: Comments on Some Commentaries," *Renaissance Quarterly* 38 (1985): 615–49; Lisa Jardine and Anthony Grafton, " 'Studied for Action': How Gabriel Harvey Read His Livy," *Past and Present* 129 (1990): 30–78; John Kerrigan, "The Editor as Reader: Constructing Renaissance Texts" in *The Practice and Representation of Reading in England*, ed. James Raven, Helen Small, and Naomi Tadmor (Cambridge: Cambridge University Press, 1996), 102–24; and Eugene R. Kintgen, *Reading in Tudor England* (Pittsburgh: University of Pittsburgh Press, 1996).

26. Robert Hume, "Texts Within Contexts: Notes Toward a Historical Method," *Philological Quarterly* 71.1 (Winter 1992): 74.

27. Ian Maclean, *The Renaissance Notion of Woman: A Study in the Fortunes of Scholasticism and Medical Science in European Intellectual Life* (Cambridge: Cambridge University Press, 1980), 52.

28. Katherine Duncan-Jones, ed., *Sir Philip Sidney* (Oxford: Oxford University Press, 1989), 227.

29. Jacques Du Bosc, *The Compleat Woman* (1639), sig. I1r. Subsequent references to *CW* will be cited in the text.

30. Vives's *De institutione foeminae Christianae* (1523), translated into English by Richard Hyrde in 1529 as *A Very Fruteful and Pleasant Boke called the Instruction of a christen woman*, was a popular work throughout the sixteenth century. It might well have been read by readers of *The Faerie Queene*; Retha Warnicke notes that Vives's book "was reissued as late as 1592" ("Eulogies for Women: Public Testimony of Their Godly Example and Leadership," in *Attending to Women in Early Modern England*, ed. Betty S. Travitsky and Adele F. Seeff [Newark: University of Delaware Press, 1994], 174–75). I have used the 1557 edition throughout. Castiglione's *Il cortegiano* was translated by Sir Thomas Hoby in 1561; I have cited the 1577 edition throughout except where otherwise noted. For Guazzo, see *The civile Conversation of M. Stephen Guazzo*, trans. George Pettie (Books 1–3, 1581) and Bartholomew Young (Book 4, 1586). Subsequent references to these three works will be cited parenthetically in the text as *ICW*, *C*, and *CC*, respectively.

31. "Nymphs" functioned as a common epithet for Elizabeth's courtly attendants; for example, they are addressed as "Ye worthy Nymphes of chast Dyanaes traine" in Henry Lok's dedicatory sonnet in *Ecclesiastes*.

32. Carol Neely, "Constructing the Subject: Feminist Practice and the New Renaissance Discourses," *English Literary Renaissance* 18.1 (Winter 1988): 15.

Chapter 1. "Some comfortable and wise discourses"

1. Robert Darnton, "First Steps Toward a History of Reading," in *The Kiss of Lamourette*, 182; Elizabeth Flynn, "Women as Reader-Response Critics," *New Orleans Review* 10 (1983): 25. Robert Hume has also called for a critical approach that endeavors "to recapture the outlook of various subgroups of readers in the past" (80).

2. Studies of English women readers that have informed my own include Margaret Ferguson, "A Room Not Their Own: Renaissance Women as Readers and Writers," in *The Comparative Perspective on Literature: Approaches to Theory and Practice*, ed. Clayton Koelb and Susan Noakes (Ithaca: Cornell University Press, 1988), 93–116; Hull, *Chaste, Silent and Obedient*; Mary Ellen Lamb, "The Agency of the Split Subject: Lady Anne Clifford and the Uses of Reading," *English Literary Renaissance*, 22.3 (Autumn 1992): 347–68; Mary Ellen Lamb, "Women Readers in Mary Wroth's *Urania*," in *Reading Mary Wroth: Representing Alternatives in Early Modern England*, ed. Naomi Miller and Gary Waller (Knoxville: University of Tennessee Press, 1991), 210–27; Jacqueline Pearson, "Women Reading, Reading Women," in *Women and Literature in Britain, 1500–1700*, ed. Helen Wilcox (Cambridge: Cambridge University Press, 1996), 80–99; Louise Schleiner, *Tudor and Stuart Women Writers* (Bloomington: Indiana University Press, 1994), particularly 3–29; Frances Teague, "Judith Shakespeare Reading," *Shakespeare Quarterly* 47.4 (Winter 1996): 361–73; and Louis B. Wright, "The Reading of Renaissance English-women," *Studies in Philology*, 28 (1931): 139–56. On women's devotional reading (particularly during the seventeenth century), see Kenneth Charlton, *Women, Religion and Education in Early Modern England* (London: Routledge, 1999), 178–87. For information on the reading of medieval women and the methodological challenges of compiling evidence for women's book ownership and ascertaining women's literary tastes, see Carol M. Meale, " '. . . alle the bokes that I haue of latyn, englisch, and frensch': laywomen and their books in late medieval England," in *Women and Literature in Britain, 1150–1500*, ed. Meale (Cambridge: Cambridge University Press, 1993), 128–58.

3. Cited in Peter Clark, "The Ownership of Books in England, 1560–1640: The Example of Some Kentish Townfolk," in *Schooling and Society: Studies in the History of Education*, ed. Lawrence Stone (Baltimore: Johns Hopkins University Press, 1976), 97.

4. David Cressy, *Literacy and the Social Order: Reading and Writing in Tudor and Stuart England* (Cambridge: Cambridge University Press, 1980), 128, 176; Cressy, "Literacy in Context: Meaning and Measurement in Early Modern England," in *Consumption and the World of Goods*, ed. John Brewer and Roy Porter (London: Routledge, 1993), 315; Keith Thomas, "The Meaning of Literacy in Early Modern England," in *The Written Word: Literacy in Transition*, ed. Gerd Baumann (Oxford: Clarendon Press, 1986), 101–3.

5. Richard Mulcaster, *Positions* (1581), 177.

6. Erasmus, *Paraclesis* (1516), reprinted in *Christian Humanism and the Reformation: Selected Writings of Erasmus*, ed. John Olin, rev. ed. (New York: Fordham University Press, 1975), 97. Erasmus's rationale, that the scriptures veritably taught themselves to the faithful, was, however, not the heartiest of endorsements of women's learning. Meale's introduction to *Women and Literature in Britain, 1150–1500* notes that the argument based on "the spiritual

benefits to be gained from the acquisition of the skill of reading is one which is familiar from the time of Jerome onwards" (1–2).

7. Retha Warnicke, *Women of the English Renaissance and Reformation* (Westport, CT: Greenwood Press, 1983), 91–92.

8. *The Court of good Counsell* (1607), sig. H3r–v.

9. Mulcaster, 181–82.

10. Grace Mildmay's autobiography, reprinted in *With Faith and Physic: The Life of a Tudor Gentlewoman, Lady Grace Mildmay 1552–1620*, ed. Linda Pollock (London: Collins and Brown, 1993), 26.

11. Cited in Kenneth Charlton, *Education in Renaissance England* (London: Routledge and Kegan Paul, 1965), 211.

12. Retha Warnicke, "Women and Humanism in England," in *Renaissance Humanism: Foundations, Forms, and Legacy*, vol. 2 of *Humanism Beyond Italy*, ed. Albert J. Rabil, Jr. (Philadelphia: University of Pennsylvania Press, 1988), 2:39, 44–45.

13. Mulcaster, 180.

14. More cited in Warnicke, "Women and Humanism," 40.

15. Mulcaster, 168, 169, 177.

16. Hyrde's dedication of Margaret More Roper's translation of Erasmus's *A devout treatise upon the Pater noster*, c. 1526, cited in Mary Ellen Lamb, *Gender and Authorship in the Sidney Circle* (Madison: University of Wisconsin Press, 1990), 8. At least, Lamb argues, Hyrde represents reading "as signifying chastity, rather than sexuality." See also Valerie Wayne's response to such "defenses" of women in "Some Sad Sentence: Vives' *Instruction of a Christian Woman*," in *Silent But for the Word*, 19–20.

17. Violet Wilson, *Queen Elizabeth's Maids of Honour and Ladies of the Privy Chamber* (London: John Lane, 1922), 66; Pearl Hogrefe, *Women of Action in Tudor England* (Ames: Iowa State University Press, 1977), 60.

18. Meale, 130–31.

19. Sears Jayne and Francis R. Johnson, *The Lumley Library: The Catalogue of 1609* (London: Trustees of the British Museum, 1956), 196, 209, 254.

20. John Aubrey cited in Hannay, *Philip's Phoenix*, 48.

21. Dorothy Meads, ed., *Diary of Lady Margaret Hoby 1599–1605* (London: Routledge, 1930), 242 note 172; Myra Reynolds, *The Learned Lady in England, 1650–1760* (1920; reprint, Gloucester, MA: Peter Smith, 1964), 32.

22. Clifford, *The Diary of the Lady Anne Clifford*, ed. Vita Sackville-West (London: William Heinemann, Ltd., 1924), 68; Meads, 59.

23. "A Catalogue of my Ladies Bookes at London taken October 27th 1627." Ellesmere Papers: EL 6495 (Huntington Library). See also Heidi Brayman, "Ladies, Lapdogs, and Libraries: Women and Their Books in Early Modern England," talk given at the Huntington Library, 25 August 1993, and Margaret Ezell, *The Patriarch's Wife: Literary Evidence and the History of the Family* (Chapel Hill: University of North Carolina Press, 1987), 15–16.

24. Anne Southwell, *The Southwell-Sibthorpe Commonplace Book: Folger MS. V.b.198*, ed. Jean Klene (Tempe, AZ: Medieval and Renaissance Texts and Studies, 1997), 98–101.

25. The women listed in the *STC* who owned books and marked them accordingly with bookplates (prior to 1641) include Anne Barnes (1591), Philippa Bragg (1634), Anne Childe (1634?), Mabel Clemetson (1618), Lady Mary Cokayne (1626–30), Catherine Dod (1630?), Anne Harington (1616–20), Anne Lake (1638), Abigail Moundeford (1630), Alice Paulett (1640), Dorothy Paynton (1626),

Elizabeth Pindar (1608), Margaret Raworth (1604), Katherine and Elizabeth Shakespeare (1598), Elizabeth Stow (1599), Frances Stuart, Duchess of Richmond and Lenox (1630), and Elizabeth Walter (1615?). See *STC*, 1.145–53 and 3.267–69.

26. Paul Morgan, "Frances Wolfreston and 'Hor Bouks': A Seventeenth-Century Woman Book-Collector," *The Library*, sixth series, 11.3 (September 1989): 197–219.

27. Vives, *de Officio Mariti*, translated into English as *The office and duetie of an husband* by Thomas Paynell (1550), sig. P8v. Subsequent references to *ODH* will be cited in the text.

28. Salter, *The Mirrhor of Modestie* (1579), sig. D3r. Reprinted in *Illustrations of Old English Literature*, ed. J. Payne Collier (London: Privately printed, 1866), vol. 1. Subsequent references to *MM* will be cited in the text.

29. Brathwait, *The English Gentlewoman* (1631), 186–87. Subsequent references to *EG* will be cited in the text.

30. Hoby, 153, 107, 111.

31. Ibid., 125, 172–73, 77.

32. Daniel, *The Civile Wares* (1609), sig. A3r.

33. Danett, preface, *The Historie of France* (1595), sig. A2r; A3v; A5r–v.

34. Michael Drayton does the same in his *Englands heroicall epistles* (1598), as he explains his practice of matching dedicatory epistles to individual epistles within the text: "every one is the first in theyr particular interest, having in some sort sorted the complexion of the Epistles, to the character of their judgments to whom I dedicate them" (sig. A2v).

35. Danett, sig. A5r; A3v; A5r–v.

36. Ibid., sig. A5r–v.

37. William Harrison, *The description of England* (1587), ed. Georges Edelen (Ithaca: Cornell University Press for the Folger Shakespeare Library, 1968), 228. Although Suzanne Hull argues that "histories" in this context refers to prose fiction (*Chaste* p. 29, note 3), Harrison would more probably boast of women reading national histories rather than romances, given the disdain romances generated and the approbation history received as a suitable genre for women. As he himself was writing a history, it would be in his own interests to represent women as having a taste for the genre.

38. Mildmay, 23.

39. Josephine A. Roberts, "Extracts from *Arcadia* in the Manuscript Notebook of Lady Katherine Manners," *Notes and Queries*, n.s., 28 (1981): 35.

40. Anne Dowriche, *The French Historie. That is; A lamentable Discourse of three of the chiefe and most famous bloodie broiles that have happened in "France" for the Gospell of Jesus Christ* (1589), sig. A2v.

41. Hoby, 132; 267, note 354; 172.

42. Penelope Devereux, according to her brother Essex's confession, had helped to foment the failed rebellion of 1601. Female courtiers were not exempt from the queen's ire when they expressed their opinions too freely, especially when they had some claim to the throne; Margaret, Countess of Derby, and the Earl of Bedford's daughter were placed under arrest for discussing the proposed Alençon marriage. See Martin A. S. Hume, ed., *Calendars of Letters and State Papers Spanish, 1568–1579* (London: Eyre and Spottiswoode, 1894), 692.

43. Clifford, 41; 47; 66; 111. See also 87 and 91 for references to Wat reading theological works aloud.

44. For an overview of the literature that informed Wroth's work, see Jose-

phine Roberts, ed. *The First Part of The Countess of Montgomery's Urania* (Binghamton, NY: Medieval and Renaissance Texts and Studies, 1995), xviii–xxxix. See also Jacqueline T. Miller, "Lady Mary Wroth in the House of Busirane," in *Worldmaking Spenser*, 115–24, and Shannon Miller, " 'Mirrours More Than One': Edmund Spenser and Female Authority in the Seventeenth Century," in *Worldmaking Spenser*, 125–47.

45. Clifford, 52, 76.

46. Barbara Lewalski notes that Florio completed his translation "while resident with the Haringtons, and . . . Lucy read, encouraged, and offered helpful suggestions for the work in progress." Florio singled out not only the Countess of Bedford but also her mother, Lady Harington, the Countess of Rutland, and Lady Penelope Rich, Lady Elizabeth Grey, and Lady Marie Nevill. See "Lucy Countess of Bedford: Images of a Jacobean Courtier and Patroness," in *Politics of Discourse: The Literature and History of Seventeenth-Century England*, ed. Kevin Sharpe and Steven N. Zwicker (Berkeley and Los Angeles: University of California Press, 1987), 60.

47. Clifford, 104. Isabella Whitney also mentions reading Ovid, along with Virgil and Mantuan in "The Auctor to the Reader" prefacing *A Sweet Nosgay* (1573), although she is feigning weariness with the course of reading she has pursued: the Scriptures, histories, and the "wonders" contained in the three classical authors she cites.

48. Clifford, 110; Donne cited in Meads, 60.

49. Anne(?) Cary, *The Lady Falkland: Her Life* in *The Tragedy of Mariam the Fair Queen of Jewry*, ed. Barry Weller and Margaret W. Ferguson (Berkeley and Los Angeles: University of California Press, 1994), 186, 187–8.

50. Ibid., 189.

51. Ibid., 194; 248; 268.

52. See Weller and Ferguson's introduction, 2.

53. Cary, 190. See p. 188 for her father's conclusion that she had a "spirit averse from Calvin."

CHAPTER 2. "HOW DOUBTFULLY ALL ALLEGORIES MAY BE CONSTRUED"

1. Kerrigan, 113.

2. Plutarch, *The Philosophie, commonly called, the Morals written by the learned Philosopher Plutarch*, trans. Philemon Holland (1603), 39.

3. See Jardine and Grafton, " 'Studied for Action.' "

4. Du Verger, *Admirable Events* (1639), sig. A7r.

5. Wallace, " 'Examples Are Best Precepts': Readers and Meaning in Seventeenth-Century Poetry," *Critical Inquiry* 1 (December 1974): 275. See also Annabel Patterson, *Censorship and Interpretation: The Conditions of Writing and Reading in Early Modern England* (Madison: University of Wisconsin Press, 1984), 58, on the multiple interpretations generated by altering the context of a given utterance, and Kerrigan's argument that early modern texts were not as immutable, fixed, or sacrosanct as we might believe, given that their authors seemed quite amenable to altering them in accord with powerful patrons' responses (107).

6. Alpers, *The Poetry of "The Faerie Queene"* (Princeton: Princeton Uni-

versity Press, 1967), 137. See also Susan Suleiman and Inge Crosman, eds., *The Reader in the Text: Essays on Audience and Interpretation* (Princeton: Princeton University Press, 1980), 37, for a reminder that "even in the distant past and in a single society there was no such thing as a single homogeneous reading (or listening) public." Some useful recent studies of reading include Tony Bennett, "Texts in History: The Determinations of Readings and Their Texts," in *Post-structuralism and the Question of History*, ed. Derek Attridge, Geoff Bennington, and Robert Young (Cambridge: Cambridge University Press, 1987), 63–81; Roger Chartier, "Texts, Printing, Readings," in *The New Cultural History*, ed. Lynn Hunt (Berkeley and Los Angeles: University of California Press, 1989), 154–75; Robert Darnton, "History of Reading," in *New Perspectives on Historical Writing*, ed. Peter Burke (University Park: Pennsylvania State University Press, 1992), 140–67; and Kintgen. Because few women received what we would term a humanist education, we might question the degree to which Kintgen's conclusions apply to them, but on the other hand, it is unlikely that women would be completely unaware of the dominant mode of interpretation taught to and practiced by their fathers, brothers, husbands, and sons.

7. Kerrigan, 111.

8. Harington, *Orlando Furioso in English Heroical Verse* (1591), 7; hereafter cited in the text as *OF*.

9. Alastair Fowler and Michael Leslie, "Drummond's Copy of *The Faerie Queene*," *Times Literary Supplement*, 17 July, 1981, 822.

10. Graham Hough, "The First Commentary on *The Faerie Queene*," *Times Literary Supplement*, 9 April, 1964, 294.

11. Alpers, 153, note 20.

12. Riddell and Stewart, *Jonson's Spenser: Evidence and Historical Criticism* (Pittsburgh: Duquesne University Press, 1995), 81, 86.

13. Tuvil, *Asylum Veneris, or a sanctuary for ladies* (1616), 16, 24. The quotations may have been included partly to compliment the dedicatee, Lady Alice Colville, a member of the "noble Familie the Spencers" (sig. A4r). On Robert Allott's *Englands Parnassus* (1600), see Alpers, 158–59.

14. Beilin, *Redeeming Eve: Women Writers of the English Renaissance* (Princeton: Princeton University Press, 1987), 268–70.

15. See Betty Travitsky, "The New Mother of the English Renaissance: Her Writings on Motherhood," in *The Lost Tradition: Mothers and Daughters in Literature*, ed. Cathy N. Davidson and E. M. Broner (New York: Frederick Ungar, 1980), 37.

16. Walter Oakeshott, "Carew Ralegh's Copy of Spenser," *The Library*, 5th series, 26.1 (1971): 9–10, 4, 6, 17.

17. Reprinted in Wells, 124.

18. This is not to say that women readers did not or could not extrapolate morals and personal meaning from male literary figures, but rather that they may have read from (at least) two different subject positions: that of the generic (male) reader and the gendered (female) reader.

19. Holland in Plutarch, 17, 18.

20. Plutarch, 43.

21. Mulcaster, 175.

22. Hake, *A Touchestone for this time present* (1574), sig. C5r. The seventeenth-century use of the term "pamphlet," according to the *OED*, included "issues of single plays, romances, poems," etc. Lyly describes his *Euphues and*

his England (1581) as a "Pa[m]phlet . . . co[n]teining the estate of England" in his dedicatory epistle to the Earl of Oxford (sig. A4v).

23. Sidney, 236–37.

24. Despite Du Bosc's confidence in recommending history as a "safe" genre for women, even it could be subversively appropriated, as I will suggest in chapter 3.

25. Whitney, "The Auctour to the Reader," *A Sweet Nosgay.*

26. Beilin, 3. See also Warnicke, "Women and Humanism," 50. This concern about women and other marginalized groups gaining power by taking control of texts obviously predates the sixteenth century. Susan Schibanoff has analyzed marginalia in copies of the Wife of Bath's Tale, claiming that Alison's bookishness ("a woman's literal and metaphorical taking of texts into her own hands") dramatizes an "extreme act of new reading" ("The New Reader and Female Textuality in Two Early Commentaries on Chaucer," *Studies in the Age of Chaucer* 10 [1988]: 77).

27. Margaret Ferguson discusses this phenomenon in her essay "A Room Not Their Own," 115.

28. See Lamb, "Women Readers," 219. On passive and active female readers being two variants of the same type, see Susan Noakes, "On the Superficiality of Women," in *The Comparative Perspective in Literature*, 354–55. According to Kintgen, "Reconstructing Elizabethan Reading," *Studies in English Literature* 30 (1990): 13, many Tudor readers were "ignoring the allegorical significance of works for the literal." Such a practice gains added significance in light of the attempted restrictions of women's hermeneutic strategies.

29. Lamb, *Gender and Authorship*, 8. One of my goals in the present study is to attend to the gendered climate in which early modern women read but to do so without perpetuating the assumption that women's reading is inevitably and always sexual. On the association of women with carnal misreadings of texts, see also Noakes, 339–55; Sasha Roberts, "Reading the Shakespearean Text in Early Modern England," *Critical Survey* 7.3 (1995): 300; Louis B. Wright, "The Reading of Renaissance Englishwomen," 150–51.

30. Bullinger, *The christen state of matrimonye* (1541, 1546), trans. Miles Coverdale, sig. M7v–M8r.

31. Hake, sig. C4r.

32. Harington, "A Preface, Or Rather A Briefe Apologie of Poetrie and of the Author and translator of this Poem," *Orlando Furioso*, v. Intended to illustrate the thoroughness of female vice, this sly observation can be read instead as revealing the extent to which shame is a patriarchal construct—Lucrece is not guilty unless Brutus is there to say she is.

33. Brathwait, *The English Gentleman* (1630), 27–28.

34. Ibid., 29, 32.

35. Davies, "Papers Complaint, compild in ruthfull Rimes Against the Paper-Spoylers of these Times," in *The Scourge of Folly* (1611), 231–32.

36. Middleton, *A Mad World, My Masters*, ed. Standish Henning (London: Edward Arnold, 1965), 1.2.43–46. Henning explains (p. 12, note 46) that *The first booke of the christian exercise, apertayning to resolution* (1582) was a very popular devotional work written by the Jesuit Robert Parsons.

37. Ibid., 1.2.49–52, 86–90; 3.1.75–79.

38. Lyly, *Euphues and his England*, sig. A5v–A6v. Juliet Fleming discusses the erotic implications of this passage in "The Ladies' Man and the Age of Elizabeth" in *Sexuality and Gender in Early Modern Europe*, ed. James Grantham Turner (Cambridge: Cambridge University Press, 1993), 159.

39. Elyot's *Defence* may also have covertly promoted Catherine of Aragon's role as regent; see Constance Jordan, "Feminism and the Humanists: The Case of Sir Thomas Elyot's *Defence of Good Women*," in *Rewriting the Renaissance: The Discourses of Sexual Difference in Early Modern Europe*, ed. Margaret Ferguson, Maureen Quilligan, and Nancy Vickers (Chicago: University of Chicago Press, 1986), 242–58. Jordan's argument encourages us to explore what seem to be relatively straightforward, oppressive works of courtesy literature for their more subtle political nuances and subtexts.

40. Henry Willoby, *Willobie his Avisa. Or the true picture of a modest maid* (1594; 1609).

41. Rather than discuss romances with other proscribed texts in chapter 1, I do so here because the condemnation of the genre is inextricably linked to sexualized assumptions about women's interpretive practices, the focus of this chapter.

42. Hull, *Chaste*, 7, 35. See also Louis Wright, "Reading," 156.

43. See Roberts, ed. *The First Part of The Countess of Montgomery's Urania*, xvii.

44. Hamilton, "Elizabethan Prose Fiction and Some Trends in Recent Criticism," *Renaissance Quarterly* 37.1 (Spring 1984): 22, 28.

45. Ascham, *The Scholemaster* (1570), in *English Works of Roger Ascham*, ed. William Aldis Wright (Cambridge: Cambridge University Press, 1904), 230–31.

46. Consider, for example, the fates of Mary Fitton, Elizabeth Throckmorton, and Mary Wroth, all of whom suffered harsher consequences from their affairs than did their lovers. As Anne Laurence observes, "the poor were more likely to be punished for their sexual lapses than the rich, and women more likely than men" (*Women in England 1500–1760* [New York: St. Martin's Press, 1994], 47).

47. Verney cited in Reynolds, 25.

48. See Sara Heller Mendelson, *The Mental World of Stuart Women: Three Studies* (Amherst: University of Massachusetts Press, 1987), 66.

49. See Hamilton's gloss discussing Redcrosse's frequent slippage from his spiritual to literal knightly role (1.1.31).

50. One of the ways Spenser managed to defend his choice of the romance genre against residual humanist criticisms of its valorized violence and depictions of lust was his eclectic incorporation of motifs from a variety of genres; see John King, *Spenser's Poetry and the Reformation Tradition* (Princeton: Princeton University Press, 1990), 182. Carol Kaske's assessment of Spenser's dialogue with Ascham's critique in "How Spenser Really Used Stephen Hawes in the Legend of Holiness" in *Unfolded Tales: Essays on Renaissance Romance*, ed. George M. Logan and Gordon Teskey (Ithaca: Cornell University Press, 1989), 120–21 ("While his heroes still 'kill without any quarrel,' thus preserving the open manslaughter, Spenser purges his romance of any hint of adultery between characters for whom we have sympathy") may underestimate the problematic role of sexual desire in the text. See Cavanagh, *Wanton Eyes*, and Silberman, *Transforming Desire: Erotic Knowledge in Books III and IV of "The Faerie Queene"* (Berkeley and Los Angeles: University of California Press, 1995), passim.

51. See Watkins, 165–67, on Paridell and Hellenore's derivation from Chaucerian fabliau. Unlike Amoret, who is forced to play a role in Busirane's Petrarchan masque, Hellenore participates willingly in the antimasque dance with the satyrs.

52. See Suzuki, 159–73, on Spenser's allusions to Virgil and Ovid in the Paridell and Hellenore episode and p. 167 on Hellenore as a "reductive" reader.

53. See Suzuki, 166, on Britomart's and Paridell's different readings of history, and Theresa Krier, *Gazing on Secret Sights: Spenser, Classical Imitation, and the Decorums of Vision* (Ithaca: Cornell University Press, 1990), 181, on Britomart's heroic Virgilian identity and Paridell's more trivial Ovidian eroticism.

54. Hake, sig. C5v–C6r.

55. James Nohrnberg, *The Analogy of "The Faerie Queene"* (Princeton: Princeton University Press, 1976), 433, points out that Homer's Helen also "envisages her own life as designing itself in the form of literature."

56. Celeste Wright, "The Elizabethan Female Worthies," *Studies in Philology* 43.4 (1946): 640. See also Pamela Benson, *The Invention of the Renaissance Woman* (University Park: Pennsylvania State University Press, 1992), 1, on the "drawing of ethical rather than political morals from the exemplary lives" in Boccaccio's *De mulieribus claris*.

57. Pettie, *A Petite Pallace of Pettie his pleasure* (1576), sig. N1v.

58. Ferne, *The Blazon of Gentrie* (1586), 157–58.

59. Lanyer, *The Poems of Aemilia Lanyer*, ed. Susanne Woods (New York: Oxford University Press, 1993), 49.

60. Southwell, 147.

61. Mendelson, 185.

62. Maclean, 63.

63. Steen, "Fashioning an Acceptable Self: Arbella Stuart," in *Women in the Renaissance: Selections from "English Literary Renaissance,"* ed. Kirby Farrell, Elizabeth H. Hageman, and Arthur F. Kinney (Amherst: University of Massachusetts Press, 1990), 137.

64. Furman, "Textual Feminism," in *Women and Language in Literature and Society*, ed. Sally McConnell-Ginet, Ruth Borker, and Nelly Furman (New York: Praeger, 1980), 52.

65. Catherine Belsey, *The Subject of Tragedy: Identity and Difference in Renaissance Drama* (London: Methuen, 1985), 149–50.

66. Greville, "A Letter to an Honorable Lady," in *The Prose Works of Fulke Greville, Lord Brooke*, ed. John Gouws (Oxford: Clarendon Press, 1986), 152, 166. Similarly, young boys today are considerably less comfortable reading what are perceived to be books for girls than girls are reading books for boys.

67. Karen Newman, *Fashioning Femininity and English Renaissance Drama* (Chicago: University of Chicago Press, 1991), xviii.

68. Krueger, "Desire, Meaning, and the Female Reader: The Problem in Chretien's *Charrete*," in *The Passing of Arthur: New Essays in Arthurian Tradition*, ed. Christopher Baswell and William Sharpe (New York: Garland, 1988), 35; Cavanagh, *Wanton Eyes*, passim.

69. From *The womens sharpe revenge* (1640), cited in Betty Travitsky, "The Lady Doth Protest: Protest in the Popular Writings of Renaissance Englishwomen," *English Literary Renaissance* 14 (1984): 281.

70. Steen, 153.

71. Elizabeth Abel, ed., *Writing and Sexual Difference* (Chicago: University of Chicago Press, 1982), 2.

72. Susan Schibanoff, "Taking the Gold Out of Egypt: The Art of Reading as a Woman," in *Gender and Reading: Essays on Readers, Texts, and Contexts*, ed. Elizabeth A. Flynn and Patrocinio P. Schweickart (Baltimore: Johns Hopkins University Press, 1986), 98, 100.

73. Wogan-Browne, " 'Clerc u lai, muïne u dame': women and Anglo-Norman hagiography in the twelfth and thirteenth centuries," in *Women and Literature in Britain,* ed. Meale, 64–65.

74. Jonathan Culler, *On Deconstruction: Theory and Criticism after Structuralism* (Ithaca: Cornell University Press, 1982), 48; Judith Fetterley, *The Resisting Reader: A Feminist Approach to American Fiction* (Bloomington: Indiana University Press, 1978).

75. Weller and Ferguson, 26–27.

76. Barbara Lewalski believes that these women writers "rewrite discourses which repress or diminish women—patriarchy, gender hierarchy, Petrarchanism, Pauline marriage theory, and more—by redefining or extending their terms, or infusing them with new meaning: it is the way any orthodoxy is first opened to revisionism." Lewalski also suggests that fictional images of "vigorous and rebellious female characters" may have worked "to undermine any monolithic social construct of woman's nature and role. There is some evidence that women took the oppositional support they needed or wanted from plays and books." See her "Writing Women and Reading the Renaissance," *Renaissance Quarterly* 44.4 (Winter 1991): 795, 797.

77. Newman, *Fashioning,* 30; Lamb, *Gender,* 4.

78. Cecily Macwilliam Ridgway was the wife of Sir Thomas Ridgway, Lord Treasurer of Ireland from 1606–1616. Barnabe Rich dedicated *A catholicke conference* (1612) to her.

79. Jean C. Cavanaugh, "Lady Southwell's Defense of Poetry," reprinted in *Women in the Renaissance,* 175–77.

80. Southwell, 42.

81. Cavendish's quote from *Sociable Letters* (1664) is cited in Mendelson, *Mental World,* 35.

82. Hull, *Chaste,* 8.

83. Bradford, *Elizabethan Women,* ed. Harold Ogden White (Cambridge, MA: Houghton Mifflin, 1936), 35.

84. Du Verger, sig. A6r–v.

85. Ibid., sig. a2r.

86. On Tyler, see Tina Krontiris, "Breaking Barriers of Genre and Gender: Margaret Tyler's Translation of *The Mirrour of Knighthood,*" reprinted in *Women in the Renaissance,* 48–68; E. D. Mackerness, "Margaret Tyler: An Elizabethan Feminist," *Notes and Queries* 190 (1946): 112–13; Louise Schleiner, "Margaret Tyler, Translator and Waiting Woman," *English Language Notes* 29.3 (March 1992): 1–8; and Schleiner, *Tudor and Stuart Women Writers,* 18–22. Subsequent references to *The Mirrour* will be cited in the text.

87. Schleiner, *Tudor and Stuart Women Writers,* 253, note 21, also comments on Tyler's use of both the "alarming" amazonian metaphor and traditionally "feminine" virtues.

88. Weller and Ferguson observe, "Translation itself had been personified as a 'female' phenomenon by John Florio in the preface to his English version of Montaigne's *Essays,*" 12.

89. Roche, 78.

90. My reading of this episode, as will be apparent, is indebted throughout to Lauren Silberman, "Singing Unsung Heroines: Androgynous Discourse in Book 3 of *The Faerie Queene*" in *Rewriting the Renaissance,* 259–71; Silberman, *Transforming Desire,* 58–70; and Susanne Lindgren Wofford, "Gendering Allegory: Spenser's Bold Reader and the Emergence of Character in *The Faerie Queene* III," *Criticism* 30.1 (Winter 1988): 1–21.

91. Dorothy Atkinson, "Busirane's Castle and Artidon's Cave," *Modern Language Quarterly* 1 (1940): 185–92.

92. Maureen Quilligan suggests that Amoret's torture could be read as "a Petrarchan metaphor literalized. . . . Like a sadistic sonneteer, Busyrane cruelly 'pens' Amoret in both senses of the word, trying to persuade her to love him by all the Petrarchan arts of seduction hideously literalized in the masque" ("Words and Sex: The Language of Allegory in the *De planctu naturae,* the *Roman de la Rose,* and Book III of *The Faerie Queene,*" *Allegorica* 1 [1977]: 209–210). In 3.7.7, Florimell passes through a door to discover the witch "Busie . . . about some wicked gin," a scenario enacted by Britomart first with Merlin and later with Busirane, both of whom are engaged in ordering the female imagination. The witch creates a perverted Petrarchan image of Florimell as Busirane does with Amoret, although the witch's False Florimell constitutes a more scathingly sarcastic rereading of the literary tradition's image of the sexually desirable female.

93. Winkler, *The Constraints of Desire: The Anthropology of Sex and Gender in Ancient Greece* (New York: Routledge, 1990), 11.

94. See Frye, 127–28, on the constant Amoret's resistance to Busirane's attempts to remove her heart. See also Wofford, "Gendering," 11.

95. Quilligan, "Lady Mary Wroth: Female Authority and the Family Romance," in *Unfolded Tales: Essays on Renaissance Romance,* ed. George Logan and Gordon Teskey (Ithaca: Cornell University Press, 1989), 262–63.

96. Wofford, "Gendering," 10.

97. Broaddus, "Renaissance Psychology and Britomart's Adventures in *Faerie Queene* III," *English Literary Renaissance* 17 (1987): 199. See also Cavanagh, *Wanton,* 141, and Frye, 129.

98. Watkins, 174.

99. *The Rape of Lucrece,* in *The Riverside Shakespeare,* ed. G. Blakemore Evans, 2nd ed. (Boston: Houghton Mifflin, 1997), line 1444. All references to Shakespeare's poetry and plays will be to this edition and cited in the text.

100. Nicholas Breton, *The Wil of Wit* (1597), sig. R3v.

101. Claridiana first learns of Artidon's powers when she encounters the lady Elizea and her knight, whom she then accompanies to Artidon's.

102. Wofford, "Gendering," 11–12, argues that "Busyrane's magic letters, written in blood, serve to transform women (in this case, Amoret) into allegorical figures. The literalization of writing with 'liuing blood' marks out the implicit violence of his poetic praxis, and shows that Busyrane's art functions by denying the woman any interiority. Though Merlin's plot does so benignly, both Merlin and Busyrane pen the female character into a specific plot that depends not only on female stereotypes but also on making female characters serve allegorical ends. . . . Busyrane comes to stand for the potential abuses of allegory itself. . . . In this self-interrogation, then, Spenser looks at Busyrane's art from the point of view of a woman and condemns it. He uses a more fictional mode of writing to challenge and reveal the limitations of allegory in its most static and extreme form." Although my own reading is clearly very close to Wofford's, I think she may underestimate the agency of women, who are capable of exercising creative resistance to Merlin and Busirane during the reading process. Frye, 134, articulates a much more negative view of a Spenser who fails to provide an alternative to the destructive Petrarchan paradigm.

103. See Pearson, 87.

104. Frye, 130.

CHAPTER 3. "DON QUIXOTE'S SISTERS"

1. *Hic Mulier: Or, The Man-Woman: Being a Medicine to cure the Coltish Disease of the Staggers in the Masculine-Feminines of our Times* (1620), sig. B3r–v. See also Wofford, *Choice*, 221, and Roberts, ed., *Urania*, xxi–xxii, for discussion of this passage.

2. L. A., "To the Friendly and Courteous Readers," *The Seventh Booke of the Myrrour of Knighthood* (1598).

3. Robert Burton, for example, links *The Faerie Queene* with *The Mirrour* and other popular romances in the fourth edition of *The Anatomy of Melancholy* (1632); see part 3, section 2, member 3, subsection 1: "Our Knights errant, and the Sir Lancelots of these days, I hope will adventure as much for Ladies' favours, as the Squire of Dames, Knight of the Sun, Sir Bevis of Southampton, or that renowned Peer *Orlando*" (*The Anatomy of Melancholy*, ed. Floyd Dell and Paul Jordan-Smith [New York: Tudor Publishing Co., 1941], 746.

4. *Hic Mulier*, sig. C2r–v.

5. Krueger undertakes a similar project in *Women Readers*, exploring "how the female reader *in* romance problematizes the role of the female reader *of* romance" (xiii).

6. Plutarch, 22.

7. Dramatists of the period satirized the same dynamic: the Beadle calls Doll Tearsheet a "she knight-arrant" in Shakespeare's *2 Henry IV* (5.4.22); Sir Epicure Mammon calls Dol Common "a Bradamante, a brave piece" in *The Alchemist* (2.3.225); and Gertrude in *Eastward Ho!* holds her ridiculous knight to the romance standard of the Knight of the Sun (2.2.180 ff. and 358 ff.; 5.1.28). See *Ben Jonson*, ed. C. H. Herford and Percy Simpson (Oxford: Clarendon Press, 1937), vols. 4 and 5. See also Simon Shepherd, *Amazons and Warrior Women: Varieties of Feminism in Seventeenth-Century Drama* (New York: St. Martin's Press, 1981), 71.

8. See also Du Bosc: "But this is not all that is evill in these Pamphlets, after they have made many *women* bold, it makes them practick in it, they finde out subtilties, with safty in them, and learne therein not only the evill they should not know, but even the fayrest wayes to perpetrat the same" (*CW*, sig. H4v).

9. See Wofford, "Gendering," 9, on Britomart's association with "several images of inner spaces, themselves connected both to female sexuality and textual interpretation."

10. Maclean, 41, citing Luis Mercado (Mercatus), *De mulierum affectionibus* (1579).

11. "An Homilie of the state of Matrimonie," in *Certaine Sermons or Homilies Appointed to be Read in Churches in the Time of Queen Elizabeth I (1547–1571)*, ed. Mary Ellen Rickey and Thomas B. Stroup (Gainesville, FL: Scholars' Facsimiles and Reprints, 1968), 241.

12. David Miller, *The Poem's Two Bodies*, 253, cites Ambroise Paré, *On Monsters and Marvels*, trans. Janis L. Pallister (Chicago: University of Chicago Press, 1982), the ninth chapter of which is entitled "An Example of Monsters that Are Created through the Imagination" (38–42). See also Maclean, 41, citing Mercado and Levinus Lemnius, *Occulta naturae miracula* (1559; Antwerp, 1574) on the imagination affecting children in utero.

13. Nashe, *The Anatomie of Absurditie* (1589), sig. A1v.

14. See Robert M. Durling, *The Figure of the Poet in Renaissance Epic* (Cambridge, MA: Harvard University Press, 1965), 223, on Ariosto and Spenser

adopting variations of Ovid's stance as a *praeceptor amoris*. See also Patrick Cheney, " 'Secret Powre Unseene': Good Magic in Spenser's Legend of Britomart," *Studies in Philology* 85.1 (Winter 1988): 26; Frye, 128; A. Bartlett Giamatti, *Play of Double Senses: Spenser's "Faerie Queene"* (Englewood Cliffs, NJ: Prentice Hall, 1975), 114, 118; and Wofford, "Gendering," 1, for discussions of Merlin, Busirane, and other poets manqué.

15. Wofford, "Britomart's Petrarchan Lament: Allegory and Narrative in *The Faerie Queene* III.iv," *Comparative Literature* 39.1 (Winter 1987): 28.

16. Quilligan, "Words and Sex," 202. On Britomart as a reader, see Silberman, *Transforming*, 21–26.

17. On Bradamante as a reader, see Albert Russell Ascoli, *Ariosto's Bitter Harmony: Crisis and Evasion in the Italian Renaissance* (Princeton: Princeton University Press, 1987), 23–24.

18. The plates in Harington's translation were probably done by Englishman Thomas Coxon, who followed those of Girolamo Porro in the 1584 Franceschi edition. See Robert McNulty's introductory commentary, *Ludovico Ariosto's Orlando Furioso Translated into English Historical Verse by Sir John Harington, 1591* (Oxford: Clarendon Press, 1972), xiii–xliii; xlv–xlvi.

19. See Jonathan Goldberg, *Endlesse Worke: Spenser and the Structures of Discourse* (Baltimore: Johns Hopkins University Press, 1981), 63, on the irony of Scudamour's substituting the story of his initial conquest of Amoret for her actual restoration to him.

20. The motif of male knights falling in love with portraits of their ladies also occurs in the Amadis cycle (Amadis de Grece and Agesilan fall in love with painted images and then disguise themselves as amazons). See John J. O'Connor, *Amadis de Gaule and Its Influence on Elizabethan Literature* (New Brunswick, NJ: Rutgers University Press, 1970), 187. Although a detailed comparison of male and female figures falling in love with visual images is beyond the scope of this study, the transformative process seems to reinforce early modern gender assumptions (i.e., women are "perfected" by loving a man, often evidenced by their adoption of male attire as knights, whereas men renounce their unequivocal masculinity in assuming the more sexually ambiguous amazonian costume).

21. See Walker, *Medusa's Mirrors*, 77–113, on Britomart's mirror vision.

22. Whether or not Spenser was aware of it, an historical analogue for Britomart's vision occurred in 1575 when Queen Elizabeth viewed magician John Dee's mirror. Dee, who was occasionally called Merlin (see Frances Yates, *The Occult Philosophy in the Elizabethan Age* [London: Routledge and Kegan Paul, 1979], 107), recalls: "The Queene's Majestie, with her most honourable Privy Council, and other her Lords and Nobility, came purposely to have visited my library: but finding that my wife was within four houres before buried out of the house, her Majestie refused to come in; but willed to fetch my glass so famous, and to show unto her some of the properties of it, which I did; her Majestie being taken down from her horse by the Earle of Leicester . . . did see some of the properties of that glass, to her Majestie's great contentment and delight." This entry in Dee's *Compendious Memorial* for 16 March, 1575, is cited in *The Private Diary of Dr. John Dee*, ed. James Orchard Halliwell (New York: AMS Press, 1968), 9–10. Here, the British queen commands the mage rather than, as in the Britomart episode, the mage scripting the British princess into a courtship narrative.

23. Stump, "Britomart's Mock-Romantic Quest" in *Spenser and the Middle*

Ages, ed. David A. Richardson (Kalamazoo, MI: Proceedings from a Special Session at the Eleventh Conference on Medieval Studies, 1976), 158. See also Thomas Bulger, "Britomart and Galahad," *English Language Notes* 25.1 (September 1987): 10–17, for Britomart's medieval precursors.

24. On Britomart as an autonomous woman subject, see Silberman, "Singing," 261.

25. Burton, *Anatomy*, part 3, section 2, memb. 3, p. 758.

26. See Silberman, *Transforming*, 13–33, on Britomart's mirror vision.

27. For a similar argument, see Margaret Thickstun, *Fictions of the Feminine: Puritan Doctrine and the Representation of Women* (Ithaca: Cornell University Press, 1988), 49.

28. Mildmay cited in Weigall, 122.

29. Silberman, Quilligan, and Wofford all note Britomart's excessive use of Petrarchan discourse. According to Quilligan, "Spenser makes Britomart speak Petrarchese with such a vengeance that her description of love's sufferings sounds more like a clinical account of stomach cancer than a conventional complaint of love" ("Words and Sex," 200). Silberman concurs: Britomart "is an anti-Petrarchan heroine. . . . [whose] uncertainty, as she falls in love with Artegall having seen nothing more than his image, about whether her love is true and destined to be fulfilled or whether it is a perverse and cruel delusion, shows up the too-pat Petrarchan strategy of making of the poet's own mental state the primary, objective reality" ("Singing Unsung Heroines," 260). See also Wofford, "Gendering," on Britomart as a reader.

30. Pettie, sig. O3v–O4r.

31. Spenser vaguely suggests this possibility in his omitting any reference to Britomart's mother and in describing Ryence as "reserving nothing apart" from his daughter, hinting at the incest motif characteristic of several Renaissance romances, Shakespeare's *Pericles* being a well-known example.

32. Artegall's appearance at the tourney in Book 4 is so unprepossessing that even though Britomart engages him in battle, she fails to recognize him; his petulant exit, motivated by disappointed lust for the False Florimell, causes Britomart no regret. Artegall will also fail to fulfill her romantic idealization of him when she views him in his cross-dressed condition in Book 5. Camille Paglia, *Sexual Personae: Art and Decadence from Nefertiti to Emily Dickinson* (New Haven: Yale University Press, 1990), 183, also notes that Artegall "falls dismally short of Britomart's daydreams."

33. Wofford, "Gendering," 8.

34. Silberman, "Singing," 262.

35. Walker, *Medusa's Mirrors*, 15.

36. Alciati, *Omnia Andreae Alciati Emblemata* (Paris, 1583), 273–74.

37. See also Silberman, *Transforming*, 19, and Linda Gregerson, "Protestant Erotics: Idolatry and Interpretation in Spenser's *Faerie Queene*," *ELH* 58.1 (Spring 1991): 20.

38. Wroth, *Urania*, p. 90, lines 21–23.

39. Pettie, sig. L3v.

40. This vicarious pleasure helps to explain the enormous popularity romance narratives still command today. See Laurie Langbauer, *Women and Romance: The Consolations of Gender in the English Novel* (Ithaca: Cornell University Press, 1990) and Janice Radway, *Reading the Romance: Women, Patriarchy, and Popular Literature* (Chapel Hill: University of North Carolina Press, 1984).

41. Tina Krontiris notes that "the author has no control over how the reader will construct meaning" (57) and speculates that women readers might have read amazon figures for vicarious pleasure, giving them "the opportunity to identify with members of their sex who at least on the printed page were engaging in traditionally male activities" (56). Like Krontiris, I am suggesting that such vicarious pleasure may have fueled genuine acts of resistance, however limited in scope.

42. As Susanne Woods puts it, "Her woman's love makes her a manlike warrior" ("Spenser and the Problem of Women's Rule," 152). See also the tale entitled "The Amazon" in Du Verger, trans., *Admirable Events*, in which "*Yoland* who had taken mans apparell to follow her Lover, found her selfe so well in that habit, and tooke such delight in all the exercises of armes, that she became an Amazon; she learned in short time to shoot with a piece, to fence, to ride a horse" (346).

43. For this reason, Benson, 261, claims that Britomart "does not threaten patriarchal order" in the poem.

44. Benson, 270. See also Lillian Robinson, *Monstrous Regiment: The Lady Knight in Sixteenth-Century Epic* (New York: Garland, 1985), 300–301, and Walker, *Medusa's Mirrors*, 88–89, on Glauce's history lesson.

45. Walker, *Medusa's Mirrors*, links "Glauce" with "glossing" (93); the *OED* indicates that the word was often used in "a sinister sense" to indicate a "sophistical or disingenuous interpretation."

46. Suzuki, 171.

47. Eugene Vinauer, ed. *The Works of Thomas Malory*, 2nd ed., 3 vols. (Oxford: Clarendon Press, 1973), 1:371–72.

48. Benson argues that "found" means discovered (and not "established" as Hamilton surmises) because law was assumed to exist naturally (270).

49. Carrie Harper, *The Sources of the British Chronicle History in Spenser's Faerie Queene* (Philadelphia: John Winston, 1910), 119.

50. Ibid., 59, 61.

51. Ibid., 60. Britomart will prove to be similarly violent in her response to Artegall's betrayal, but, rather than attack Artegall directly, her anger is channeled into her attack on Radigund. Claridiana's response, in contrast, resembles that of Guendolen: the inconstant Knight of the Sun sees Claridiana in a vision "with so great majestie and beautie, that it dazeled the sight of his eies, equall unto the shining of the Sunne when he appeareth out of the Orient, her bodie all armed, saving her head & face was wholie discovered with her yeolow golden haire, which was disparsed behinde her eares, and hung downe unto the grounde like threeds of golde, she had hir swoord naked in her hand, and with an irefull semblaunce, lifting up her arme for to strike him, she said. Oh false and traiterous knight, thou art now at the extremitie and point to receive the guerdon for thy great disloialtie" (1586, *Third part of the first booke*, ch. 1, 2v). In his dream he falls at her feet asking pardon, but she "alwaies seemed for to strike him with the sword she had in her hand" (3r). Claridiana will later chide herself for reproaching her knight, but at least is depicted as venting her anger more directly than does Britomart.

52. Harper, 62.

53. See Henry Ten Eyck Perry, *The First Duchess of Newcastle and Her Husband as Figures in Literary History* (Boston and London: Ginn and Company, 1918; reprint, 1968), 215–16.

54. Benson, 271.

55. Harper, 166. It is unclear whether Holinshed's opinion indicates disapproval of bad scholarship or resistance to depicting a powerful woman leader.

56. Ibid., 168.

57. Cavanagh observes that "The new warrior . . . betrays no explicit debt to the female warrior tradition which the narrator claims to miss" in 3.4.1 (*Wanton Eyes*, 152), yet I would suggest that the implicit debt is apparent.

58. Villeponteaux, 64, also notes, "Nor is the idea of the masculine disguise Merlin's." Although I make this point to emphasize literary appropriation rather than castration anxiety, we're heading to a similar conclusion; as Villeponteaux puts it, "Britomart's ability to don a masculine identity and the authority it confers, even as she can don her armor and weapons, is potentially subversive in what it suggests about the nature of power and authority—that they are constructs that can be adopted, even by a woman, rather than innate and 'natural' traits of maleness" (64–65).

59. Claridiana is also notably tall; the Knight of the Sun is able to wear a suit of armor that has been made for the princess, "for that in stature they were almost equall" (Bk. 1, pt. 3, ch. 32, 153r).

60. Buncombe, 172; Cavanagh, *Wanton Eyes*, 202, note 32. See also Silberman, *Transforming*, 20 and 148, note 29 on Britomart's story of her upbringing as a martial maid and the fictional "constructedness" of Britomart as a character. Walker believes Britomart's story to be "a revising and re-presenting of history and of her identity before she looked into Merlin's mirror, . . . that of a masculine childhood—coming as close as she can to self-denial and self-revision by seeing herself as the knight in the mirror" (*Medusa's Mirrors*, 79), whereas I view it as an emblem of the facility of female readers to appropriate literary paradigms.

61. See Janet Arnold, *Queen Elizabeth's Wardrobe Unlock'd* (Leeds: W. S. Maney, 1988), 201, for a warrant itemizing the feathers purchased to trim the queen's hats and a reproduction of a 1573 portrait by George Gower of Elizabeth Cornwallis, Lady Kyston [*sic*; presumably an error for Kytson], wearing a high-crowned, feather-trimmed hat.

62. *Hic Mulier*, sig. B2r.

63. Silberman, *Transforming*, 20.

64. Lamb, *Gender*, 8; Rozsika Parker, *The Subversive Stitch: Embroidery and the Making of the Feminine* (London: The Woman's Press Ltd., 1984), 15.

65. Lewalski, *Writing Women in Jacobean England*, 45–65, 89.

66. See lines 37–42, cited by Constance Jordan, *Renaissance Feminism: Literary Texts and Political Models* (Ithaca: Cornell University Press, 1990), 175, note 33.

CHAPTER 4. "PUT ON YOUR VAILES"

1. Whigham, *Ambition and Privilege: The Social Tropes of Elizabethan Courtesy Theory* (Berkeley and Los Angeles: University of California Press, 1984), 38, 191 note 36.

2. Quilligan, *Milton's Spenser*, 197. All women, according to T. E., the author of *The lawes resolutions of Womens Rights* (1632), were "understood either married or to bee married" (cited in Betty Travitsky, "Introduction: Placing Women in the English Renaissance," in Anne M. Haselkorn and Betty S. Travit-

sky, eds., *The Renaissance Englishwoman in Print: Counterbalancing the Canon* [Amherst: University of Massachusetts Press, 1990], 23).

3. Quilligan, *Milton's Spenser*, 37.

4. Patricia Fumerton, *Cultural Aesthetics: Renaissance Literature and the Practice of Social Ornament* (Chicago: University of Chicago Press, 1991), 51, also notes the similarity of Amoret's progress (from Chrysogone to Venus to Psyche to the Fairy Queen) to the educational training of such Elizabethan girls as Bridget Manners and Penelope Devereux.

5. This seems to have been the approach of Margaret Lucas as she strategically sought to engage the attentions of the Earl of Newcastle. Mendelson observes that "during courtship, . . . young women exploited the very conventions that were intended to circumscribe their activities. Margaret Lucas used her modesty (along with other traditional female weapons) as an aggressive lure" (24, 187).

6. Ann Rosalind Jones, "Nets and Bridles: Early Modern Conduct Books and Sixteenth-Century Women's Lyrics," in *The Ideology of Conduct: Essays on the Literature and History of Sexuality*, ed. Nancy Armstrong and Leonard Tennenhouse (New York: Methuen, 1987), 41. Carol Neely, *Broken Nuptials in Shakespeare's Plays* (New Haven: Yale University Press, 1985), 10, comments on the intense competition for husbands during the period; the average size of dowries doubled from 1570 to 1590 and increased even more in subsequent years. See also Hull, *Chaste*, 123–24, on the surplus of marriageable women.

7. Jones, 40–41, 43.

8. Murray, *The Ideal of the Court Lady 1561–1625* (Chicago: University of Chicago Libraries, 1938), 1, 22.

9. Jones, 43.

10. Giamatti, *Play of Double Senses: Spenser's "Faerie Queene"* (Englewood Cliffs, NJ: Prentice Hall, 1975), 68.

11. Lockerd, *The Sacred Marriage: Psychic Integration in "The Faerie Queene"* (Lewisburg: Bucknell University Press, 1987), 122, 151.

12. Trafton, "Politics and the Praise of Women: Political Doctrine in *The Courtier*'s Third Book," in *Castiglione: The Ideal and the Real in Renaissance Culture*, ed. Robert Hanning and David Rosand (New Haven: Yale University Press, 1983), 33, 36.

13. Rebhorn, *Courtly Performances: Masking and Festivity in Castiglione's "Book of the Courtier"* (Detroit: Wayne State University Press, 1978), 42. Spenser exhibits a similar concern in his description of Calidore in 6.1.2. Calidore's courtesy, his gentleness of spirit, mild manners, comely appearance, and gracious speech are all itemized, but then, as if these qualities will be construed as too effeminate, the narrator hastens to assure us, "Nathlesse thereto he was full stout and tall, / And well approu'd in batteilous affray, / That him did much renowme."

14. Sir Thomas Elyot, *The Boke Named the Governour*, sig. J5v. I use the 1580 edition throughout.

15. Buncombe, 165, links Castiglione's ideal gentlewoman with Florimell, who serves "as the allegorical symbol of a combination of the Neo-Platonic concept of love and the Christian virtues of the chaste, unmarried noblewoman at court." Yet Amoret seems to me an even more compelling exemplar than Florimell, given the emphasis on her socialization and her precise placement in Womanhood's lap in the Temple of Venus.

16. Lewis, *Spenser's Images of Life*, ed. Alastair Fowler (Cambridge: Cambridge University Press, 1967), 60.

17. Henry Smith, *A Preparative to Mariage* (1591; Lowell, MA: E. A. Rice and J. E. Short, 1847), 40. See Robert Cleaver, *A Godlie Forme of Householde Government* (1598), 105, for a close parallel.

18. Miller, 219.

19. One way to interpret the link between Britomart and Amoret can be found in Du Bosc's chapter "Of Chastitie and Courtisie": "It is fit to joyne these two goodly qualities together to reduce them into a perfect temper; since there are some who become curst for being chast, and others refuse nothing for being curteous" (*CW*, sig. O2v). Britomart and Amoret must each incorporate aspects of the other.

20. Watkins, 127, reads Alma and Medina as shadows of Elizabeth "in their personal chastity and in their rational government of their estates." I would suggest, however, that many Elizabethan and Jacobean women had experience in governing family estates and that these characteristics need not limit our reading of the characters to the queen.

21. See Greenblatt, 157–92. See also Watkins: "Book II dispels epic's long-standing anxieties about female magistracy by recasting the Renaissance distinction between the chaste and concupiscent Didos as a contrast between Italianate temptresses like Phaedria and Acrasia and surrogates of the Virgin Queen like Medina, Alma, and Belphoebe. . . . By privileging starkly allegorical places of instruction like Medina's Castle and the House of Alma over the luxuriance of the Bower of Bliss, Spenser establishes himself as a writer of explicitly didactic verse in contrast to Ariosto's and Tasso's luxuriance" (8). Watkins' point is well taken, but his focus remains on the male recipient of Spenserian didacticism.

22. A. Kent Hieatt discusses the parallels between Phaedria's and Medina's interventions in "A Spenser to Structure our Myths," in *Contemporary Thoughts on Edmund Spenser*, ed. Richard Frushell and Bernard Vondersmith (Carbondale: Southern Illinois University Press, 1975), 114–16.

23. Miller, 178. Less sexually charged than the depiction of the female body in the Garden of Adonis, Spenser's House of Alma is used in William Austin's *Haec homo, wherein the excellency of the creation of woman is described* (1636) (cited in Louis Wright, *Middle-Class Culture in Elizabethan England* [Chapel Hill: University of North Carolina Press, 1935], 503).

24. See also Jones's discussion of this misinterpretation by William Guazzo in "Nets and Bridles," 44.

25. Krier, *Gazing*, 67.

26. Jones, 46.

27. See Hamilton's gloss and Watkins, 132.

28. Tilney, *Flower of Friendshippe* (1568), sig. D7v.

29. According to Thomas Wright's *The passions of the minde* (1601), one could identify harlots by "the light & wanton motions of their eyes" and "honest matrons, by their grave and chaste lookes" (54).

30. The oxymoron "carelesse modestee" derives from Britomart's disarming at Malbecco's castle in 3.9.21.

31. Yeazell, *Fictions of Modesty: Women and Courtship in the English Novel* (Chicago: University of Chicago Press, 1991), 5–6, 11.

32. Wroth's *Urania* details the multiple uses to which the blush could be put: Orilena, beloved of Philarchos, communicates by blushing (205); Dalinea wants to tell Parselius of her love but modesty forbids it; however, her "modestly amorous" looks prompt him to take her in his arms without her having to say the

words "I love you," and he eventually marries her (126–27); Lucenia's blush is duplicitous—"desiring to bee thought bashful, but more longing to bee intreated for the rest" (163).

33. The false Una and False Florimell, as well as Duessa, are skillful practitioners of the tactics of feigning shamefastness.

34. Jones, 44–45.

35. Lyly, *Euphues and his England*, sig. P2v–P3r.

36. See Carol Cook, " 'The Sign and Semblance of Her Honor': Reading Gender Difference in *Much Ado about Nothing*," *PMLA* 101 (1986): 186–202.

37. Thickstun, 49.

38. Krier, " 'All suddeinly abasht she chaunged hew': Abashedness in *The Faerie Queene*," *Modern Philology* 84.2 (November 1986): 142, 132.

39. Biblical texts and glosses are taken from the Geneva Bible (1560), henceforward cited parenthetically in the text.

40. *Hic Mulier*, sig. B3r. See also 6.1.13 on the discourtesy of cutting men's beards and women's hair. Spenser conspicuously diverges from his source by adding an insult to the lady to parallel that given the man.

41. A. Bartlett Giamatti's "Spenser: From Magic to Miracle," in *Four Essays on Romance*, ed. Herschel Baker (Cambridge, MA: Harvard University Press, 1971), 15–31, addresses the wonder-inspiring quality of Britomart's hair. See also John Bean, "Cosmic Order in *The Faerie Queene*: From Temperance to Chastity," *SEL* 17 (1977): 71–72, on the hair of Spenserian heroines.

42. See David Lindley, "Embarrassing Ben: The Masques for Frances Howard," *English Literary Renaissance* 16 (1986): 349. On the common Elizabethan practice of virgin brides wearing their hair loose, see Roy Strong, *The Cult of Elizabeth: Elizabethan Portraiture and Pageantry* (Berkeley and Los Angeles: University of California Press, 1977), 17.

43. John Davies, *Wittes Pilgrimage* (1605), sig. Q3r.

44. David Miller, 229.

45. Watkins, 119.

46. *Haec Vir* reprinted in Katherine Usher Henderson and Barbara F. McManus, eds. *Half Humankind: Contexts and Texts of the Controversy about Women in England, 1540–1640* (Urbana: University of Illinois Press, 1985), 288.

47. Juliet Dusinberre, *Shakespeare and the Nature of Women* (London: Macmillan, 1975), 66.

CHAPTER 5. COURTSHIP AND THE FEMALE COURTIER

1. Woodbridge, *Women and the English Renaissance*, 134.

2. For example, Watkins points out that Hellenore's behavior would be judged harshly by epic standards but much more positively by those of the fabliau (164–67).

3. Thickstun, 41–42.

4. See also Cavanagh, *Wanton Eyes*, 76, and Anne Shaver, "Rereading Mirabella," *Spenser Studies* 9 (1988): 217, on the manipulability of the term "chaste."

5. William Baldwin, *A treatise of morall phylosophie* (1547; "Now the sixt time inlarged" by Thomas Palfreyman, 1620), 115v. As the rest of this chapter will suggest, Baldwin's word "sincere" is highly problematic.

6. Kelso, *Doctrine for the Lady of the Renaissance* (Urbana: University of Illinois Press, 1956), 23–24.

7. Maclean, 62. See also Cavanagh's observation that "Arthur's . . . absence during Britomart's adventure supports the suggestion that chastity is . . . primarily a female virtue" (" 'Beauties Chace': Arthur and Women in *The Faerie Queene*," in *The Passing of Arthur*, 215.

8. Jones, 45. The modern-day equivalent of this dynamic is the insidious accusation that a raped woman "asked" for it.

9. Iser, *The Act of Reading: A Theory of Aesthetic Response* (Baltimore: Johns Hopkins University Press, 1978), 78. In one sense, *all* readers are participants in the construction of a text's meaning, but Iser's distinction is nevertheless useful.

10. See Lamb, *Gender*, 15, for one possible explanation of the sexual license granted to Rich, who carried on a blatant extramarital affair with Charles Blount, Lord Mountjoy. Mary Fitton, however, was dismissed from court after bearing a stillborn child to William Herbert; Ann Vavasour was also punished for bearing a child to Edward de Vere. Even in the rather notorious moral climate of the Jacobean court (Anne Clifford had noted in 1603 that "all the ladies . . . had gotten such ill names that it was grown a scandalous place," 16–17), Lady Mary Wroth's affair with her cousin William Herbert contributed to her being exiled from court. Her romance *The Countess of Montgomery's Urania* "heroizes constant women who remain true to lovers, not necessarily to their husbands" (Lamb, *Gender*, 18). This stance seems closer than Spenser's to the spirit of the medieval romance tradition and plays out Ascham's fears of the romance's privileging of adultery.

11. *Speeches Delivered to Her Majestie This Last Progresse* (Oxford: Joseph Barnes, 1592), A3r. See also Jean Wilson, ed. *Entertainments for Elizabeth I* (Totowa, NJ: D. S. Brewer, 1980), 45; 149, note 108. For a more extensive discussion of this episode and the role of Elizabeth's attendants, see my essay "Reading the Margins: Female Courtiers in the Portraits of Elizabeth I," *Ben Jonson Journal* 2 (1995): 31–58.

12. Harington, *Nugae Antiquae*, 2:137.

13. For a less-than-flattering interpretation of Elizabeth's relations with younger male courtiers as represented in *The Faerie Queene*, see Judith Anderson, "Arthur, Argante, and the Ideal Vision: An Exercise in Speculation and Parody," in *The Passing of Arthur*, 193–206. If one adopts this less-charitable view, the description of Belphoebe's gloating over Lust's corpse gains heightened meaning: his soul had fled, "Yet ouer him she there long gazing stood, / And oft admir'd his monstrous shape, and oft / His mighty limbs" (4.7.32).

14. Lawrence Stone, "Marriage among the English Nobility in the Sixteenth and Seventeenth Centuries," *Comparative Studies in Society and History* 3 (1961): 195.

15. Quilligan, "Lady Mary Wroth: Female Authority and the Family Romance," in *Unfolded Tales*, 268.

16. *DNB*, "Robert Devereux, Second Earl of Essex."

17. Breight, "Realpolitik and Elizabethan Ceremony: The Earl of Hertford's Entertainment of Elizabeth at Elvetham, 1591," *Renaissance Quarterly* 45.1 (Spring 1992):40–41.

18. Violet Wilson, *Queen Elizabeth's Maids of Honour and Ladies of the Privy Chamber* (London: John Lane, 1922), 107, 151, 230.

19. Rowland Whyte, *Letters and Memorials of State*, ed. Arthur Collins, 2 vols. (London: T. Osborne, 1746), 2:203.

20. Lewalski, "Writing Women," 813.

21. On the relationship between Britomart and Amoret, see Dorothy Stephens, "Into Other Arms: Amoret's Evasion," *ELH* 58.3 (Fall 1991): 523–44.

22. Goldberg, 60, observes that the narrator here addresses his audience specifically as readers. This designation reaffirms my point about chastity being a highly contextual and almost subjective virtue, one that depends on the assumptions of the viewer or "reader" of female behavior.

23. Cavanagh, *Wanton Eyes*, 84; on men's reconstructing women's chastity, see pp. 81–84.

24. Spenser may be commenting here on the vulnerability experienced by the masculine as well as the feminine when participating in romance. Without his armor, Calepine—a man "dis-made"—is susceptible to attacks on his martial valor, just as the lady is left open to attacks on her sexual honor.

25. Cited in Robert Lacey, *Sir Walter Ralegh* (New York: Atheneum, 1974), 171.

26. See William A. Oram, "Spenser's Raleghs," *Studies in Philology* 87 (1990): 341–62.

27. Agnes M. C. Latham, ed., *The Poems of Sir Walter Ralegh* (Cambridge, MA: Harvard University Press, 1951), 20.

28. See Oakeshott on the Raleighs and Roberts, ed., *Urania*, lxx–lxxi, on the topicality of romance fictions.

29. Kintgen, 188.

30. Lacey, 147, 150, 166–69.

31. Rowse, *Sir Walter Ralegh: His Family and Private Life* (New York: Harper & Brothers, 1962), 164.

32. Jordan, *Renaissance Feminism*, 29.

33. Nohrnberg, 714.

34. Poggioli, *The Oaten Flute* (Cambridge, MA: Harvard University Press, 1975), 57.

35. Adrian Wilson, "The Ceremony of Childbirth and Its Interpretation," in *Women as Mothers in Pre-Industrial England*, ed. Valerie Fildes (London: Routledge, 1990), 73. For information on churching, see also David Cressy, *Birth, Marriage, and Death: Ritual, Religion, and the Life-Cycle in Tudor and Stuart England* (Oxford: Oxford University Press, 1997), 197–229. Spenserian depictions of childbirth rarely, if ever, conform to the social norm. Charissa is perhaps the only Spenserian mother to enjoy her "fruitfull nest" within a predominantly female space, that of the House of Holiness. Chrysogone (rather spectacularly) gives birth alone and in her sleep, after fleeing into the wilderness to hide her shame; Amavia is also isolated, recounting plaintively that "The woods, the Nymphes, my bowres, my midwives weare, / Hard helpe at need" (2.1.53); and Satyrane's mother bears him in the forest, accompanied only by the satyr who raped her.

36. *The famous, pleasant, and variable historie, of Palladine of England* (1588), translated from the French by Anthony Munday, contains an analogous episode, in which the mother of the child in the wild beast's jaws is, unlike Serena, very much present. Palladine and Manteleo "beheld a lion comming toward them, carying a yong Infant (wrapped in swadling clothes) in his mouth, and a yong Woman running after the beast, with verie pitifull cries and acclamations. . . . The poore woman, seeing how readie they were to helpe her, cryed aloude to them, that they should get between the lion and his cave." Once the lion (and his mate) have been slain, "the poore woman . . . took up her child,

which when she beheld had escaped all danger, on her knees she humbly thanked the Princes." Cited in *The Works of Edmund Spenser: A Variorum Edition*, ed. Edwin Greenlaw et al. (Baltimore: Johns Hopkins Press, 1938), 6:203. William Oram argues in "Elizabethan Fact and Spenserian Fiction," *Spenser Studies* 4 (1984):43–45, that Amoret, Aemylia, and the Hag represent various aspects of Throckmorton's disgrace.

37. Ovidius Naso, Publius. *Shakespeare's Ovid Being Arthur Golding's Translation of the Metamorphoses*, 1567, ed. W. H. D. Rouse (Carbondale, IL: Southern Illinois University Press, 1961), Book 2, pp. 51–54, lines 504–663.

38. Edward Topsell, *The Historie of Foure-footed Beastes* (1607), 37. Subsequent references will be cited parenthetically in the text. Radigund is likened to a "greedie Beare" when attacking Artegall in 5.5.9, which underscores both her violence and her lust.

39. Gail Kern Paster also connects the bear's hibernation with the woman's lying-in in *The Body Embarrassed: Drama and the Disciplines of Shame in Early Modern England* (Ithaca: Cornell University Press, 1993), 275.

40. On bears and Candlemas, see Michael Bristol, "In Search of the Bear: Spatiotemporal Form and the Heterogeneity of Economies in *The Winter's Tale*," *Shakespeare Quarterly* 42.2 (Summer 1991): 159, and François Laroque, *Shakespeare's Festive World: Elizabethan Seasonal Entertainment and the Professional Stage*, trans. Janet Lloyd (Cambridge: Cambridge University Press, 1991), 48. Jeanne Addison Roberts also discusses Candlemas in relation to the churching of women and notes, too, that February was the Roman month of purification and time of the Lupercalia, a festival enacted to ensure fertility. See "Shakespeare's Maimed Birth Rites," in *True Rites and Maimed Rites: Ritual and Anti-Ritual in Shakespeare and His Age*, ed. Linda Woodbridge and Edward Berry (Urbana: University of Illinois Press, 1992), 135. See also Paster, *Body Embarrassed*, 194–97, on churching and shame.

41. Aristotle, *Historia Animalium*, trans. Richard Cresswell, cited in *The Bedford Companion to Shakespeare*, ed. Russ McDonald (New York: St. Martin's, 1996), 275.

42. Perdita's baptism is not represented (Paulina's ostensible errand in 2.3.40 is to confer with Leontes about the choice of the child's gossips, a business that is never completed, except by default, leaving Antigonus as godfather; the child is furnished with a bearing cloth, but the text is unclear about whether the actual rite has been performed). Mothers were often excluded from the baptism service, since children were generally baptized soon after the birth and before the woman's month was accomplished, but Leontes' refusal to claim the child provokes Hermione to provide her with a name. Hermione's request is particularly appropriate, given that infants who seemed unlikely to live (as Perdita does at this point, left to the mercy of a storm and wild beasts of prey) were eligible to be baptized by female midwives, who had the church's reluctant sanction to administer baptismal rites.

43. These girls do indeed disappear from the text, almost as if Paulina loses her own daughters at the same time Hermione loses Perdita.

44. Andrew Gurr, "The Bear, the Statue, and Hysteria in *The Winter's Tale*," *Shakespeare Quarterly* 34 (1984): 420–21.

45. *Macbeth*, 3.4.99, alludes to the "rugged Russian bear." Daryl W. Palmer has also commented on Shakespeare's deviation from his source; see "Jacobean Muscovites: Winter, Tyranny, and Knowledge in *The Winter's Tale*," *Shakespeare Quarterly* 46.3 (Fall 1995): 324–25.

46. Dennis Biggins, " 'Exit pursued by a Beare': A Problem in *The Winter's Tale*," *Shakespeare Quarterly* 13.1 (Winter 1962): 11.

47. Harington's moral to Book 11 of the *Orlando* links bears to the sexual intemperance of young men. Perhaps this explains why Wroth's *Urania* genders male the bear pursuing Veralinda (a princess disguised as a shepherdess); Leonius saves his beloved Veralinda, but not without attention being drawn to the seductive sight of Veralinda's legs as she runs and the amorous thoughts this inspires in Leonius, whose name links him to a wild beast (426–27). *The Winter's Tale* also acknowledges male complicity in sexual coupling. For example, in his vehement denial of Hermione's fault, Antigonus first vows to geld his daughters (aged eleven, nine, and five), then blusters that he'd rather castrate himself than see them bring forth illegitimate children. Such an act would guarantee that he would have no more daughters to disgrace him, but it also underscores the man's role in conception. Unlike Antigonus, the Shepherd speaks as a father to a son, and he wishes no age existed between ten and twenty-three, "for there is nothing in the between but getting wenches with child." His son's sexual escapades with Mopsa and Dorcas and Autolycus's song of tumbling in the hay with his "aunts" provides a corrective discourse to Leontes' self-righteous accusations.

48. Edward Edwards, *The Life of Sir Walter Ralegh*, 2 vols. (New York: Macmillan, 1868), 2:46.

49. Linda A. Pollock, "Embarking on a Rough Passage: The Experience of Pregnancy in Early-Modern Society" in *Women as Mothers*, 39.

50. Hoby, entry for 7 October, 1603, p. 206. See also Patricia Crawford, "The Construction and Experience of Maternity in Seventeenth-Century England," in *Women as Mothers*, 19, and Pollock, "Embarking," 39–41, on infertility.

51. Topsell cites this persistent myth only to dismiss it: "yet is the truth most evidently otherwise" (37).

52. For example, Alice Spencer, Lady Strange, was churched with a big celebration three weeks after the birth of her third daughter Elizabeth in 1588. See Fogle, 11.

53. David Cressy notes that during the month of privilege, a woman's husband was expected to serve her and perform her usual domestic chores. See "Foucault, Stone, Shakespeare and Social History," *English Literary Renaissance* 21.2 (Spring 1991): 133.

54. See Cavanagh's useful reminder of the ambiguity of "coy," whose meanings range from "appropriately modest" to "reprehensibly aloof" (*Wanton Eyes*, 113).

55. See Harry Berger, Jr., "Narrative as Rhetoric in *The Faerie Queene*," *English Literary Renaissance* 21.1 (1991): 3–49, on distinctions between the narrator and Spenser.

56. Sanders, *Gender and Literacy on Stage in Early Modern England* (Cambridge: Cambridge University Press, 1998), 35.

57. See George Rowe, "Privacy, Vision, and Gender in Spenser's Legend of Courtesy," *Modern Language Quarterly* 50.4 (December 1989): 325, on Serena's silence and shame.

58. Paster argues that "Hermione's trial displaces the churching ceremony. . . . What Hermione experiences is precisely the public shame that the churching ceremony, however implicitly, sought to contravene for any newly delivered woman" (272). See also p. 278 for a discussion of the statue scene's echoes of the churching ceremony. Richard Wilson, "Observations on English Bodies: Li-

censing Maternity in Shakespeare's Late Plays," in *Enclosure Acts: Sexuality, Property, and Culture in Early Modern England*, ed. Richard Burt and John Michael Archer (Ithaca: Cornell University Press, 1994), 143, also notes the parallel between Hermione's release and the churching ceremony.

59. For a discussion of tournament prizes and tourneys, jousts, and barriers held to celebrate the nuptials of various courtiers in the late sixteenth and early seventeenth centuries, see Alan Young, *Tudor and Jacobean Tournaments* (Dobbs Ferry, NY: Sheridan House, 1987), 50, 201–7. On Florimell's girdle, see Silberman, *Transforming*, 101–6.

60. Erasmus, *The Colloquies of Erasmus*, trans. Craig R. Thompson (Chicago: University of Chicago Press, 1965), 1:124.

61. See Marina Warner, *Alone of All Her Sex: The Myth and the Cult of the Virgin Mary* (1976; reprint, New York: Vintage, 1983), 278–79.

62. Elyot, *The Boke Named the Governour*, sig. Q6v–Q7r. See also Jonson's *Hymenaei* (1606) on the girdle around a virgin's waist being removed at the time of her marriage (*Ben Jonson*, ed. C. H. Herford and Percy and Evelyn Simpson [Oxford: Clarendon Press, 1941], 7:220).

63. Cited in *The Renaissance Englishwoman in Print*, 235, note 15. See also Jeanne Addison Roberts, "Horses and Hermaphrodites: Metamorphoses in *The Taming of the Shrew*," *Shakespeare Quarterly* 34 (1983): 164, for a discussion of the equation of women with horses in Elizabethan culture.

CHAPTER 6. CHASTE BUT NOT SILENT

An earlier version of this chapter appears in the *Huntington Library Quarterly* 60.4 (1997): 1–26.

1. R. B. McKerrow and F. S. Ferguson, *Title-Page Borders Used in England and Scotland, 1485–1640* (London: Bibliographical Society at Oxford University Press, 1932), 145–46.

2. Jewel is cited in Yates, *Astraea*, 78, note 2; the Leonard Wright quotation is from *A Patterne for Pastors*, annexed to *A Summons for Sleepers* (1589), 56 (misnumbered 54).

3. Thickstun maintains that Una "remains allegorical, indeed becomes more so as her story progresses, because she so explicitly represents the True Church rather than a female believer; her sufferings reflect not on her own spiritual inadequacies but on the failings of her champion, the Red Cross Knight. . . . The bride of Christ operates as a metaphor for the soul or the church but not as a model for individual Christian women" (26). Similarly, Cavanagh, *Wanton Eyes*, 31, claims that "Rarely in the epic does the allegory remain as flat and obvious as it does in association with women such as Fidelia, Speranza, and Charissa, for instance, who primarily serve to reinforce the picture of holiness being presented to Red Crosse." However, I would hesitate to dismiss so categorically the potential of Una and her holy nurse counterparts as religious exemplars, given their resemblance to didactic ideals prescribed in other literature of the period. My reading of Book 1 does not deny Una's allegorical significance as the bride of Christ or as a type of Elizabeth I, nor condone the inequality of early modern discussions of female piety, but attempts to read Spenser's depictions of "mother church" intertextually. Despite the iconicity of details such as Fidelia's book or Charissa's breast, such details could also resonate with early modern social practices and concerns; they are not limited to

theological or emblematic meaning, particularly if one considers them from a female rather than male subject position.

4. Betty Travitsky describes this ideal in "The New Mother of the English Renaissance: Her Writings on Motherhood," in *The Lost Tradition: Mothers and Daughters in Literature*, ed. Cathy N. Davidson and E. M. Broner (New York: Frederick Ungar, 1980), 33–43, an article to which my own analysis is obviously indebted. See also Kenneth Charlton, " 'Not publike onely but also private and domesticall': Mothers and Familial Education in Pre-Industrial England," *History of Education* 17.1 (1988): 1–20, and Valerie Wayne, "Advice for Women from Mothers and Patriarchs," *Women and Literature in Britain, 1500–1700*, ed. Wilcox, 56–79. See also Jacqueline T. Miller, "Mother Tongues: Language and Lactation in Early Modern Literature," *English Literary Renaissance* 27.2 (Spring 1997): 177–96.

5. Spenser, *A view of the state of Ireland*, in *The Works of Edmund Spenser: A Variorum Edition*, ed. Rudolf Gottfried (Baltimore: Johns Hopkins University Press, 1949), 9:119–20. John Foxe also records the potent influence of childhood caregivers; Vitus, who was sacrificed by his pagan father, "had been instructed in the principles of Christianity by the nurse who brought him up" (*Fox's Book of Martyrs*, ed. William Forbush [Philadelphia: John C. Winston, 1926], 26). The final "worldly" action taken by several of John Foxe's female martyrs is their arrangement for alternate nurses for their children, thereby reiterating women's responsibility for the physical and spiritual well-being of their children. Prior to their deaths, for example, Hellen Stirke and Agnes Bongeor consign their children to suitably Protestant friends and then prepare to die (*The Actes and Monuments*, 1632, 2:616, 3:849). Incidentally, "most of the prose redactions" of *The Faerie Queene* "were written by women acting in their feminine capacity as moral instructors of young children" (David Hill Radcliffe, *Edmund Spenser: A Reception History* [Columbia, SC: Camden House, 1996], 125).

6. Bentley, *The Monument of Matrones* (1582), sig. B1v. Bentley conflates a variety of female figures in his work (Old Testament women such as Deborah and Esther, characters from New Testament parables such as the five wise virgins, and allegorical symbols such as the bride of Christ), a practice remarkably similar to Spenser's wide-ranging use of historical, mythological, and allegorical female figures.

7. John King, "The Godly Woman in Elizabethan Iconography," *Renaissance Quarterly* 38.1 (Spring 1985): 41, 50.

8. Reprinted in *The Acts and Monuments of John Foxe*, ed. S. R. Cattley and G. Townsend (London: Seeley and Burnside, 1837), 5:527.

9. The woodcut is reproduced in King, "Godly," 48.

10. On women's transmission of religious texts, see *Silent But for the Word*. Pursuits recommended to women that looked like forms of limitation—such as translation of religious works—could also be empowering, as Elaine Beilin has argued (*Redeeming Eve*, 61).

11. Plutarch, 17.

12. Bentley, in "The sixt Lampe of Virginitie," *The Monument of Matrones* (1582), 31.

13. Gouge, *Of Domesticall Duties* (1622), 546. Subsequent references to Gouge will be cited parenthetically in the text.

14. Clifford, 56–57, 60, 64, 87, 91, 103.

15. Hoby, 76, 80, 81, 105, 111, 130, 173, 175.

16. Hoby's monument inscription is cited in Margaret P. Hannay, " 'O Daughter Heare': Reconstructing the Lives of Aristocratic Englishwomen," *Attending to Women in Early Modern England,* ed. Betty S. Travitsky and Adele F. Seeff (Newark: University of Delaware Press, 1994), 42. See also Susan Groag Bell, "Medieval Women Book Owners: Arbiters of Lay Piety and Ambassadors of Culture" in *Women and Power in the Middle Ages,* ed. Mary Erler and Maryanne Kowalski (Athens, GA: University of Georgia Press, 1988): 149–87.

17. Provoked by the recusant Lady Egerton of Ridley, Sir Christopher Hatton commented with mild exasperation on the ways religious zeal inspired women to defy social custom: "she hath not hitherto conformed herself to her Majesty's proceedings, upon a certain preciseness of conscience *incident to divers of her sex,* without reason or measure oftentimes" (my emphasis). Hatton continues, however, that "in other respects she hath always showed herself very dutiful" in maintaining an Anglican chaplain to lead household services. In his relatively irenic letter he urges the Earl of Derby and Bishop of Chester to employ gentle persuasion rather than imprisonment on account of the lady's age and ill health. See Nicholas H. Nicolas, ed. *Memoirs of the Life and Times of Sir Christopher Hatton* (London: Richard Bentley, 1847), 309, for this letter of 10 January, 1582.

18. Claire Cross, " 'Great Reasoners in Scripture': The Activities of Women Lollards, 1380–1530" in *Medieval Women,* ed. Derek Baker (Oxford: Blackwell, 1978), 378.

19. Hooker, *Of the Laws of Ecclesiastical Polity* (1593), ed. Arthur McGrade (Cambridge: Cambridge University Press, 1989), section 3.13, 17–18.

20. Colin Atkinson and Jo B. Atkinson, "Subordinating Women: Thomas Bentley's Use of Biblical Women in *The Monument of Matrones* (1582)," *Church History* 60.3 (1991): 299. See also Patrick Collinson, "The Role of Women in the English Reformation Illustrated by the Life and Friendships of Anne Locke," *Studies in Church History* 2 (1965): 258–59; Richard L. Greaves, "Foundation Builders: The Role of Women in Early English Nonconformity," in *Triumph Over Silence: Women in Protestant History,* ed. Greaves (Westport: Greenwood Press, 1985), 75–92; Marie B. Rowlands, "Recusant Women 1560–1640" in *Women in English Society, 1500–1800,* ed. Mary Prior (London: Methuen, 1985), 165; Diane Willen, "Women and Religion in Early Modern England," in *Women in Reformation and Counter-Reformation Europe: Public and Private Worlds,* ed. Sherrin Marshall (Bloomington: Indiana University Press, 1989), 142; and Sherrin Marshall Wyntjes, "Women in the Reformation Era," in *Becoming Visible: Women in European History,* ed. Renate Bridenthal and Claudia Koonz (Boston: Houghton Mifflin, 1977), 169, 185.

21. Mildmay, 28–30.

22. George C. Williamson, ed. *Lady Anne Clifford, Countess of Dorset, Pembroke, and Montgomery, 1590–1676: Her Life, Letters, and Work,* 2nd ed. (1922; Yorkshire: S. R. Publishers, 1967), 495, 465.

23. Cary, 191–92.

24. On Bacon, see Beilin, *Redeeming Eve,* 60; on Falkland see Margo Todd, *Christian Humanism and the Puritan Social Order* (Cambridge: Cambridge University Press, 1987), 107. William Fitzwilliam's 1598 will is cited in Richard L. Greaves, *Society and Religion in Elizabethan England* (Minneapolis: University of Minnesota Press, 1981), 311.

25. See Retha Warnicke, "Eulogies for Women: Public Testimony of Their Godly Example and Leadership," in *Attending to Women,* 179.

26. Cleaver, 234.

27. Daniel Rogers, *Matrimoniall Honour* (1642), 284.

28. Sibbes, "Lydia's Conversion," *The Riches of Mercie* (1638), 9–10.

29. Maclean, 64.

30. See Debora Shuger on "the trend toward feminizing Christianity . . . during this period," in tension with the residual assumption that women were "weaker, more sensual" than men (*Habits of Thought in the English Renaissance: Religion, Politics, and the Dominant Culture* [Berkeley and Los Angeles: University of California Press, 1990], 223–24, note 21). See also Ruth Kelso's characterization of the behavioral ideal for women as predominantly Christian and that for men as predominantly pagan (36).

31. King, *Spenser's Poetry*, 6.

32. See Salter, *MM*, sig. D3v, and Mildmay, who urges others to read *The Actes and Monuments* (23). See Warnicke, "Lady Mildmay's Journal," *Sixteenth Century Journal* 20 (1989): 56–58, 61 on Mildmay finding female role models in Foxe's text. See also Carole Levin, "Women in *The Book of Martyrs* as Models of Behavior in Tudor England," *International Journal of Women's Studies* 4 (1981): 196–207, and Ellen Macek, "The Emergence of Feminine Spirituality in *The Book of Martyrs*," *Sixteenth Century Journal* 19.1 (1988): 63–80.

33. See Wilhelm Schneemelcher, ed., *New Testament Apocrypha*, trans. R. McL. Wilson (Philadelphia: Westminster Press, 1964), 2:355–64, for the story of Thecla, who is also mentioned in Caxton's translation of *The Golden Legend* (in the narratives of John the Baptist and St. Martin). Vives includes Thecla in his frequent catalogs of exemplary female saints in his *ICW*, as Bentley does in *The Monument of Matrones*. I am grateful to Debora Shuger for drawing my attention to potential links between Una and Thecla.

34. The lamb also alludes to St. Agnes, who, like Una, manages to retain her innocence despite sexual assaults and is noted for the light of her countenance.

35. Winkler, 97, notes that blaming erotic magical rites rather than a girl's wantonness provided parents in ancient Greece with a means of saving family honor.

36. Richard Halpern, "Puritanism and Maenadism in *A Mask*," in *Rewriting the Renaissance*, 94.

37. Peter Brown, *The Body and Society: Men, Women, and Sexual Renunciation in Early Christianity* (New York: Columbia University Press, 1988), 329. See also p. 155 for a discussion of the late classical romance as a model for many of the stories in the Apocryphal Acts.

38. John E. Booty, ed. *The Book of Common Prayer 1559: The Elizabethan Prayer Book* (Charlottesville: University Press of Virginia/Folger Shakespeare Library, 1976), 291.

39. Ibid., 296.

40. Naomi Yavneh's assessment of Sofronia in Tasso's *Gerusalemme Liberata* ("as in the life of Saint Agnes, the female has greater spiritual strength than the male") also pertains to Una's relationship with Redcrosse. See "The Ambiguity of Beauty in Tasso and Petrarch" in *Sexuality and Gender in Early Modern Europe: Institutions, Texts, Images,* ed. James Grantham Turner (Cambridge: Cambridge University Press, 1993), 152.

41. Cited in Atkinson and Atkinson, 294.

42. Women of the period may or may not have suspected that bearing fewer children and nursing them at home could have improved their children's chances of survival. In any case, aristocratic women were expected by their

husbands to bear as many children as possible and to employ wet nurses; consequently, their fertility was extremely high. Since it was commonly assumed that sexual intercourse tainted a mother's milk, and the church elevated the wife's responsibility to satisfy her conjugal responsibilities before her maternal ones, wet-nursing was a standard practice.

43. Elyot, sig. B5v.

44. More, *Utopia*, trans. Paul Turner (Harmondsworth: Penguin Books, 1965), 82.

45. On the popularity of Erasmus's work, and the ready availability of "The New Mother" to early modern readers, see Wayne, "Advice," 61.

46. *Colloquies of Erasmus*, 1:283.

47. See Dorothy McLaren, "Marital Fertility and Lactation 1570–1720," in *Women in English Society*, 22–53; Linda Pollock, *Forgotten Children: Parent-Child Relations from 1500 to 1900* (Cambridge: Cambridge University Press, 1983), 213, and Patricia Crawford, "The Construction and Experience of Maternity in Seventeenth-Century England," in *Women as Mothers*, 24.

48. Newdigate-Newdegate, 16–17, 20.

49. Cary, 202.

50. Taylor, "The Rule and Exercises of Holy Living," in *The Whole Works of Jeremy Taylor*, ed. Reginald Heber (London, 1828), 4:157.

51. Smith, 99.

52. Cleaver, *Godlie*, 235. See also Bentley, "The sixt Lampe," 30.

53. Tusser, *Five hundreth points of . . . huswiferie* (1599), 139.

54. Clinton, *The countesse of Lincolnes nurserie* (1622), reprinted in *The Female Spectator: English Women Writers Before 1800*, ed. Mary Mahl and Helene Koon (Bloomington: Indiana University Press, 1977), 91, 92, 97–98. See also Patricia Crawford, " 'The sucking child,' " *Continuity and Change* 1.1 (1986): 32.

55. Mildmay, 30.

56. Dod and Cleaver, *A Plaine and familiar Exposition of the Ten Commaundements* (1606), 195.

57. Strong, *Cult*, 85–89; Emerson, 195–97.

58. Hooker, 17–18.

59. See Quilligan, *Milton's Spenser*, 90, on Error as "a parodic, perverted version of the good-mother figure."

60. Error's indigestion may allude to the collect for the second Sunday in Advent in the Elizabethan *Book of Common Prayer*: "Blessed Lord, which hast caused all holy Scriptures to be written for our learning: Grant us that we may in such wise hear them, read, mark, learn, and inwardly digest them: that by patience and comfort of thy holy Word, we may embrace and ever hold fast the blessed hope of everlasting life, which thou hast given us in our Saviour Jesus Christ." See William Keatinge Clay, ed., *Liturgies and Occasional Forms of Prayer Set Forth in the Reign of Queen Elizabeth* (Cambridge: Cambridge University Press for the Parker Society, 1847), 79.

61. Suzuki, 203, suggests that the Blatant Beast signifies "the faulty reader who violates texts by misinterpreting them"; "unlike female Errour, he cannot be readily contained or destroyed" (206). I would argue that the female Error's misreadings are less easily contained than Suzuki suggests, partly because the potential for "misreading" inheres in the good Una as well as the bad Error.

62. Cleaver, *Godlie*, 61.

63. This detail occurs in stanza 31, a possible allusion to Proverbs 31, which

describes the virtuous woman's "price" as "farre above the pearles." Red-crosse should have been more discerning in his assessment of Duessa's attire, which identifies her as the whore of Babylon; clothing is one of the key indicators of the suitability of a pious bride, according to Cleaver: "It is convenient that he that will be a suter to a woman, that he marke what apparell she customably useth to weare, whether it bee vaine, whorish, wanton, light, or comely, modest, and mannerly, and beseeming her estate and condition: to wit, honest and sober raiment" (103). Other signs of female godliness include reputation, looks, speech, and companions.

64. Thickstun, 44, also reads Charissa within a context of social rather than allegorical discourse, observing that Charissa, Womanhood, and the virtues in the Temple of Venus "form a composite picture of the Christian wife—modest, loving, fruitful, and obedient," but relates these images to Britomart rather than to Una. Since Charissa's husband never appears, however, I would argue that the text emphasizes her spiritual, maternal authority rather than her wifely obedience.

65. See Hamilton's annotation of 1.10.29 and David Miller, 112–13, on Redcrosse's second gestation and rebirth.

66. King, *Spenser's Poetry*, 63. On Una as a teacher, see Susanne Woods, "Women at the Margins in Spenser and Lanyer," in *Worldmaking Spenser*, 101–114.

67. Whitgift, *The Works of John Whitgift*, ed. John Ayre (Cambridge: Cambridge University Press for the Parker Society, 1852), 500–501, 504–5.

68. Richey, " 'To Undoe the Booke': Cornelius Agrippa, Aemilia Lanyer and the Subversion of Pauline Authority," *English Literary Renaissance* 27.1 (Winter 1997): 106–7, note 3.

69. Mulcaster, 181.

70. Richard A. Levin also draws a parallel between Una and Thyamis, although his discussion suggests that Thyamis was impregnated immediately; see "The Legende of the Redcrosse Knight and Una, or Of the Love of a Good Woman," *Studies in English Literature* 31.1 (Winter 1991): 12.

71. Clinton, 94.

72. Cleaver, *Godlie*, 88. Amavia is another wife who must take her husband firmly in hand; Acrasia had Mordant "In chaines of lust and lewd desires ybound," but Amavia cures him through "wise handling and faire gouernaunce" (2.1.54).

73. Nohrnberg notes that "the Christian is said to be 'begotten' by the word of truth (James 1:18), and this in part accounts for Una's somewhat maternal character in relation to her knight" (128); the "other part" may be the social construction of feminine piety as maternal.

74. Sibbes, 13.

75. Smith, 61, 79.

76. Wright, 55.

77. Whitgift, 504; on Calvin see Jane Dempsey Douglass, *Women, Freedom, and Calvin* (Philadelphia: Westminster Press, 1985), 106–7. King, in *Spenser's Poetry*, argues that Fidelia's role as a "wise tutor conforms to the Protestant doctrine of the priesthood of all believers," but he does not comment on the ways gender complicated the public expression of this doctrine (63).

78. Cleaver, 60–61. Cf. 2.3.2: Guyon names Ruddymane but gives the child to Medina, who is "In vertuous lore to traine his tender youth, / And all that gentle noriture ensu'th."

79. Erasmus, "New Mother," 273.

80. Elyot, sig. C1r.

81. Ong, "Latin Language Study as a Renaissance Puberty Rite," *Studies in Philology* 56.2 (April 1959): 108. See also William Kempe, *The Education of children in learning*: "when the child is about five yeares old, the Father . . . shall commit him to some Phoenix . . . that can teach him all things, framing him to eloquence in talke, and vertue in deedes" (sig. E4v). A similar pattern can be discerned in Dante's *Divine Comedy* when Beatrice's maternal guiding role is superseded by that of the holy "father," Saint Bernard.

82. Elyot, sig. B8v. See also Bartholomew Batty, *The Christian mans closet*, trans. William Lowth (1581), 54r.

83. Batty, 53v.

84. Askew cited in Beilin, 44.

85. Mildmay, 68.

86. Rich, *Of Woman Born: Motherhood as Experience and Institution* (reprint, 1976; New York: W. W. Norton, 1986), 119.

Afterword

1. For a more extensive analysis of this painting, see my essay "Reading the Margins."

2. Lamb, "Women Readers," 218.

Bibliography

Primary Sources

Ariosto, Ludovico. *Orlando Furioso in English Heroical Verse.* Translated by Sir John Harington. London, 1591.

Ascham, Roger. *The Scholemaster.* In *English Works of Roger Ascham,* edited by William Aldis Wright. 1904. Reprint, Cambridge: Cambridge University Press, 1970.

Batty, Bartholomew. *The Christian mans closet.* Translated by William Lowth. London, 1581.

Bentley, Thomas. *The Monument of Matrones.* London, 1582.

Blundeville, Thomas. *The true order and Methode of wryting and reading Hystories.* London, 1574.

The Book of Common Prayer 1559: The Elizabethan Prayer Book. Edited by John Booty. Charlottesville: University Press of Virginia for the Folger Shakespeare Library, 1976.

Brathwait, Richard. *The English Gentleman.* London, 1630.

———. *The English Gentlewoman.* London, 1631.

Burton, Robert. *The Anatomy of Melancholy.* London, 1632.

Cary, Anne(?). *The Lady Falkland: Her Life.* In *The Tragedy of Mariam the Fair Queen of Jewry, with The Lady Falkland: Her Life,* edited by Barry Weller and Margaret W. Ferguson. Berkeley and Los Angeles: University of California Press, 1994.

Castiglione, Baldassare. *The Courtyer.* Translated by Sir Thomas Hoby. London, 1577.

Cleaver, Robert. *A Godlie Forme of Householde Government.* London, 1598.

Clifford, Lady Anne. *The Diary of the Lady Anne Clifford.* Edited by Vita Sackville-West. London: William Heinemann, 1924.

Clinton, Elizabeth Knyvet. *The countesse of Lincolnes nurserie.* (1620). In *The Female Spectator: English Women Writers Before 1800,* edited by Mary Mahl and Helene Koon. Bloomington: Indiana University Press, 1977.

The Court of good Counsell. London, 1607.

Daniel, Samuel. *The Civile Wares.* London, 1609.

Davies, John. *The Scourge of Folly.* London, 1611.

Dod, John, and Robert Cleaver. *A Plaine and familiar Exposition of the Ten Commaundements.* London, 1606.

Drayton, Michael. *Englands heroicall epistles.* London, 1598.

Du Bosc, Jacques. *The Compleat Woman.* Translated by N. N. London, 1639.

284

Du Verger, S[usan], trans. *Admirable Events*. John Peter Camus. London, 1639.

Elyot, Sir Thomas. *The Boke Named the Governour*. London, 1580.

Erasmus, Desiderius. *Christian Humanism and the Reformation: Selected Writings of Erasmus*. Edited by John Olin. Revised edition. New York: Fordham University Press, 1975.

———. *The Colloquies of Erasmus*. Translated by Craig R. Thompson. Chicago: University of Chicago Press, 1965.

Erondell, Peter. *The French Garden: for English Ladyes and Gentlewomen to walke in*. London, 1605.

Ferne, John. *The Blazon of Gentrie*. London, 1586.

Foxe, John. *The Actes and Monuments*. London, 1632.

The Geneva Bible. London, 1560.

Gibson, Anthony. *A Womans Woorth, Defended against all the men in the world*. London, 1599.

Golding, Arthur. *Shakespeares Ovid being Arthur Golding's Translation of the Metamorphoses*. Edited by W. H. D. Rouse. Carbondale: Southern Illinois University Press, 1961.

Gouge, William. *Of Domesticall Duties*. London, 1622.

Greene, Robert. *Mamillia. A mirrour or looking-glasse for the ladies of Englande*. London, 1583.

———. *Penelopes web: wherein a christall myrror of faeminine perfection represents vertues and graces*. London, 1587.

Guazzo, Stefano. *The civile Conversation of M. Stephen Guazzo*. Translated by George Pettie (Books 1–3) and Bartholomew Young (Book 4). London, 1581, 1586.

Hake, Edward. *A Touchestone for this time present*. London, 1574.

Harington, Sir John. *Nugae Antiquae*. Edited by Henry Harington. 3 vols. London: J. Dodsley, 1779.

Haec Vir. In *Half Humankind: Contexts and Texts of the Controversy about Women in England, 1540–1640*, edited by Katherine Usher Henderson and Barbara F. McManus. Urbana: University of Illinois Press, 1985.

Hic Mulier: or, The Man-Woman: Being a Medicine to cure the Coltish Disease of the Staggers in the Masculine-Feminines of our Times. London, 1620.

The Historie of France: The Foure First Bookes. Translated by Sir E. Hoby from Lancelot Voisin, with a prefatory epistle by Thomas Danett. London, 1595.

Hoby, Lady Margaret Dakins. *Diary of Lady Margaret Hoby 1599–1605*. Edited by Dorothy M. Meads. London: Routledge, 1930.

"An Homilie of the state of Matrimonie." In *Certaine Sermons or Homilies Appointed to be Read in Churches in the Time of Queen Elizabeth I (1547–1571)*, edited by Mary Ellen Rickey and Thomas B. Stroup. Gainesville, FL: Scholars' Facsimiles and Reprints, 1968.

Hooker, Richard. *Of the Laws of Ecclesiastical Polity*. Edited by Arthur McGrade. Cambridge: Cambridge University Press, 1989.

Kempe, William. *The Education of children in learning*. London, 1588.

Lanyer, Aemilia. *The Poems of Aemilia Lanyer.* Edited by Susanne Woods. New York: Oxford University Press, 1993.

Lok, Henry. *Ecclesiastes, Otherwise Called the Preacher.* London, 1597.

Lyly, John. *Euphues and his England.* London, 1581.

Mildmay, Grace Sharington. "Autobiography." In *With Faith and Physic: The Life of a Tudor Gentlewoman, Lady Grace Mildmay 1552–1620,* edited by Linda Pollock. London: Collins and Brown, 1993.

The Mirrour of Princely Deedes and Knighthood

The First Part of the Mirrour of Princely Deedes and Knighthood. Translated by Margaret Tyler from Diego Ortuñez de Calahorra. London, 1578.

The Second Part of the First Booke of the Myrrour of Knighthood. Translated by R. P. London, 1585, 1599.

The Third Part of the First Booke of the Mirrour of Knighthood. Translated by R. P. London, 1586.

The Second Part of the Myrror of Knighthood. Translated by R. P. London, 1583.

The Seventh Booke of the Myrrour of Knighthood. Translated by L. A. London, 1598.

Mulcaster, Richard. *Positions wherin those primitive circumstances be examined, which are necessarie for the training up of children.* London, 1581.

Nashe, Thomas. *The Anatomie of Absurditie.* London, 1589.

———. *Christes Teares Over Jerusalem.* London, 1593.

———. *The Terrors of the night Or, A Discourse of Apparitions.* London, 1594.

Pettie, George. *A Petite Pallace of Pettie his pleasure.* London, 1576.

Plutarch. *The Philosophie, commonly called, the Morals written by the learned Philosopher Plutarch.* Translated by Philemon Holland. London, 1603.

Rich, Barnabe. *Riche his farewell to militarie profession.* London, 1581.

Rogers, Daniel. *Matrimoniall Honour.* London, 1642.

Salter, Thomas. *A Mirrhor mete for all Mothers, Matrones, and Maidens, intituled the Mirrhor of Modestie.* London, 1579.

Saltonstall, Wye. *Picturae Loquentes.* London, 1635.

Shakespeare, William. *The Riverside Shakespeare.* Edited by G. Blakemore Evans. 2nd ed. Boston: Houghton Mifflin, 1997.

Sibbes, Richard. *The Riches of Mercie.* London, 1638.

Sidney, Philip. *The Defence of Poesy.* In *Sir Philip Sidney,* edited by Katherine Duncan-Jones. Oxford: Oxford University Press, 1989.

Smith, Henry. *A Preparative to Mariage.* London, 1591.

Southwell, Anne. *The Southwell-Sibthorpe Commonplace Book: Folger MS. V.b.198.* Edited by Jean Klene. Tempe, AZ: Medieval and Renaissance Texts and Studies, 1997.

Speeches Delivered to Her Majestie This Last Progresse. Oxford: Joseph Barnes, 1592.

Spenser, Edmund. *The Faerie Queene.* Edited by A. C. Hamilton. Longman Annotated English Poets Series. New York: Longman, 1977.

———. *Spenser's Faerie Queene.* Edited by J. C. Smith. Oxford: Clarendon Press, 1909.

———. *The Works of Edmund Spenser: A Variorum Edition.* Edited by Frederick Morgan Padelford. Baltimore: Johns Hopkins University Press, 1932.

———. *The Yale Edition of the Shorter Poems of Edmund Spenser.* Edited by William A. Oram et al. New Haven: Yale University Press, 1989.

Tilney, Edmund. *A briefe and pleasant discourse of duties in Mariage, called the Flower of Friendshippe.* London, 1568.

Topsell, Edward. *The Historie of Foure-footed Beastes.* London, 1607.

Travitsky, Betty, ed. *The Paradise of Women: Writings by Englishwomen of the Renaissance.* Westport, CT: Greenwood Press, 1981.

Tuvil, Daniel. *Asylum Veneris, or a sanctuary for ladies.* London, 1616.

Vives, Juan Luis. *A very fruteful and pleasant boke called the Instruction of a christen woman.* Translated by Richard Hyrde. London, 1557.

———. *The office and duetie of an husband.* Translated by Thomas Paynell. London, 1550.

Wells, William, ed. *Spenser Allusions in the Sixteenth and Seventeenth Centuries.* Chapel Hill: University of North Carolina Press, 1972.

Whitney, Isabella. *A Sweet Nosgay.* London, 1573.

Wright, Leonard. *A Summons for Sleepers* with *A Patterne for Pastors.* London, 1589.

Wright, Thomas. *The passions of the minde.* London, 1601.

Wroth, Lady Mary. *The First Part of the Countess of Montgomery's Urania.* Edited by Josephine A. Roberts. Binghamton, NY: Medieval and Renaissance Texts and Studies, 1995.

SECONDARY SOURCES

Abel, Elizabeth, ed. *Writing and Sexual Difference.* Chicago: University of Chicago Press, 1982.

Alpers, Paul. *The Poetry of "The Faerie Queene."* Princeton: Princeton University Press, 1967.

Anderson, Judith. "Arthur, Argante, and the Ideal Vision: An Exercise in Speculation and Parody." In *The Passing of Arthur: New Essays in Arthurian Tradition,* edited by Christopher Baswell and William Sharpe, 193–206. New York: Garland, 1988.

———." 'In liuing colours and right hew.' " In *Poetic Traditions of the English Renaissance,* edited by Maynard Mack and George de Forest Lord, 47–66. New Haven: Yale University Press, 1982.

Armstrong, Nancy, and Leonard Tennenhouse, eds. *The Ideology of Conduct: Essays on Literature and the History of Sexuality.* New York: Methuen, 1987.

Arnold, Janet. *Queen Elizabeth's Wardrobe Unlock'd.* Leeds: W. S. Maney, 1988.

Ashelford, Jane. *Dress in the Age of Elizabeth I.* London: Batsford, 1988.

Atkinson, Colin, and Jo B. Atkinson. "Subordinating Women: Thomas Bentley's

Use of Biblical Women in *The Monument of Matrones*." *Church History* 60.3 (September 1991): 289–300.

Atkinson, Dorothy F. "Busirane's Castle and Artidon's Cave." *Modern Language Quarterly* 1 (1940): 185–92.

Bates, Catherine. *The Rhetoric of Courtship in Elizabethan Language and Literature*. Cambridge: Cambridge University Press, 1992.

Bean, John C. "Making the Daimonic Personal: Britomart and Love's Assault in *The Faerie Queene*." *Modern Language Quarterly* 40 (1979): 237–55.

Bednarz, James P. "Ralegh in Spenser's Historical Allegory." *Spenser Studies* 4 (1984): 49–70.

Beilin, Elaine V. *Redeeming Eve: Women Writers of the English Renaissance*. Princeton: Princeton University Press, 1987.

Bell, Susan Groag. "Medieval Woman Book Owners: Arbiters of Lay Piety and Ambassadors of Culture." In *Women and Power in the Middle Ages*, edited by Mary Erler and Maryanne Kowalski, 149–87. Athens, GA: University of Georgia Press, 1988.

Belsey, Catherine. *The Subject of Tragedy: Identity and Difference in Renaissance Drama*. London: Methuen, 1985.

Bennett, H. S. *English Books and Readers 1558–1603*. Cambridge University Press, 1965.

———. *English Books and Readers 1603–1640*. Cambridge University Press, 1970.

Bennett, Tony. "Texts in History: The Determinations of Readings and Their Texts." In *Post-structuralism and the Question of History*, edited by Derek Attridge, Geoff Bennington, and Robert Young, 63–81. Cambridge: Cambridge University Press, 1987.

Benson, Pamela Joseph. *The Invention of the Renaissance Woman: The Challenge of Female Independence in the Literature and Thought of Italy and England*. University Park: Pennsylvania State University Press, 1992.

Berger, Harry, Jr. "Kidnapped Romance." In *Unfolded Tales: Essays on Renaissance Romance*, edited by George M. Logan and Gordon Teskey, 208–56. Ithaca: Cornell University Press, 1989.

———. "Narrative as Rhetoric in *The Faerie Queene*." *English Literary Renaissance* 21.1 (1991): 3–49.

Berry, Philippa. *Of Chastity and Power: Elizabethan Literature and the Unmarried Queen*. London: Routledge, 1989.

Boehrer, Bruce. " 'Carelesse modestee': Chastity as Politics in Book 3 of *The Faerie Queene*." *English Literary History* 55.3 (Fall 1988): 555–73.

Brayman, Heidi. "Ladies, Lapdogs, and Libraries: Women and Their Books in Early Modern England." Unpublished paper given at the Huntington Library, 25 August 1993.

Breight, Curt. "Realpolitik and Elizabethan Ceremony: The Earl of Hertford's Entertainment of Elizabeth at Elvetham, 1591." *Renaissance Quarterly* 45.1 (Spring 1992): 20–48.

Brill, Lesley. "Chastity as Ideal Sexuality in the Third Book of *The Faerie Queene*." *Studies in English Literature* 11 (1971): 15–26.

Broaddus, James W. "Renaissance Psychology and Britomart's Adventures in *Faerie Queene* III." *English Literary Renaissance* 17 (1987): 186–206.

Bulger, Thomas. "Britomart and Galahad." *English Language Notes* 25.1 (September 1987): 10–17.

Buncombe, Marie H. "Faire Florimell as Faire Game: The Virtuous, Unmarried Woman in *The Faerie Queene* and *The Courtier*." *College Language Association Journal* 28 (1984): 164–75.

Cain, Thomas H. *Praise in "The Faerie Queene."* Lincoln: University of Nebraska Press, 1978.

Camden, Carroll. *The Elizabethan Woman*. Houston: Elsevier Press, 1952.

Cavanagh, Sheila T. " 'Beauties Chace': Arthur and Women in *The Faerie Queene*." In *The Passing of Arthur: New Essays in Arthurian Tradition*, edited by Christopher Baswell and William Sharpe, 207–18. New York: Garland, 1988.

———. *Wanton Eyes and Chaste Desires: Female Sexuality in "The Faerie Queene."* Bloomington: Indiana University Press, 1994.

Cavanaugh, Jean C. "Lady Southwell's Defense of Poetry." *English Literary Renaissance* 14 (1984): inset between 284–285.

———. "The Library of Lady Southwell and Captain Sibthorpe." *Studies in Bibliography* 20 (1967): 243–54.

Charlton, Kenneth. *Education in Renaissance England*. London: Routledge and Kegan Paul, 1965.

———. " 'Not publike onely but also private and domesticall': Mothers and Familial Education in Pre-Industrial England." *History of Education* 17.1 (1988): 1–20.

———. *Women, Religion and Education in Early Modern England*. London: Routledge, 1999.

Chartier, Roger. "Leisure and Sociability: Reading Aloud in Early Modern Europe." In *Urban Life in the Renaissance*, edited by Susan Zimmerman and Ronald F. E. Weissman, 103–20. Newark: University of Delaware Press, 1989.

Cheney, Patrick. " 'Secret Powre Unseene': Good Magic in Spenser's Legend of Britomart." *Studies in Philology* 85.1 (Winter 1988): 1–28.

Clark, Peter. "The Ownership of Books in England, 1560–1640: The Example of Some Kentish Townfolk." In *Schooling and Society: Studies in the History of Education*, edited by Lawrence Stone, 95–111. Baltimore: Johns Hopkins Press, 1976.

Collinson, Patrick. "The Role of Women in the English Reformation Illustrated by the Life and Friendships of Anne Locke." *Studies in Church History* 2 (1965): 258–72.

Crawford, Patricia. "The Construction and Experience of Maternity in Seventeenth-Century England." In *Women as Mothers in Pre-Industrial England*, edited by Valerie Fildes, 3–38. London: Routledge, 1990.

———. " 'The sucking child.' " *Continuity and Change* 1.1 (1986): 23–51.

Cressy, David. *Birth, Marriage, and Death: Ritual, Religion, and the Life-Cycle in Tudor and Stuart England*. Oxford: Oxford University Press, 1997.

———. "Foucault, Stone, Shakespeare and Social History." *English Literary Renaissance* 21.2 (Spring 1991): 121–33.

———. *Literacy and the Social Order: Reading and Writing in Tudor and Stuart England*. Cambridge: Cambridge University Press, 1980.

———. "Literacy in Context: Meaning and Measurement in Early Modern England." In *Consumption and the World of Goods*, edited by John Brewer and Roy Porter, 305–19. London: Routledge, 1993.

———. "Purification, Thanksgiving and the Churching of Women in Post-Reformation England." *Past and Present* 141 (November 1993): 106–46.

Cross, Claire. " 'Great Reasoners in Scripture': The Activities of Women Lollards, 1380–1530." In *Medieval Women*, edited by Derek Baker, 359–80. Oxford: Blackwell, 1978.

Culler, Jonathan. *On Deconstruction: Theory and Criticism after Structuralism*. Ithaca: Cornell University Press, 1982.

Darnton, Robert. "History of Reading." In *New Perspectives on Historical Writing*, edited by Peter Burke, 140–67. University Park: Pennsylvania State University Press, 1991.

———. *The Kiss of Lamourette: Reflections in Cultural History*. New York: Norton, 1990.

Dasenbrock, Reed Way. "Escaping the Squires' Double Bind in Books III and IV of *The Faerie Queene*." *Studies in English Literature* 26 (1986): 25–45.

Dauber, Antoinette B. "The Art of Veiling in the Bower of Bliss." *Spenser Studies* 1 (1980): 163–75.

———. "Veils." *The Spenser Encyclopedia*. Edited by A. C. Hamilton. Toronto: University of Toronto Press, 1990.

Davies, Kathleen. "The Sacred Condition of Equality—How Original Were Puritan Doctrines of Marriage?" *Social History* 2 (1977): 563–80.

Davies, Stevie. *The Feminine Reclaimed: The Idea of Woman in Spenser, Shakespeare, and Milton*. Lexington: University of Kentucky Press, 1986.

Dolan, Frances E. "Reading, Writing, and Other Crimes." In *Feminist Readings of Early Modern Culture: Emerging Subjects*, edited by Valerie Traub, M. Lindsay Kaplan, and Dympna Callaghan, 142–67. Cambridge: Cambridge University Press, 1996.

Dusinberre, Juliet. *Shakespeare and the Nature of Women*. London: Macmillan, 1975.

Emerson, Kathy Lynn. *Wives and Daughters: The Women of Sixteenth Century England*. Troy, NY: Whitston Publishing Company, 1984.

Ezell, Margaret J. *The Patriarch's Wife: Literary Evidence and the History of the Family*. Chapel Hill: University of North Carolina Press, 1987.

Felski, Rita. *Beyond Feminist Aesthetics: Feminist Literature and Social Change*. Cambridge, MA: Harvard University Press, 1989.

Ferguson, Margaret W. "A Room Not Their Own: Renaissance Women as Readers and Writers." In *The Comparative Perspective on Literature: Approaches to Theory and Practice*, edited by Clayton Kolb and Susan Noakes, 93–116. Ithaca: Cornell University Press, 1988.

Ferguson, Margaret W., Maureen Quilligan, and Nancy J. Vickers, eds. *Rewriting the Renaissance: The Discourses of Sexual Difference in Early Modern Europe*. Chicago: University of Chicago Press, 1986.

Fildes, Valerie, ed. *Women as Mothers in Pre-Industrial England*. London: Routledge, 1990.

Fisher, Sheila, and Janet E. Halley, eds. *Seeking the Woman in Late Medieval and Renaissance Writings: Essays in Feminist Contextual Criticism*. Knoxville: University of Tennessee Press, 1989.

Fitz [Woodbridge], Linda. "What Says the Married Woman? Marriage Theory and Feminism in the English Renaissance." *Mosaic* 13 (1980): 1–22.

Fleming, Juliet. "The Ladies Man and the Age of Elizabeth." In *Sexuality and Gender in Early Modern Europe: Institutions, Texts, Images,* edited by James Grantham Turner, 158–81. Cambridge: Cambridge University Press, 1993.

Flynn, Elizabeth A., and Patrocinio P. Schweickart, eds. *Gender and Reading: Essays on Readers, Texts, and Contexts.* Baltimore: Johns Hopkins University Press, 1986.

Flynn, Elizabeth A. "Women as Reader-Response Critics." *New Orleans Review* 10 (1983): 20–25.

———. "Women Reading: A Phenomenological Approach." *Reader* 8 (July 1980): 16–22.

Fogle, French R. " 'Such a Rural Queen': The Countess Dowager of Derby as Patron." In *Patronage in Late Renaissance England,* edited by French R. Fogle and Louis A. Knafla, 1–29. Los Angeles: William Andrews Clark Memorial Library, 1983.

Fowler, Alastair. "Oxford and London Marginalia to *The Faerie Queene.*" *Notes and Queries* 206 (November 1961): 416–19.

Fowler, Alastair, and Michael Leslie. "Drummond's Copy of *The Faerie Queene.*" *Times Literary Supplement* 17 July, 1981: 821–22.

Fox, Evelyn. "The Diary of an Elizabethan Gentlewoman." *Transactions of the Royal Historical Society.* 3rd series. 2 (1908): 153–74.

Frye, Susan. *Elizabeth I: The Competition for Representation.* New York: Oxford University Press, 1993.

Fumerton, Patricia. *Cultural Aesthetics: Renaissance Literature and the Practice of Social Ornament.* Chicago: University of Chicago Press, 1991.

Furman, Nelly. "Textual Feminism." In *Women and Language in Literature and Society,* edited by Sally McConnell-Ginet, Ruth Borker, and Nelly Furman, 45–54. New York: Praeger, 1980.

George, Charles H., and Katherine George. *The Protestant Mind of the English Reformation, 1570–1640.* Princeton: Princeton University Press, 1961.

Giamatti, A. Bartlett. *Play of Double Senses: Spenser's Faerie Queene.* Englewood Cliffs, NJ: Prentice Hall, 1975.

———. "Spenser: From Magic to Miracle." In *Four Essays on Romance,* edited by Herschel Baker, 15–31. Cambridge, MA: Harvard University Press, 1971.

Gilde, Helen. " 'The Sweet Lodge of Love and Deare Delight': The Problem of Amoret." *Philological Quarterly* 50 (1970): 63–74.

Goldberg, Jonathan. *Endlesse Worke: Spenser and the Structures of Discourse.* Baltimore: Johns Hopkins University Press, 1981.

Grafton, Anthony. "Renaissance Readers and Ancient Texts: Comments on Some Commentaries." *Renaissance Quarterly* 38 (1985): 615–49.

Greenblatt, Stephen. *Renaissance Self-Fashioning.* Chicago: University of Chicago Press, 1980.

Hamilton, A. C. "Elizabethan Prose Fiction and Some Trends in Recent Criticism." *Renaissance Quarterly* 37.1 (Spring 1984): 21–33.

———. "Elizabethan Romance: The Example of Prose Fiction." *English Literary History* 49.2 (Summer 1982): 287–99.

————, ed. *The Spenser Encyclopedia*. Toronto: University of Toronto Press, 1990.

Hannay, Margaret P. "O Daughter Heare: Reconstructing the Lives of Aristocratic Englishwomen." *Attending to Women in Early Modern England*, edited by Betty S. Travitsky and Adele F. Seef, 35–63. Newark: University of Delaware Press, 1994.

————. *Philip's Phoenix: Mary Sidney, Countess of Pembroke*. New York: Oxford University Press, 1990.

Harper, Carrie. *The Sources of the British Chronicle History in Spenser's "Faerie Queene."* Philadelphia: John Winston Co., 1910.

Haselkorn, Anne M., and Betty S. Travitsky, eds. *The Renaissance Englishwoman in Print: Counterbalancing the Canon*. Amherst: University of Massachusetts Press, 1990.

Hieatt, A. Kent. "A Spenser to Structure Our Myths (Medina, Phaedria, Proserpina, Acrasia, Venus, Isis)." In *Contemporary Thoughts on Edmund Spenser*, edited by Richard Frushell and Bernard Vondersmith, 99–120. Carbondale: So. Illinois University Press, 1975.

Hogrefe, Pearl. *Tudor Women: Commoners and Queens*. Ames: Iowa State University Press, 1975.

————. *Women of Action in Tudor England*. Ames: Iowa State University Press, 1977.

Hough, Graham, ed. *The First Commentary on The Faerie Queene*. 1964. Reprint. Folcroft, PA: Folcroft Press, 1969.

————. "The First Commentary on *The Faerie Queene*." *Times Literary Supplement* 9 April, 1964: 294.

Hull, Suzanne W. *Chaste, Silent and Obedient: English Books for Women 1475–1640*. San Marino: The Huntington Library, 1982.

Hulse, Clark. "Stella's Wit: Penelope Rich as Reader of Sidney's Sonnets." In *Rewriting the Renaissance: The Discourses of Sexual Difference in Early Modern Europe*, edited by Margaret W. Ferguson, Maureen Quilligan, and Nancy J. Vickers, 272–86. Chicago: University of Chicago Press, 1986.

Hume, Anthea. *Edmund Spenser: Protestant Poet*. Cambridge: Cambridge University Press, 1984.

Hume, Robert D. "Texts Within Contexts: Notes Toward a Historical Method." *Philological Quarterly* 71 (1992): 69–100.

Iser, Wolfgang. *The Act of Reading: A Theory of Aesthetic Response*. Baltimore: Johns Hopkins University Press, 1978.

Jardine, Lisa, and Anthony Grafton. " 'Studied for Action': How Gabriel Harvey Read His Livy." *Past and Present* 129 (1990): 30–78.

Jayne, Sears. *Library Catalogues of the English Renaissance*. Berkeley and Los Angeles: University of California Press, 1956.

Jayne, Sears, and Francis R. Johnson. *The Lumley Library: The Catalogue of 1609*. London: Trustees of the British Museum, 1956.

Johnson-Haddad, Miranda. "Englishing Ariosto." *Comparative Literature Studies* 31.4 (1994): 323–50.

Jones, Ann Rosalind. "Nets and Bridles: Early Modern Conduct Books and Sixteenth-Century Women's Lyrics." In *The Ideology of Conduct: Essays on the*

Literature and History of Sexuality, edited by Nancy Armstrong and Leonard Tennenhouse, 39–72. New York: Methuen, 1987.

Jordan, Constance. "Feminism and the Humanists: The Case of Sir Thomas Elyot's *Defence of Good Women*." In *Rewriting the Renaissance: The Discourses of Sexual Difference in Early Modern Europe*, edited by Margaret W. Ferguson, Maureen Quilligan, and Nancy J. Vickers, 242–58. Chicago: University of Chicago Press, 1986.

———. *Renaissance Feminism: Literary Texts and Political Models*. Ithaca: Cornell University Press, 1990.

Kaske, Carol V. "How Spenser Really Used Stephen Hawes in the Legend of Holiness." In *Unfolded Tales: Essays on Renaissance Romance*, edited by George M. Logan and Gordon Teskey, 119–36. Ithaca: Cornell University Press, 1989.

Kelly, Joan. *Women, History, and Theory: The Essays of Joan Kelly*. Edited by Catharine R. Stimpson. Chicago: University of Chicago Press, 1984.

Kelso, Ruth. *Doctrine for the Lady of the Renaissance*. Urbana: University of Illinois Press, 1956.

Kennard, Jean E. "Convention Coverage or How to Read Your Own Life." *New Literary History* 13 (1981): 69–88.

Kerrigan, John. "The Editor as Reader: Constructing Renaissance Texts." In *The Practice and Representation of Reading in England*, edited by James Raven, Helen Small, and Naomi Tadmor, 102–124. Cambridge: Cambridge University Press, 1996.

King, John N. "The Godly Woman in Elizabethan Iconography." *Renaissance Quarterly* 38 (1985): 41–84.

———. *Spenser's Poetry and the Reformation Tradition*. Princeton: Princeton University Press, 1990.

Kintgen, Eugene R. *Reading in Tudor England*. Pittsburgh: University of Pittsburgh Press, 1996.

———. "Reconstructing Elizabethan Reading." *Studies in English Literature* 30 (1990): 1–18.

Klein, Joan Larsen. "Women and Marriage in Renaissance England: Male Perspectives." *Topic* 36 (1982): 20–37.

Krier, Theresa M. " 'All suddeinly abasht she chaunged hew': Abashedness in *The Faerie Queene*." *Modern Philology* 84.2 (November 1986): 130–43.

———. *Gazing on Secret Sights: Spenser, Classical Imitation, and the Decorums of Vision*. Ithaca: Cornell University Press, 1990.

Krontiris, Tina. "Breaking Barriers of Genre and Gender: Margaret Tyler's Translation of *The Mirrour of Knighthood*." In *Women in the Renaissance: Selections from English Literary Renaissance*, edited by Kirby Farrell, Elizabeth H. Hageman, and Arthur F. Kinney, 48–68. Amherst: University of Massachusetts Press, 1990.

Krueger, Roberta. "Desire, Meaning, and the Female Reader: The Problem in Chretien's *Charrete*." In *The Passing of Arthur: New Essays in Arthurian Tradition*, edited by Christopher Baswell and William Sharpe, 31–51. New York: Garland, 1988.

———. *Women Readers and the Ideology of Gender in Old French Verse Romance*. Cambridge: Cambridge University Press, 1993.

Lacey, Robert. *Sir Walter Ralegh*. New York: Atheneum, 1974.

Lamb, Mary Ellen. "The Agency of the Split Subject: Lady Anne Clifford and the Uses of Reading." *English Literary Renaissance* 22.3 (Autumn 1992): 347–68.

———."The Countess of Pembroke's Patronage." *English Literary Renaissance* 12.2 (Spring 1982): 162–79.

———. *Gender and Authorship in the Sidney Circle*. Madison: University of Wisconsin Press, 1990.

———. "Gloriana, Acrasia, and the House of Busirane: Gendered Fictions in *The Faerie Queene* as Fairy Tale." In *Worldmaking Spenser: Explorations in the Early Modern Age*, edited by Patrick Cheney and Lauren Silberman, 81–100. Lexington: The University Press of Kentucky, 2000.

———. "Women Readers in Mary Wroth's *Urania*." In *Reading Mary Wroth: Representing Alternatives in Early Modern England*, edited by Naomi Miller and Gary Waller, 210–27. Knoxville: University of Tennessee Press, 1991.

Langbauer, Laurie. *Women and Romance: The Consolations of Gender in the English Novel*. Ithaca: Cornell University Press, 1990.

Laqueur, Thomas. *Making Sex: Body and Gender from the Greeks to Freud*. Cambridge, MA: Harvard University Press, 1990.

Laurence, Anne. *Women in England 1500–1760: A Social History*. New York: St. Martin's Press, 1994.

Levin, Carole. "Women in *The Book of Martyrs* as Models of Behavior in Tudor England." *International Journal of Women's Studies* 4 (1981): 196–207.

Levin, Richard A. "The Legende of the Redcrosse Knight and Una, or Of the Love of a Good Woman." *Studies in English Literature* 31.1 (Winter 1991): 1–24.

———. "Women in the Renaissance Theatre Audience." *Shakespeare Quarterly* 40.2 (Summer 1989): 165–74.

Lewalski, Barbara. "Lucy Countess of Bedford: Images of a Jacobean Courtier and Patroness." In *Politics of Discourse: The Literature and History of Seventeenth-Century England*, edited by Kevin Sharpe and Steven N. Zwicker, 52–77. Berkeley and Los Angeles: University of California Press, 1987.

———. "Writing Women and Reading the Renaissance." *Renaissance Quarterly* 44.4 (Winter 1991): 792–821.

———. *Writing Women in Jacobean England*. Cambridge, MA: Harvard University Press, 1993.

Lewis, C. S. *The Allegory of Love: A Study in Medieval Tradition*. 1936. Reprint. Oxford: Oxford University Press, 1977.

———. *Spenser's Images of Life*. Edited by Alastair Fowler. Cambridge: Cambridge University Press, 1967.

Lockerd, Benjamin G., Jr. *The Sacred Marriage: Psychic Integration in "The Faerie Queene."* Lewisburg: Bucknell University Press, 1987.

Long, Percy. "Spenser and Lady Carey." *Modern Language Review* 3.3 (April 1908): 257–67.

Loris, Michelle. "Images of Women in Books III and IV of Spenser's *Faerie Queene*." *Mid-Hudson Language Studies* 8 (1985): 9–19.

Lucas, Caroline. *Writing for Women: The Example of Woman as Reader in Elizabethan Romance*. Milton Keynes: Open University Press, 1989.

Macek, Ellen. "The Emergence of Feminine Spirituality in *The Book of Martyrs*." *Sixteenth Century Journal* 19.1 (1988): 63–80.

Mackerness, E. D. "Margaret Tyler: An Elizabethan Feminist." *Notes and Queries* 190 (1946): 112–13.

Maclean, Ian. *The Renaissance Notion of Woman: A Study in the Fortunes of Scholasticism and Medical Science in European Intellectual Life*. Cambridge: Cambridge University Press, 1980.

McLane, Paul E. "Spenser's Chloris: The Countess of Derby." *Huntington Library Quarterly* 24.2 (February 1961): 145–50.

McLaren, Angus. *Reproductive Rituals: The Perception of Fertility in England from the Sixteenth Century to the Nineteenth Century*. London: Methuen, 1984.

McLaren, Dorothy. "Marital Fertility and Lactation 1570–1720." In *Women in English Society 1500–1800*, edited by Mary Prior, 22–53. London: Methuen, 1985.

McManus, Caroline. "Reading the Margins: Female Courtiers in the Portraits of Elizabeth I." *Ben Jonson Journal* 2 (1995): 31–58.

McMullen, Norma. "The Education of English Gentlewomen 1540–1640." *History of Education* (Great Britain) 6.2 (1977): 87–101.

Meale, Carol M. " '. . . alle the bokes that I haue of latyn, englisch, and frensch': laywomen and their books in late medieval England." In *Women and Literature in Britain, 1150–1500*, edited by Carol Meale, 128–58. Cambridge: Cambridge University Press, 1993.

Mendelson, Sara Heller. *The Mental World of Stuart Women: Three Studies*. Amherst: University of Massachusetts Press, 1987.

———. "Stuart Women's Diaries and Occasional Memoirs." In *Women in English Society 1500–1800*, edited by Mary Prior, 181–210. London: Methuen, 1985.

Miller, David. *The Poem's Two Bodies: The Poetics of the 1590 "Faerie Queene."* Princeton: Princeton University Press, 1988.

Miller, Jacqueline T. "Lady Mary Wroth in the House of Busirane." In *Worldmaking Spenser: Explorations in the Early Modern Age*, edited by Patrick Cheney and Lauren Silberman, 115–24. Lexington: The University Press of Kentucky, 2000.

Miller, Shannon. " 'Mirrours More Then One': Edmund Spenser and Female Authority in the Seventeenth Century." In *Worldmaking Spenser: Explorations in the Early Modern Age*, edited by Patrick Cheney and Lauren Silberman, 125–47. Lexington: The University Press of Kentucky, 2000.

Montrose, Louis. "The Elizabethan Subject and the Spenserian Text." In *Literary Theory/Renaissance Texts*, edited by Patricia Parker and David Quint, 303–40. Baltimore: Johns Hopkins University Press, 1986.

———. " 'Shaping Fantasies': Figurations of Gender and Power in Elizabethan Culture." *Representations* 1 (1983): 61–94.

Morgan, Paul. "Frances Wolfreston and 'Hor Bouks': A Seventeenth-Century Woman Book-Collector." *The Library*, sixth series, 11.3 (September 1989): 197–219.

Murray, Lucy. *The Ideal of the Court Lady, 1561–1625*. Chicago: University of Chicago Libraries, 1938.

Neely, Carol. "Constructing the Subject: Feminist Practice and the New Renaissance Discourses." *English Literary Renaissance* 18.1 (Winter 1988): 5–18.

Newdigate-Newdegate, Lady, ed. *Gossip from a Muniment Room Being Passages in the Lives of Anne and Mary Fytton 1574 to 1618*. London: David Nutt, 1897.

Newman, Karen. *Fashioning Femininity and English Renaissance Drama*. Chicago: University of Chicago Press, 1991.

Noakes, Susan. "On the Superficiality of Women." In *The Comparative Perspective in Literature: Approaches to Theory and Practice*, edited by Clayton Koelb and Susan Noakes, 339–55. Ithaca: Cornell University Press, 1988.

———. *Timely Reading: Between Exegesis and Interpretation*. Ithaca: Cornell University Press, 1988.

Nohrnberg, James. *The Analogy of "The Faerie Queene."* Princeton: Princeton University Press, 1976.

Oakeshott, Walter. "Carew Ralegh's Copy of Spenser." *The Library*, 5th series. 26.1 (1971): 1–21.

O'Connor, John J. *"Amadis de Gaule" and Its Influence on Elizabethan Literature*. New Brunswick, NJ: Rutgers University Press, 1970.

Ong, Walter. "Latin Language Study as a Renaissance Puberty Rite." *Studies in Philology* 56.2 (April 1959): 103–24.

Oram, William A. "Elizabethan Fact and Spenserian Fiction." *Spenser Studies* 4 (1984): 33–47.

———. "Spenser's Raleghs." *Studies in Philology* 87 (1990): 341–62.

Orme, Nicholas. *Education and Society in Medieval and Renaissance England*. London: Hambledon Press, 1989.

Parker, Patricia. *Inescapable Romance: Studies in the Poetics of a Mode*. Princeton: Princeton University Press, 1979.

———. *Literary Fat Ladies: Rhetoric, Gender, Property*. London: Methuen, 1987.

Parker, Rozsika. *The Subversive Stitch: Embroidery and the Making of the Feminine*. London: The Women's Press Ltd., 1984.

Paster, Gail Kern. *The Body Embarrassed: Drama and the Disciplines of Shame in Early Modern England*. Ithaca: Cornell University Press, 1993.

Patterson, Annabel. *Censorship and Interpretation: The Conditions of Writing and Reading in Early Modern England*. Madison: University of Wisconsin Press, 1984.

Pearson, Jacqueline. "Women Reading, Reading Women." In *Women and Literature in Britain, 1500–1700*, edited by Helen Wilcox, 80–99. Cambridge: Cambridge University Press, 1996.

Pollock, Linda A. "Embarking on a Rough Passage: The Experience of Pregnancy in Early-Modern Society." In *Women as Mothers in Pre-Industrial England*, edited by Valerie Fildes, 39–67. London: Routledge, 1990.

Quilligan, Maureen. "Lady Mary Wroth: Female Authority and the Family Romance." In *Unfolded Tales: Essays on Renaissance Romance*, edited by

George M. Logan and Gordon Teskey, 257–80. Ithaca: Cornell University Press, 1989.

———. *The Language of Allegory: Defining the Genre*. Ithaca: Cornell University Press, 1979.

———. *Milton's Spenser: The Politics of Reading*. Ithaca: Cornell University Press, 1983.

———. "Words and Sex: The Language of Allegory in the *De planctu naturae*, the *Roman de la Rose*, and Book III of *The Faerie Queene*." *Allegorica* 1 (1977): 195–216.

Quitslund, Jon A. "Spenser and the Patronesses of the *Fowre Hymnes*: 'Ornaments of All True Love and Beautie.' " In *Silent But for the Word: Tudor Women as Patrons, Translators, and Writers of Religious Works*, edited by Margaret P. Hannay, 184–202. Kent, OH: Kent State University Press, 1985.

Radway, Janice. *Reading the Romance: Women, Patriarchy, and Popular Literature*. Chapel Hill: University of North Carolina Press, 1984.

Radcliffe, David Hill. *Edmund Spenser: A Reception History*. Columbia, SC: Camden House, 1996.

Rebhorn, Wayne. *Courtly Performances: Masking and Festivity in Castiglione's "Book of the Courtier."* Detroit: Wayne State University Press, 1978.

Reynolds, Myra. *The Learned Lady in England, 1650–1760*. 1920. Reprint. Gloucester, MA: Peter Smith, 1964.

Riddell, James A., and Stanley Stewart. *Jonson's Spenser: Evidence and Historical Criticism*. Pittsburgh: Duquesne University Press, 1995.

Roberts, Gareth. "Amatory Magic." In *The Spenser Encyclopedia*, edited by A. C. Hamilton, 446–47. Toronto: University of Toronto Press, 1990.

Roberts, Jeanne Addison. "Shakespeare's Maimed Birth Rites." In *True Rites and Maimed Rites: Ritual and Anti-Ritual in Shakespeare and His Age*, edited by Linda Woodbridge and Edward Berry, 123–44. Urbana: University of Illinois Press, 1992.

Roberts, Josephine A. "Extracts from *Arcadia* in the Manuscript Notebook of Lady Katherine Manners." *Notes and Queries*, n.s., 28 (1981): 35–36.

Roche, Thomas P., Jr. *The Kindly Flame: A Study of the Third and Fourth Books of Spenser's "Faerie Queene."* Princeton: Princeton University Press, 1964.

Rose, Mark. *Heroic Love: Studies in Sidney and Spenser*. Cambridge, MA: Harvard University Press, 1968.

Rose, Suzanna. "Is Romance Dysfunctional?" *International Journal of Women's Studies* 8.3 (1985): 250–65.

Rowe, George E. "Interpretation, Sixteenth-Century Readers, and George Gascoigne's 'The Adventures of Master F. J.' " *ELH* 48.2 (Summer 1981): 271–89.

———. "Privacy, Vision, and Gender in Spenser's Legend of Courtesy." *Modern Language Quarterly* 50.4 (December 1989): 309–36.

Rowlands, Marie B. "Recusant Women 1560–1640." In *Women and English Society, 1500–1800*, edited by Mary Prior, 149–80. London: Methuen, 1985.

Rowse, A. L. *Sir Walter Ralegh: His Family and Private Life*. New York: Harper and Brothers, 1962.

Salzman, Paul. *English Prose Fiction 1558–1700: A Critical History*. Oxford: Clarendon Press, 1985.

Sanders, Eve Rachele. *Gender and Literacy on Stage in Early Modern England*. Cambridge: Cambridge University Press, 1998.

Schibanoff, Susan. "The New Reader and Female Textuality in Two Early Commentaries on Chaucer." *Studies in the Age of Chaucer* 10 (1988): 71–108.

———. "Taking the Gold Out of Egypt: The Art of Reading as a Woman." In *Gender and Reading: Essays on Readers, Texts, and Contexts*, edited by Elizabeth A. Flynn and Patrocinio P. Schweickart, 83–106. Baltimore: Johns Hopkins University Press, 1986.

Schleiner, Louise. *Cultural Semiotics, Spenser, and the Captive Woman*. Bethlehem: Lehigh University Press, 1995.

———. "Margaret Tyler, Translator and Waiting Woman." *English Language Notes* 29.3 (March 1992): 1–8.

———. *Tudor and Stuart Women Writers*. Bloomington: Indiana University Press, 1994.

Shaver, Anne. "Rereading Mirabella." *Spenser Studies* 9 (1988): 211–26.

Shepherd, Simon. *Amazons and Warrior Women: Varieties of Feminism in Seventeenth-Century Drama*. New York: St. Martin's Press, 1981.

Sherman, William H. *John Dee: The Politics of Reading and Writing in the English Renaissance*. Amherst: University of Massachusetts Press, 1995.

Shuger, Debora. *Habits of Thought in the English Renaissance: Religion, Politics, and the Dominant Culture*. Berkeley and Los Angeles: University of California Press, 1990.

Silberman, Lauren. "Singing Unsung Heroines: Androgynous Discourse in Book 3 of *The Faerie Queene*." In *Rewriting the Renaissance: The Discourses of Sexual Difference in Early Modern Europe*, edited by Margaret W. Ferguson, Maureen Quilligan, and Nancy J. Vickers, 259–71. Chicago: University of Chicago Press, 1986.

———. *Transforming Desire: Erotic Knowledge in Books III and IV of "The Faerie Queene."* Berkeley and Los Angeles: University of California Press, 1995.

Somerset, Anne. *Ladies-in-Waiting: From the Tudors to the Present Day*. London: Weidenfeld and Nicolson, 1984.

Spufford, Margaret. *Small Books and Pleasant Histories*. Athens, GA: University of Georgia Press, 1982.

Stallybrass, Peter. "Patriarchal Territories: The Body Enclosed." In *Rewriting the Renaissance: The Discourses of Sexual Difference in Early Modern Europe*, edited by Margaret W. Ferguson, Maureen Quilligan, and Nancy J. Vickers, 123–42. Chicago: University of Chicago Press, 1986. 123–42.

Steen, Sara Jayne. "Fashioning an Acceptable Self: Arbella Stuart." In *Women in the Renaissance: Selections from "English Literary Renaissance,"* edited by Kirby Farrell, Elizabeth H. Hageman, and Arthur F. Kinney, 136–53. Amherst: University of Massachusetts Press, 1990.

Stenton, Doris. *The English Woman in History*. London: George Allen and Unwin, 1957.

Stephens, Dorothy. "Into Other Arms: Amoret's Evasion." *ELH* 58.3 (Fall 1991): 523–44.

Stillman, Carol. "Politics, Precedence, and the Order of the Dedicatory Sonnets in *The Faerie Queene*." *Spenser Studies* 5 (1984): 143–48.

Stone, Lawrence. "Marriage among the English Nobility in the Sixteenth and Seventeenth Centuries." *Comparative Studies in Society and History* 3 (1961): 182–206.

Strong, Roy. *The Cult of Elizabeth: Elizabethan Portraiture and Pageantry.* Berkeley and Los Angeles: University of California Press, 1977.

Stump, Donald. "Britomart's Mock-Romantic Quest." In *Spenser and the Middle Ages,* edited by David Richardson, 158–66. Kalamazoo, MI: Proceedings from a Special Session at the 11th Conference on Medieval Studies, 1976.

Suleiman, Susan R., and Inge Crosman, eds. *The Reader in the Text: Essays on Audience and Interpretation.* Princeton: Princeton University Press, 1980.

Suzuki, Mihoko. *Metamorphoses of Helen: Authority, Difference, and the Epic.* Ithaca: Cornell University Press, 1989.

Swift, Carolyn Ruth. "Feminine Identity in Lady Mary Wroth's Romance *Urania.*" *English Literary Renaissance* 14.3 (Autumn 1984): 328–46.

Teague, Frances. "Judith Shakespeare Reading." *Shakespeare Quarterly* 47.4 (Winter 1996): 361–73.

Thickstun, Margaret Olofson. *Fictions of the Feminine: Puritan Doctrine and the Representation of Women.* Ithaca: Cornell University Press, 1988.

Thomas, Keith. "The Meaning of Literacy in Early Modern England." In *The Written Word: Literacy in Transition,* edited by Gerd Baumann, 97–131. Oxford: Clarendon Press, 1986.

Todd, Margo. "Humanists, Puritans, and the Spiritualized Household." *Church History* 49 (1980): 18–34.

Tompkins, Jane P. "The Reader in History: The Changing Shape of Literary Response." In *Reader-Response Criticism: From Formalism to Post-Structuralism,* 201–32. Baltimore: Johns Hopkins University Press, 1980.

Trafton, Dain. "Politics and the Praise of Women: Political Doctrine in *The Courtier*'s Third Book." In *Castiglione: The Ideal and the Real in Renaissance Culture,* edited by Robert Hanning and David Rosand, 29–44. New Haven: Yale University Press, 1983.

Travitsky, Betty. "The Lady Doth Protest: Protest in the Popular Writings of Renaissance Englishwomen." *English Literary Renaissance* 14 (1984): 255–83.

———. "The New Mother of the English Renaissance: Her Writings on Motherhood." In *The Lost Tradition: Mothers and Daughters in Literature,* edited by Cathy N. Davidson and E. M. Broner, 33–43. New York: Frederick Ungar, 1980.

Travitsky, Betty S., and Adele F. Seeff, eds. *Attending to Women in Early Modern England.* Newark: University of Delaware Press, 1994.

Villeponteaux, Mary. "Displacing Feminine Authority in *The Faerie Queene.*" *Studies in English Literature* 35 (1995): 53–67.

Walker, Julia M. *Medusa's Mirrors: Spenser, Shakespeare, Milton, and the Metamorphosis of the Female Self.* Newark: University of Delaware Press, 1998.

———. "Spenser's Elizabeth Portrait and the Fiction of Dynastic Epic." *Modern Philology* 90.2 (November 1992): 172–99.

Wall, Wendy. "Disclosures in Print: The 'Violent Enlargement' of the Renaissance Voyeuristic Text." *Studies in English Literature* 29 (1989): 35–59.

————. *The Imprint of Gender: Authorship and Publication in the English Renaissance.* Ithaca: Cornell University Press, 1993.

Wallace, John M. " 'Examples Are Best Precepts': Readers and Meanings in Seventeenth-Century Poetry." *Critical Inquiry* 1 (1974): 273–90.

Waller, Gary. "The Countess of Pembroke and Gendered Reading." In *The Renaissance Englishwoman in Print: Counterbalancing the Canon*, edited by Anne M. Haselkorn and Betty S. Travitsky, 327–45. Amherst: University of Massachusetts Press, 1990.

————. "Mary Wroth and the Sidney Family Romance." In *Reading Mary Wroth: Representing Alternatives in Early Modern England*, edited by Naomi Miller and Gary Waller, 35–63. Knoxville: University of Tennessee Press, 1991.

Warnicke, Retha M. "Eulogies for Women: Public Testimony of Their Godly Example and Leadership." In *Attending to Women in Early Modern England*, edited by Betty S. Travitsky and Adele Seeff, 168–86. Newark: University of Delaware Press, 1994.

————. "Women and Humanism in England." In *Humanism Beyond Italy*, vol. 2 of *Renaissance Humanism: Foundations, Forms, and Legacy*, edited by Albert J. Rabil, Jr., 39–54. Philadelphia: University of Pennsylvania Press, 1988.

————. *Women of the English Renaissance and Reformation.* Westport, CT: Greenwood Press, 1983.

Watkins, John. *The Specter of Dido: Spenser and Virgilian Epic.* New Haven: Yale University Press, 1995.

Wayne, Valerie. "Advice for Women from Mothers and Patriarchs." In *Women and Literature in Britain, 1500–1700*, edited by Helen Wilcox, 56–79. Cambridge: Cambridge University Press, 1996.

————. "Some Sad Sentence: Vives' *Instruction of a Christian Woman.*" In *Silent But for the Word: Tudor Women as Patrons, Translators, and Writers of Religious Works*, edited by Margaret Patterson Hannay, 15–29. Kent, OH: Kent State University Press, 1985.

Weigall, Rachel. "An Elizabethan Gentlewoman: The Journal of Lady Mildmay, c. 1570–1617." *Quarterly Review* 215 (1911): 119–38.

Weinstein, Minna F. "Reconstructing Our Past: Reflections on Tudor Women." *International Journal of Women's Studies* 1 (1978): 133–40.

Wells, Robin Headlam. *Spenser's "Faerie Queene" and the Cult of Elizabeth.* London: Croom Helm, 1983.

Whigham, Frank. *Ambition and Privilege: The Social Tropes of Elizabethan Courtesy Theory.* Berkeley and Los Angeles: University of California Press, 1984.

White, Robert. "Shamefastnesse as *Verecundia* and as *Pudicitia* in *The Faerie Queene.*" *Studies in Philology* 78.4 (Fall 1981): 391–408.

Wilcox, Helen, ed. *Women and Literature in Britain, 1500–1700.* Cambridge: Cambridge University Press, 1996.

Willen, Diane. "Women and Religion in Early Modern England." In *Women in Reformation and Counter-Reformation Europe*, edited by Sherrin Marshall, 140–65. Bloomington: Indiana University Press, 1989.

Williams, Franklin B., Jr. *Index of Dedications and Commendatory Verses in English Books Before 1641*. London: Bibliographical Society, 1962.

———. "The Literary Patronesses of Renaissance England." *Notes and Queries* 207 (1962): 364–66.

Wilson, Adrian. "The Ceremony of Childbirth and Its Interpretation." In *Women as Mothers in Pre-Industrial England*, edited by Valerie Fildes, 68–107. London: Routledge, 1990.

Wilson, E. C. *England's Eliza*. Harvard Studies in English, vol. 20, 1939. Reprint. London: Frank Cass, 1966.

Wilson, Jean, ed. *Entertainments for Elizabeth I*. Studies in Elizabethan and Renaissance Culture, vol. 2. Totowa, NJ: D. S. Brewer, 1980.

Wilson, Richard. "Observations on English Bodies: Licensing Maternity in Shakespeare's Late Plays." In *Enclosure Acts: Sexuality, Property, and Culture in Early Modern England*, edited by by Richard Burt and John Michael Archer, 121–50. Ithaca: Cornell University Press, 1994.

Wilson, Violet A. *Queen Elizabeth's Maids of Honour and Ladies of the Privy Chamber*. London: John Lane, 1922.

Wofford, Susanne. "Britomart's Petrarchan Lament: Allegory and Narrative in *The Faerie Queene* III, iv." *Comparative Literature* 39.1 (Winter 1987): 28–57.

———. *The Choice of Achilles: The Ideology of Figure in the Epic*. Stanford: Stanford University Press, 1992.

———. "Gendering Allegory: Spenser's Bold Reader and the Emergence of Character in *The Faerie Queene* III." *Criticism* 30.1 (Winter 1988): 1–21.

Wogan-Browne, Jocelyn. "Saints' Lives and the Female Reader." *Forum for Modern Language Studies* 27.4 (1991): 314–32.

———. " 'Clerc u lai, muïne u dame': women and Anglo-Norman hagiography in the twelfth and thirteenth centuries." In *Women and Literature in Britain, 1150–1500*, edited by Carol M. Meale, 61–85. Cambridge: Cambridge University Press, 1993.

Woodbridge, Linda. "Womanhood." *The Spenser Encyclopedia*. Edited by A. C. Hamilton. Toronto: University of Toronto Press, 1990.

———. *Women and the English Renaissance: Literature and the Nature of Womankind, 1540–1620*. Urbana: University of Illinois Press, 1984.

Woods, Susanne. "Spenser and the Problem of Women's Rule." *Huntington Library Quarterly* 48 (1985): 141–58.

———. "Women at the Margins in Spenser and Lanyer." In *Worldmaking Spenser: Explorations in the Early Modern Age*, edited by Patrick Cheney and Lauren Silberman, 101–14. Lexington: The University Press of Kentucky, 2000.

Wright, Celeste Turner. "The Elizabethan Female Worthies." *Studies in Philology* 43 (1946): 628–43.

Wright, Louis B. *Middle-Class Culture in Elizabethan England*. Chapel Hill: University of North Carolina Press, 1935.

———. "The Reading of Renaissance Englishwomen." *Studies in Philology* 28 (1931): 139–56.

Wyntjes, Sherrin. "Women in the Reformation Era." In *Becoming Visible:*

Women in European History, edited by Renate Bridenthal and Claudia Koonz, 165–91. Boston: Houghton Mifflin, 1977.

Yates, Frances. *Astraea: The Imperial Theme in the Sixteenth Century,* 1975. Reprint. London: Routledge and Kegan Paul, 1985.

Yavneh, Naomi. "The Ambiguity of Beauty in Tasso and Petrarch." In *Sexuality and Gender in Early Modern Europe: Institutions, Texts, Images,* edited by James Grantham Turner, 133–57. Cambridge: Cambridge University Press, 1993.

Yeazell, Ruth. *Fictions of Modesty: Women and Courtship in the English Novel.* Chicago: University of Chicago Press, 1991.

Young, Alan. *Tudor and Jacobean Tournaments.* Dobbs Ferry, NY: Sheridan House, 1987.

Index

CHESTER COLLEGE LIBRARY